Over the Glass & Into the Crowd!

Life After Hockey

**Profiles of 200
Former NHL Players
(1933-1994)**

BRIAN McFALONE

Best Wishes!

Guelph, Ontario
Canada

Published by MainStreet Press
10 Suffolk St. W.
Guelph, Ontario, Canada
N1H 2H8
(519) 766-4756 (phone & fax)
e-mail: mainst@freespace.net
web site: http://www.freespace.net/~mainst

Canadian Cataloguing in Publication Data
McFalone, Brian, 1957-
Over the Glass and Into the Crowd life after hockey : profiles
of over 200 former NHL players (1933-1994)

ISBN 0-9681460-0-7

1. National Hockey League - Biography. 2. Hockey
players - Biography. 3. Hockey players - Retirement
I. Title.
GV848.5.A1M28 1996   796.962'092'2   C96-932063-9

Production coordination by is five communications

Cover design by Sharon Adams & is five communications

Cover collage photograph by Ron Tanaka

Cover photos of Wally Stanowski and Walt Tkaczuk by Camilla Leach. Photo of Gary Bromley provided by Gary Bromley

Text illustrations by Joanne Kelly

We wish to thank the Topps Gum Co. and Parkhurst Products Incorporated who kindly gave permission to illustrate their cards in this book.

We wish to acknowledge the generosity of Guelph Museums for their loan of ancient materials used in the cover photograph of this book.

Photo Credits:
Camilla Leach - Pgs. 15, 27, 29, 77, 108, 109, 130, 131, 135, 137, 140, 253, 254, 259, 265, 266, 276, 279
Pat Payton, Sports Editor St. Marys Journal Argus - Pg. 92

Additional photographs are reproduced in this book courtesy of the players.

Printed and bound in Canada

To my parents,
Frank and Lola McFalone
Two souls, two minds, one heart

Acknowledgments ─────────

A package of gratitude is extended to my wife, Camilla Leach, a tireless editor, business manager and lifeline of support; to Tom Scanlan of *is five Communications* who offered invaluable assistance and guidance; to Sharon Adams for her cover design; to Joanne Kelly who extended her soul in addition to her pen; and to Peter Knight who brought life to the layout of these pages.

The research for this book could not have been completed without the gracious help of the following people:

Andy Bathgate	Harry Watson
Jim Peters Sr.	Ken Rootham
Wally Hergesheimer	Gary Sabourin
Tom Reid	J.P. Parisé
Fred Stanfield	Nick Nickson
Dollard St. Laurent	Bruce Affleck
Pete Conacher	Leo Labine
John Peirson	Dave Dryden
Bill Gadsby	Bill White
Bob Nystrom	Graham Fiddes
Émile Bouchard	Donna Prince
Fred Barrett	Jennifer Cole
Dickie Moore	Ken Cole
Anne Kurt	Chuck Henderson
Pat Stapleton	Kathy Best
Ron Lord	Gerry Norman
Baron Bedesky	Al Sikorski
Brian Aitken	Miranda Leung
Anatole Kung	Linda Love
Pete LeClair	J. Fred Duncan
Gary Tulk	

Contents

Introduction

The road is longer than the journey on ice ... the game goes on.

The idea for this book was not hatched in an editorial office. Its birth and evolution ran parallel with the unfolding of my own life.

It all began in Aurora, Ontario, 1962. I had just been drafted in the third round as an underaged player by my dad, coach of the Aurora Maple Leaf Atoms. My scouting report read as follows:

Age: 5
Height: 3'2"
Weight: 37 pounds
Shot: unknown
Characteristics:

• Plays all forward and defensive positions simultaneously, wandering from one to the other aimlessly.

• Refuses to play unless he gets to wear Dave Keon's #14.

• Will never speak to his best friend, Bruce McGauley, again because Brucey blocked his one and only breakaway and thus thwarted an imaginary trip to the Stanley Cup finals.

Every morning, en route to school, I revved up my bike at the expense of Earl Ingarfield and Don Simmons, their hockey cards clattering mercilessly between the spokes of my wheels as I fancied myself to be "the Wild One". I entered the grounds of Regency Acres Public School and Casino armed with hockey cards in every pocket and a bag of puree boulders strapped to my side. I'd stride the gamut of profiteers, looking to flip and roll my way to a berth into the playoffs. My take at the end of the day—too many Gordie Howe cards! I pawned them off on the kid up the street.

The passage of time, however, gently slipped the rites of youth from under my pillow as I slept. I awoke to a new life where hockey cards and gloves had long since disappeared from the floor of my messy closet. Mother did what she thought needed doing.

I forgot about the men whose hockey-card faces stared back at my boyish gaze, the men who freely lent their names to every road-hockey game I ever played. It wasn't until working as a school teacher that I overheard two young lads in conversation:

- I'll trade two Brett Hulls and a Larmer rookie for that Gretzky.

- No way! The Larmer's got a crease. How about that Gordie Howe card your dad gave you?

- Are you kidding, my dad would kill me if I traded Gordie Howe!

I thought to myself, "Kid, don't give up the Gordie Howe!! I did and it has haunted me and my assets ever since." I sat silently reflecting on the sound of my bike, clattering with the help of Earl and Don. On those cards I saw their youthful faces that now looked younger than mine. I began to wonder about what became of these men who symbolized victory, strength, discipline, vision and resilience. Where did they go? What did they do? Were they still heroic people?

In raising these questions, I realized that I was no longer the young boy who was willing to idolize men I didn't really know. To know them on a more personal level, however, required me to remove them from the pedestal for a closer look—a risky business indeed.

In the process, I had some unsettling questions to face. Were they approachable? Would I like me? Would I like them? Could our meeting sustain the weight of my expectations? Would I be disappointed, regretting the exposure of a sacred ground better left unturned?

My early efforts to contact former players bore little fruit. I sent out inquiries in all directions with hardly a stir. Then one day my voice-mail light was flashing. I pushed the play button to hear:

> *Hi Brian! This is Bill Gadsby speaking. I got your letter and I understand you want to talk. I'll be in after 7pm tomorrow night. Give me a call.*

Bill had opened the door! On the other side I found a large body of former NHL plumbers, fix-it men, hit-men, heroes and plenty in between who were willing to talk about the human side of their lives. By and large, they were approachable and likeable. They were funny and serious. They were inspiring and successful.

I observed that each of these men, at one point in time, aspired to the top of his profession in the world. And in any world-class endeavour, it takes drive, discipline, commitment and character to make it to the big leagues. The eventuality of retirement brought with it the trial of either jumping or being pushed from the equivalent of a moving train. No matter how well prepared he may have been, the departed player was headed for a tumble before he could get on his feet. Grant Mulvey described the jump as the most devastating transition a person can go through. Sometimes the fall was hard, but inner drive and resiliency soon brought them to their feet in pursuit of new successes.

I was fascinated to see the diversity of paths followed by men who at one time in their lives, all played in the National Hockey League. They made their mark on ice and through their unique and individual talents, they continue to make their mark on life. In the pages of this book you will learn of Tim Ecclestone's pursuit of lost galleon treasure; Gus Mortson's introduction of pizza into Canada; Gerry Hart's development of a groundbreaking sports facility; Ab Demarco's calling as a professional father; Lou Fontinato's farm; Randy Manery's work with the Haggai Institute; Rick Martin's gold-mining pursuits in the Ivory Coast; the Cullen brothers auto-sales dynasty; Dean Prentice's commitment to Christianity and Hockey Ministries International; Frank Brimsek's ride on the rails; and the Barrett brothers fighting fires.

And then there is the culture of charity within which these men continue to live. While on the stage of professional hockey, they made frequent visits to hospital wards to brighten the lives of sick children and to raise funds to fight diseases and improve community programmes. I observed that through this experience, giving became a powerful, life-long addiction that Red Storey described as a privilege. "I would say that about seventy-five percent of my life is spent on charity work," he noted. "People say, 'You work too hard!' I say, 'No, it's not work it's a reward'." In the end, the road may be longer than the journey on ice, but the culture of charity remains as long as the road itself.

While conducting my research for this book, I kept tabs on the kind of money being raised by alumni associations across North America. Through oldtimers' hockey games, softball outings and golf tournaments, my rough calculations came in at more than $3,000,000 secured annually for a variety of community causes. This figure does not include the incalculable initiatives of individual players who hold annual golf tournaments and fundraising drives of their own.

I was touched to learn that after the deaths of Brian Spencer and his wife, their two sons received scholarship funds to attend university as did Larry Mickey's son and daughter, thanks to the efforts of Fred Stanfield and the Buffalo Sabres' alumni association. I felt a sense of gratitude for the Montreal Canadiens' alumni association when they provided a specially equipped van to improve mobility for Dave Balon, now crippled by the effects of multiple sclerosis. I felt compelled to give more to my own community while listening to Ted Irvine talk about his association with the Special Olympics programme and the Winners' Foundation. I had the same response to Tom Reid who described his work with the Make A Wish Foundation. I can still feel the vibration of a thousand motorcycles circling Minneapolis, each carrying a cloth that represented a child's wish.

In researching this project, I observed that the absence of accurate information leads to generalizations. We've seen the image of "Big Bobby Clobber", the hockey caricature invented by *The Royal Canadian Air Farce*. We've had the lives of John Kordic, Bill Goldsworthy and Brian Spencer paraded before our eyes. We've heard that former hockey players drink too much; that they're not well educated or intelligent; that their only prospects after hockey are to sell beer, coach in the minor leagues or scout for the next generation of players.

In writing this book, my goal has been to provide a more focused and specific body of information that will allow us to extend our thinking beyond generalizations fostered by a media that more often than not, operates on the notion that good news is no news and bad news is good news. I do not seek to consciously challenge or analyze these preconceived notions. My goal is to present a series of stories that will allow you as the reader to draw your own conclusions. To that end, I wish you as much pleasure in reading these pages as I had in researching and writing them.

Brian McFalone
Guelph, Ontario

Nicknames

Hockey players are the greatest at coming up with nicknames for one another. If there's any abnormality, something about a guy ... they don't look the other way, they call it the way they see it. Nothing is sacred. There was a guy I played with in the WHA whose head looked out of shape, as if somebody had squashed it. His nickname was "Firestone". They called him that because it looked like somebody drove over his head with a car.

Dave Dryden

It is your true friends who care enough to tell you if there's a spot on you lapel or a bit of goo on your nose or lip. The warning you receive hardly sounds solemn and yet the underlying intent signals a degree of care and comradery that is not restricted by social conventions. Nicknames, as cruel or unfriendly as they may sound, also signal a bond between friends that serves to maintain a unique space within which the relationship can unfold. When retirement comes and the dressing-room socials are gone, the nickname is one of the few tangible items that can be taken, intact, into the next phase of a player's life. When the phone rings and the caller says, I want to speak with "Kong" or "Pie", the name serves as a password to indicate that someone on the inside, someone who understands, is on the line. It is for this reason that the nicknames and their origins have been included in this work.

N.B. The Nickname Challenge series is based exclusively on players profiled in this book.

Ken Dryden
The Mantle Of Fame

THE

p u b l i c

e y e

Ken Dryden speaks about public figures with private lives who must live by the deceptive rules of fame.

The Remarkable Obligations Of The Sports Hero

Professional athletes are literally characters of somebody's life, of somebody's childhood. And I think it's why when we read in the newspaper of some tragic incident happening to some [celebrity], or even something that isn't so tragic ... it really hits hard... As that person's story changes, or at least what you know of it changes, then it starts to affect your own... For a lot of [people], they're only a passing parade of characters in somebody's life. But for some, they're not. For some they are fairly central... I see it when I go on book tours or out giving talks in some public place and somebody will come up. You come to realize in a sense, the life-long responsibility you have because you know that you were a real character in this person's life. And just because you stopped playing doesn't mean that you have left their lives... And I think it's why it is so difficult for somebody to go to a card show or be somewhere where their hero is disrespectful to them, or is shorter than they should be or something else... It's quite a remarkable obligation that in fact is an ongoing one and you never realize that that was part of the bargain—but it is. And you [as a professional athlete] have to be really conscious of it or otherwise you're messing around with someone else's life.

The Stalwart Hero: An Object Of Our Own Creation

One of the difficult things of being a public figure of some sort is that you may have been trained all your life to be a fifty-goal scorer. But what we tend to do with our heroes, any kind of hero, is that we fill out the portrait with the equivalent of a fifty-goal scorer in every other dimension of that person's life. And so they're a fifty-goal scorer in terms of being funny, of being nice, of being generous, of being courageous, of being family-centred or whatever it happens to be... And chances are, they're not fifty-goal scorers in lots of other aspects of their lives. And it's the sort of thing that's at the root of what goes wrong... It's why our public figures are

almost always disappointing to us, if we get close to them...
They're just not quite that height, that look, that nice, that
approachable. So all of us will turn our heroes into full-
dimensioned people. But they are, for the most part, people
of our own creations. And of course the people we create in
our heads are always well beyond what people in real life
can ever be. And that's the dilemma of ... the very
successful public person. The person who never allows
himself to be the real person ... the Beliveau or somebody
else who never once in their lives puts at risk that public
person—never gets into the mire and mix of real life that
may make them disappointing as a real person. They've
decided, "No, I have this image as the public person and so
anytime that I am out in front of anybody, that is the person
that I'm going to be." So you either end up changing
personalities or you end up carefully selecting where you
are going to be in your life and how you decide to live in it.

The Contract's Hidden Clause

You're always told when you're playing that you are a
model in some way. But in fact, most of us spend that time
denying that in fact we are. We don't want that baggage...
We figure that the responsibility that we have is to be us
and that anything else is a cheat and is a lie. Probably only
after you've stopped playing ... you realize, no, that [being
a role model] is part of the bargain. I mean the million
dollars that's there in your contract that says it's to play
first base for the Toronto Blue Jays, that's only part of it.
The reason that you're getting paid a million bucks is only
in part because you bat .300 and hit twenty home runs. The
rest of it is because millions of people like you in some way
and look to you in some particular way... And you think
it's just to hit twenty home runs. But you're wrong! A
major reason that you're paid what you are is for the rest of
it. And that's really ... the bargain that you're making
when you're signing that contract, and you can't pretend
otherwise. You can't have it both ways... So no kidding
around, that's it! That's the deal...

The Search For A Full And Integrated Hero

I don't know enough about Albert Belle but ... I
remember reading a quote from the general manager in
Cleveland, John Hart. And at some point, somebody is
saying to him about Belle that, "Jeez, if he would just
loosen up a bit, smile and be pleasant with people, he could

> *"So all of us will turn our heroes into full-dimensioned people. But they are, for the most part, people of our own creations."*
>
> Ken Dryden

> *"With Albert Belle, it's just brutal... He's got to pretend to play their game enough to make himself invisible, uninteresting... Then the microphones will go away."*
>
> Ken Dryden

own Cleveland!" John Hart's quoted response was, "He doesn't want to own Cleveland, he just wants to be the best baseball player the Indians have ever had." And I think that's Albert Belle. And in fact, the fans and the people in the media are the first [ones] to say, "Jeez, the athletes that we have ... it just doesn't seem important to them anymore to play left field for the ball team. They want to be these business people and be surrounded by these agents and lawyers and hangers-on... And so it seems as if baseball or hockey isn't important to them anymore." Well, if John Hart is right, Albert Belle is in fact the guy that we say we want. This is a guy who doesn't seem to care about anything else except playing baseball for the Cleveland Indians and hitting fifty home runs. So that's what [the public] says on the one side, but then when he behaves in a way that is not consistent with the way we want fifty-home-run hitters to [behave], then we crucify the guy. We don't allow him to live. We're just in his face all the time, taunting him, just waiting for him to blow and hoping that we're around when it happens. And then it's just hell for him... But I think in a way, what Albert Belle has to understand is that what the fans and the media say about just playing baseball, isn't enough. That they're lying... That they are looking for this full, integrated person and that you've got to give at least enough ... of the other part to make your life invisible. If you try to give nothing to make yourself invisible, that only makes you visible. You have to be just pleasant enough. Talk to them enough... You play the [media] game in that kind of way and then you're allowed to be a left fielder who hits fifty home runs and people will focus on that. But if you do it any other way, they won't allow you.

With Albert Belle, it's just brutal. It's the Albert Belle watch. I mean you've got people there who have an incentive now to taunt [him] and to stick a microphone in his face at a moment that might be an awkward one... [He] gets it in every city within which he goes and he doesn't have a chance. The only way he's going to stop it is to make some sort of pronouncement that sounds like he's playing their game. Then he can go on and play his own game. But he's got to pretend to play their game enough to make himself invisible, uninteresting... Then the microphones will go away.

Ken Dryden played goal for the Montreal Canadiens from 1971-1979. He is an author, lawyer, consultant, social commentator and president-general manager of the Toronto Maple Leafs.

The Players ──────────────

"Guys from another era... Believe me, it makes me feel like a little kid again to listen to them talk. There's a lot to be learned from them all... The life experiences that they've gone through are far-reaching and I'll tell you, just to hear them talk is a great benefit to all of us."— Rob Ramage

(Left to right) Lou Fontinato, Harry Howell, Chuck Henderson and Andy Bathgate together for a recent Guelph Biltmore Madhatters' Memorial Cup reunion.

Affleck, Bruce: *Played defense for St. Louis, Vancouver and the New York Islanders between 1974 & 1984. Born: Salmon Arm, British Columbia, 1954.*

"I feel I should have done more," Bruce Affleck said honestly, reflecting back on his career and the era in which he played. "I just felt that I should have been more dedicated to the sport now that I see the way players act today. They look after themselves much better than we did. We didn't look at hockey as a job back then. I didn't realize what it could mean for the future of both my family and myself...

"On the other side, I feel good about making it when there were only sixteen teams and coming up through college instead of through the junior route. I played at the University of Denver. I was the highest drafted college player ever picked at that time."

Bruce cleared his final zone for the Canucks in 1980 and moved on to experience a different brand of hockey in Switzerland for two seasons. "I played in a suburb just outside of Zurich called Kloten," he recounted. "It was a great experience. During the summer before we went over, my wife and I went to school and took German. I found that we were a little more accepted. Although we weren't fluent by any means, we were able to go to someone's house and have an enjoyable evening without having to worry about the language too much."

He completed his sojourn in Europe and then returned to the NHL for a brief stint with the New York Islanders in 1983 before retiring from hockey. "I had made a promise to my wife

Bruce Affleck

that once our daughter had started school we would try and settle down," he explained. "So we moved back to St. Louis and I returned to the real-estate field, working full-time for a corporate relocation firm."

Bruce described his initial transition from hockey as unsettling. "The biggest thing I had to put up with was every afternoon at two o'clock, I felt like taking a nap ... as though I was getting ready for a hockey game," he related. "As for the transition out of the limelight, I was in the minors for most of my last couple of years, so that probably helped to let me down slowly."

In 1987, Bruce rejoined the St. Louis Blues' organization. "I came on as director of sales and to do colour on the radio," he reported. "The purpose of that was to get my name back out with the public in order to make my sales calls easier. After three or four years here, I was named vice president of sales, although the job hasn't changed too much." He also handles pregame and intermission interviews for the Blues' television broadcasts.

These days, Bruce devotes much of his spare time to his wife, Cecily, and their two children as well as to supporting local charities. To that end, he has taken on the role as president of the March of Dimes Golf Tournament and as president of the Blues' alumni association.

Nickname: *Scratch*

"Everybody gets called by their initials," Bruce observed. "In my case, B.A. was 'Bare Ass' back in the sixties and seventies. My first year in St. Louis, they scratched me for the first twelve games I was there. They used to say, 'Scratch #4 from your programme, Bruce

Affleck!' So Chuck Lefley started calling me 'Scratch'."

Aldcorn, Gary: *Played left wing for Toronto, Detroit and Boston from 1956-1961. Born: Shaunavon, Saskatchewan, 1935.*

If necessity is the mother of invention, then Gary Aldcorn, by definition, is in a constant state of necessity. As such, his collective callings as an athlete, scientist, inventor, businessman and artist were the natural offspring of a mind bubbling with conceptual adventure.

"I'm probably what you'd call your classic entrepreneur," he affirmed. "I'm a great starter-upper—that's my strength. I get highly motivated and I'm bright enough to [follow through]."

During the 1950's, Gary was in hot pursuit of dream number one—to make it as a professional hockey player. He realized his goal in 1956, as he slipped his head through the blue and white passage of a Maple Leaf jersey. But his choicest hour came three years later when the Red Wings picked him up and dropped him onto a line with Gordie Howe. With "Mr. Hockey" in the wings, Gary's production vaulted to a career-high twenty-two goals and twenty-nine assists.

"Playing with Gordie tended to do that to a person," he conceded with modesty. "It was a big experience—a big thrill! I found that I could think with Gordie. I wasn't the greatest skater in the world, but on a hockey-comprehension level, I was almost with him. We would project the same way. Like I'd go to A and he'd go to B and we'd both know that I was going to C..."

But in spite of the on-ice magic, Gary's exploits remained the lesser servant of a greater passion for learning and innovation. The forces that compelled him to play hockey were equally strong in swaying his mind to explore other fields.

"I'd been taking part-time university courses during all of my hockey career," he related. "Bobby Pulford, Billy Harris and I had gone to school since the time we played junior. And during the summertime, I'd go back to my home in Winnipeg to attend the University of

Manitoba. I'd decided to go into a science stream, which meant that I had to take labs, which weren't available for those attending part-time. So inevitably, I needed to go back to school to complete my degree. As well, I had a little catharsis, if you will, on the road to Damascus... A teammate of mine, Billy McNeil, had a wife who contracted polio and died within three weeks. That affected me in the direction of studying medicine. So when I was traded to Boston along with Murray Oliver in 1960, I told Lynn Patrick [Bruins' GM] that I was going to retire at the end of the year. At the time, I figured I was single with no responsibilities per se, so that's what lead me to quit hockey."

But to break the med-school barrier, Gary would first have to complete years three and four of his undergraduate programme. To that end, he returned to the University of Manitoba where lab coats and test tubes became his tools of trade.

"I did pretty well!" he exclaimed. "But when I applied for medicine, the guy ahead of me got in and I didn't. That was the first time in my life that I couldn't really control my own agenda. I'd just assumed that when I made my decision, I'd be there. So having finished my BSc and then not getting accepted, I was sort of flabbergasted because I didn't know what to do."

The dust of bewilderment soon cleared off, however, exposing an alternative path to a satisfying end. "I continued with my education," he affirmed. "I took my Master's in virology and that lead me, along with a partner, to establish a company called National Biological Labs. The University of Manitoba Medical School had four sheep that they used to provide sheep red-blood cells for everybody in Winnipeg [doing research]. They were wrestling with these sheep every week to bleed them. So my partner and I said, 'Look we'll do that so you won't have to, and that was the basis of our biological business. And that's what got me into an entrepreneurial mode'."

It also landed him back at school, this time on the trail of a Master's of Business Administration. "My business was weak, there's no question about it," he admitted. "It still is weak because I'm more of a conceptual guy than a numbers guy."

In spite of his predisposition, Gary chipped away at his programme until, by the early seventies, he could finally hang an MBA on his wall.

In the meantime, he also stoked his career in hockey by playing at the senior level in Manitoba. In 1968, he was then invited to join Father Bauer's Canadian National Team, an opportunity that stirred Gary's sense of patriotism.

"You know, back in 1960, Billy Harris, Bobby Pulford, Bobby Nevin and I were over in Europe all summer," he recounted. "The point being that when you get out of Canada, you become nationalistic—you become a little prouder of your heritage. So my involvement with the National team—representing Canada—was very emotional, very impactful as far as my Canadiana."

After a stint as the National Team's coach in 1970, Gary was summoned by Hockey Canada to head up the development side of their agenda. Cutting his ties with National Biological Labs, he then headed east to grapple with the creation of a national coaches' certification programme.

"The singular purpose of the project was to improve coaching in Canada," he explained. "It was like an educational stepladder to assist coaches in moving up the ranks. This certification was the first ever in ... the world. It's the basis for the whole coaching programme in Canada today.

"I also did some consulting work with *Hockey Night in Canada*. At that time, they were doing a series on the development of hockey in the Soviet Union, Czechoslovakia and Sweden. So they sent four of us over, with me being in charge, to take film footage and to gain information on their development process. It was extremely interesting. Later, it was used in between periods of *Hockey Night in Canada* broadcasts."

In 1976, Gary revisited the entrepreneurial zone, by founding a national sports magazine called *Hockey Player*. "We provided instructional information in an entertaining fashion, covering all levels of hockey," he reported. "It was a consumer product where our advertising paid for most of the expenses. But the problem was, the Canadian Hockey Association were upset that our production was [infringing on their territory]. The long and the short of it was, they knocked off all of our big advertisers by saying, 'If you advertise with the magazine, we won't do any work with you.' So in the end, the CHA absorbed us."

Undaunted, however, Gary simply zeroed his inventive radar onto a new target. Observing room for improvement in the hockey-pad industry, he jumped in with a new innovation called "Flak Equipment".

"I was putting air bags underneath the different pads to absorb more impact and shock," he explained. "We supplied the big houses like Sears as well as retail shops across the land. Eventually I sold out to my venture capital people in 1987 who, in turn, sold the company to Bauer.

"Then I started another company on my own called *Mr. Hockey*. I produced a different line of products based on my experience with Flak. I tried a different method of selling directly to the hockey associations. My concept was, instead of paying the markup to retailers, I'd pay it to sales agents at twenty-five percent and motivate them to sell to their local communities. I did that for two or three years, but I ran out of gas, so I gave the concept to a couple of my agents in 1994."

In the interim, Gary has allowed himself to drift into artistic semi-retirement. His artistry, as such, was gently coaxed by the most subtle of his creative voices—the sculptor's.

"I've always had a little artistic inclination," he revealed. "I was particularly drawn to the three-dimensional aspect of sculpting.

"While my daughter was attending chiropractors' college, I did a project for her graduation. In response, people said that I should market it—which I did, and that got me into the commercial sculpture area. Then, once I looked at the market and my own interests, I thought I'd just do sports sculpture.

"So what I did is like any entrepreneur does,

"I'm having so much fun doing this!" — Gary Aldcorn

I went right back to Rodin. I looked at the history of sculpture—and eventually I found a contemporary technique called 'cold-cast sculpture' to cast the bronze. I searched in Canada, but nobody knew how to do it. So I went down to the States to learn the technique. So I think I'm the only one in Canada who knows how to do it.

"Now having played on a line with Gordie Howe in Detroit, I naturally have a great deal of respect for the man. So the first project I did was a thirty-six-inch-high statue of him. I'm very happy with it. It's a limited edition of seventy-five. I also wanted to honour the legends of the game, so I made a large maple leaf and placed the busts of King Clancy, the 'Kid Line': Primeau, Conacher and Jackson ... right up to Bob Baun and Punch Imlach. Then I did the Montreal Canadien legends—eighteen faces on their logo including George Vezina, Howie Morenz ... right up to 'Pocket' Rocket, Cournoyer and Guy Lafleur. I'm having so much fun doing this! I get

to honour these guys and I get to select who's included. It's like publishing ... what power! You're the final arbiter of what goes in there! I also have the legends of golf: Hogan, Snead... And right now I'm working on Stevie Yzerman. I'm also considering doing a portrayal of the current Red Wings who won the Stanley Cup this year."

And as his mind sifts through a myriad of possibilities, each choice made is ultimately screened through values honed to weed out the smallest trace of productive monotony.

"Creation by my definition is creating something that hasn't been there before," he asserted. "If you're creative and you've maximized your abilities in that mode, whether it's painting, writing or sculpture, the challenge is to yourself. You have to create within your own value structure, whether you're out to make money or to create something that will have some kind of permanence. The nice thing about sculpting is that I know it's going to be around for X number of years. In fact I have one piece that I give to each new-born child in the family. I call it my 'Madonna'. I put the child's name on the bottom so I know it's going to be with them for their whole lives."

(Gary can be contacted at P.O. Box 5072, Claremont, Ontario L1Y 1A4)

Anderson, John: *Played right wing for Toronto, Quebec and Hartford from 1977-1989. Born: Toronto, Ontario, 1957.*

As John Anderson first stepped onto Maple Leaf Gardens' ice in 1977, his most obvious asset was scintillating speed that, in the early years, sometimes outran other aspects of his game. Experience, however, plus the arrival of Bill Derlago and Rick Vaive in 1980, placed him dead over centre on a thirty-goal lane.

In the company of his linemates, he continued to put up steady numbers for the Leafs until he was shipped to Quebec in 1985. After a brief stay with the Nordiques, he moved on to his final destination in Hartford.

By the start of the Whalers' training camp in 1989, John's career-point number 700 was within walking distance. Business was as usual until a quick twist of events stopped him cold in his tracks.

"The hard thing was, I had had a really good training camp in Hartford that year," he recounted. "But because of my age, I was the first to go—so I headed overseas. I played about fourteen games in Milan, Italy where they were building a brand new rink that could seat 14,000 people. They were going to get the Russian ballet, the circus and the ice skaters to come as a show the following year. But in return, the team had to use two Russian players as their imports. After I played a few games, the Russian people got wind of it. They said they were going to cancel the ballet and circus if I continued to play. So the team paid me for the rest of the year and sent me home! The Whalers still owed me another year on my contract as well. I guess that year I made the most money in my whole career and I only played fourteen games!"

In spite of his gilded earnings John's career shuffle had suddenly vaulted him beyond the edge of his own foreseeable future. It was from this uncertain vantage point that he began to navigate uncharted waters.

"I thought I could get into the coaching end," he explained. "Well, I found out quickly that it's a really tough clique to crack. But Bruce Boudreau called and said, 'I'm going to be an assistant coach in Fort Wayne in the IHL.' Bruce asked me if I wanted to come down for a week. 'If you don't like it,' he said, 'you can go home. Nothing will be lost.'

"I was really upset because the owner didn't pay me all the money he owed me."

John Anderson

"So I came down and had a great time! Then the following year, I went to New Haven [of the AHL] as a player-assistant under head coach Doug Carpenter and GM Pat Hickey. I finished the season as Most Valuable Player."

John continued to edge his way towards management by spending two seasons as a player-assistant with the San Diego Gulls of the IHL, joining former NHLers Lindy Ruff, Tony McKegney and Scott Arniel.

But in 1994, he severed his on-ice continuum to work for Mica Sportswear based in Bracebridge, Ontario. "They were into wet-suit manufacturing," he explained. "They'd taken on Scott ski goggles and poles. I was their Canadian sales manager for that year. It was fun and the people I worked with were tremendous—and of course I got to live up in Muskoka for a winter! My whole life, I'd wanted to spend a winter up north, ice fishing and ski-dooing. But my wife and kids were still living in Hartford and I found that going down every couple of weeks was getting to be too much. So I went to look for a coaching job so we could get the family back together."

John found his solution in the Southern

Hockey League where he landed as head coach of Winston-Salem. During the semi-finals of the 1996 playoffs, he lead his charges to victory against Daytona, a team coached by his former teammate, Walt Poddubny.

But the bestowal of year-end laurels came in words without deeds as John was pressed to a sour departure by unscrupulous double-dealings. "When I left the Southern Hockey League," he reported, "I was really upset because the owner didn't pay me all the money he owed me. I was really pissed off needless to say! I wasn't sure if I wanted to stay in coaching, although I loved the coaching aspect—it was the other stuff that was so upsetting."

During his time of indecision, word of his availability travelled to the owner of the Colonial League's Quad City Mallards. A few meetings in the Muskokas salted the deal and John was hurtled on his way to a 1997 league championship. And now the fans come out in droves from along the Illinois-Iowa border to catch a look at this new, frozen phenomenon.

"It's really a hockey anomaly," he explained. "They got their first rink about four years ago. Now, our main rink seats 9,700 people and you can't get a ticket on the weekend! It feels good! After the championship, they gave us a parade televised live—it was like their Stanley Cup!"

But despite his on-ice success, advancement up the ranks remains as hard as a coconut's shell. "I'll give you an example of how tough it is out there," John warned. "I took Winston-Salem, a new franchise, to the finals in my first year and I took the Mallards, a team that ended up eighth out of nine teams the year before, to a championship this year. Now, I could not get an interview for an American League or an IHL job! They always want to hire somebody they're comfortable with. So a lot of coaches, even though not successful for whatever reasons, keep getting recycled back into the system. But I think you'll see a slow changing of the guard as the older hockey echelon dies off. Then you'll see a new guard come in, and they'll bring their friends in. I probably won't get a chance unless one of the people I played with, whom I know

very well, gets a general manager's position"

In the meantime, John will have to settle for celebrity status along the Illinois-Iowa divide.

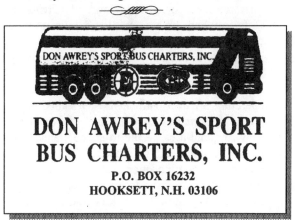

DON AWREY'S SPORT BUS CHARTERS, INC.

P.O. BOX 16232
HOOKSETT, N.H. 03106

Awrey, Don: *Played defense for Boston, St. Louis, Montreal, Pittsburgh, the New York Rangers and Colorado from 1963-1979. Born: Kitchener, Ontario, 1943.*

As a hockey player, Don Awrey savoured a scrappy round of defense the way a train loves its track. Known as "Elbows" around the league of his day, he preferred a full-throttle bodycheck to a dipsy-doodle and relished the thrill of hurling his body into the path of oncoming shots. His reckless brand of play made him a popular man amongst the hometown fans.

Over the course of his sixteen years in the NHL, he played 979 regular-season games. With tongue in cheek, he claims to have never officially signed the form to certify his retirement. "I'm still waiting by the phone for a chance to play my 1000th game," he maintains.

After his final outing with the Colorado Rockies in 1979, Don returned to the familiar turf of Boston where he established his own tavern called "Don Awrey Food and Spirits". The transition into a state of self-employment, however, was not without its afflictions. "I missed hockey," he confided. "I missed the guaranteed paycheque that would come every two weeks versus being in business for myself. The restaurant was successful, but it required a lot more time and energy than I wanted to put out. So I sold it."

From 1983 to 1986, he and the steady paycheque were reunited. He worked first as a sporting-goods sales rep in the Boston area. He then returned to his hometown of Kitchener, Ontario where he was employed by a moving company until they went bankrupt. "I'm not sure if that says much for me and the moving business..."

At present, Don is in his fourth year of operating a travel outfit in Boston called "Don Awrey's Sports Bus Charters, Inc". "I arrange for New England-area people to attend Canadiens' games in Montreal," he reported. "The package includes accommodation, a pregame party, tickets and transportation. I keep them entertained by showing movies of old games that I played in. And of course when I'm seen carrying the puck, they throw comments at me to try and get me going like, 'Oh there's Gretzky'!"

Once he arrives in Montreal, Don knows how to sustain the good spirits. "This year the pregame party is going to be from 3:00 till 6:30," he announced. "I give them three-and-a-half hours of drinks, two for the price of one. I always try and walk around and talk to them and touch base on a personal level."

He organizes about fifteen trips per season. The easy part of his job is arranging for hotels and transportation. The tough part is getting tickets for the game. "In the past, I haven't been able to work directly with the Canadiens," he related. "I've had to go to the scalpers and of course they want your eyeteeth... But if I want a business, I've got to pay them!"

Don also pays attention to how the NHL has evolved since his day. "I don't want to be like a lot of the old guys who downgrade today's game," he stressed. "It's like being an ostrich and sticking your head in the sand. Things do change and time is progress."

He did find one aspect of this progress to be objectionable, however. "Years ago," he commented, "I never saw where a player like Gretzky could go to the Kings and say, 'Look you guys, make a commitment [to improve the team] and I'll sign with you.' Then he goes to St. Louis because they claim to want to win the Stanley Cup. But he wasn't happy there with the six million dollars he was offered. To me that's baloney. Since when do players dictate to teams? The teams are the employers. That's where I don't see eye to eye."

When confronted with spare time, Don enjoys boating, skiing and playing oldtimers' hockey with the Boston Bruins' alumni.

He currently makes his home close to the Massachusetts border in Hooksett, New Hampshire.

Nickname: *Bugsy*

"Phil Esposito gave me the name because I used to bug people in the dressing room and during off-ice activities," Don recollected with pride.

Balon, Dave: *Played left wing for the New York Rangers, Montreal, Minnesota, Vancouver (NHL) and Quebec (WHA) from 1959-1973. Born: Wakaw, Saskatchewan, 1937.*

Although Dave Balon broke into the NHL with the New York Rangers in 1960, his hockey scrapbook didn't begin to swell until he joined the Montreal Canadiens as part of a 1963 blockbuster trade. Jacques Plante, Phil Goyette and Don Marshall headed south to Broadway in exchange for Dave, Leon Rochefort and Gump Worsley.

On Forum ice, Dave began to realize his potential as a solid left winger with a touch around the net. He potted twenty-four goals during his first campaign and by the time he moved on to the North Stars in 1967, he had two Stanley Cups in the bank.

He then returned to the New York Rangers in 1968 where, as a member of the "Bulldog Line", he saved his best for last. By 1971, he was scoring at a personal high in spite of a disquieting sensation that began to make waves deep in his soul.

"I knew something was wrong," he disclosed. "I had thirty-six goals that year and I was on my way to at least forty or more. I was loosing my coordination. After that it was just a nightmare!"

Dave was experiencing the onset of multiple

Dave Balon's sternwheeler, the Neo-Watin, on the waters of Lake Waskesiu

sclerosis, a disease which attacks the central nervous system, resulting in partial or complete paralysis.

"Then I got traded to Vancouver," he recounted. "The next year, I got a shot on my leg and it never healed. I guess with this disease you don't heal properly. After that I gave up hockey. But then I got a call from Jacques Plante in Quebec. He wanted me to join the club. So I went out there and I made the team. At that time though, I didn't realize I was a full-fledged victim of MS. About the second or third game of the season I got hit in the foot ... and broke a bone. I never played again."

Dave retreated to his native Saskatchewan where he coached the Humboldt Broncos of the Saskatchewan Junior League until 1980. He also took on three partners to purchase a fifty-passenger sternwheeler—a Mississippi-style boat. They called it the *Neo-Watin* and operated it on Lake Waskesiu. "I eventually bought out my partners and I operated it myself for a while," he explained. "Then my wife and I ran it for about

seven years. Now, I'm fully licensed. I cook food on board and take out groups and company members. I still own [the boat] but now my son's old enough to operate it. I can't do any manual labour. All I do is drive it and stuff like that. That's about all I can do with MS."

In 1995, however, Dave suffered a setback. "I really had a bad attack this fall," he revealed. "I'm a shut-in now. I'm paralyzed in my legs so I don't get around at all." Dave has been fortunate to be surrounded by a caring family—his son, daughter and wife, Gwen. "She's my biggest support, that's for sure," he declared. "I couldn't do anything if it wasn't for her."

Word of his worsened condition travelled east to the Montreal Canadiens' alumni association. The troops were mobilized and over $50,000 was raised to purchase a van equipped with a mechanical lift. Sporting the license plate "HABS 20", the van was awarded to a surprised Dave Balon at a dinner held in his honour in Prince Albert.

With Burt Olmstead, Dickie Moore, Emile Francis and Bill Hicke in attendance, Dave was treated to a heart-warming and emotional evening that buoyed his spirits and brought mobility back to his shrinking world.

At home, Dave savours his haven of personal mementos and press clippings that attest to the fruits of his labours in the NHL. It is from this vantage point that he reflects on how times have changed. "We didn't wear any shields," he recalled. "We were fearless but we had respect for each other. We respected a guy's head. Now they're so well protected, it looks like they're head hunters out there... The next thing you know, they'll be demanding windshield washers to keep their visors clean!"

Barrett, Fred: *Played defense for Minnesota and Los Angeles between 1970 & 1984. Born: Ottawa, Ontario, 1950.*

Fred Barrett was acquired by the Minnesota North Stars in the 1970 amateur draft. He joined their line-up the following autumn and initiated his fourteen-year career as a bruising, stay-at-home rearguard. Known as "Swoop" because of his quick lateral movement, he specialized in spreading the opposition along the boards in the manner of a rinkboard advertisement.

The nucleus of Fred's physical brand of play was consistently fuelled by the simple love of lacing up the blades and hitting the ice. By 1983, near the end of his career, nothing had changed. "I felt that the best part of hockey was playing the game," he asserted. "I still felt I could play but they decided in Minnesota to go with some younger people. They offered me a position as player-coach in the minors, but I said no. I didn't want to start bouncing around with my family... It's the price you pay to get into management or coaching—you have to pack your bags and be ready to go!

"They traded me to Los Angeles right after training camp. I was in the last year of a contract. I figured if I was going to move out to L.A., I wanted some guarantee that I'd be there for at least one year."

Fred didn't get any assurance from Kings' general manager George McGuire. "I wasn't making big money," Fred declared. "And moving my wife and kids from Minnesota to L.A. is culture shock. So at that point I said I was retired."

Later that year, Roger Neilson became the Kings' head coach and coaxed him to join the club for one final season. To grease the wheels, the team arranged to fly his wife, Lois, out to Los Angeles once a month so the family could remain based back in Minnesota. At the close of the season, in spite of the sweet deal, he then stayed true to his word and retired for good.

> *"Playing pro hockey is basically glorified shift work."*
>
> **Fred Barrett**

"Maybe it would have worked out differently if I had been a little more flexible," he speculated. "But I don't regret that now. We're very happy where we are. The family's intact and that's really the most important thing. There is a lot of life after hockey."

With walking papers in hand, Fred then returned to the reliable ambiance of Minnesota to contemplate his next move. While sorting through the loose ends of transition, he visited a career counsellor who prompted him to look inward and realize that through his career on ice he had developed life skills that transcended the arenas from which they were born.

With fresh resolve on the rise, he embarked on a trial run under the aegis of a custom home builder in Minneapolis. But after two years, he realized that construction work was not his calling. Instead he responded to a hunch that his native Ottawa, with extended family and friends was a better wager—and it was. In 1987, he found his niche with the Gloucester Fire Department.

"Playing pro hockey is basically glorified shift work," he explained in comparing hockey to firefighting. "My work involves teamwork and, when the alarm goes off, there's that same rush I got as a player. There aren't many professions that offer this!

"Sometimes you run into situations that are really tough. You have to deal with death and with people who are badly hurt. But it's also similar to hockey in that there's a bit of a boys-will-be-boys attitude... Certain people are easy to get a rise out of. I remember when this guy ... came in just after we'd cleaned all the floors. He walked all over them with rubbers on. He was going to do a talk on fire prevention at the school and we happened to get some peanut butter on the inside of his rubbers. When he took them off at the school, he had this brown stuff all over his shoes. He looked like he'd been tramping through a manure pile!"

Fred still keeps in touch with hockey through his work with the Ottawa Senators' alumni association and as coaching chairman of the Leitrim Hockey League.

He closed our conversation by reflecting back on his experience in the NHL: "In some ways I think it was a great time to play because I was able to go against my boyhood idols like Howe, Delvecchio and Beliveau. From 1970 to 1983, I went from those people right through to the Gretzky's and Lemieux's. From that point of view it was a real pleasure to be involved."

Barrett, John: *Played defense for Detroit, Washington and Minnesota from 1980-1987. Born: Ottawa, Ontario, 1958.*

Long before his days in the NHL as a strong, physical blueliner, John Barrett lived and worked on his father's 160-acre dairy farm near Ottawa. While in high school, he met his future wife, Cheryl, and gradually set a solid, community root deep into the Gloucester soil.

Throughout his career and transition out of the game, the farm, the family and the community were always there to serve as a compass and a point of reference. "I was very lucky ... that I knew where my home was," John affirmed. "I know guys I played with that met their wives in different cities. When their careers were over, they had to ask, 'Where are we going to go?' There's a lot of pressure there to make that decision.

"Many players leave home at such a young age and don't keep their ties. I used to come home every summer to help my dad with the farm, so I still have that network of friends that I grew up with. We're all still a big, close group."

There was little question about where John wanted to be when he left the NHL. The real question, however, was what to do for a second career.

Friends had suggested that he get into business for himself. John and Cheryl felt otherwise. "From the time I was fifteen or sixteen years old," he recalled, "I was given a paycheque, meal money and ... they made all my travel arrangements. There's nothing you do in the game of hockey that prepares you for a business venture. When you're thirty years old and you've never been in charge of anything, it's kind of a scary thing to do."

John opted to pursue a more secure profession. He and his brother, Fred, had had their eyes on firefighting as a career of choice. Fred had already hooked up with the Gloucester Fire Department, but John had to wait for an opening with one of the regional departments.

During the next two years, he picked up odd jobs to hold himself over while preparing for various firefighting exams. He drove a furnace-oil truck, cleared snow and did landscaping work to make ends meet.

"Going eight to five, six days a week. That's the hard part to get used to after you've played hockey for fifteen years," he observed. "That going to work every day is a bitch (laughs)! We worked long hours in landscaping. We were up at six and worked till dark. That was a real big eye opener. You say to yourself, 'Whooof! This is life'!"

John got his break with the Napean Fire Department in 1990. "I really enjoy it," he declared. "We have a thirty-man platoon with eight guys in a shift. We're a bit like a team. When we go out on a call, everybody has a job to do. I like it that way—there's a lot of comradery.

"I know some people at the department find themselves very nervous when the tone goes off. I don't find any pressure myself, because of the intense pressure I had playing hockey. I know there are times when there are unfriendly things that have to be done. We see a lot of car accidents and stuff like that. You don't want to see any more of that than you have to—but you realize that you have a job to do. I saw lots of injuries and lots of blood in hockey, so it doesn't bother me."

"We worked long hours in landscaping. We were up at six and worked till dark. That was a real big eye opener. You say to yourself, 'Whooof! This is life'!"

John Barrett

Outside the fire hall, John enjoys raising his three children and coaching minor hockey. He and his brother, Fred, helped establish the Ottawa Senators' alumni association which generates about $50,000 a year for important local causes.

John still rates tending the family farm as his number-one source of satisfaction. "We were a dairy farm until I left to play junior hockey," he recalled. "Now we just take the hay off and grow some cash crops. So it's not a daily commitment."

Nicknames: *Buff*; *Bear*

"They called me 'Buff' first, as in buffalo because I was big and had long hair then," John mused. "But 'Bear' was the name the guys in Detroit called me all those years. I was a stand-up bodychecker and I really wasn't much of a fighter. But anytime I got into a fight, if somebody punched me once, I knew he was going to punch me again. So I used to put a big bear hug on him, squeeze him, lift him up and throw him to the ice."

Bassen, Hank: *Played goal for Chicago, Detroit and Pittsburgh between 1954 & 1968. Born: Calgary, Alberta, 1932.*

Hank Bassen was a feisty redhead who was as adept at swatting goal-crease transgressors as he was at shoring up gaps between the pipes.

He made his first NHL break with the Chicago Blackhawks in 1954-55. After two seasons of spot duty, he was dealt to Detroit in a blockbuster exchange that saw Ted Lindsay and Glenn Hall move to Chicago.

Hank enjoyed his most heated action in 1960-61 when the Red Wings made a run to the Stanley Cup finals. The Wings came close against a powerful Blackhawks' squad, but were eventually vanquished, four games to two.

In 1967, he was traded to the expansion Pittsburgh Penguins where he played one additional season before closing out his career with an overall goals-against average of 2.99. Fourteen seasons of minor- and major-league hockey were enough to leave him yearning for a well-planned transition.

During his days in the NHL, Hank had joined forces with a partner to establish an excavation business in his hometown of Calgary, Alberta. He was now more than ready to make a full-time leap into the operation of Kitsul/Bassen Excavation Ltd. which specialized in preparing foundations for new home construction.

Their company was equipped with heavy-duty earth-moving machinery and, at its height, employed as many as thirty-five workers. Being a sociable type, Hank focused on the public relations and business end of the operation.

A recession hit Alberta in 1980, however, bringing a sustained slowdown to the construction industry. Many companies went down including Kitsul/Bassen. After twenty-four years of service they were forced to close their doors.

"Everyone used to come to us and say, 'You lost it all'," Hank's wife, Shirley, reported. "I think it should be made known that we didn't lose it all. Sure we felt bad because we lost a good company. But we didn't lose the best part—we still have each other. We have our family, we have our health and we have the Lord!"

In the wake of Kitsul/Bassen's disquieting demise, Hank returned to the world of hockey as general manager of the Calgary Wranglers of the Western Hockey League. He stayed on for two successful seasons before the club folded as a result of financial difficulties experienced by the team's owner. From 1988 until his retirement in 1992, Hank worked as a salesman for a local printing company.

He and Shirley have raised four sons and a daughter. One of their sons, Bob Bassen, followed his father's footsteps to the NHL where he currently plays for the Dallas Stars.

"A real highlight for our family has been our experience of Christianity," Hank added. For sixteen consecutive summers, he volunteered his teaching services to Hockey Ministries International, a training programme combining Christian values with effective hockey skills.

These days, Hank and Shirley reside in Calgary where they are enjoying family life which includes frequent visits from their nine grandchildren.

Bathgate, Andy: *Played right wing for the New York Rangers, Toronto, Detroit, Pittsburgh (NHL) and Vancouver (WHA) between 1952 & 1975. Born: Winnipeg, Manitoba, 1932.*

Scouting in professional hockey has become a business of turning over stones, sifting gravel and speculating on tiny particles of talent. In Andy Bathgate's day, however, a boulder of skill and potential could crash through the rink window and catch as much attention as a custodian gives to a wrapper on the floor.

"I went to Guelph because my older brother Frank was taken there by the Rangers," Andy explained of his efforts to join the Ontario Hockey Association's Biltmore Madhatters. "I was not invited... Actually, they weren't even going to give me a chance. But Frank said, 'If you're not going to give Andy a tryout with the team, then I'm going to Oshawa with him!' He really threw a fit and said, 'If you don't give me my release, you fellows are not going to get out of this room!'

Andy Bathgate enjoying a summer day in Guelph

"So they gave me a tryout and I made the team. We played together on the same line. I scored twenty goals that first year and we won the OHA... It was the only time I ever played with my brother, Frank. We had lots of fun together and a lot of good memories.

"When you're kids, you've got to stand up for yourself. My father had passed away when I was thirteen. So we had to stick together a little bit and sometimes, we took the law into our own hands (laughs)."

Andy went on to flourish as an elite member of the New York Rangers starting in 1952. As an early proponent of the slap shot, he racked up a career-high forty goals and forty-eight assists in 1958-59. The following season he tagged Jacques Plante in the face with a shot that was instrumental in precipitating Plante's introduction of a mask into regular-league play.

In 1964, Andy was traded to the Toronto

Maple Leafs as part of a high-stakes gamble by Punch Imlach to maintain buoyancy amongst his troops. Andy seized the moment, scoring five vital goals during the playoffs to claim his lone Stanley Cup victory.

The following season, he had a falling out with Imlach and was shipped to Detroit where he toiled until the league underwent its first expansion. "I went to Pittsburgh with the draft in 1968," he recalled. "I played there for the full year and I think I got the most points of anybody playing for an expansion team that year. The next season at training camp, they advised me that I had been traded to the Montreal Canadiens. They wanted me to retire and coach the Montreal Voyageurs in the American League. But I decided that I was prepared mentally and physically to play another season. So I went out west and played two years with the Vancouver Canucks."

In 1970, Red Kelly invited Andy to return to the Penguins. "I said, 'I'll come back and play, but if I'm not helping the team, I don't want to stay'," he recounted. "After January, I wasn't getting much ice time. It was getting to be a real bore. I needed one goal to end out my career at 350. But I never got an opportunity to score it because I didn't get any ice time... So I thought it was time to hang 'em up."

In 1971, Andy became the first NHL import to play in Europe. He, his wife, Merle, and their two children relocated to the Swiss village of Ambri-Piotta where he coached and played with the local villagers.

It took little time for the opposition to figure out that to beat Ambri-Piotta—you had to beat Andy Bathgate. "I had to be very careful over there," he confided. "Being the pro, I had to keep my mouth shut. I didn't want to be critical of their style or system. I took a lot of abuse because the other teams would come up and spit right in my face. They knew if I dropped my gloves it was an automatic suspension. I didn't

know how to handle it. I used my stick because when somebody spits in your face, you want to whack them! You don't care if you get beat up! Some of them really got me upset at times, so I didn't take any mercy on them."

After one season in Europe, Andy returned to Canada and resumed his association with the world of golf. "I've been in the golf business since I was playing junior in Guelph," he recalled. "My brother and I had a driving range out along Highway 6. When I was traded to the Leafs in 1964, I bought a range in Mississauga and I've been at it ever since."

Andy Bathgate Golf Centre is located one mile from the town centre known as Square One. "The location is convenient," he noted. "I get a couple of hundred thousand cars going by a day. We usually keep 150 tees open at all times.

"My son works full-time with me and my wife is there almost every day. I enjoy it. I like working for myself and being outdoors."

In 1972, Andy went into partnership with Harry Howell and Vic Hadfield to develop the Indian Wells Golf Club in Burlington, Ontario. "We bought a farm," Andy recounted. "Harry Howell wanted to stay in California. He sold out before we started building. So Vic Hadfield and I were partners. I thought that the place could have been developed into one of the top, public golf courses around. But Vic wanted to go private. I said, 'Well, if that's what you want, you better buy me out,' which he did."

In 1975, Andy spent a year and a half coaching the Vancouver Blazers of the World Hockey Association. "I enjoyed Vancouver, but I didn't like the direction that the WHA was going," he asserted. "I thought it was better to get back into business for myself."

Twenty years have now passed since Andy left professional hockey. In reflecting on the conditions and experiences of his era, he is sometimes amazed at what was achieved in the

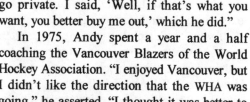

"I had to take a $1,500 cut to join the NHL. We had no choice. They had complete control over us."

Andy Bathgate

Some forty-five years after the fact, Madhatters Andy Bathgate, Chuck Henderson, Harry Howell and Lou Fontinato continue to uphold the tradition of lifting cars for reasons other than repairs.

face of adversity.

Playing hockey in Madison Square Gardens, for example, had little of the shine associated with the bright lights of New York City. "In my eleven years there, we practised seven times on the Garden ice!" he remarked. "We were upstairs on the fifth floor on a little dinky rink with aluminum boards. It was chaos when you think of how archaic our times were. We had Gump Worsley at one end and a piece of plywood with four holes at the other end. And I've got pictures to prove it!"

Andy also keyed in on salaries as another example of how the world turns: "I was just thinking today that what Gretzky or Messier gets for playing one shift, I got for a whole year! My last year in Guelph, I was helping my mother and I needed some money. I got $125 playing for the Biltmores and I worked for Muller Collision Service for $64 a week, if I got my forty-two hours in. So basically, I was earning $200 a week and forty weeks would give me $8,000 a year. But then I had to go to New York to play for

$6,500. I had to take a $1,500 cut to join the NHL! We had no choice. They had complete control over us."

Andy concluded that the real fortune earned in hockey came from the relationships that evolved while growing up. "Junior is the most memorable time for any young boy," he affirmed. "You go from a peach-fuzzed little kid to a young man. And you make life-long friends like Louie Fontinato, Harry Howell and Dean Prentice. All of us keep in touch. And if I needed some help from Louie or Harry ... they would be here in a minute. And I know that I would be there for them too... Sure you meet different guys in pro hockey, but they come and go. The junior boys, you seem to remember. Winning is one thing, but we had a lot of fun growing up together.

"In fact we did a lot of fun things like hiding Louie's car. Every time the police chief moved his car, we'd put Louie's there. Louie was pretty well always the last one out of the dressing room. So about six of us would put his car between two parking metres. We'd lift it up on the curb and he

30

couldn't get it out. He'd get so mad at us. We'd have a few battles on the ice about it, but it was all in good fun."

Nickname: *Tubby*

"They called me different names in New York, but nothing stuck at all," Andy reported. "But a lot of guys used to call me 'Tubby', just because of a bathtub I guess."

Bennett, Curt: *Played centre for St. Louis, the New York Rangers and Atlanta from 1970-1980. Born: Regina, Saskatchewan, 1948.*

The name Bennett had been ringing a vague bell around the NHL since long before Curt Bennett arrived on the scene with the St. Louis Blues in 1971. His father, Harvey, played twenty-four games in goal for the Boston Bruins in 1944-45. His dispiriting claim to fame occurred on the night of March 18th, 1945 when he surrendered one of the more famous goals scored in league history—Rocket Richard's fiftieth marker in his fiftieth game of that season.

Curt made reference to the event with a kind of filial pride that dwells not on the negativity, but rather on the virtue of his father and the Rocket making hockey history together.

Curt followed his father to the big leagues, and, as if to avoid any possible relapse of the family name, played every position during his decade in the NHL—*except goal.*

Spending most of his time at centre ice, his forte was as a special-teams man, killing penalties and serving on the power play.

As he began to slow a step by 1980, Curt left the NHL in search of a more manageable adventure—this time in the Orient. He packed his bags, his stick, plus a *Berlitz* phrase book and headed to Japan.

"We played in a little town called Mikko, which is about two hours north of Tokyo," he recalled. "My brother, Harvey, and I both played there for two years. We were the *gijan* or foreigners and the rest were all Japanese guys. There were six teams, like the old NHL—it was their version of pro hockey. The difference was

Curt Bennett & Company

Commercial Real Estate

Curt Bennett
Owner

5200 Northside Drive - Atlanta, Georgia 30327
Fax: (770) 952-4261 - Beeper: 638-0222
e-mail: cbennet@onramp.net
home page: http://rampages.onramp.net/~cbennett

we usually all traveled to one city and played a tournament against each other...

"We enjoyed the experience just as much as the hockey. I wrote some articles on the difference in mentality when I was over there. They had a veneration for older players. Here, we get rid of you when you're old and put in a young guy. There, they'll do it too, it's just that they have more of a protocol. They're very sly. They just kind of put the players out of the way. We short-circuited [their process] a couple of times. We made the younger guys play because we were player-coaches. It backfired on us though because the kids played terribly. They were embarrassed! We won the battle but lost the war."

In 1982, Curt returned to his home base in Atlanta to enter the field of commercial real estate. "It was a big change," he said of his transition. "First of all, you were used to shorter hours and doing something you were skilled at. Then you enter business and you're doing something you're not skilled at. I compare it to when you first learn how to box. You get punched a lot. Someone asks, 'Do you like boxing?' You say, 'No, I don't like it because I get hit so much!' Well business is the same way. You have to readjust. It's somewhat of a problem though because hockey players are used to making a lot of money. They go into a business and think, 'Well, I'll make a lot of money here too.' But you can't jump from one peak to another. You have to climb the mountain again. But some guys figure, 'I made $300,000 in hockey, I'll just work half as hard and make $150,000 in business.' It just doesn't work that way!"

By 1988, Curt had set up his own commercial office-leasing firm under the name *"Curt Bennett & Co."*, which he still operates. "I was working with a couple of developers, trying to get some form of hockey back here," he explained. "We ended up getting the Knights of the IHL, so I needed some flexibility. That's one of the reasons I went into business for myself. Also, I like being able to make my own decisions. Almost all of my brothers own their own businesses. I don't know why—it must be something my dad did. We don't like authority!"

"Then you enter business and you're doing something you're not skilled at. I compare it to when you first learn how to box. You get punched a lot."

Curt Bennett

Curt joined the club as part owner and assistant coach during the Knights' first year of operation. He then sold his shares but continued to assist the team until their departure from Atlanta in 1996.

He now has his eyes set on something bigger. "My main goal is getting an NHL team here. It's got to be!" he exclaimed. "How can they pass it up? I mean they're hitting every other city. I think [Ted] Turner will get us a team. He owns the basketball and baseball teams. They're in the process of building a new stadium, so they're going to need another tenant."

Any spare time Curt has on his hands is quickly replaced with a tennis racquet. He maintains a court at his home and is presently ranked third in the state of Georgia in the forty-five-year-old category. He also slips away on occasion with former Toronto Maple Leafs' defenseman Kurt Walker for some scuba diving.

Nickname: *Vas-y*

"I got the name from Guy Chouinard while playing for the Flames," Curt related. "He and some of the other French players would look at me and say '*Vas-y*', which means 'go on'!"

Berenson, Gordon (Red): *Played centre for Montreal, the New York Rangers, St. Louis and Detroit from 1961-1978. Born: Regina, Saskatchewan, 1939.*

During the 1996 NCAA playoffs, Red Berenson stood behind the bench of his Michigan Wolverines and watched along with the world as Mike Lake lifted the puck onto the blade of his stick, came out from behind the net and neatly dropped the puck over the shoulder of the opposition's unsuspecting goaltender. It was an unusual move that seemed to defy conventional thinking. But for Red, the unexpected was nothing new.

During the late fifties, as a college-aged kid, he faced the dilemma of whether to play junior-A hockey or to continue with his schooling. "The mentality of the day was, 'You'll never be a pro if you go to college'," he remarked. "But I really believed in education, so I got my bachelor's degree... When I got into pro hockey, there were six teams and I was sent down and up. I could see ... the fact that my career could be over in a minute or that it might go in a direction I didn't feel comfortable with. But what were the choices? I didn't want to be a career minor-leaguer. I just wanted to have some options and at least have a step up on the dilemma the average hockey player finds himself facing when he's finished."

Once Red joined the NHL, he used his summers to complete a Master's degree in Business Administration. He could then play a full hand in hockey and still have a spare deck to deal in the bigger game of life.

By 1978, he had not only proven that a college player could make it to the NHL, he had demonstrated his staying power as well. With over 1,000 games and 695 points to his credit, he had made his point and, at the age of thirty-nine, was ready for the comfortable fit of an office chair.

The mercurial path of transitions, however, dealt him a curve which lead straight back to the Blues' fold as an assistant coach under Barclay Plager. "The main reason I did that was to keep our family in a stable environment," Red

32

explained. "I really never had an aspiration to be a coach."

During his second season behind the bench, Red took over the head coach's position and survived its precarious hazards until midway through the 1981-82 season.

He then jumped from the pan to the edge of the burner, joining Scotty Bowman and Jim Roberts as an assistant coach in Buffalo. "I felt that we made a good coaching team," he said. "We were building a young team there. I think a coach can contribute more with younger players than with the older players. They need you more in terms of their development and in helping them adjust to pro hockey."

In 1984, Red intensified his commitment to young, aspiring hockey players by assuming his present role as head coach at his Alma Mater, the University of Michigan. "The experience has been excellent," he remarked. "Hockey is very popular in this area and the cause of combining hockey development with education is something I really believe in.

"I made a tough call to go to school when [very few] did at that time. I proved that you could do it and I guess I'm a good role model for young kids who are ... trying to accomplish their dreams. I'm encouraging kids to get an education, to have something when hockey's over. But they're still being told by a lot of people in hockey that they'll never be a pro if they go to college. So we're still fighting that same mentality thirty-five years later."

Away from the rink, Red has devoted much of his spare time to his four children and his wife, Joy, whom he married while in college. "She's been through it all with me," he respectfully noted. Their family tradition has been to pack up the trailer and canoe for a two-week camping trip every year. "I'm a serious canoeist and camper," he added. "I've gotten together with Jim Roberts and his family every summer for the past twenty years. We'll pick some spot and all meet there with our trailers and gear."

Bladon, Tom: *Played defense for Philadelphia, Pittsburgh, Edmonton, Winnipeg and Detroit from 1972-1981. Born: Edmonton, Alberta, 1952.*

On December 11, 1977, Tom Bladon and the Philadelphia Flyers squared off against the Cleveland Barons in a lopsided affair that vaulted Tom into the NHL record books on the force of his four goals and four assists—the most ever scored by a defenseman in one game.

His feat was highly indicative of his style of play as a hard-shooting, offensive-minded defenseman who made his home on the Flyers' point for six seasons. He scored the bulk of his offensive output during that time before being bounced to Pittsburgh, Edmonton, Winnipeg and Detroit during his final three seasons in hockey.

The moves from city to city were unsettling and retirement only brought more of the same. "I don't think it's easy for anybody," he admitted. "I don't think you've heard too many people say that it was a snap to walk out of hockey and into something else. I can tell you that it's a difficult transition."

After his departure from Detroit in 1980, Tom returned to his native Edmonton and, for the next eleven years, worked for United Van Lines. "I dealt with all the major corporations in Alberta, handling their personnel and office relocations," he explained. "I ended up in a dispute with my employer, an agent for United. This agent ended up switching van lines, bouncing around doing some goofy things and to boot, decided down the road that he wanted me to take a substantial pay cut. Then we ended up with problems in the courts which was a real pleasant experience!"

Tom eventually put the agent, the courts, United and Alberta behind him, opting to resettle in Victoria, British Columbia. He bought a local business called "Action Awards and Sportswear Ltd." which specializes in engraving awards and trophies as well as selling sports clothing and accessories. "It's been a challenge to say the least," he admitted. "We took a business that was going downhill.

I've certainly tried to improve on it. We've got it going in the right direction but it's still not there." He noted that although turning the enterprise around has required a great deal of time and energy, he remains hopeful that his company's bottom line will continue to resist the gravity of slow markets and stiff competition.

When spare time overtakes his workload, Tom likes to hang loose on the golf course and at the local ice rink in the company of old pros like former NHLer Lyle Moffat.

At home, he and his wife, Diane, are raising four daughters. "It's been terrific!" Tom exclaimed. "The kids are our life. They are your entertainment for a lot of years."

Nicknames: *Bomber; Sparky*

"I was called a lot of things," Tom joked. "'Bomber' just meant that I could shoot the puck. I got it from Dale Tallon in ... Pittsburgh.

"Joey Watson used to call me 'Sparky'. I don't know what it meant. He just hung it on me. I wasn't that crazy about it. I always thought it sounded more like a dog (laughs)."

Blight, Rick: *Played right wing for Vancouver and Los Angeles between 1975 & 1983. Born: Portage la Prairie, Manitoba, 1955.*

Rick Blight's first three seasons with the Vancouver Canucks were the most stable and productive of his career. As a mainspring of the Canucks' power play, he used his effective shooting skills and goal-crease radar to tally 187 points.

His final three seasons, by contrast, were characterized by uncertainty, instability and itinerancy. After being dispatched by the Los Angeles Kings in 1983, he and his wife, Donna, earned enough travel points to buy their own airplane. He saw action in Dallas, Cincinnati, Switzerland, Wichita, Moncton and New Haven before hanging up his blades—and his wings. He was homourously emphatic about his final experience in New Haven in 1987: "That was it! I knew I was never going back to the NHL. I was getting slower and slower."

In retirement, Rick hit Vancouver again, this time with plans to become a stockbroker. "It seemed like a nice life, so I thought I'd try it," he recalled. While with the Canucks he had gotten to know a few brokers and had made a few bucks for himself while dabbling in the market. So, on the crest of bullish resolve, he completed a Canadian-securities course and then entered the fray. His shot at the market soon wavered,

"I think that last year in Vancouver cost me about twenty grand. The market was terrible!"

Rick Blight

however, flying well over the target and into the investors' mire. Luckily, the family business back in Manitoba was in urgent need of his help. "Dad phoned and said they'd bought the place in Carmen," Rick recalled. "Actually I didn't come back soon enough. I think that last year in Vancouver cost me about twenty grand (laughs). The market was terrible!"

Having evaded the claws of the great financial bear, Rick retreated to his native Manitoba to manage an outlet of the family farming equipment business, Blight's Portage Ltd., in the town of Carmen. Seven years later, his father retired and Rick returned to Portage la Prairie to take over management of the entire operation. The business and its manager are still thriving today.

"We do a million-and-a-half dollars in parts business each year between the two places," he said. "We also sell farm equipment, tractors, combines and four-wheel drives. In fact I just sold Chuck Lefley and his brother a swather!"

Observing his rural clientele, Rick mused: "Farmers are the sanest group of people you've ever met for fifty-one weeks of the year. But the first week of harvest, lots of guys go brain dead. We're in an extreme business. When we're busy, we're way too busy and when we're not busy, we're nowhere near busy."

In his off time, Rick enjoys family life with Donna and their two children. As well, he likes to golf and has taken up what he humourously called "that stupid curling game".

—⟨⟨⟨⟨⟨⟩⟩⟩ –

Bodnar, Gus: *Played centre for Toronto, Chicago and Boston from 1943-1955. Born: Fort William, Ontario, 1925.*

Gus Bodnar was a crafty, fleet-footed centreman who joined the Toronto Maple Leafs at age eighteen in 1943. During his first-ever shift, he stepped into the face-off circle, watched the puck fall amongst smashing sticks and adroitly whisked it free and through to the twine in fifteen seconds flat—a league record as the fastest marker by a rookie.

Gus used the remaining forty-nine games of his opening season to secure an additional sixty-one points and a Calder Trophy as the league's top rookie.

His first campaign was his best although he continued to gain notoriety as a member of the "Flying Forts"—a line comprised of Gus, Gaye Stewart and Bud Poile, all natives of Fort William, Ontario.

Gus won two Stanley Cups with the Leafs before moving on to Chicago where he made more league history on the night of March 23, 1952. Right winger Bill Mosienko caught fire with an intense flash, scoring three goals in twenty-one seconds—a league record that remains untouched to this day. Gus was the feed man and, as such, holds the record for the fastest three assists.

But there's much more to Gus Bodnar than mere clever dekes and passes. If he hadn't chosen hockey for a profession, he might have pursued a career as a storyteller. Some fifty years later in retirement he requires only a slight nudge to launch himself and his listeners into the NHL of the 1940's.

When asked if he had a nickname as a player, Gus began to unravel one of his tales: "I

> *"You had to watch every transaction, because people ... had itchy fingers. The night clerk used to rent two or three rooms for himself and one for Gus!"*
>
> Gus Bodnar

didn't have any monikers as far as the press was concerned. But the players called me 'Little', which I was! I was only 145 pounds—but they had to catch me! The best lesson I ever learned happened during my first year of training camp. I got a real awakening. Bucko McDonald's on defense and I was a fresh kid coming from Fort William-Port Arthur—you know, with lots of curly locks of hair and nineteen years old. I'd get out on the ice puttin' the puck between their legs and going around them and all this kind of stuff. Bucko McDonald said, 'You're making us look bad you know son!' So I came along one time with my head down, looking at the puck with my hair over my eyes and, Jeez, he stepped into me. Ho, lights out!! Did he ever cork me. He rattled my teeth! Of course when Bucko expanded his chest, I think it was sixty-five [inches]. God, when he hit you, he hurt you! He just lifted me up and carried me to the bench, put me down there and said, 'I told ya, you're making fools of us. I recommend that you go get your hair cut.' So I went right back to the hotel and, Jeez, I got a brushcut. Cut it all off! That's the best lesson I ever learned about keeping my head up!"

Gus also kept his eyes open during his time in the NHL for career options outside of professional hockey. "I didn't have any leisure summers," he said. "I just kept busy." He spent his off-season time working first for a brewery and then for an engineering firm.

"I turned down a contract for the '55-56 season," he remarked of his departure from the NHL. "I had a pretty good job and I was married with a couple of children. I thought I'd better stay with a job that I knew well because hockey wasn't too stable—one year in and one year out."

Gus made the transition, directing his full-time energy to Corman Engineering where he had spent his summers. "We were doing general machine shop work and we were in the tool-and-die business," he explained. "Then they went hog wild, going strictly for aircraft parts, but they didn't look after their other customers." As a result, Corman went under.

Although working full-time, Gus always reserved his evenings and weekends for some kind of hockey enterprise. He coached the Lakeshore Bruins for a season before taking the helm of the Brampton Rangers until about 1960.

After Corman went down, he struck out in a new direction, purchasing the Benson Hotel in Lindsay, Ontario. "Boy, was it tough work! It had fifty rooms, a dining room, a coffee shop and a beverage room. I bought myself a pretty good job ... oh and how!" he exclaimed. "You had to watch every transaction, because people ... had itchy fingers. The night clerk used to rent two or three rooms for himself and one for Gus! I didn't have a good partner there—not until I caught on and let them all go. I decided, 'Boy, if I have to do this, I'm going to drive myself up a wall!' So I sold the place."

Drawing on his previous experience at Corman Engineering, Gus was able to land a job as a Toronto-area sales rep on behalf of Dahmers Steel, based in Kitchener, Ontario. As before, he devoted his days to Dahmers and his evenings and weekends to his new coaching post with the Toronto Marlboros. He maintained this harmonious union until the late sixties when Punch Imlach invited him to coach the Sabres' Western Hockey League affiliate in Salt Lake City.

With a leave of absence from Dahmers in hand, he promptly headed west to Utah. "The team owner at the time wanted a winner," Gus recalled. "He wanted some oldtimers. All Punch had was a bunch of overaged juniors which he sent to me to bring up to the NHL level!"

Of course that wasn't the only point of contention that Gus had to field between Salt Lake's owner and the Sabres. "We'd have attendance of 14,000 for a game and the owner of the club would report that all we had was 7,500," Gus related. "Punch would get on the line and I didn't have to hold the phone to my ear! He'd

Nickname Challenge #1

Big Sam

"When I first went away to play hockey years ago, a fellow with the Associated Press in Boston called me 'Big Sam'. I happen to see him most every year and he doesn't remember why he gave me the name. Maybe I was a bit bigger than the average hockey player then. 'Big Sam' always meant to be a big, friendly guy."

Who is he?

Clues

a. He played defense for the New York Rangers, Chicago, Boston, Toronto and Philadelphia from 1948-1969.

b. He was a second-team all-star in 1960 & 1966.

c. He won four Stanley Cups.

If your point shot was deflected wide, see page 285.

say, 'What the hell is he talking about? How many people did you have?' I heard him right from Salt Lake to Buffalo! There was some skulduggery going on, so Buffalo dropped their affiliation with Salt Lake."

Gus then reinstated himself in Ontario and eventually became head coach of the Oshawa Generals of the OHA for six seasons. During the shuffle he transferred his services to Gatt Steel, working as a sales rep in the Toronto area.

By the late seventies, he had retired from the Generals and from the steel industry, although he initiated the latter in stages because Gatt found it hard to live without his services.

He rounded out his long and variegated hockey career with a season of coaching the Team Canada juniors and another as president of an earlier incarnation of the Ontario Hockey Association.

These days, he and his wife, Etta, spend winters at their home in Florida and summers in Oshawa. Gus's great love is the game of golf. He even goes so far as to make his own clubs and occasionally takes requests from admirers. "They look at my clubs and say, 'Where'd you buy those?' And I say, 'Well, I made them.' It's just a hobby. I don't go out and make a business out of it."

Gus and Etta have raised four girls and a boy. Etta hails originally from the Isle of Lewis in the north of Scotland, where on a recent pilgrimage to her birthplace, Gus underwent a cultural transformation: "When I got there," he quipped, "they initiated me as *Mc*Bodnar!"

Quizature #1

Clues

A. He broke into the NHL with the Chicago Blackhawks in 1970-71.

B. He also played for the Canucks and the Kings before retiring from the Sabres in 1984.

C. His nickname comes from a 1930's movie starring Fay Wray.

If you're still short-handed, see page 285.

Boivin, Leo: *Played defense for Toronto, Boston, Detroit, Pittsburgh and Minnesota from 1951-1970. Born: Prescott, Ontario, 1932.*

Leo Boivin was born and raised along the banks of the St. Lawrence River in the small town of Prescott, Ontario. Like any young lad, he was entranced by the allure of the seaway in all its forms. When the currents were at flow, Leo was at play, faithfully swimming, fishing and exploring nature with the consummate methodology of a child. When winter came, the seaway stood still and became host to throngs of gliding tykes, tots and teens.

"We had many a hockey game on the St. Lawrence River," Leo recounted. "We had some open-air rinks close by and anytime the river was frozen, we'd go there and skate too. I remember being on skates since I could walk!"

Leo's career in professional hockey took him to cities, towns and hamlets throughout North America, but Prescott and the St. Lawrence have always remained his home port.

"Many years ago, I started out with a three-bedroom cottage overlooking the river with a boathouse underneath," he explained. "We'd go there all summer.

"But one day, my wife, Patricia, said to me, 'We're going to start staying in one place.' So about nineteen years ago, I made a permanent home of it. My three boys and I added eighty feet.

"The house looks both ways up and down the St. Lawrence River. The big ships that pass by aren't any more than a quarter of a mile out in front of my place. I've got a window on the west side and patio doors on the east side, so I can see them coming up and I can see them going down."

Back in the early fifties, as a young up-and-comer, Leo got his first crack in the NHL with the Toronto Maple Leafs where his titanic hip checks quickly earned him the name "Snake Hips". Standing 5'7" and weighing 190 pounds, he was as durable as a fire hydrant and difficult to ignore in close quarters or on open ice.

By 1970, as a grizzled veteran, Leo had completed training camp en route to his nineteenth NHL campaign when word came from above that his blueliner days were done. "I was in Minnesota at the time," he recalled. "I was thirty-eight and it seemed that management wanted to go with younger players. But it didn't bother me one bit. I said, 'Fine!'—I was about to retire anyway. So I just packed it up.

"Punch Imlach was with Buffalo at that time and he bothered me for a month, wanting me to play for him. But I said, 'No, when I retire, I'm going to stay retired,'—which I did."

Leo stayed on with the North Stars as a scout for two additional seasons before trying his hand as head coach of the Ottawa 67's of the Ontario Hockey Association. "I enjoyed coaching the 67's," he confided. "But it was quite a chore to coach those kids."

He then returned to the realm of the NHL in 1975. "I was scouting for St. Louis until they fired the coach [Lynn Patrick]," he explained. "I was asked to fill in as an interim coach..." By 1976, Emile Francis took over but was fired and again, Leo stepped in as head coach until February of 1977, when he surrendered his sword, preferring to stick with his role as a scout.

"Coaching is a tough job," he confessed.

"We had many a hockey game on the St. Lawrence River. We had some open-air rinks close by and anytime the river was frozen, we'd go there and skate too. I remember being on skates since I could walk!"

Leo Boivin

"It's not so bad if you're the coach, general manager and president. If you've got all the strings you're all right. But otherwise, with the players making lots of money, you can't threaten them or do very much. It's not like you have to have them under your thumb, but you do need a little authority. So I really only liked the scouting end of things. I was on my own. I just had my general manager and chief scout to deal with."

Leo continued to scout for the Blues until the early eighties when general manager Emile Francis invited him to transfer his services to the Hartford Whalers. It is there that he remained until his retirement in 1993.

At present, with his easy-chair lifestyle now thoroughly rehearsed, Leo gazed back on the well-worn path he had travelled as an NHL scout. "It's like I was in a suitcase and every night I was going somewhere," he related. "We covered all the leagues, high schools and colleges all over the country. We did everything! For example, I'd go into Boston to see some high school games. I might see as many as four or five games in a day! I'd see a game, drive maybe twenty-five miles, see another and then drive to the next one and so on."

The search, however, was rarely for undiscovered gold. The nature of his work centred more on the verification of league-wide collective grubstake. "There were no Bobby Orr's... I mean everything was covered," he explained.. "Each team had five or six scouts and they'd seen them all. You couldn't draft a guy till he was seventeen. So when your turn came in the draft, you knew who you wanted and you just hoped that the guy was still there."

Since packing it in, Leo has given his luggage the same well-deserved rest as he bestowed upon himself. "I haven't moved out of here except for my trip to Boston for the last hurrah at the Gardens in '95," he said with peaceful resolve.

He is now content to savour his life from the vantage point of his perch overlooking the St. Lawrence. He takes great pleasure in doing woodworking and construction projects around the house and for friends in need of help. "I don't have any trouble puttin' in my time," he mused.

Hockey is now limited to an occasional trip to Ottawa to see his grandsons play and his Saturday night trips to see the South Grandville junior B's play at a local rink.

In reflecting back on his own career in the NHL, Leo cited hard work as the backbone of his prolonged existence at the top. "You worked so hard to get there as a youngster," he revealed. "Then you had to work twice as hard to stay there."

In 1986, he received the ultimate acknowledgment for his commitment to hockey—he was inducted into the Hockey Hall of Fame along with Dave Keon and Serge Savard.

"I was just so happy and elated," Leo beamed. "To be in with guys like Howe, The Rocket, Beliveau, George Armstrong and Timmy Horton... Jeez, I'll tell you, I was on cloud nine for a while. It was a great thrill and an honour!"

Nickname: *Billy*

"They used to call me 'Billy' when I was in Boston," Leo remarked. "It had no real meaning. It's just that we had Leo Labine playing there. So that with two Leo's, everybody called me Billy."

⊂▥▻ –

Bolton, Hugh: *Played defense for Toronto from 1949-1957. Born: Toronto, Ontario, 1929.*

As Hugh Bolton matured in the midst of the Toronto sports scene, his greatest passion was reserved for baseball rather than hockey. He could certainly shoot and skate with the best of his peers, but a ball on the sweet part of the bat lead straight to his heart. Since Canada offered few professional baseball opportunities at the time, he made the pragmatic choice of playing hockey while satisfying his eccentricities by means of his other passion—electricity.

He juggled his love for sports and academics until he entered his first year at the engineering department of Queen's University in Kingston, Ontario. That's when the balancing act came undone. Hugh's on-ice exploits had caught the eye of the Toronto Maple Leafs who made him an offer he couldn't refuse: a chance to play for the Maple Leafs' affiliate, the Toronto Marlies. There was, however, one condition attached to the offer made by Leafs' owner Conn Smythe: "Hugh, you have to either think hockey or school, but not both." So he elected to think hockey first and school later.

"Hugh, you have to either think hockey or school, but not both."

Conn Smythe

He soon found himself teamed on the Marlies' blueline in the company of a revitalized Flash Hollett. When the Leafs' Stanley Cup hero of 1951, Bill Barilko, met with a premature death, Hugh was promoted to fill his skates. It was a tall order to live up to the bashing-Barilko style of play, but Hugh threw his 6'3", 190-pound frame into the fray without reservation.

He stayed with the Leafs' organization until 1957, when a severe leg break ended his career. He promptly entered the University of Toronto where he completed his degree in electrical engineering. He then pursued his career in education, teaching grade thirteen physics at various secondary schools in the greater Toronto area. In 1988, he retired as head of the science department at Scarlett Heights.

These days, Hugh enjoys spending his leisure time puttering around the cottage and playing bridge. He and his wife are occasionally joined by their two sons and spend the remainder of the year at their home in Weston, Ontario.

Boschman, Laurie: *Played centre for Toronto, Edmonton, Winnipeg, New Jersey and Ottawa from 1979-1993. Born: Major, Saskatchewan, 1960.*

When Laurie Boschman joined the Toronto Maple Leafs as a rookie in 1979, he made no bones about his deep commitment to Christianity. Skeptics bristled, claiming that a man of religious beliefs would lack the necessary killer instincts to succeed in the majors. Laurie wasted little time in demonstrating that, to the contrary, a belief in the Lord and an old-fashioned round of knock-em-down hockey were quite compatible.

Laurie was an excellent skater who could gun for his share of the offensive spoils while staying the course through an abundance of scraps and scrums along the boards. By the time he retired from the Ottawa Senators in 1993, he had amassed 598 career points and 2,405 penalty minutes.

Over the course of his fourteen seasons in the NHL, he had also frequently donated his spare time to various Hockey Ministries International camps along with fellow NHLers such as Ryan Walter and Mike Gartner. After stepping out of his Senators' jersey, Laurie took a breather for a year to enjoy time with his wife, Nancy, and their three sons. He then accepted his present position as the Ottawa and Eastern Ontario Director for Hockey Ministries International.

"I do a lot of speaking engagements, awareness weekends and hockey clinics," he reported. "In that context we talk about hockey skills and we also talk about life skills. Our aim is to develop the whole person and not just the physical aspect of things. We incorporate Bible principles that have helped us in our lives and in our careers. We feel that we are passing along something that has proved to be very valuable... We believe these values work and will certainly stand the test of time! It's very rewarding when we are able to share that with young people, their parents and grandparents."

"This year they will have twenty-eight camps across Canada, the U.S., the former Soviet Union, the Czech Republic, Sweden and Switzerland," he added.

Since his days with the Jets, Laurie has also maintained a sideline interest in some shoe stores in Manitoba. "It's more of an arms-length investment," he added. "It continues to go quite well. I'm very pleased with it."

At home, family life and leisure time are integrally linked for Laurie and Nancy. "Like so many parents who have children involved in activities, we spend a lot of time shuttling them around," he remarked. "We like to build family memories together. My wife and I enjoy each other's company and we enjoy being with our kids ... snowmobiling, boating, fishing and water-skiing."

Bouchard, Dan: *Played goal for Atlanta, Calgary, Quebec and Winnipeg from 1972-1986. Born: Val d'Or, Quebec, 1950.*

Dan Bouchard's father, Marcel, was a shrewd, semi-pro who was sautéed and seasoned in the oil of minor-league hockey. He once played for Eddie Shore's Oakland Oaks of the U.S. Hockey League; he skated stride for stride with Dave Keon in Noranda; and although he never made it to the NHL, he was the first-round draft choice of the Montreal Canadiens in 1950.

When son, Dan, came of age, Marcel brought him along for a firsthand look at life as a semi-pro in northern Ontario and Quebec. "I became a rink rat," Dan fondly recounted. "I followed him everywhere."

As a youngster in Val d'Or, Dan's life was a goal-mouth scramble of ice, sticks and blades at every turn. He had only to look out his window to see five backyards in succession bound together into one solid rink with a perimeter of boards.

It took him little time to gravitate towards his position of choice. "My attraction to become a goalie was the equipment," he confided. "One of my uncles was a goalie and I always thought that was neat. For me, to carry the equipment and strap it on was a real fascination and obsession. I was mimicking goaltenders and then the first thing you knew I was playing in Ville La Salle for Jacques Lemaire's father, Émile."

As Dan set his sights on higher goals, his

father, Marcel, was there to help him forge a vision. "I came back from a pee-wee tournament in Quebec City one day," Dan recounted. "I found it extremely exciting to play in front of twelve, fourteen thousand people. I remember when my father came to pick me up at the train station. I said, 'You know Dad, I'm going to become a hockey player.' He said, 'Well, that's great!'

"So one day, coming home from church, we stopped at a convenience store. He went in and bought some hockey cards. He opened a pack and gave me Terry Sawchuck. He said, 'There's a very good goalie. You can learn a lot from that guy.' Then he goes to throw the other cards away and I said, 'Don't do that! I can trade them.' He said, 'What do you want to be a goalie or a forward?' I didn't know what he was getting at. Then he opened another pack and there was a Jacques Plante, then a Glenn Hall and then a Johnny Bower. He said, 'Here, you've got those four guys. When we get home, I'll tell you what to do.'

"When we got home, he gave me a cardboard liner from a new shirt and said, 'Glue a card on each corner and learn everything you can about those guys—imitate everything they do—you'll learn a whole lot'!"

Dan followed his father's advice and by 1970, he was playing for the Hershey Bears of the American Hockey League, an affiliate of the Boston Bruins. In 1972, he caught his major-league break as a draft pick of the expansion Atlanta Flames.

At the outset of his NHL career, Dan received good advice from another old pro. "It was my first official game in the NHL," he recalled. "We were playing in the Montreal Forum. Frank Mahovlich came down the wing about fifteen feet inside the blueline. He took a slapper about two or three inches off the ice, binged it off the post and it went in. Big Frank skated by and said, 'One of many kid! One of many!'

"Years later, when we played in a Canada-Russia series in '77, my roommate was Frank Mahovlich. I walked in the room and said, 'You were right Frank, it was one of many!' He laughed and said, 'You remembered!'

"When Frank said, 'One of many', he didn't mean *he* was going to score many. He meant that if I played a long time, I was going to give up goals. A guy beans it in off the post—you've got to live with those. The other guy's got talent too!"

Dan played out his final days in the NHL at the Winnipeg Jets' training camp in 1986. "All the young guys would come around me," he explained. "I used to help them out. Dan Maloney was the coach that year. I don't know if he felt threatened by that or not? I always lived under the motto: 'If I can bring success to someone else's life, I'll always have mine.' One day Fergie [general manager John Ferguson] called me and said, 'It's not going to work. I'd like to keep you here. You helped us make the playoffs last year ... but [Maloney] doesn't want you around'."

So Dan left the Jets' camp to play in France for three weeks when he tore the anterior-cruciate ligament of his left knee—that was the nudge he needed to retire. He stayed on as the team's coach until the end of the season at which time he began a four-year stint as a goaltending coach for the Quebec Nordiques.

With his wife, Janet, and their two children based in the Atlanta suburb of Marietta, Dan commuted north to Quebec once a month to oversee the development of Stephane Fiset and Jocelyn Thibeau.

When his relationship with the Nordiques ended in 1994, he shifted to his current post as vice president of S.P.T. Product Development which specializes in the development and marketing of sports performance technologies.

"We just finalized our patent in late December [1996]," Dan said with pride and anticipation. Their unique line of products includes special garments that regulate body temperature; golf clubs that enhance drives; as well as shoes and skates that reduce vibration, absorb shock from impact and channel the energy into the next stride.

This new technology, known as "Power Skin", was developed in conjunction with the

Omar Rice Sports Enhancement Centre at Georgia Tech University.

"It can enhance anyone's daily life," Dan emphasized. "A guy who works in a factory or a guy bent over in a garage—the sky's the limit!"

"I had brain surgery in 1990. I gave some as a test to the doctor who performed the fifteen-hour operation. He said that after the operation, he wasn't as tired; his legs weren't as dead; his back wasn't as sore. He reorders the stuff all the time.

"It's been really interesting. But we've had to spend all kinds of money to secure the patents. Everybody put in just about everything they had. It's been very hard to work two years for nothing. But we have something here we believe in!"

With legal rights firmly in hand, Dan and his partners are close to securing deals with larger corporations that will put Power Skin around the bodies of athletes, workers and seniors around the world.

Bouchard, Émile (Butch): *Played defense for Montreal from 1941-1956. Born: Montreal, Quebec, 1920.*

In the old-time era of smallish, hard-nosed hockey players, Butch Bouchard towered as a mountain among foothills. Standing 6'2" and weighing 205 pounds, his shorter adversaries were hard pressed to scale him or to circumvent his long reach. As one of his opponents once observed, "He wasn't fast but he got around."

Butch was first discovered by Montreal Canadiens' coach Dick Irvin who, through strong faith and encouragement, transformed the gangly blueliner into one of the league's premier defensemen.

He joined the Canadiens in 1941 and immediately brought stability to a struggling line-up. From that day forward until his retirement, he served as a rearguard mainstay winning three first-team all-star awards and was eventually appointed to the team's captaincy.

At the start of the 1948-49 campaign, however, Butch's future was dimmed by the glare of a serious injury. "The doctors thought I couldn't play anymore," he noted with a dash of determined pride.

"I was just married in 1947, so I got a business going to fall back on," he added. That business was the Butch Bouchard Restaurant which he established in Montreal in 1948.

Butch Bouchard

Of course he roundly outlasted his doctor's predictions. "I played hockey and ran the restaurant for another eight years!" he exclaimed.

When he first launched his venture, Butch had no experience in the food industry, so he worked with a knowledgeable partner for three years before becoming the sole proprietor.

In 1951, however, things began to heat up in his kitchen. While on a road trip in Detroit, the restaurant caught on fire. "It did quite a bit of damage," he recalled. "And the city would not give me a permit to repair it. So I had to rebuild the restaurant completely. I spent about $350,000! That was a lot of money in those days and I don't have to tell you that I didn't have it. I had to put a mortgage on the place and it took me twenty-five years to pay it off.

"When it was finished, there was room for a banquet. All totaled with the basement, it was four-stories high. I could seat about sixteen hundred people..."

By the mid-fifties, Butch's tenure on the Canadiens' blueline was drawing to a close. "After fifteen years in hockey, you're not getting any better," he observed. "My intention was to retire the year before, but Toe Blake asked me to stay on because he wanted an experienced defenseman. [Jean Guy] Talbot was a rookie and Toe Blake figured he wasn't ready for the game yet. Talbot finally replaced me in the middle of the '56 season, but I stayed on with the club until the end. We won the Stanley Cup and that club went on to win five in a row."

Shortly after leaving hockey, Butch was approached by the Brooklyn Dodgers' organization to serve as president of their triple-A affiliate, the Montreal Royals. The club's storied past included such baseball players as Jackie Robinson, Duke Snyder and Roy Campanella.

"When I was there, Sparky Anderson was playing with us and Tommy Lasorda was pitching," he said. "He was a very good minor-league pitcher."

By 1980, however, the encompassing pace of restaurants, ball parks and fame took their toll on Butch's health. Experiencing heart trouble, his doctors advised a change of lifestyle. So he sold his restaurant and is taking life easier—although according to his son, Pierre, not too easy: "He got himself one of those exercise bicycles. We've been teasing him with that. He's never used one in his life and now at seventy-seven, he's finally riding one!"

Butch and his wife, Marie-Clare, currently maintain a winter home in Belair, Florida, a condominium in Montreal and a country home across the road from their son, Pierre, who has a farm outside of Montreal. "I like to have my grandchildren at my house in Verchers," Butch says. "My wife and I enjoy their presence. I have a swimming pool and eight acres. I like to garden and play a game of golf here and there."

Bouchard, Pierre: *Played defense for Montreal and Washington from 1970-1982. Born: Longueuil, Quebec, 1948.*

Pierre Bouchard frequently refers to directing his life on the basis of dreams and visions. The earliest source of those visions came through his birth into the hustle-and-bustle world of hockey and restaurants.

"I was still very young when my father retired," he recalled. "I was only about seven years old, so I probably only saw him play about ten times. I remember going to practices though and going into the Montreal Canadiens' dressing room when I was four or five years old. I saw Jean Beliveau, Maurice [Richard] and all the guys sitting with my dad. I still remember the smell of the wintergreen they used to rub on themselves to help their muscles."

"I lived in Fort Lauderdale for six months and took some real-estate courses. But then I saw that there were more people with real-estate licenses than drivers' licenses!"

Pierre Bouchard

As Pierre grew older, his father Butch's restaurant became the starting point for his life-long association with the hospitality industry. "My first job was as a cook in La Sapinière ... and after that I was a bellboy in a hotel," he recounted. "I took some courses at *L'École d'Hôtelerie* in Montreal. Now I'm still with a chain of sports restaurants called *La Cage aux Sports*, which has forty-two [outlets] around Quebec. I'm on the board of directors plus I do some public relations. I'm also a shareholder."

Pierre took a cue from his father's on-ice example as well. As a hockey player back in 1970, he was plucked from the Montreal Voyageurs by general manager Sam Pollock to add toughness to the Canadiens' defensive corps. Like his father, he played a physical, stay-at-home brand of defense and at times could be confused for Ken Dryden's third goal pad. Pierre joked about the Bouchard family's scoring prowess by noting that it took him and his father only twenty-seven years to notch eighty-seven career goals.

By 1981, Pierre was a battle-worn member of the Washington Capitals. "I was tired," he recalled. "It was the end of the line—I was thirty-four. I went to the minors with the Hershey Bears for about half a season. But when I saw that I was going nowhere and that I had no chance to go back up, I retired."

With his blades and stick in storage, Pierre

unearthed his well-defined plan for the future. "My dream was to farm in the summertime in Montreal and do real estate during the winter months," he explained. "So I went from Washington to Florida. I lived in Fort Lauderdale for six months and took some real-estate courses. But then I saw that there were more people with real-estate licenses than drivers' licenses (laughs)! Everybody who goes to Florida is semi-retired and thinks they'll do some real estate on the side. Once I realized this I said, 'Uh oh, that's not for me'."

He then reestablished himself in his native Quebec and accepted an offer to be a television colour analyst for the Nordiques. "I jumped right in," he declared. "The only experience I had had was being interviewed between periods. And it was a big thing for me because I was very shy when I was young. I couldn't be in a theatre play or talk in front of people. I just couldn't do it. But then you get the roll of things and learn what people like to hear."

After one year with the Nordiques, Pierre returned to Montreal to step up his broadcasting career. From 1984 to 1990, he hosted a two-hour sports phone-in show on CKC radio. A year later, the CBC also hired him to be an analyst between periods for Canadiens' games on Saturday nights.

In 1993, he left the CBC to assume his present post as a colour analyst for hockey coverage with RDS, the French counterpart to The Sports Network.

And although absorbed in the transitions and excitement of real estate and broadcasting, Pierre never lost sight of his dream to farm.

"I have a farm where I'm living now. That's my main job during most of the summer," he noted. "Starting in April till about November, we raise grain and beef cattle. We've got twelve hundred acres ... and a few horses."

Sharing the farm with Pierre is his wife, Kathleen, and their children, Émile and Sophie. Looking back, Pierre observed, "I've been very, very lucky. I thank hockey for that and I thank my father for being there."

Boutette, Pat: *Played right wing for Toronto, Hartford and Pittsburgh from 1975-1985. Born: Windsor, Ontario, 1952.*

Although small in stature, Pat Boutette was big enough at heart to stick his nose into any hornets' nest that stood between him and success in the NHL. He was a feisty winger who could mix things up with whatever it took: fisticuffs, checking, jousting or scoring. Through ten seasons split between Toronto, Hartford and Pittsburgh, Pat, otherwise known as "Bouter", racked up 477 career points and roughly twenty-five hours of game-time in the penalty box.

When his big-league days were finally up in 1985, he packed his bags along with his practical approach to the game, and as was the case with any adversary, he looked retirement straight in the eye.

"I think at the end you basically had to say, 'Hey, it's over.' Which I did," he explained. "I had a young family and you've got to go on with your life. So you start wherever you can. I say it wasn't easy ... it's a big transition in your life. You're thirty-two, thirty-three years of age and you've got to start a whole new career. You've basically got to put everything behind you, look forward—and away you go!"

Pat's friends and relations were still very much a part of life in southern Ontario. So he, his wife, Betsy, and their two daughters reestablished themselves in Toronto. Once settled, Pat soon found work through a family connection as a manager of The Old Mill Restaurant in Etobicoke.

"In hockey, you control your own destiny," he asserted. "But when you get into business, it's not only the people you're working with, it's also the customer that is number one. So the service industry is quite a bit different. It's hard work, but it's like anything, you've got to be attentive. You've got to be well focused..."

Since 1991, Pat has been president of a company that owns and operates The Doctor's House, a restaurant-banquet facility in Kleinburg, Ontario. He keeps himself right in the thick of the project. "We've got about sixty full-time staff," he reported. "From an operations point of view, I make sure that everything runs on an even scale from day to day. We've got so many things going on: weddings, corporate functions and social functions. We've got food costing to do, menus to do. There are millions of jobs that have to be done. You just try to keep things as organized and as smooth as possible.

"Yesterday we had almost five hundred people here: three hundred for brunch and three weddings. It can get pretty hectic around here at times."

As a healthy contrast to the rush, Pat puts the squeeze on his spare time to play squash, golf and keep pace with the evolving dynamics of fatherhood.

Brimsek, Frank: *Played goal for Boston and Chicago between 1938 & 1950. Born: Eveleth, Minnesota, 1915.*

The phone rings. Frank Brimsek picks up the receiver to hear, "Have you got a moment to talk hockey?" With a warm and seasoned voice, he replies, "I'm retired now. I've got all the time in the world. Hang on a second, I'm going to pull up a chair..."

He eases his way into a comfortable spot and begins to tell the tale of a remarkable life.

Frank was born in Eveleth, Minnesota where winter culture was not unlike that found in Canada. As a teenager, he watched his brother perform second-string duty in the nets at Eveleth High School. One day, however, his brother's fantasy to play defense boiled over thus clearing the way for Frank to don the pads. He liked the fit and persisted with the game right up the ranks to the Providence Reds of the American Hockey League.

In 1938, Boston Bruins' general manager Art Ross put his neck on the line by selling the inimitable Tiny Thompson to Detroit to make way for his colossal hunch—Frank Brimsek.

At risk of being run out of town on a rail, a nervous young Frank stepped into Tiny's giant skates and stunned the hockey world with seven consecutive shutouts. By season's end he had ten goose eggs, a 1.58 goals-against average, a Calder Trophy as the league's top rookie, a Stanley Cup and a Vezina Trophy as the league's best netminder.

With Frank in goal, the Bruins' fortunes soared. They finished in first place three years in a row and, in 1941-42, claimed another Stanley Cup. That same season, he was named a first-team all-star and skated away with his second

Nickname Challenge #2

The Duke of Discount

"Dave Babych called me 'the Duke' when we were in Hartford. I thought, 'Yeah, John Wayne.' But he said, 'No, the Duke of Discount', because I could usually find good deals around town. But of course I would say it was my resemblance to John Wayne."

Who is he?

Clues

a. He played left wing and right wing for Toronto, Hartford and Minnesota from 1980-1993.

b. His initials are S.G.

If you missed the five-hole, see page 285.

Vezina Trophy.

By 1943, however, the magic thread hit a snag. World War II was screaming louder than the Gardens' fans as Frank left the NHL to enlist in the United States Coast Guard. During his eighteen months on the deck of a patrol craft in the Pacific, his perspective of life underwent a profound and inexplicable change. "When I got out of the war I knew I wasn't going to play long because I didn't have that same feeling for the game," he recounted. "Actually I had a hard time even going back to training camp. Before the war I couldn't wait. When the snow fell, I was ready to go.

"I had spoken to Art Ross in 1947. I told him that I would like to leave Boston in '49 to go to Chicago in '50. My brother was starting a business there and I thought I might help him open a few doors. Art Ross agreed, but when it got to '49, he didn't like the idea anymore. I told him, 'If that's the way you feel, I'll quit hockey altogether!' I was going to quit right on the spot."

In the end, Frank prevailed, winning his ticket to Chicago where he endured one final, arduous season before packing in the pads for good. "It didn't bother me at all," he insisted. "I had that feeling five, six years before, so I knew it wouldn't bother me to quit."

To set the foundation for the next phase of his life, Frank returned to Virginia, Minnesota to build a house. He rolled up his sleeves and got in up to his elbows. "I'll tell you, in our neighbourhood, we had to learn to do it all!" he exclaimed. "Repair cars, carpentry work, everything. We started building in May and we moved in at the end of November. Holy Jeez that was tough work! I had to mix the concrete for the bricklayers. They had two separate batches. I had to deliver one to them and I had to keep the other one mixed so they would never run out. The two bricklayers were working on different parts of the house, so I had to carry the bricks to them in different directions!"

By 1951, the house was complete, the bricks were arrayed, and Frank was free to join the Duluth, Winnipeg & Pacific branch of the Canadian National Railway. "I had to start first in the roundhouse where they service the engines," he recollected. "Those were steamers then. We didn't get diesels till 1956. You had to learn about the engines first. You took an exam and when they thought you were ready, they'd give you a job firing.

"And that was quite a job! They had stokers then, so you didn't have to shovel coal, but you had to keep the back end of the boiler banked and then you got a better fire and better steam. I liked it more than diesel because it kept you so busy you got from one point to another before you knew it."

After three years on the firing line, Frank was promoted to an engineer. When asked about his experience of driving a train, he replied: "When you get on the train, the rails take care of the driving. But you've got to make sure you read your orders because we had a single track and you met oncoming trains. So you had to make damn sure you didn't go past the point of meet. I got so I knew every tie on that rail, all the way."

He also gained an intimate knowledge of the rural scenery between Virginia and the Canadian border. "I enjoyed it because I saw a lot of game: wolves, moose, deer, lynx and bobcat. I saw one lynx so big, I thought it was a deer at first!" he exclaimed.

"One time, I hit a wolf. There was deep snow that winter and the wolf wouldn't get off the track. I tried to slow down for him, but I

"One time I hit a wolf. There was deep snow that winter and the wolf wouldn't get off the track. I tried to slow down for him but I scraped his side... The section crew told me they mounted the wolf. They said, 'Jeez, that was the perfect job' ... The skin wasn't even broken."

Frank Brimsek

46

couldn't. I scraped his side. I told the section crew when I got up to Canada. So a week later, when I made the trip up north again, the section crew told me they'd mounted the wolf. They said, 'Jeez, that was a perfect job.' I didn't damage the wolf at all. The skin wasn't even broken!"

When Frank managed to get himself off track, he found great pleasure in slipping away for some fly casting and hunting. "He'd take his dog and go duck hunting all the time," observed his wife, Marguerite. "He loved it!" Now in his eighties, Frank is no longer up to the vigours of the hunt, opting instead for an easier lifestyle.

Married in 1940, he and Marguerite are approaching their fifty-eighth wedding anniversary. They've raised two daughters and now have five grandchildren plus two great grandchildren.

Bromley, Gary: *Played goal for Buffalo, Vancouver (NHL), Calgary and Winnipeg (WHA) from 1973-1981. Born: Edmonton, Alberta, 1950.*

Gary Bromley was a stand-up goalie who weighed in at a slight 5'10" and 160 pounds. He usually played a conservative-style game relying on his small frame to generate quickness and agility with whatever limbs were needed.

He opened his NHL career with the Buffalo Sabres in 1973 as a backup to Dave Dryden. The following season, he got his one and only shot as a major-league workhorse, appearing in fifty games while leading the Sabres to an Adams Division championship. From that point on, he would have to draw straws for his share of the goal crease, whether in Buffalo, Calgary, Winnipeg or his final stop, Vancouver.

By the start of the 1980-81 campaign, Gary found himself as the third man in a trio comprised of Canuck goaltenders Glen Hanlon and newly arrived "King" Richard Brodeur. Something had to give and in the end it was Gary, whose rights were traded to the Los Angeles Kings. Having read the fine print on his new contract, he knew it was time to look for a day job. "I had applied to the Vancouver Fire

Gary Bromley of the Vancouver Firefighters

Department the summer before my last season," he recalled. "Because when I signed a two-way contract with L.A., I pretty well knew which way it would be no matter how well I played. I was a bit disappointed because I did have a good training camp.

"So they sent me down to New Haven for the year. But I still had the idea that I was going to get on with the fire department. When I came back to Vancouver at the end of the season, I applied to the department again and got on. So I took the secure job.

"I've been at it now for almost fourteen years. It's been a terrific experience. Like hockey, firefighting is a team game with comradery and shift work ... so the transition was easy."

The firefighters of British Columbia pull for one another when the going gets hot and they're a keen bunch to hit the cold ice for a good cause.

There are approximately twenty hockey teams in their league, each representing a different fire department from Vancouver and the lower mainland area. During Gary's third year on the force, they took a team to Toronto to compete for the national title. "We won the whole thing," he declared with pride. "It was the first time that a team from Western Canada had ever won the Canadian Firefighters' Championship, so that was a nice little thing to add onto hockey."

A man of strong family values, Gary enjoys spending time with his wife, Kathy, and their three children, camping during the summer and skiing during the winter.

He, Kathy and the kids currently make their home in Coquitlam, British Columbia.

Nickname: *Bones*

"I was a skinny guy at 160 pounds," Gary admitted. "During my first year in the Eastern League, Bob Shupe, who weighed 230 pounds, was standing next to me and said I was skin and bones—'so we'll call you "Bones" from here on in.' And so they did."

Brown, Arnie: *Played defense for Toronto, the New York Rangers, Detroit, the New York Islanders, Atlanta (NHL), Michigan and Vancouver (WHA) between 1961-1975. Born: Apsley, Ontario, 1942.*

"You don't choose to quit hockey," Arnie Brown remarked of a path well worn by many veterans of the NHL. "You either get too old, you're not fast enough or you've got injuries. In my case I had eight operations, four in each knee. I just couldn't play anymore."

Long before Arnie's legs were hobbled by errant twists and turns, he was regarded as a promising prospect in the Toronto Maple Leafs' farm system. In 1964, New York Rangers' general manager Muzz Patrick took notice and had Arnie's rights thrown in amidst the throng of players who flew south to Broadway in exchange for Andy Bathgate and Don McKenney. For the next six seasons, Arnie served the Rangers as a hard-hitting defenseman with a taste for the elegance of an up-ice rush.

By 1971, his legs began to falter as he experienced a rapid succession of placements in Detroit, New York, Atlanta, Michigan and Vancouver. "You tend to not feel so much a part of the team when you start getting traded," he explained. "So I felt fairly bitter when I had to quit. I remember calling Mr. Eagleson at the Players' Association office, trying to find out if there were any opportunities for me... I didn't even get a phone call back. So I decided that I was going to get away from the game and make it on my own. I felt that it was important ... to prove that I could do something else."

> *"So I felt fairly bitter when I had to quit. I remember calling Mr. Eagleson ... trying to find out if there were any opportunites for me. I didn't even get a phone call back."*
>
> Arnie Brown

With convincement on the boil, he plotted a new course as a salesman in Toronto for the plastics department of the Monsanto Corporation in the spring of 1975. After two years, however, he was lured back into hockey on the basis of his friendship with Orland Kurtenbach. Arnie stepped in as an assistant coach for the Vancouver Canucks throughout the 1977-78 season. "The Canucks were in the depths of despair as far as talent and position in the league," he lamented. "It didn't work out very well. Unfortunately Orland got fired and so did I."

Retreating over an unburned bridge, Arnie recouped his position with Monsanto as a salesman at their Vancouver office. By 1981, he was promoted to sales manager for Monsanto's central region of Canada, a post which he assumed at the company's office in Toronto.

Since 1990, he has enjoyed an appreciable advancement as an account manager for the Safe Flex group in Detroit. "Safe Flex" is Monsanto's brand name for a type of plastic that holds windshields together in spite of shattering impact. He flies coast to coast and throughout Europe, handling Monsanto's world-wide contracts in his particular field.

Outside of his regular job, Arnie has played alumni hockey wherever he has worked. As well, he harbours a sacred devotion for the wilds of the north: "My wife and I still have a home and a cottage up in Canada," he notes. "We go up there as many weekends as we can. I like to fish and hunt."

Over the years, he and his wife, Sandra, have raised a daughter and a son and currently maintain their principal residence in Detroit.

Bucyk, Johnny: *Played left wing for Detroit and Boston from 1955-1978. Born: Edmonton, Alberta, 1935.*

Johnny Bucyk is hockey's answer to the character actor who dependably supports and bears witness to the stars and story lines that rise and climax—year in and year out.

His first important role was to perform on the Bruins' "Uke Line" with Bronco Horvath and Vic Stasiuk. Success ran high for Johnny and the Bruins until 1960, when the team entered a seven-year dearth at the bottom of the standings. Johnny knows, he was there.

When the Bruins resurged to claim two Stanley Cups under the aegis of Bobby Orr and Phil Esposito, Johnny knows, he was there too.

As Orr and Espo gave way to Terry O'Reilly and the "Big Bad Bruins", Johnny's work in the corners fit right in until age and injuries dictated a change of script.

"My last season in '78," he recalled, "I didn't dress for the playoffs. So I did some colour on the radio. I just dove into it..."

His new role as the media curator of Bruins' tradition was both logical and appropriate for the man whose life thread is woven through two decades of the team's history.

"Right after I retired as a player, I kind of took a year off, but I still worked for the Bruins' organization," he continued. "We had thirty-four

stations all through New England carrying the broadcasts. I spent the year doing promos for them, going out to different stations, doing interviews and meeting all the people. The following year, I got into doing a little bit of the marketing and became part of the broadcast team with Bob Wilson."

"Since Bob retired, I'm just doing the pregame, post-game and intermission shows. I'm *really* enjoying it." Johnny travels with the team while the show's host remains in their Boston studio. If a guest is available, Johnny does an interview. Otherwise he and the host discuss current affairs around the league.

In addition to broadcasting, Johnny coordinates public relations events for the Bruins' alumni. "I'm listed as the director of the alumni association," he pointed out. "We do a lot of functions for different charities, raising about $300,000 a year. We play about twenty hockey games a season and some baseball during the summertime."

All told, Johnny's stock-in-trade of sticks, bats, clubs, mikes and timetables has him yearning for an eighth day of the week. "It's quite an operation to work: running the alumni, putting the games together, going to different charitable events. I just don't get any time off!" he exclaimed. The only breaks he insists on are for his participation in the annual Hall of Fame golf tournament in Toronto and to spend his summers out west with his wife, Anne. "I go to my little place in British Columbia and retreat to play golf and fish," he added. "They've got some big trout out there!"

Nickname: *Chief*

"'The Chief' was my most popular nickname," Johnny recalled. "Bronco Horvath tagged me with it years ago when we played with the Edmonton Flyers, a farm club for the Detroit Red Wings. He called me 'Chief' because I was always putting things together. They also used to say I was the chief of the corners. With my dark complexion, I guess everybody thought I was an Indian ... a lot of people still do. But actually, I'm full-blooded Ukrainian."

Burrows, Dave: *Played defense for Pittsburgh and Toronto from 1971-1981. Born: Toronto, Ontario, 1949.*

Dave Burrows was born into a world of console radios and televisions which beamed their black-and-white renderings of the *tricolore* and the blue and white into living rooms across the country. The wispy signals and muted, silver images were, in turn, recolourized by the voice of Foster Hewitt who, in a single evening, could etch the names Mahovlich, Richard, Beliveau and Horton into the impressionable minds of young Canada.

"As a kid you grow up watching those guys," Dave remarked. "Then, when you actually get on the ice with them and get to know them, it's a thrill! I remember watching Tim Horton as a kid. Then when I got to Pittsburgh, I ended up playing with him. So that was a real highlight for me."

As a rookie in 1971, Dave hopped over the boards and into a career filled with the excitement of joining Tim Horton in fending off players whose careers lingered on longer than the echo of Foster Hewitt's voice.

A decade later, however, the greats from his youth had gone back stage and the magic was fading. "To be honest with you," he confessed, "the game kind of lost its fun for me. So I thought, 'It's time to move on.' I figured it was the right thing to do—to leave when *I* wanted to rather than when the management told me I was done. I was at the stage where I'd had a good career. I knew it wasn't going to get any better..."

At the conclusion of the 1980-81 season, Dave called it a day. "I was very unprepared for retirement as far as what I was going to do with the rest of my life," he admitted. "It was nice that hockey gave me enough money that I could take a couple of years to sort that out.

"My wife, Carol, and I had always liked the country. We wanted some acreage where we were going to build our dream home. We found a piece of property that we really liked near Shelburne. We wanted to retire there and we were going to live happily ever after. But then after a year or two of that, I thought, 'Boy, I'm going to have to do something sooner or later.' You get too much

time on your hands."

To rustle up some excitement, Dave took charge of a miniature golf course and driving-range facility for the year that followed. "The place was close by," he added. "I thought it would be fun and it was."

"In 1984, my family and I moved to Caledon where I became director of hockey operations for Teen Ranch, a Christian sports camp," he continued. "We had a hockey team which toured to raise money for different youth activities. The camp was also rented out to different churches and youth groups. We ran programmes for them ... everything from horseback riding to tobogganing."

Dave Burrows

But beyond the surface of merriment and games, Teen Ranch had a deeper objective. "We tried to meet the kids not only on a physical level, as far as sports go, but also on their mental, emotional and spiritual levels as well," he explained.

In 1992, Dave left Teen Ranch and moved north to Parry Sound where he carries on his commitment to young people as manager of the Optimists Youth Centre. The facility was built recently through the efforts of the local Optimists Club under the motto: A Friend of Youth.

"I do everything from developing programmes for kids to renting the facility out for weddings and meetings," he reported. "The space is given out to a gymnastics club, Girl Guides and so on. Renting the facility only helps to pay a few of the bills."

He and Carol presently live in a house overlooking a Muskoka lake in the region of Parry Sound—an ideal setting for his prime interests of hunting, fishing and "anything to do with the outdoors".

Nickname: *Bone Rack*

"While I was in Pittsburgh, some of the guys used to call me 'Bone Rack' because I was pretty thin," Dave recalled. "I got it around Halloween when all the skeleton pictures were up. Some of the guys like Bob Paradise would say, 'Look, there's Davy Bone Rack'!"

———⟨※⟩———

Carleton, Wayne: *Played left wing for Toronto, Boston, California (NHL), Ottawa, Toronto, New England, Edmonton and Birmingham (WHA) from 1965-1977. Born: Sudbury, Ontario, 1946.*

Wayne Carleton was on the edge of his first break into professional hockey when a serious knee injury sidelined him into hospital for nearly eight months. "I was sixteen years old," he recounted. "And I tell you, I saw people with sickness at Sunnybrook, people dying! Guess what? Your perspective changes a lot. Things like that shape your life. Change is what makes everybody better. We can all look at the small print, but life's a big picture. Nobody is infallible... It doesn't matter what you do or how good you think you are—you're only passing through."

"Nobody is infallible... It doesn't matter what you do or how good you think you are—you're only passing through."

Wayne Carleton

Wayne eventually got back onto his skates and carried his new perspective forward to claim the Memorial Cup and the Stanley Cup before his hockey days were done. "I look back at my career between the WHA and the National Hockey League and I ended up with close to 600 points in ten years," he remarked. "And I know that doesn't sound like a lot in today's terms but back then, there weren't that many guys who scored 600 points. And I say to people who claim that the WHA was a whatever league: Guess what? The Bobby Hull's played in it. The Gordie Howe's played in it and the Wayne Gretzky's started in it."

Wayne ended his career in 1976 as a result of a contract dispute with Peter Pocklington in Edmonton. "I think it was a ploy by

Pocklington ... to put me down," he contended. "At the time I was the fourth- or fifth-leading scorer in the league since the WHA had started!"

After the dispute, he took life in hand by retiring to his two farms in Collingwood, Ontario. "I farmed and raised standard-bred horses," he related. "I did it as a hobby and I liked being able to train and raise them to be winners. It's not like coaching a player who whines and gripes. With horses, they don't say anything, it's a perceptive thing. Making them competitive just like I was competitive was a good fit."

Two years of full-time work, however, convinced Wayne that horses made a better hobby than business. "I trained them and had some successes but it's very time consuming," he explained. "There's a lot of travel involved and I didn't want to be trucking all over. I put my family ahead of that type of business."

As an alternative, he settled for the world of auto sales at Blue Mountain Chrysler, a dealership in Collingwood owned by former NHLer Darryl Sly. "Sales is geared to enjoying people," he affirmed. "You've got to be able to read them just like you've got to read a horse. And where did I get all this? Obviously, when you play hockey you meet a lot of different characters and you develop a feel for them.

"My goal at the time was to be part owner of a dealership and that wasn't going to materialize, so I got a chance to go with The Investors Group out of Winnipeg. I went back to school and took my C.F.P. ... chartered financial planner [course] in 1983, and I've been with Investors ever since. I do everything from tax to investment strategies to estate planning."

In 1987, Wayne and his wife, Elizabeth,

simplified their lives by selling their farms and moving into town. But horses do continue to be an important part of their lives. "It never leaves you," he said. "I've been at it thirty years now. In fact we were just breaking a filly this morning. It's a joy to go out and watch them, to see them improve."

With his hockey career now in the distant past, Wayne reflected on his transition from the game. "Life goes on," he affirmed. "I've seen people live and die hockey all their lives. And they're still living and dying today because they can't find happiness doing anything else. Thank God I'm not in that boat. I love to do the horses. I love the world of financial planning and I love to see my boy grow up and make something of himself."

Nickname: *Swoop*

"Buck Houle, the GM of the Toronto Marlboros gave me that nickname when I was a kid," Wayne recalled. "I used to start behind my own net and sort of swoop out and down the other end of the ice, or sometimes I'd swoop around the defenseman."

Chartraw, Rick: *Played defense for Montreal, Los Angeles, the New York Rangers and Edmonton from 1974-1984. Born: Caracas, Venezuela, 1954.*

During the early fifties, the country of Venezuela launched itself on a course of expansion and modernization. Foreign experts were recruited to assist in the construction of a modern infrastructure upon which the country's future could be built. Rick Chartraw's father was among those recruited to fill the bill.

The Chartraw family left the United States and spent the next four years living in the city of Caracas. "I was born while they were down there," Rick noted. "My father was an engineer, managing this group who were doing the building. They were putting electrical power into the interior of the country for mineral and mining development."

Rick's earliest images of life were as far removed from hockey as hindsight is to the present moment. It would require a return to the stable setting of the north-eastern United States before he could begin to make the connection between ice and hockey.

"We moved around a number of times," he recalled. "Finally, when I was ten years old, we landed in Erie, Pennsylvania.

"We lived kind of out in the country. There was a pond about a block from my house where a number of kids played hockey during the winter. I remember the first time I skated: A number of us kids in the neighbourhood went with a dad out onto the large bay in Erie. He drove us out onto the ice, stopped the car and all the kids jumped out. So out I got and then he drove away! I didn't know what to do, I'd never skated before. I was a half a mile out and all the kids skated away from me. So it was either sit down and freeze to death or learn how to skate to catch them. I learned how to skate real quickly!"

Rick persisted with hockey until age sixteen. To turn his game up to the next level, he signed with the Kitchener Rangers of the Ontario Hockey Association for the following three seasons. In 1974, he was selected in the NHL entry draft by the Montreal Canadiens who were in need of his size, toughness and mobility.

Ten years and five Stanley Cups later, Rick began to have pragmatic thoughts about his future. At age thirty, his back was bad, his legs were slowing and he'd experienced life in the exchange lane, having been dealt to Los Angeles, New York and finally, Edmonton by 1984.

"I decided to move on to the next chapter," he recalled. "I knew a person with a real-estate business in Florida that was growing very quickly. He had a position for me. It was kind of intriguing and put me into a new world. He needed to open a number of offices up and down the Gulf Coast of Florida in a very short period of time. He said, 'Why don't you do it for me?' I really hadn't had any experience but he gave me a little guidance.

"All the time that I was building these offices, I was also buying used boats that were somewhat distressed. I would rehab them both mechanically and cosmetically ... and then resell them for a profit—in most cases. I enjoyed boating and the water. I said to myself, 'How can I make a livelihood out of this?' So I went to work for a couple of marinas. I worked my way through various positions, learning the business. It took me about four years.

"Then I purchased a small marina in Newport Beach, California. Our services included selling

Nickname Challenge #3

Knobby

"When I first started out in Boston, the guys started calling me 'Knobby'. I was bald and there was a knob on the top of my head. Then for a few years, I wore a rug, a toupee—so everybody had fun with that! After the game I'd go to find my rug. Somebody would have hidden it and I couldn't leave the room till I'd found it."

Who is he?

Clues

a. He played centre for Boston, Pittsburgh and Atlanta of the NHL and Calgary of the WHA between 1962 & 1976.
b. His initials are B.L.

If you've been hooked from behind, see page 285.

boats, motors, tackle, accessories and providing storage and repairs."

Rick sold the marina in 1989, so he and his wife, Maureen, could head east to Rochester, New York in order to be near Maureen's father. Rick managed a marina there while rebuilding an old farmhouse.

"We spent about a year and a half in New York," he noted. "After her father passed away, we closed up family business. We were both not happy living in the Northeast anymore. After living on the Gulf Coast of Florida and the Pacific Coast of California, the winters became unappealing to us."

In 1991, the couple returned to Sierra Madre, California where Rick made playing golf his primary focus. For the following year and a half, he aimed to get his game back on track. His objective, however, was cut short as a result of an injured tendon in his finger that would have required extensive surgery to repair. He decided instead to stop golfing.

As an alternative he channeled his essential energies into remodelling and expanding his home. For the next two years he walked the handyman's path with power tools in one hand and renovation books in the other.

More recently, he has established a consulting business under the name "Strong-Side Hockey". "I consult on the building and operation of skating facilities, both ice and roller," he explained. "Hockey is going very well, so we've opened a number of projects in the last three years. It looks like we may be doing a lot of work with a number of municipalities across the country."

As a sideline since 1991, Rick has also been developing an educational package designed to teach hockey players and coaches about the thinking side of the game. "There are lots of schools out here that will teach you basic skills," he pointed out. "Our aim is to teach players when and why skills are used at certain times." He believes that in addition to learning specific skills, each player must attain a global perspective of the game by learning the requirements of all positions. As with consulting, he calls his programme "Strong-Side Hockey" and promises that it will be coming to your neighbourhood sometime in the future.

⌥ –

Conacher, Pete: *Played left wing for Chicago, the New York Rangers and Toronto between 1951-1958. Born: Toronto, Ontario, 1932.*

Pete Conacher's father, Charlie, was skating for the New York Americans in 1940—his final season in the NHL. It was then that Pete grabbed his one and only opportunity to catch a glimpse of his father on National League ice.

"I can remember going down to the Gardens to see him, but I don't remember the game or how he played," Pete said in describing what amounted to a hazy, childhood memory.

He did not come away with a strong visual reference to his father's success, but he did respond to its presence. "I don't think my dad influenced me on a hands-on basis," he surmised. "He influenced me because of his reputation—who he was and what he stood for. So the hero worship was there."

The most sustaining ingredient in Pete's career, however, was not the allure of fame, money and fast rinks; it was the simple fact that he loved the game.

"The other night my uncle, Burt Conacher, was here along with my cousin, Murray Henderson, who played for Boston," Pete reported. "And I was saying to them—never, ever did I say I wanted to play in the NHL. All through my time in minor hockey and junior, I don't think I heard anybody say, 'I want to play in the NHL.' All they ever said was that they wanted to play, period!"

Many of Pete's most significant hockey memories were formed before he ever made it to the big show. Like Andy Bathgate, he spoke of a special bond that forms between young players on the rise—particularly those sharing the same line. "I played junior with Kenny Wharram for two years and in Buffalo we played together before he joined Chicago," Pete recalled. "It was a real treat being on the same line with Kenny and Larry Wilson!"

By 1958, Pete had taken his final stride across the NHL stage. He still had plenty of fire left in his stick and some old tricks to teach young players. So he spent the next eight seasons playing for Buffalo and Hershey in the American Hockey League. It was there that he teamed up with Mike Nykoluk and Myron Stankiewicz on another personally memorable line.

"I started working at the Toronto Stock Exchange on the trading floor ... It was like a big dressing room."

Pete Conacher

"In hindsight," he mused, "you never remember the bad times, the slumps, the losses. If you make a scrapbook, there aren't many poor write-ups in it. You always remember the good times though—playing with great guys for thirteen years was a real highlight."

By the mid-sixties, the foundation for Pete's transition out of hockey was solidly in place. "When I was still playing in 1954," he recounted, "I started working at the Toronto Stock Exchange on the trading floor. I'd come back every summer. So when I finished playing in 1966, I stayed on full-time until April of '95."

In Pete's lengthy experience, the frenzied action of the Exchange was not unlike that of an outing on ice. "It was almost like playing on a big team because you were with the same guys day in and day out," he concluded. "It was like a big dressing room. The comradery was terrific and we had a lot of fun."

The other essential link in Pete's transition out of hockey was his experience in the Sans Souci area of Georgian Bay. "I bought crown land on an island in 1960," he recalled. "It was a fourteen-mile boat ride to get out to the place. We built a home there in 1965. That project took the place of missing hockey because I put all my effort and energy into building the cottage and other buildings."

Married in 1966, Pete and his wife, Ann, currently live in Toronto.

54

Wayne F. Connelly
General Manager

Teck News
Agency (1977) Ltd.

5 Kirkland Street, P.O. Box 488
Kirland Lake (Ontario) P2N 3J6
Fax: (705) 567-6101

Connelly, Wayne: *Played right wing for Montreal, Boston, Minnesota, Detroit, St. Louis, Vancouver (NHL), Minnesota, Cleveland, Calgary and Edmonton (WHA) between 1960 & 1977. Born: Rouyn, Quebec, 1939.*

As the World Hockey Association became a reality in 1972, six-figure salaries were splashed around the NHL in a bid to purchase credibility. Wayne Connelly was the first in line to accept an offer and to make the jump. The uncertainty of change consistently spelled opportunity in Wayne's books and the WHA was at the top of his page.

By 1977, however, he had made the rounds and was ready for another fortuitous leap—this time out of his Edmonton Oilers' jersey and into a new career. Good fortune continued its sustain thanks to a timely offer from his brother, Cliff, to work at Tech News Agency, a magazine and book wholesaler in Kirkland Lake, Ontario.

As the agency's general manager, Wayne has exchanged the road trips, trades and media rumours for a quieter, more stable livelihood, overseeing the warehouse, the office and the sales departments to ensure that all orders are filled to standards. "We deliver magazines and books to corner stores and so on, throughout the northern Ontario region," he reported. "We handle about 300 different titles per week."

Wayne's shift from newsmaker to news distributor has advanced at a steady pace. "I didn't have any problems at all," he affirmed. "I'd played seventeen years of pro hockey and it was time to do something new. I enjoyed getting into the work force. I think the habits that I developed in hockey have really helped me in the

business world. I adapted to it and enjoyed it.

"Of course I had no business experience. But my brother was a great teacher. I would be in his office almost every night learning how to do things so I could run the place myself. It was nothing for me to work fifteen hours a day at the start!"

Farther down the road, Wayne took another step up by obtaining a partnership with his brother in two other news agencies: The Kingston News Service based in Kingston, Ontario and National News based in Ottawa. He meets on occasion with the managers of these agencies, although they are, for the most part, arms-length investments.

Wayne is thriving in his current lifestyle which he shares with his wife, Reg. "I love Kirkland Lake," he mused. "I golf two to three times a month and I'm only ten minutes away from my cottage. During the warmer season, I leave work early on Friday afternoons and head off to my cottage to fish and relax. I don't return again until Monday."

"It was nothing for me to work fifteen hours a day at the start!"

Wayne Connelly

Wayne also saves time to observe and speculate on today's incarnation of the NHL. He offered some sage thoughts about how players might extend the length of their careers: "I think the reason players don't survive that long is because they're making the big dough. Teams are saying let's cut this guy, he's making himself maybe a million dollars... Let's bring in a rookie instead. So you have to be really consistent in order for a team to keep you. I remember when Lou Nanne signed with the North Stars. I think he signed for five years. Usually a player gets yearly increases in a long-term contract. But Lou went the opposite way, figuring that when he was finished his contract, he wasn't going to be as good—but he'd be making less money, so they would keep him!"

Corrigan, Mike: *Played left wing for Los Angeles, Vancouver and Pittsburgh between 1967 & 1978. Born: Ottawa, Ontario, 1946.*

As a product of the Toronto Maple Leafs' farm system of the mid-sixties, Mike Corrigan had to toil patiently in the American Hockey League until NHL expansion created more employment for young tradesmen such as himself. In 1967, he got his first audition with the Los Angeles Kings where he saw limited duty before being drafted by the expansion Vancouver Canucks in 1970. In a Canuck jersey, he finally got enough open ice to establish himself as a league regular with a knack for puck handling and robust play.

In 1971, the Kings reacquired Mike on waivers and let him freewheel to the tune of a career-high thirty-seven goals and 136 penalty minutes. For the next four years, Los Angeles became home to the most productive phase of his career. He then played two additional seasons for the Pittsburgh Penguins before stepping behind the bench as the club's assistant coach in 1978.

"When you get into coaching the first couple of years, it's very tough," he recounted. "You're leaving the regiment of the players and now you're on the other side. I had to listen to the players' problems *and* I had to listen to the problems of management."

Mike's struggles as a middleman eventually smoothed themselves over, although the same could not be said for his experience of relentless nights away from home. After six years, he figured it was time to trade in the known for the unknown. He resigned from his coaching position and hit the pavement for some hard lessons in the job market.

"When I went out into ... the world, a lot of people were intimidated," he confided of his initial search. "I mean I played about eleven years and then I was an assistant coach for nearly six—so that's about seventeen years in

> *"There were jobs that I should have easily gotten, but they'd call back and say I was over-qualified."*
>
> Mike Corrigan

the game. When I interviewed for a job, I put that up front ... and it was like I was intimidating them! There were jobs that I should have easily gotten, but they'd call back and say I was over-qualified."

Two years of waiting rooms and resumes were enough. Mike felt he no longer had a future in Pittsburgh. "I had to leave," he confided. "There was nothing there! What gets me is you spend all this time in a city and you work your butt off and then you can't get anything... It doesn't make sense to me. I think there are a lot of things that you could do."

Through persistence, his job search took a northeast spiral to Connecticut where he was eventually hired by a company called "Waste Management". "I coordinate environmental protection," he explained. "I had to do training ... and get my licenses. I know every environmental thing from trees, shrubs and grass to chemicals and waste." Mike's job consists of ensuring that proper standards are maintained whenever his company is involved in the transport, storage or application of toxic materials within the state of Connecticut.

Now far removed from the emotional intensity of his transition, Mike is better able to summarize the perspective that brought him down the bumpy turnpike of life after hockey. "If you have a chance to get in the door somewhere and you take advantage of it," he affirmed, "you can have some success." In other words, attitudes giveth and attitudes taketh away!

When spare time calls, Mike either golfs or shares his heritage and know-how at hockey schools and clinics in Connecticut and New York state.

Over the years, he and his wife, Claudette, have raised three daughters and a son and are grandparents four times over. They currently make their home in Windsor Locks, Connecticut.

56

Creighton, Dave: *Played centre for Boston, Toronto, Chicago and the New York Rangers from 1948-1960. Born: Port Arthur, Ontario, 1930.*

Dave Creighton's career in hockey was full of promise as he and teammate Danny Lewicki powered the West End Bruins of Port Arthur to a Memorial Cup victory during the late forties. In 1948, Dave was quickly scooped up by the Boston Bruins who were eager to translate some of his Memorial magic into a championship of their own.

The NHL, however, was a much tougher soup to stir than the broth of the junior ranks. Dave's scoring output was initially limited to an average of twenty-three points per season through 1954. After a brief detour in Toronto and Chicago, he rose to his scoring stride in New York while centering Camille Henry and Andy Hebenton, netting 142 points in three seasons.

"I probably could have lasted a lot longer," he related. "But the Rangers left me off of the protected list with about five others: Gump Worsley, Danny Lewicki, Jack Evans..! And I'd ended up eleventh overall in scoring that year, so to get left off of the protected list seems a little bit strange... Then Montreal picked me up and after training camp, Frank Selke Sr. tells me, 'Dave, you had a good camp but I can't use you. I didn't really want you anyhow. I just picked you up to teach Phil Watson [the Rangers' head coach] a lesson.' So that kind of stuff really affected my career!"

Life as a professional commodity continued to undermine Dave's potential even after resurfacing with the Leafs. "I was with Rochester most of that year [1959-60]," he recounted. "They'd just brought Red Kelly in and of course they cherished Red a little more than they cherished me. But I played pretty well for them when they brought me up for one game. I got the winning goal with about five minutes left... Punch said, 'Well, we can't get rid of him if he plays like that!' So the next day I'm down in the minors again.

"Now I was making about $8,000 to play for Rochester and that was pretty good money for the

American League. That's like a $100 a game. But then they brought me back up to Toronto at the end of the year. So I went to see King Clancy—he was like an assistant manager who did a lot of the dirty work for Punch. I said to him, 'King, I made as much money in Rochester during a regular season game as you guys are paying me to play in the Stanley Cup finals! It really doesn't sound good. It isn't right!'

"So King comes back later and says, 'Dave, I talked with Punch and he said, "Take it or leave it!"' And I didn't know if I was going to be playing or not—and I didn't think I was. But first thing you know, Punch is playing me on the power play, playing me here, playing me there! Now had he told me I was going to be used, I could have prepared myself. But he didn't tell me anything. He just threw me out there—and I think that was pretty piss poor when you're coming into the Stanley Cup finals... But that was Punch..."

Dave tolerated the abuses of life in the NHL until 1960, at which point he receded to his final run in the American Hockey League with Rochester, Buffalo and Baltimore. "I was a player, a player-coach and I finished as a player-manager with Providence," he recounted.

During his final AHL season, an invitation from friends, including Eddie Shack, brought home an inkling of the creative license that would one day be the cornerstone of Dave's second career. He accepted their offer to invest in Vaughan Valley, a Toronto-based executive golf course. "They talked me into coming up to look at the land," he related. "I liked it and so I got involved."

It soon became evident that, as a partner, Eddie Shack had more energy than Mother Nature herself. "Eddie's a real go-getter," Dave revealed. "But at that time, he didn't understand the golf business. He just thought that if you ... open up a course, that automatically, you're going to be going full tilt for the first year. Well it just doesn't happen that way because you don't have any grass on your fairways or greens. First, we had to sell the place, and that took time."

In the interim, Dave was lured from his

NORTHDALE
GOLF CLUB

4417 Northdale Blvd.   **DAVE CREIGHTON**
Tampa, Florida 33624   Owner

fairway to pilot the fledgling Philadelphia Blazers of the WHA. "It was hard to pass up that good money," he disclosed. "I was their first general manager, but I wasn't too thrilled with the owner. He brought in Derek Sanderson himself. And most of the players available had been picked over before I got there—I had no creative input. I just wasn't happy and that was the crunch of it. So I got bought out of my contract and went on my merry way back to the golf business."

Dave returned to Ontario and continued to acquire valuable experience in golf-facility management while working for Burlington Springs Golf Course.

Some years later, as a seasoned veteran, he took on a new partner and together, they launched themselves into a flurry of acquisitions.

First they bought and ran a course in Welland, Ontario. Next, they acquired the Northdale Golf Club in Tampa, Florida, and finally, the Rosemont Golf Course in Orlando.

Lifesyle changes, however, eventually required a parting of ways, so Dave and his partner split their kingdom asunder. Dave gave up his shares in the Rosemont course while retaining full ownership of the Northdale club in Tampa.

But the thought of owning only one course was intolerable. As a cure, he went out on another shopping spree to enlarge the domain upon which, after all the years of restrictions, he now finally wields his unhindered talents. "Now I also have interests in three other

courses!" he added. "One near Disney World. It's doing very well. We've rebuilt the whole place. Besides that I have a half interest in an executive course in Tampa and then we bought a course in Mt. Hope [Ontario] and expanded it to twenty-seven holes."

Management of his empire now keeps the Creightons as one big, extended clan. "There's family involved at all of the courses," he related. "And now that my son, Adam, is coming to the end of his NHL career, we're looking to branch out with something for him. I don't think he's going to starve to death (laughs)!"

Cullen, Barry: *Played right wing for Toronto and Detroit from 1955-1960. Born: Ottawa, Ontario, 1935.*

An early draft of this book brought distressing news to former Leafs' right winger Barry Cullen—his biography was less than half the length of his more talkative brothers, Brian and Ray. In a humourous display of fraternal rivalry, Barry unleashed a succession of anecdotes and family facts that would force his brothers into submission.

"I don't see any reason why I should get fewer lines than those other two guys!" he asserted. "Right? They're no better than I am, that's for sure!"

Whether on the ice or in the world of business, the Cullen brothers have always kept their eyes on the big picture and the bottom line. "One of the number-one concerns for hockey players was what would they be doing with the rest of their lives when they were finished playing," he remarked. "It was a real concern, especially in those days. People weren't making very much money. My brother, Brian, had quit hockey at twenty-nine because his wife wasn't in great health... He went to work at Hearne Pontiac, running the leasing division.

"One year later, now I'm twenty-nine and he's telling me how busy he is and that he's going to hire an assistant. At the time, I was at training camp with Buffalo and I said, 'I'll take the job!' I asked, 'What does the job pay?' and he said, 'A hundred dollars a week.' Even in the early sixties, that was not a lot of money. I had four kids. I took the job anyway..."

It was a lean beginning but Barry recognized what it took to succeed. "When you're playing professional hockey, you have to be a competitive person," he declared. "You have to have discipline and you have to practise a lot and take care of yourself. It's the same thing in the business world. There is an awful lot of competition in the car business. So you have to work harder than the guy down the street..."

The Cullen brothers seemed to have outworked everyone on the block. The value of their stock with General Motors rose quickly. "In two years, Brian got his own G.M. dealership and then I took over his position," Barry recalled. "Then about three years went by and I got my own dealership in Guelph."

Barry has owned and operated Barry Cullen Chev-Olds Cadillac Ltd. since 1969 and he's still at it today. "It's been just great!" he exclaimed. "I'm running my own business so I have the final decision. You can do anything you want. I love the car business. I love the excitement. The new models come out every year and it's something that everybody likes to talk about."

On the home front, Barry and his wife have raised four boys and two girls. Mark works as Barry's general manager in Guelph, while two other sons work at a dealership in Atlanta, Georgia. His most well-known son, John, was a member of the Tampa Bay Lightning until being sidelined with Hodgkin's disease.

Barry and his wife currently live in Puslinch Township, a rural setting just outside Guelph.

Cullen, Brian: *Played centre for Toronto and the New York Rangers from 1954-1961. Born: Ottawa, Ontario, 1933.*

"The last four years," Brian Cullen reported, "I've sort of been, if you want to use the word, 'semi-retired'." The word "semi-retired" did not come out of his mouth easily. Perhaps it's because, in his own life's context, he is not the retiring type.

His interests in life have been diverse and the outcomes of his focus have always born fruit. He is readily willing to share his formula for success: "You have to have the commitment. In sports, you're trained to be a winner. You're not trained to be a loser. And when you get into the business world, that same theory applies. You get paid to win, you don't get paid to lose!"

Back in the early fifties as a junior player, Brian was one of Canada's most prolific scorers. In 1954, he graduated to the Toronto Maple Leafs where he soon discovered that NHL goaltenders, by comparison with their junior counterparts, seemed to play with the equivalent of six arms and four legs. Goals were hard to come by although he did manage to pot twenty markers and twenty-three assists in 1957-58. During his tenure with the Leafs, he also began to take a few sales courses on the side to make way for life after hockey. When the time came in 1961, he had only to wait for an opportunity to put his sales skills to the test.

"There was a fellow in Toronto named Herb Kearney who was a real Leafs fan," Brian recounted. "He supplied a lot of hockey players with their cars. He took a liking to me. When I quit hockey at age twenty-nine, he asked me if I'd come to learn the car business. So I went into Hearne Pontiac-Buick in Toronto."

Following three-and-a-half years under Kearney's wing, Brian landed his own establishment in Grimsby, Ontario. "It was a small Pontiac-Buick dealership," he noted. "We sold about 300 new cars a year."

Cullen, Ray: *Played centre for the New York Rangers, Detroit, Minnesota and Vancouver from 1965-1971. Born: Ottawa, Ontario, 1941.*

Ray Cullen was the youngest of the three Cullen Brothers. He made his NHL debut with the New York Rangers in 1965-66 although he didn't obtain full rank until he caught on with the Minnesota North Stars in 1967. During the next three seasons, he raked in a career-high 162 points. He was then drafted by the expansion Vancouver Canucks in 1970 where he played one final season before stepping off the only path he'd ever known.

"I just didn't have the education," Ray admitted of his experience outside of a rink. "As soon as we made junior hockey, a lot of us quit school. Fortunately enough, the years that I was playing, I worked for Labatts as a sales representative. I was always very good at sales and so I felt that that was the only future I had.

"I almost went into the real-estate business. But in '71, when I retired, my brother's sales manager talked me into the car business. Fortunately for me, from that day on to this day, I've just loved the automobile business."

Temptation, however, was thrown in Ray's path at the point of his transition. "A year after I quit hockey," he recounted, "the World Hockey [Association] came in and Glen Sonmor ... was the general manager of the new Minnesota Fighting Saints. He flew down to Niagara Falls and I met him in a hotel. He offered me twice as much money as I had ever made in hockey. The most money I made was in my last year in Vancouver—I think I made $30,000. He offered me a two-year contract for $125,000! I'd only been in the car business six or seven months. I'd just be going for two years, but I'd started a career I really enjoyed. So it was a tough decision. I anguished over it for four or five days."

Of course Ray's dilemma was not based exclusively on money. His love for hockey and the auto business stood shoulder to shoulder. "I think in my career," he reflected, "I had had at least two hat tricks in the NHL ... maybe three. But I remember as a salesman, I sold three cars

Four years later, in 1970, he caught the attention of General Motors and was awarded a very large Chev-Olds-Cadillac dealership in St. Catharines. In spite of the move, he continued to operate under the same name he had used in Grimsby, "Brian Cullen Motors Ltd."

"I've been here now for twenty-six years," he declared. "We have about eighty employees and we do approximately fifty million dollars in sales a year."

Brian handed the day-to-day operations over to his sons, Bobby and Brian Jr. in 1992. They will carry the Cullen family into its second generation in the automobile business. "You have to know when to step back and give the reigns to somebody else," Brian added.

Of course, he continues to keep a few other reigns in hand. "I've been a breeder and I've raced horses since 1963," he remarked. "We have a farm out here in the country outside of St. Catharines. We've run horses in the Queen's Plate and I've had some real nice horses over time."

Since the death of his long-time trainer, Art Warner, however, Brian has pulled back on his involvement in the sport. "I'm only racing a couple of horses this year," he reported. "I'm getting older and I just don't have the time to do everything."

One of his current priorities is to spend time with his steadily growing family which is comprised of his wife, Carol, three daughters, two sons and twelve grandchildren.

and I got as much of a thrill out of that as scoring three goals in the National League."

Having weighed the potential impact that such a move might have on his children and the fact that he loved his work, he declined Sonmor's offer.

With his hockey bridge now aflame, Ray was free to concentrate on learning the inner workings of the car business while in the employ of his brother Brian's dealership in St. Catharines. Over the next eight years, he progressed through the ranks from salesman to general manager.

"I had a chance to get my own dealership in London, Ontario," he added. "We came here in 1977, and we've been very, very fortunate."

Ray's success in business is born from an attitude of commitment he nurtured while learning to play hockey. "I look at anybody who made the National Hockey League out of the hundreds and hundreds of thousands of kids who played minor hockey," he observed. "You had to give 100% to hockey to make it to that level and it's the same thing in business. In hockey, when you practised, you might stay out a half hour longer. Whereas in the automobile business the difference was, you might put in thirteen-hour days instead of the average ... eight hours. If you didn't mind the thirteen hours, you were rewarded. You learned more, you sold more and you made more money."

These days, Ray has brought his sons on board to manage the day-to-day affairs of the dealership. With five boys to integrate into the business, however, he has his eyes open for a second operation.

With his sons at the helm, he is now freer to keep tabs on the business at arms length while enjoying his passion for playing golf.

Ray and his wife, Jackie, bought a home in Florida which allows him to swing the clubs all year round.

Debol, Dave: *Played centre for Cincinnati (WHA) and Hartford (NHL) from 1977-1981. Born: Clair Shores, Michigan, 1956.*

"It seems like sometimes my wife looks at me on the weekend and says, 'I thought you retired from hockey?' But my wife's very understanding. She knows we raise a lot of money for charity."

Dave Debol was referring to his play with the Detroit Red Wings' alumni team. "Just a couple of weeks ago we had a game in Plymouth," he continued. "Gordie Howe had come in to play with us the year before. We had raised money for a kid who had a double lung transplant. So this year, with Gordie back again, you see the kid walk out on the ice and they gave him a standing ovation. My wife might be mad and then

Dave Debol

she'll see something like this and say, 'I can't be mad can I?' And I say, 'No you can't'."

Dave revealed the gruelling practices and late nights that form the backbone of life on the alumni circuit. "We try to practise at least once every other week down at Joe Louis," he said. "It's usually from six to seven p.m. By the time I shower and we have a few pops and some food afterwards, I'm home at 9:15. The odd time, I come home at midnight and my wife says, 'Oh, what do you do, go over the border to those strip joints?' And I say, 'Honey, ten years ago I might have done that but now we sit in the dressing room and talk.' And she says, 'Yeah, right!' 'But honey,' I say, 'you've go to understand, there's Alex Delvecchio and all these guys there and every once in a while they get going on a story and sure enough we'll sit in that dressing room till eleven or twelve o'clock.' And finally, she started coming to some games and admitted, 'You guys really do that'!"

According to Dave, in addition to serving the community, the alumni also serves its members by sustaining the essential qualities that made professional hockey worthwhile in the first place. "It's one of the only sports where when you retire, you can really continue doing it," he observed. "We have a couple of old guys that skate with us. These guys are seventy-three years old—Jimmy Peters Sr. and Joe Klukay. Joe once said to me, 'If it wasn't for the Red Wings' alumni, I'd be dead. I'm out here skating, trying to stay in shape.' He has more fun... Those guys don't miss a practice or a game."

As a Michigan native, Dave first gained notoriety for himself during the mid-seventies as an All-American scoring ace at the University of Michigan where he set records for goals scored and assists. He then graduated to the Cincinnati Stingers of the World Hockey Association in 1977 before finishing up his NHL career in Hartford.

After his departure from the Whalers in 1981, he bounced around in the minors with the Oklahoma Stars, the Cincinnati Tigers and the Birmingham South Stars before closing out his career with one final season in Wetzikon, Switzerland in 1985.

He then resettled in Ann Arbor, Michigan to manage a bowling centre for two or three years. With a preference for his sport of choice, however, he jumped at a chance to join Louisville Slugger sporting goods as a sales rep. "I figured, if you're going to sell something, you might as well sell something you know about," he surmised. "It was good to be back in the hockey business."

Dave stayed with Louisville for three years and then made the leap to Wilson Sports, a company that distributes twenty-three different lines of sporting goods including Sherwood and Christian Brothers hockey sticks. "I do all the team sales for college, junior and pro," he explained. "I also do retail sporting-goods stores in Michigan and Illinois."

Nickname Challenge #4

Bep

"My mother, being Italian, tended to pronounce the letter *b* like a *p*. When she said *baby*, it came out like *bepy*—so I became known as 'Bep'. Years later as a pro, Foster Hewitt said, 'I can't use your regular name ———.' I said, 'Bep' is fine with me and it's stuck ever since."

Who is he?

Clues
a. He played left wing for Boston, Detroit and Chicago from 1942-1952.
b. He was the youngest player to have ever broken into the NHL.

If you were crosschecked,
see page 285.

Delvecchio, Alex: *Played centre for Detroit from 1950-1974. Born: Fort William, Ontario, 1931.*

It was in his native Fort William, Ontario, that a young Alex Delvecchio fell under the watchful eye of Larry Aurie, the tiny dynamo who was instrumental in powering the Detroit Red Wings to their first ever Stanley Cup in 1936. Under Aurie's direction, Alex learned the old-time tricks of the trade before moving on to the Oshawa Generals of the Ontario Hockey Association. In 1950-51, he lead the league in assists—a clear indication of intelligent things to come.

The following season, he played six games for Indianapolis of the American Hockey League before making his debut in a Detroit Red Wing jersey—the only NHL sweater he'd ever wear.

By the end of his rookie campaign, Alex had laid claim to fifteen goals, twenty-two assists and his first Stanley Cup. With Sid Abel's departure to Chicago in 1952, the famous "Production Line" faced a work slowdown until Alex stepped into the centre lane between survivors Gordie Howe and Ted Lindsay. His fluid skating and reverence for fine passing kept the "Production Line" pistons moving at full tilt.

For the next quarter of a century the history of the Detroit Red Wings and Alex Delvecchio would remain intertwined in mutual respect. He served as team captain from 1962 onwards. He was a three-time winner of the Lady Byng Trophy for gentlemanly play and by the time retirement came in 1974, he had tallied 1,385 points in 1,670 games. It had been a momentous career and the ailing Wings were in no hurry to see it end. His laid-back personality was hoped to be the perfect antidote to the traditional discipline doled out by outgoing head coach Ted Garvin. Enter new head coach

Alex Delvecchio.

"It was a difficult task because you're playing with these guys all season and then, when I went in as a coach in February, I was telling them what to do," he recollected. "I think it was probably just as tough on them accepting the leadership from me as it was for me to be changing my tune. So it wasn't an easy transition."

As had always been the case, Alex performed and the Red Wings liked what they saw. During the following season, Bruce Norris, the team's owner, tempted him with the general manager's position to complement his job as coach. "Sure, it was a great opportunity," he admitted. "You feel that you should grab it. But I think, just like playing the game of hockey, you've got to start at the bantam or the midget level and work your way up, because it's a big responsibility. We had a peculiar situation in Detroit with Bruce Norris—we could do nothing without his approval! There were times when we would be negotiating with someone for a trade and then we couldn't reach [Norris]. He'd be in Europe or wherever. We'd get the deal worked out but then we'd have to wait to discuss it. It was just like buying a car. If you figured it was a great deal or you were making a steal, well you grabbed it! But by the time we got back a couple of times [with Norris], the deal would have cooled right off. I never had the flexibility. So it kind of goofed up some of the ways I wanted to move the team."

Alex attempted to resign from the Wings' helm early in the 1976-77 season. "I told them that I didn't want to do it anymore," he confided. "I knew that coaching and management were not for me. I wasn't comfortable with it. I'd had enough. I couldn't get enough *Maalox* in me. That's that stuff for when you've got ulcers (laughs)!

"But they asked me if I would stay on until they could get a replacement. Eventually they got Ted Lindsay to come in."

Midway through the 1976-77 season, Alex brought his twenty-six-year association with the Red Wings and the NHL to a close.

"I figured, 'Hey, why don't I just get out of the game, settle back and get to know my family'?" he related. "You look back and think, 'Boy I never did spend much time with them.' But if you wanted to make a career of sports, that had to be your number-one priority or else you were not going to be around. So something had to be given up, and unfortunately, a lot of that was the family."

When he retired in 1976, his youngest son, at age fifteen, represented his last chance to make up for lost ground at home.

"He's the only one I had the opportunity with," he said regretfully. "The others were already grown and on their own by that time."

Alex also had to contend with the psychological adjustment of leaving a familiar domain. "It's like waking up in the morning. You say, 'Where am I going today? What's going on here? I've got no place to go'," he admitted. "It's tough because you've been in hockey all those years. Then all of sudden, you're on your own, even though I did have a business where I could go."

Back in 1969, he had established Alex Delvecchio Enterprises as a sideline. He was now ready to focus his full-time energy on expanding the business.

"It's what we call customer-appreciation products where different companies or organizations give you a memento with their name on it," he explained.

In this capacity, A.D.E. serves as a broker between the manufacturers of ball caps, golf shirts and scratch pads and the organizations that want them personalized. Alex also has an extensive engraving system on site. His company provides engraved plaques for the Michigan and Alabama Sports Halls of Fame.

Drumming up business for the company has usually been a soft sell which suits Alex just fine. "In the Detroit area, if you're connected with sports, it opens a lot of doors," he remarked. "A lot of the people you meet in the business world seemed to be more interested in your sport than what you're trying to sell them. So there was no real hard sell. They either liked you and would buy from you or they didn't."

Alex relishes spending his recreational time with the Detroit Red Wings' alumni. "They're a good bunch of guys," he affirmed. "I think it's a great tonic for the mind and the body. We play a lot of charity hockey games. In the vicinity of twenty-five every year. And damn near all summer, we attend golf outings in the Detroit area. We're a close-knit organization and we do it all for charity. We're not looking for a payout for what we do, we just have a lot of fun."

He and his wife, Teresa, have raised three sons and two daughters. There are now nine Delvecchio grandchildren in the area who keep Alex and Teresa hopping.

In critiquing today's NHL, Alex is an advocate for good, clean play. "I don't really care for the goon network," he observed. "I don't think that's good for the game. It's a wonderful sport to watch when you're making some good passes and good plays. It's really a great satisfaction for the players ... plus the people who are watching. The scrubby stuff of hitting everything that moves—I don't care for that type of play. Maybe that's why I got out of the game. Good hockey people that love the sport, love to see the teamwork out there—the passing and the cooperation... It's a tough enough game and you're going to get hit, so you don't have to go out of your way to look for it."

Ab & Susan Demarco with their daughters, Marina, Lucia and Micaela.

Demarco Jr., Ab: *Played defense for the New York Rangers, St. Louis, Pittsburgh, Vancouver, Los Angeles, Boston (NHL) and Edmonton (WHA) from 1969-1979. Born: Cleveland, Ohio, 1949.*

"I come from an Italian background," Ab Demarco affirmed. "So for me, life is a big table, a bowl of spaghetti and family."

He and his wife, Susan, waited for Ab's retirement from hockey before raising three daughters who are, at present, their primary focus.

"Parenting is my priority," he insisted. "The most exciting event these days is that I've got everybody out of diapers. I spend as much time as I can with my kids. I'm a member of our parent-teacher organization and I'm at school every day."

Ab's reverence for parenthood, however, was not apparent during his time in the NHL as an offensive-minded rearguard with the stinging point shot. "When I played, my attitude was different," he confessed. "After a practice it would be, 'Let's go down to a little pub, have a sandwich, a couple of beers, talk and relax.' But there were always those few guys that never showed up. They went home with their wives and kids and I couldn't understand that. It was like, 'No way, we have to gel as a team!' But now I understand—I'm

older. I look back and I say, 'Of course they went home. If I was married when I played, I would have been home too!'

"But for me, my whole twenty-four hours was involved in getting ready for the game—the big show at eight o'clock. I'd be in the dressing room early and other guys would show up just a few minutes before they had to or even a few minutes late. Why? Well they were doing something with little Johnny or bringing Maria to a dance lesson and I couldn't comprehend that.

"Now when I look back, it's like, 'Thank God I had the opportunity to have both careers.' And I look at this as the greatest career, which is of course, raising a family.

"I hear friends of mine say that they can't wait for their kids to leave home. But hey, I've got three little girls. There's no way they're leaving home. I mean I'm putting an electric fence around the house. I've got a great big home I built here. This is where everybody's going to live. 'You want to get married? Yeah, you can move in here with me. What? I'm going to let you go out into that world with some goof? I don't think so!' Because I know enough about men and I'm sure you do too. Men, we're a different breed than the female breed. Although the beautiful little things, they yap a lot in the car. 'He did this! She did that'!"

In his paternal maturity, Ab reflected on some of the missed opportunities that came with pursuing a career in hockey: "I was about fourteen and my brother, Dave, was about eleven. We'd come home after school and have about an hour to kill. It's a chilly November day and there's David and I dropping our books off and playing hockey in the driveway with a tennis ball.

"Then my mother comes to the front door

and says, 'You know you have music lessons in half an hour and you haven't practised all week!' And I stood there and I made the only stand I ever made in my life to my mother who I dearly love. I said, 'Mom, I don't want to play the piano, I want to play hockey.' Now I'm waiting for her to yell at me. She just looked at me and said, 'You're going to be very sorry.' And she turned and walked away. So that gave us the opportunity to play hockey. But I always remembered what she said and I've been sorry ever since because now my little girls play the piano and I can't."

It is not surprising then that Ab found family values as the basis for his real calling in life. His venture into professional hockey was more like a trip to the carnival. He enjoyed the ride but recognized that the merry-go-round only goes in a circle. Hockey served its purpose, but the road was longer than his journey on ice.

"At the age of seventeen, I remember seeing a guidance counsellor in high school," he recounted. "The counsellor said, 'Okay Ab, what do you want to be when you grow up?' He gave me some brochures and I went home. I kind of panicked. I thought, 'What the hell do I want to do? doctor? lawyer? Indian chief? I guess I could be a mechanic.'

"I was sitting at home with this hanging over my head. 'Jeez, I've got to make a decision as to which direction I want to take.' The phone rang. It was Emile Francis of the New York Rangers. He says, 'Hi, do you want to play for New York?' And I said, 'Holy (bleep), thanks for making up my mind!' All of a sudden I got a job offer to play this silly game for money and it was like, 'Jeez, thanks'!"

So Ab set out for the Big Apple to seek his fortune on big-city ice. The problem was, fortune was seeking him in ways that his youthful mind couldn't fathom.

"I remember when I first joined the Rangers in 1970," he recounted. "My first-ever roommate was Tim Horton! Now here I am, twenty years old and Tim was forty at the time. And I mean I grew up with his picture on my bedroom wall and now we're rooming together—now that was a rush! He said to me, 'I'd like you to meet my daughter.' And I'm thinking, well hold it, first of all things are nuts here—Tim Horton's my roommate and now he wants me to meet his daughter! Well she's got to be ugly! Well she turns out to be gorgeous, right? And not only that, she likes me! Well, that was a scary thing. We went out for a number of years. And I remember Timmy always said to me, 'Listen, I'm opening up some donut chains. Why don't you buy one in North Bay?' I'm twenty, twenty-one years old. Like what do I want to do, make donuts—are you nuts? ... *I could have been a multi-millionaire!* Can you believe that? Even to this day, I'd die to have one of those!!"

Nickname: *T-bone;*

"Barclay Plager used to call me 'T-Bone'," Ab recalled. "Playing against him when I was with New York, he figured I was kind of tough, so he never wanted to take a run at me. Then when I played with him in St. Louis, we got in the dressing room and he realized that I was rather thin. He said, 'You goddamn T-bone. Here I was worried about you. I could have kicked the hell out of you'!"

Derlago, Bill: *Played centre for Vancouver, Boston, Winnipeg, Quebec and Toronto from 1978-1987. Born: Birtle, Manitoba, 1958.*

Bill Derlago joined the Brandon Wheat Kings of the Western Hockey League in 1974. For the next four seasons, he turned the heads of fans and scouts by scoring enough goals to rewrite the record books in his own image and likeness. He was a savoury pick, chosen fourth overall in the 1978 entry draft by the Vancouver Canucks. The Canucks were impatient, however, and quick to leap at the chance to pry Dave "Tiger" Williams away from the Leafs in exchange for Bill and teammate Rick Vaive. Although he never recaptured his junior form at the NHL level, Bill did fall into a successful mix with Vaive on his left and John Anderson on his right. Bill used his strong acceleration and knack for setting up Vaive's rocket launcher to

66

post 317 points during his five full seasons in Toronto.

After bouncing around on behalf of Boston Winnipeg and Quebec, Bill had had his fill of the big leagues and decided to join former NHLer Dale McCourt in Switzerland for the 1987-88 season. "We played for Ombri-Piotta," he explained. "Ombri and Piotta were two little towns with a rink situated in the middle. Together they had a population of about 1,000 people and yet, attendance for our games was around 14,000. The trains would arrive before

Nickname Challenge #5

Diesel

"When I went down to Barrie, Ontario to play with the junior team, I had a reputation for being a pretty good, strong skater. While we were in the dressing room one day, one of the defensemen, Ralph Willis, just came out with, 'Hey, Diesel!' So they picked it up and then everyone began to use it."

Who is he?

Clues

a. He played defense and left wing for Boston, Chicago, Minnesota, Atlanta and Washington from 1953-1975.

b. He was a member of Chicago's "Scooter Line".

c. His initials are D.M.

*If you received a misconduct,
see page 285.*

game time and all these people would flood in."

Bill received an offer to play in Germany for the 1988-89 season but opted instead to return to Canada. "I'd done too much moving around," he declared. "So I decided to pack it in."

Having settled into the Toronto area, he spent the next year and a half selling insurance for Canada Life.

"Then I got my broker's license and along with a partner, we set up our own shop serving the Mississauga-Toronto-Hamilton area," Bill related.

Following three or four years of operation, he retired from the insurance business to spend six months as an auto salesman along with former NHLer Brad Selwood at Al Palladini Motors in Toronto. Car sales seems to have suited Bill just fine. In 1995, he hooked up with Cooksville Dodge Chrysler Jeep in Mississauga, Ontario where he presently works.

Bill spends his leisure time playing golf and tennis although he emphasized his love for all sports. He draws particular enjoyment from his participation with the Maple Leaf oldtimers' team: "We made $300,000 for various charities playing twenty games last year, and I like the comradery of getting together with the guys."

Desjardins, Gerry: *Played goal for Los Angeles, Chicago, the New York Islanders, Buffalo (NHL), Michigan and Baltimore (WHA) from 1968-1978. Born: Sudbury, Ontario, 1944.*

Very few people would aspire to make their living as a target for expert marksmen. Gerry Desjardins, as part of a rare breed and its tradition, relished every moment of every shot that came his way.

"I had the greats shooting at me," he recollected. "Jean Beliveau, Gordie Howe, Phil Esposito, Doug Harvey... And I played against Glenn Hall and my idol, Jacques Plante!

"I remember when I first started with the Kings, it was my second or third game. We were in the Detroit Olympia and I came up against Howe, Delvecchio and Mahovlich on the same line. I mean these guys were all my heroes!"

After logging five seasons in the NHL, Gerry jumped to the World Hockey Association's Michigan Stags in 1974. By Christmas of that year, the Stags had folded, moved to Baltimore and became the Blades. Gerry went along until the phone rang in February. "Punch Imlach got wind that I was a free agent," he related. "He called to see if I'd like to join the Sabres that same year. So I went to Buffalo just before the trade deadline."

Gerry prospered in the Sabres' net until the night of February 10, 1977. "I got hit in the eye with the puck," he recalled. "I was operated on that summer for a cataract extraction. I tried to come back the following year but it was a hopeless case. There was no focusing power in my right eye... I was misplaying long shots from the blueline."

Gerry gave up the crease but stayed on as a goaltending consultant for Don Edwards and Bob Sauvé until 1978. Then it was time to move on.

"It's not an easy thing to adjust to," he stressed. "Hockey is your whole life. That's all you live for and all of sudden it's no longer there. Business or no business, afterwards, it's quite the adjustment to make."

Gerry resettled in Sherbrooke, Quebec where he got into the mortgage field. "At the time I was looking to invest the little bit of money I had," he explained. "A friend of mine had quite a lot of experience with real estate and mortgages. So I got into business with him."

By 1983, however, interest rates had erupted to twenty-two percent, melting many institutions in its path. Gerry and his partner withstood the heat until it was time to get out of the kitchen. "We just wound the company down and figured we'd go our separate ways," he said.

"While I was still in Sherbrooke, I began working with Pat Stapleton's Minor League

> *"... it's amazing ... in life when you give it all you've got and never say give up. Amazing things happen to you."*
>
> *Gerry Desjardins*

Hockey Association," he continued. "I liked the idea of working with kids and I liked the programme that Pat had put together. It involved teaching in 500 different communities across Canada.

"After being associated with the programme, Pat asked me to come to London, Ontario, near their head office, to become more involved. So I did in 1986. The project ran until our sponsors pulled out and that was the end."

Gerry stayed on in London and eventually settled into the steel industry as a sales representative for St. Thomas Steel, just south of the city. Over the next ten years he learned the ropes and built up a strong network of relationships.

The expertise he gained gave him the confidence and connections to strike out on his own as part owner of Canada Steel. "I'm a partner with the individual who gave me my first job in the steel business ten years ago," he related. "We have a brand-new warehouse in London. It's very exiting. I'm really looking to a bright future for Canada Steel. There's no doubt in my mind that this company is going to flourish."

Gerry directs most of his energy to developing and maintaining accounts with welding shops, automotive plants, construction businesses and machine shops within a sixty-mile radius of London. "I'm out on the road meeting people face to face and that's what I like!" he affirmed.

In pondering his past in the NHL, Gerry marveled at the common and yet magical essence of fulfilling his ambition. "I guess it's every Canadian boy's dream to someday play in the National Hockey League and I wasn't any different," he reflected. "You're fourteen, fifteen years old. You dream about playing, but it's so far away that you don't think it will ever come to be. So it's amazing what happens in life when you give it all you've got and never say give up. Amazing things happen to you!"

Dionne, Marcel: *Played centre for Detroit, Los Angeles and the New York Rangers from 1971-1989. Born: Drummondville, Quebec, 1951.*

No airborne insect looks less apt to fly than a bee; few hockey players looked less apt to take flight than the short and stocky Marcel Dionne. Yet like the bee, Marcel was a natural aviator more than able to sting his opponents.

"When you saw him standing there," one of his adversaries recalled, "he looked like he was weighed down... But once the puck was dropped, he was as fast and graceful as a ballerina!"

Marcel's fourth season with the Detroit Red Wings brought him a career-high 121 points and the resolve to escape an organization marked by turmoil and inconsistency. In June of 1975, he became the league's first marquee player to exercise free agency. He signed with the Los Angeles Kings, where like a jewel on the back side of a crown, his lustre became more known than seen.

It was not until the late eighties that Marcel came east to New York to soak up the rays of a traditional hockey market. By then, however, his career was in decline as were his hopes for winning a Stanley Cup. With age no longer an ally, he was forced to change his course.

"When I retired from the Rangers in 1989," he recalled, "we were living in Westchester County, New York, north of Manhattan. I wanted to stay close to home at the time so I decided to work in real estate, having had experience at it since age twenty. At about the same time, I set up Dionne, Feldman Dry Cleaning with a partner

and operated it for about three years."

Marcel's next venture was to move north to the Buffalo area where he bought a struggling business called "D&T Brothers Plumbing". "I gave it an infusion of cash, cleaned up the books and it's running just fine," he declared with an air of quiet confidence.

In 1993, he bought a share in the Carolina Stingrays of the East Coast Hockey League, a club presently coached by former NHLer Rick Vaive. As with D&T, Marcel perceived that there were problems with their day-to-day operations. He soon set things straight and ended up as the club's president. He sold his share, however, in May of 1995 as a result of some legal wranglings. "I felt it best to sell rather than turn our profits over to lawyers during the course of a lawsuit," he noted wryly.

When free of the entanglements of business, Marcel enjoys spending time with his wife, Carol, their two sons and daughter at their home in Buffalo, New York. "We love to go outdoors ... skiing, golfing and fishing, lots of stuff!" he exclaimed. Marcel also stays active playing oldtimers' hockey, touring across Canada with the Greatest Legends of Hockey.

Dorey, Jim: *Played defense for Toronto, the New York Rangers (NHL), New England, Toronto and Quebec (WHA) from 1968-1979. Born: Kingston, Ontario, 1947.*

Jim Dorey was born into the hockey hotbed of Kingston, Ontario. With Quebec at his right and Ontario in his midst, the culture of hockey was as much a part of Jim's upbringing as water is to a seedling.

"My father and my uncles played hockey and I saw hockey equipment around," he recollected. "I was about five or six years old when I started out on the old aluminum bob skates with double blades on a pond at my grandfather's farm. Then I started playing outdoor hockey. I just seemed to have skates on all the time after that. There was nothing else to do—you went to school and you played hockey.

"When I was eighteen, I got picked to play

with the OHA all-stars. We played against a Russian and a Czechoslovakian touring team in Maple Leaf Gardens. I came home for Christmas after the game and got a phone call from the Toronto Maple Leafs. They gave me a Christmas gift—they said, 'You've played so well, we'd like to reward you by having you go down and spend a weekend playing for Rochester of the American Hockey League.' I guess Turk Broda, my coach at the time, had put my name down saying, 'Get this guy a taste of the pros.' My dad drove me down to Rochester and lo and behold, there were guys like Don Cherry, Bronco Horvath, Gerry Ehman, Dick Gamble, Warren Godfrey and Al Arbour playing there!

"When I left, they gave me a $100 cheque for the game. I saw how it was with the pros and I thought, 'Jeez, I like this life. So I went back to junior and really worked hard."

Jim later went on to play eleven seasons of hard-nosed hockey in the NHL and the WHA before a contract dispute with the Nordiques in 1979 put the final punctuation to his career at the top.

"The Nordiques offered me a coaching position, but at the time, I wasn't ready mentally to launch into coaching," he insisted. "Besides, I had no French fluency."

In 1981, Jim was recruited as extra insurance by the Rangers' organization who were planning a run for the Cup that year. He spent the season, however, playing for New Haven of the American Hockey League.

"The following year, Craig Patrick offered me the positions of coach and GM in New Haven—but I refused," Jim reported. "I looked at what was available to me and I looked at my two kids and thought, 'Yeah, maybe I should listen to my wife a little more now and take a look at getting my feet planted. Besides, I didn't

"...we spent five or six hours with Rocket, sharing his Scotch while talking about all of his phenomenal stories. I mean, can you imagine an American sitting with Mickey Mantle for five or six hours uninterrupted?!"

Jim Dorey

want to ride the bus circuit having tasted life in the NHL."

His decisions made, Jim closed out his accounts in professional hockey and began to investigate the field of insurance as a second career.

"Tony Featherstone, who used to play for the Seals, and I, used to play in the World Hockey League," Jim recalled. "I came across him in a restaurant and he said he was working for All State Insurance. I'd been talking to a couple of insurance companies and he said, 'You should have a look at All State.' I interviewed with them and hit it off. I came away thinking, 'I can deal with all aspects of people and it doesn't look like I've got a dull moment in any of my day'!"

Since 1982, Jim has worked steadily at the Kingston offices of All State Insurance Company of Canada "The rules in insurance are the same as in hockey," he concluded. "The bottom line is, 'What are you going to do for me tomorrow?' It's hard work and a challenge every day and I really love it. I put the same work and energy into my job as I did in hockey—it's much like a rink. Every day you step in there, you think you know what you're going to do. But a bodycheck or a phone call can change whatever momentum you've got going, so you've got to learn to adapt."

From the comfort of his office chair, Jim contemplated the high points of his career in professional hockey.

"I think that my highlight was to have played for the Toronto Maple Leafs and to have been around at a time when the whole United States, Canada and Europe was opening up," he mused. "Being in hockey in that era, I went to places that people didn't even dream of going to—Houston, California ... on a routine basis."

Since the early nineties, Jim has played

thirty to forty games a year with the Greatest Legends of Hockey tour. It was while with the Legends that his other great magical moment occurred.

"We had just played a promotional hockey game in northern British Columbia with the Legends," Jim recounted. "After we'd play a game, each guy would go his own way after having a couple of cocktails and doing some PR work for the clients. Some guys go out for supper and some guys for a movie. This particular night I was rooming with Red Storey. I was just going to watch TV and Red was asleep. I got a phone call from one of the guys and he said, 'Jim, what are you doing?' And I said, 'I'm just sitting here watching TV, baby-sitting Red.' He said, 'Why don't you put on your clothes, Rocket Richard wants you to come up and have a drink with him.' I'd had a drink with Rocket in a bus or in a bar before, but never in this kind of setting.

"So I went up and along with a couple of other guys, we spent five or six hours with Rocket, sharing his Scotch while talking about all of his phenomenal stories. I mean, can you imagine an American sitting with Mickey Mantle for five or six hours uninterrupted?! I got to ask questions and talk about his hockey. He's not an outgoing person, but when he has your confidence, he's quite the storyteller! He's an excellent person—I was just stunned by that."

—⚬⚬⚬—

Douglas, Kent: *Played defense for Toronto, Oakland, Detroit (NHL) and the New York Raiders (WHA) between 1962 & 1973. Born: Cobalt, Ontario, 1936.*

By the time Punch Imlach plucked Kent Douglas from the untamed world of Eddie Shore's Springfield Indians, Kent had been thoroughly grounded in the art of tough and heady defense.

During his first campaign as a Leaf blueliner, he put his skills to effective use, finishing the season with a Calder Trophy as the league's top rookie in one hand, and a Stanley Cup in the other. It would never get any better than that.

Kent toiled for the Leafs until 1967 before

rounding out his NHL career with Oakland and Detroit.

With the advent of the World Hockey Association in 1972, Kent resurfaced in a New York Raider jersey for one season before joining the Baltimore Clippers of the American Hockey League for his final three years in professional hockey.

"My last season, I served as player-coach. I found that hard to do," he admitted. "I was playing and coaching thirty-five to thirty-eight minutes a night! If I'd been younger it might have been okay, but I was older and I was tired.

"I also found it hard to be critical with people when I'm making the same mistakes they were. I found that to be the most difficult [point]."

Kent finally called it quits in 1976. And being highly proficient in the fine art of conversation, he chose real estate for the next phase of his career. Specializing in Baltimore's residential market, he had little trouble setting people as his first priority. "I'm still friends with a lot of the customers I've sold houses to," he noted. "I'm not sure how many real-estate people are (laughs)."

Kent sighted an example of his personal approach to sales. While representing a builder, he was showing three model homes to a couple who, to this day, are still his friends. "The wife's looking through the house and the husband and I are talking," Kent related. "He's into making golf clubs and so am I. So she came back after looking through the houses and we were *still* sitting there discussing golf. And she said, '*Well, I want to buy a house*!!!' Of course we told her there are priorities in life and [the house] was down the list a little bit. We were discussing golf and that was much more important."

And as that conversation went, Kent's career was soon to follow. The sweet sensation of a hard drive and a soft green was too much to resist—he put real estate on hold to become a golf pro at Sparrow's Point Golf Club in the Baltimore suburb of Dundock. Having held his Professional Golf Association card since 1967, he was quite comfortable in his role as an instructor. The course was a private club maintained by

Bethlehem Steel for their employees. "You got people who worked for a living and some of them didn't start at being the boss ... and that was good," he observed. "It was easy for me to associate with them. We always had something to talk about. They were down to earth unlike what you find in some private clubs where there's a hierarchy... They're not quite sociable with everyone because you might be on a different level. I know we're not living in India or anything like that but there are still tiers as people are well aware of and I don't feel there should be."

After a healthy stint on the fairways, Kent retired from the golf business and resumed his career in real estate. He also reentered the world of sports by volunteering to coach the hockey team at the Naval Academy in Annapolis, Maryland. "I told them, 'I'm doing this for free! You couldn't afford me if you had to pay me'!" he exclaimed.

Kent soon developed a regard for the dedication and character of the Academy players. "They weren't the most talented players in the world," he admitted. "But they seldom quit and they never lost a close game. They were a great group of kids. The commitment was there. Hell, they'd go right through the boards.

"Of course in college, they're not allowed to fight. And that was okay. I said, 'Look, you guys are pretty damn strong. You're probably stronger than most of the people you're ever going to play against. So if you ever get into trouble—you've got long arms—just grab ahold of them, and smile...' If you really want to get somebody upset with you, just put a little grin on your face when they can't hit you."

Kent also stressed the importance of academics in conjunction with his programme: "We had three of the top thirteen kids in the senior class playing hockey. And the two highest ones were goaltenders which makes no sense. I asked them, 'How could people with your kind of intelligence want to play goal of all positions'?"

Although his focus has been on college hockey, Kent hasn't lost sight of the NHL. "It's an offensive game today although if you watch the playoffs, they still win with defense," he observed. "But the onus is on entertainment and people want to see goals and exciting plays."

If he has a qualm about today's style of play, it is the tendency to consistently dump the puck in over the blueline rather than to practise effective puck control. Coming from the school of Eddie Shore, Kent quoted his former teacher who said, "Why do you want to give the puck away when you worked so hard to get it?"

Over the years, he and his wife, Jacqueline, raised two boys at their home in Lutherville, Maryland. Athletics and the Douglas family have continued to roll over into the next generation as one of their sons became an All-American lacrosse player, representing Team Canada in the 1984 Olympics in Los Angeles.

Dryden, Dave: *Played goal for the New York Rangers, Chicago, Buffalo, Edmonton (NHL), Chicago and Edmonton (WHA) between 1961 & 1979. Born: Hamilton, Ontario, 1941.*

"When I graduated from junior hockey at age twenty, there was no way I was considering a pro career," Dave Dryden said, reflecting back on his ascent to the NHL.

"When I was nineteen," he continued, "I had been seriously thinking about going to the States on a hockey scholarship. But what happened was one of those flukes. The goalie for the New York Rangers [Gump Worsley] got hurt midway through the game one evening when they were playing the Leafs. They only carried one goalie in those days, so I got called out of the stands to fill in for Gump! By doing that, I was then considered a professional. No college in the States would offer me a scholarship, so that really shot me down!"

The event seemed to narrow Dave's options. Since he had earned a teaching certificate at age nineteen, he chose to shift his focus from hockey to education. After three years of teaching, he took a year off to pursue his bachelor's degree at the University of Waterloo. The birth of his son the following year, however, necessitated his return to the classroom.

And then another one of those life-shaping flukes occurred. "I was playing senior hockey as it was called at the time and a couple of goalies got injured," he recollected. "I landed at the pro level ... filled in for them and did okay. Then the Blackhawks offered me a contract, so I quit teaching and went to play pro."

Although he had made it to the NHL, Dave never lost sight of the bigger picture, which for him, included education. "All of the years that I played pro, I would always come back in May and teach the last month or so," he recounted. "I also took courses by correspondence, and in the summertime at Wilfred Laurier—so I had my degree after about five years."

By 1979, Dave and the Edmonton Oilers had just made their transition back into the NHL. Looking ahead, Dave had arranged his final contract to stipulate that he would assume an assistant-coaching role with the team upon his retirement.

That transition was close at hand. "I just felt that I'd lost the enthusiasm for playing in November of that ... year," he confided. "I was skating on the ice in Denver and I just said to Glen [Sather], 'As of tomorrow, get a new goaltender because I'm retiring'."

Dave completed that season as an assistant coach. He also had an agreement with Sather that if the head coach's position opened up that he would get it.

The following summer Sather brought Bryan "Bugsy" Watson on board as an assistant coach. "Bugsy and I were just shooting the breeze," Dave reported, "when he said, 'You know Dave, I've been promised the head-coaching job when it comes up next.' I said, 'Well, I'd been promised the same thing.' So I talked to Glen about it and he said, '*Well*, I changed my mind.' And I said, '*Well*, I quit'!"

Dave had yet to fully satisfy his coaching aspirations, so he accepted a position as the manager-coach of the Peterborough Petes of the Ontario Hockey Association. "I stayed there for a year and a half," he recounted. "And then I was fired about ... midway through the second year. By Christmas of that second year, I knew I didn't want to coach for a career. I just didn't enjoy it one bit—and I don't think I was very good at it."

"I just thoroughly enjoyed getting back into teaching."

Dave Dryden

Dave then went full circle by returning to the field of education. "I just thoroughly enjoyed getting back into teaching," he observed. "And I knew that that was what I was going to do."

He reentered the profession as a supply teacher in Toronto and progressed through the ranks until, in 1991, he assumed his first term as a principal of Thorn Lodge Public School.

To get to that level, he underwent intensive training that included specialist courses and the completion of his Master's degree in Niagara Falls, New York.

Dave is now principal of Tecumseh Public School in Mississauga.

Although education has been his primary focus, he also continues to keep a finger in the world of hockey. From 1985 to 1991, he served as a goaltending coach for the Detroit Red Wings. During the summer of 1996, he initiated an ongoing term as goaltending consultant for the Nippon Cranes in Japan.

For leisure, Dave enjoys athletics in general as well as spending time with his wife, Sandra, their two children and their first, newly born grandchild. Their son, Greg, is an international auditor for the Coca-Cola Corporation. So Dave and Sandra have enjoyed visiting him in settings throughout the world.

Over the past few years, they have travelled to such places as Argentina, Australia, China,

Russia, New Zealand—where Dave taught hockey, and India—where he distributed bed kits on behalf of his father's children's aid programme.

Dave and Sandra make their home in Oakville, Ontario.

Nickname: *Sod*

"I didn't tend to swear very much," Dave recalled. "I'd just say, 'You sod'!"

Duguay, Ron: *Played centre for the New York Rangers, Detroit, Pittsburgh and Los Angeles from 1977-1989. Born: Sudbury, Ontario, 1957.*

Ron Duguay's life, both on and off the ice, was characterized by a kind of big-screen magnetism. His devilish good looks won him modelling contracts and made female fans swoon. His image was made for Broadway and Madison Square Gardens was an ideal stage.

In Ranger blue, Ron chased pucks the way a prospector digs for gold. He'd zoom up and down his wing with short, choppy strides, leaving his long, curly hair struggling to keep up. Within the range of the opposing net, the Rangers' #10 could unleash a deceptively quick shot that brought home a career-high forty goals in 1981-82.

After six seasons in New York, Ron was traded to the Detroit Red Wings where he continued to perform with panache. By 1985, however, his career became a rambling road in the service of Pittsburgh, New York and finally, Los Angeles.

With twelve NHL seasons and 672 career points in the bank, he decided to make a withdrawal to Manheim, Germany for a year. "It was so different from the NHL," he observed. "There was very little travel ... so it wasn't really hard on your body. As for the rinks, a lot of them were outdoors or half rinks with just a roof on them. I was like a little kid in Canada, playing on a rink outside all season."

Ron then came back to North America to play for the San Diego Gulls of the International Hockey League from 1990 to 1992. He pointed out that what he lost in salary going from the NHL to the IHL was made up for by the comradery and

respect that he felt with teammates and management.

With a strong desire to continue playing, he attempted a comeback with the Tampa Bay Lightning in 1992. "They were giving me a chance, and only one chance," he revealed of his experience. "Then I had the bad luck of getting hurt and so they offered me a radio job."

Ron described the challenge he faced in moving upstairs to the broadcast booth: "It was very difficult—especially because I wanted to play so badly. I was so disappointed at not getting that chance ... sitting up in the stands, watching some of these younger players not play that well—it was very frustrating! And when you're doing radio, you always have to fill in the gap when there is a quiet time. I had to talk to a lot of players so I'd have information to share... But I didn't want to hang around the dressing rooms because I wanted to play so badly. It was hard for me..."

Ron's radio job only served to increase the intensity of his desire for competitive action. In response, he turned to the world of roller hockey in search of satisfaction.

"I found it difficult because as a big man, you slide a lot on the blades," he recounted. "A lot of my game is to start and stop quickly. I couldn't do that with the rollerblades, so I was frustrated with it. After a while, I just learned to make those big turns that they make to try to be at the right place at the right time—but it was a whole different game."

It was a game Ron preferred to leave behind, so he decided to move west. "It was more a family decision," he explained. "My two girls from my first marriage lived in California and I really missed them while I was in Tampa. And then my wife got pregnant which meant that she was going to need help with the house, so I decided to leave hockey and spend time with the kids."

After almost three years of focusing primarily on family, Ron reentered the hockey world, playing home games for the San Diego Gulls. "I just practise when I need to practise," he added. "It doesn't get any better than that!"

Ron spends his leisure time enjoying his three

children as well as attending to his house and menagerie. "I have a big yard," he said. "I've fenced off an area where we have a couple of pigs, a couple of goats and a couple of dogs. I also do a lot of landscape work on the property."

He and his new wife, Kim Alexis-Duguay,

have a son and make their home in Newport Beach, California.

Dumart, Woody: *Played left wing for Boston between 1935 & 1954. Born: Kitchener, Ontario, 1916.*

During the 1996 induction ceremony for the Hockey Hall of Fame, the men who fashioned the "Kraut Line"—one of the Boston Bruins' most exciting and effective trios—came as close to a complete reunion as is humanly possible.

The late Bobby Bauer's two sons stepped to the podium to speak on the occasion of their father's induction. Bobby Bauer Jr. spoke eloquently about the rare chemistry that existed between his father, Milt Schmidt and Woody Dumart. Milt and Woody sat in the front row, absorbing every spark of a moment charged with emotion, dignity and sentiment.

As the two men stood to be acknowledged, it was apparent that neither age nor death could keep the spirit of these three men apart.

During his prime, Woody Dumart played in the spirit of Lady Byng, relying on a hard shot and persistent checking to maintain his place amongst the illustrious Bauer and Schmidt.

By 1954, Woody's on-ice career had played out its course. He retired and snapped up the first job that came available—as a salesman in a Boston sporting goods store. The position was not to his liking, but it kept the wolf from the door until, six months later, a better opportunity surfaced.

His kindred pal, Bobby Bauer, had married the boss's daughter, creating the connection through which Woody became a manufacturer's rep for Bauer skates in the New England area.

During his first year out of hockey, Woody found he thoroughly missed being associated with his former teammates. Becoming a Bruins' supplier over the next couple of decades, however, allowed him to stay in close touch with the organization and its players.

In addition to marketing Bauer products, he set up a small warehouse to stock hockey-related items that the Bauer company didn't handle. "I

Nickname Challenge #6

Flash

"When I was still in Buffalo of the International League, I was known as 'Busher'. But when I got called up to the Leafs, Busher Jackson was there. The team trainer, Tim Daly, said, 'We can't call you Bush, so we'll call you Flash!'—so 'Flash' it was."

Who is he?

Clues

a. He played defense for Ottawa, Toronto, Boston and Detroit from 1933-1946.
b. He was a first-team all-star in 1945.
c. With an assist from Milt Schmidt, he scored the winning goal against the Leafs' Turk Broda to claim the Stanley Cup for the Boston Bruins in 1939.

If you broke your stick on the drive, see page 285

bought hockey equipment up in Canada and brought it down here to sell to my dealers," he recollected. "I kept a good inventory of jerseys and stock that no one else had down here. Local dealers could come and get everything they wanted in the same day."

Business remained brisk until a groundswell of interest hurled Woody and his warehouse to a new level. His jerseys and sticks became celebrities in themselves—being mobbed by delirious fans. "During the Orr, Esposito days in the late sixties and early seventies, hockey down here just boomed!" he exclaimed. "Twelve months a year you could sell everything that you could get!"

By 1980, Woody was ready to punctuate a great run in the sporting goods-business. Being sixty-three and with money in the bank, he was ready to get down to some serious porch sitting and paper reading. More recently he remains active playing the odd round of golf and supporting the Boston Bruins' oldtimers. "I can't skate anymore, so I act as coach behind the bench," he noted. "It's just getting together with the fellas that I look forward to. It's all for charity and a lot of fun."

He also keeps an eye on today's NHL. "It's a different style of hockey now," he observed. "Most of the time they take the puck up to the red line and shoot it into the corner and everybody chases it instead of passing their way in. As for bodychecking, you can stay in centre ice and they'll try to poke the puck away from you. If you get into the corners, why they're coming from all over just to put you through the boards. That's where I find all the bodychecking is."

The pinnacle of Woody's post-playing career, although late in arriving, finally came in 1992 with his induction into the Hockey Hall of Fame. "That was probably the greatest thrill of my life!" he exclaimed. "It's something I'd always hoped for when I was through playing. But I had to wait a long time—I was nominated about three years in a row. I really didn't think I would make it because I had lost out on other years."

He and his wife, Phyllis, have raised two sons and a daughter, who in turn, have added seven grandchildren to the clan. For Woody and Phyllis, they represent seven reasons to enjoy life at their home in Needham, Massachusetts.

Dunlop, Blake: *Played centre for Minnesota, Philadelphia, St. Louis and Detroit from 1973-1984. Born: Hamilton, Ontario, 1953.*

During his final season as a junior with the Ottawa 67's of the Ontario Hockey Association, Blake Dunlop became a hot property on the force of his record-setting sixty goals and ninety-nine assists. He was quickly scooped up by the Minnesota North Stars in 1973 where he began a five-year odyssey in search of the scoring touch that seemed to abandon him. It was not until he entered his second five-year phase, first with Philadelphia and then with St. Louis, that a burst of the old playmaking savvy returned. Before all was said and done, he had secured an additional bounty of 355 points.

But even as the crowds were still cheering and the reporters were still reporting, Blake's mind began to wander into the field of his own mortality where athletes must face the issues of their own demise.

"I think that the problem a lot of players have coming out of hockey is that it's a very structured environment," he reasoned. "You constantly have somebody telling you what to do, when to do it and how to do it. So it becomes difficult for the players to step out and say, 'Well, now what can I do?' There are so many choices out there. They don't know where to start."

During the summer before his final season in the NHL, Blake sought to address this problem in advance. "I had a friend who was an industrial psychologist," he recalled. "He did a lot of work with corporations. I took some preferential testing to try and help narrow down what fields I might be interested or capable of working in. Basically, they pointed out that I would be good at sales. I was a more independent, entrepreneurial type."

"Then," Blake continued, "he introduced me to a number of firms in St. Louis to see if I could get an opportunity to work in the summer. Instead of having a shotgun, it was more of a bullet approach, where you could try these two or three companies. I ended up at A.G. Edwards Brokerage Firm."

Blake finished up the 1983-84 season in Detroit. He then had to face a difficult decision: Should he try to stretch out his NHL career for a few more years at the risk of having to relocate his family or, would it be better to remain at his home base in St. Louis and leave pro hockey behind?

"The easy decision is to stay and play hockey somewhere because that's what you've been doing since you were a little boy," he remarked. "You know what it takes. The hard decision is to step away and realize that it might be tougher the first year. But if you're successful in the long run, then it's the right thing to do. Fortunately for me, it was the right thing. The business I got into has worked out very well..."

Blake settled in with A.G. Edwards, where he'd started the previous summer. "I'm what you'd call a stockbroker or investment broker," he noted. "I'm currently a vice president in sales. The last four years I've managed a branch in St. Louis that has about fifty employees. I have sort of a dual role if you will. A lot of my day is spent talking to my own clients and prospects about various investments. I also supervise and run the branch."

Blake has found success in both the hockey and the business worlds. He offered some insight into his approach in both cases: "When I got established in the NHL, I didn't do that over night. I played hockey since I was five years old—learning, working and honing my skills. So I looked at my second career in the same way. I wasn't going to be able to be the manager or the president of the company in my first year. I needed to learn the business. I needed to work hard and to put in my time. And if I did that successfully, then I would be rewarded. I think that's where some players have a hard time with

the transition. They're used to being at a certain level, being recognized. [They'll] say, 'Well, I should be able to just go from here ... and be the head of this company.' I try to tell people, 'You played many years of junior and got beat up. You did whatever you had to do to get there. Starting a second career is no different. You have to start at a lower level and find a way to build it up'."

Blake spends much of his spare time with his wife, Nora, and their four children. He also coaches his son's triple-A midget hockey team and runs an annual hockey school. His leisure interests include traveling, golfing and playing tennis; and with some partners, including former NHLer Rob Ramage, he purchased a junior-A hockey team that started play in St. Louis in the fall of 1996.

Nickname: *Gunner*

"If I ever scored a goal, which wasn't too often," Blake quipped, "they'd call me 'Gunner' while I was in St. Louis."

Dupère, Denis: *Played left wing for Toronto, Washington, St. Louis, Kansas City and Colorado from 1970-1978. Born: Jonquière, Quebec, 1948.*

Denis Dupère sustained his career in professional hockey on the basis of fine penalty killing and a knack for winning face-offs. "He was a great big Frenchman with a tremendous wrist shot off the wrong foot," his former teammate, Ab Demarco stated. "Goaltenders were often deceived by his shot because he gave no indication that it was coming."

Well in advance of his NHL debut, Denis was biding his time with Omaha of the Central Hockey League. To make his mark off ice, he made it known that any rough stuff would be summarily dealt with by him—or by members of his family.

Ab Demarco related an example of just such a case: "We had a big, three-bedroom apartment in Omaha. There were four of us staying there: Denis, myself, Bryan Lefley and the late Burt Wilson. So it was two guys to a room and then the other two got their own rooms for a month

Denis Dupère with his diningroom masterpiece: a picture of his first NHL goal which he scored against Rogie Vachon at the Montreal Forum in 1970

until the next time we drew straws. Now beyond hockey, Denis's other claim to fame was being related to the world-famous Vachon brothers. You know, 'Mad Dog' Vachon, the professional wrestler? They were icons in the province of Quebec. Well, one day, they showed up in Omaha and of course, they came over to visit Denis. Now 'Dupy' as we called him, had been rooming with Bryan Lefley, and he was upset that Bryan wasn't cleaning up after himself. So 'Dupy' said, 'My cousins are comin' an der gonna get choo!'—the way he would talk. Well the door opened up and these two monsters gaped in, and I mean they were huge—6'5", 330 pounds, both bald and mean looking. They could have starred in any horror show you could imagine. Now Denis had already told 'Mad Dog' about Bryan. So 'Mad Dog' lumbers in and says, 'Where's dat Bryan Lefley?' and Bryan's face turned white as the Vachon's were staggering towards him. They grabbed ahold of him and picked him right up. Of course Bryan didn't know what to do, he was scared shitless. So when our little laugh was complete, one of them sat down in a big, livingroom chair and, I'm not kidding you, the four legs crumbled to the floor, Kerplunk! And while he was sitting there, 'Dupy' had the laugh of his life."

All humour aside, Denis remained with Omaha as a Ranger prospect until the Leafs secured his rights and brought him to the Gardens in 1970. For the next four seasons, he performed as an effective utility man until the inevitable trades of the journeyman's life set in. He was first secured by the expansion Washington Capitals in 1974 and then dealt to St. Louis, Kansas City and finally, Colorado.

By age thirty, and on the far end of his prime, Denis's rights were held by the tottering Rockies who retained his services like an undervalued insurance policy.

"They sent me down to the minor leagues at Christmas of my last year," he recounted. "They told me that my contract would terminate at the end of the season. Then the Rockies had a shot at the playoffs and [Wilf] Paiement wasn't scoring. So, they decided to bring me back up. I had twenty points in fifteen games! I negotiated with the team's owner to get a full, one-way contract. But Mr. Vickers sold the team in June before we closed the deal. The new ownership would only offer me a two-way deal when I went to training camp and so that's when I went home. I didn't want to play in the minors for a minor-league salary. But then later, I said, 'I'll go down to the minors as long as you guarantee to add one more year's contributions to my pension. They'd have had to put in three or four thousand bucks, but they wouldn't even do that. So I just went home. It was kind of a sad note, but there's no point in being bitter—it's a fact of life."

Denis now stood alone in the eerie midst of involuntary change. "Hockey was something I'd been doing for fifteen, sixteen years," he related. "Then, all of a sudden, the door was shut—you're not prepared for it! It was just a big blank. And all the good friends I'd made in hockey were living all across the country—I didn't see them anymore. So it was a big adjustment that takes awhile. But that's part of life. I compare it to someone who looses their job in business at age fifty and they say, 'Well, what do we do now'?"

As his bearings came into focus, Denis knew the NHL would be a hard act to follow—but follow it he did by accepting a two-year offer to play and coach in Lyon, France. "It was good as an experience," he recalled. "But, at the time, the hockey over there was pretty poor. I made some good friends too, but I felt I was beginning to lose my contacts and friends back here [in North America]. So I decided to come home to face the parade of readjusting here."

Time would be a necessary ally in sorting out the loose ends of where to go from there. He retreated to his native Jonquière, Quebec to hammer out some decisions on what to do and where to call home.

Ontario, the cradle of Denis's junior days, won out as his *pieds-à-terre*. Shortly thereafter, he landed a job as a salesman for a baseball-cap distributor based in Mount Forest. "I handled East Coast and Quebec sales for three years," he noted. "But I found that working in sales was not really me, so I packed it in."

Since 1985, he has enjoyed the next best thing to hockey he's yet to find, working in the inventory department for Tournament Sports, a wholesale sporting-goods company based in Kitchener, Ontario. "We're a successful, growing company dealing in everything from golf shoes to sports shirts," he remarked. "It's been a great trade for me to get into. There's always something different happening every day."

These days, Denis lives a comfortable, bachelor's life amidst a few choice symbols from his past. His diningroom centrepiece is an action shot of his first NHL goal, scored against Rogie Vachon in 1970. But his greatest prize stands sentinel over his livingroom easy chair: a commemorative team picture of his trip to the All-Star Game. "When I was with Washington in '74, I had scored twenty goals before the all-star break," he proudly recounted. "Since they had to invite one member from each team, I got my chance. The game was played in Montreal and being from Quebec, seeing all those guys—Lafleur, Dryden, Esposito, Orr—I was shaking when I hit the ice. You can't beat a thrill like that! It was the fulfillment of a dream that money can never buy."

Ecclestone, Tim: *Played right wing for St. Louis, Detroit, Toronto and Atlanta from 1967-1978. Born: Toronto, Ontario, 1947.*

Tim Ecclestone approached his hockey career with the mind set of an entrepreneur who knows that survival is based on a finely tuned blend of creativity, adaptability and above all, usefulness. When the coach had a problem, Tim came through with a pocket full of solutions. He could play all three forward positions as well as the point on power plays. When short-handed, he was a topnotch checker who could smother penalties with a firm hand. At even strength, he was an artful playmaker who tallied 243 career assists.

Although a product of the New York Rangers' system, Tim got his first NHL break with the expansion St. Louis Blues in 1967. As his career advanced, he saw action with the Detroit Red Wings and the Toronto Maple

Leafs. On November 2, 1974, he found himself as the property of three different teams in one day. He had breakfast as a Maple Leaf, lunch as a Washington Capital and dinner with his final team, the Atlanta Flames.

By 1977, Tim was beginning to see the horizon of his career on ice. "I'd hurt my knee and they approached me about being the assistant coach and perhaps playing on an occasional basis," he recalled. "I just played sparingly that year and then in '78, they named me assistant coach.

"I was in management obviously. But I still had a rapport with the players that sometimes the head coach didn't have. So if some communication problems came up, it was easier for me to approach them and work things out."

Tim stayed on as an assistant coach with the Flames until 1980. "The team was moving and I was already in the restaurant business by then," he explained. "Cliff Fletcher offered me a post in Calgary but I decided to stay on in Atlanta and branch out on my own."

Back in 1978, he and a friend had opened a sports bar called "Timothy John's". "My partner only lasted a couple of years while I continued on until I sold the place in 1989," Tim related. "Then I opened another sports bar called TJ's in 1990. The original Timothy John's became known as TJ's, so when I opened my current place, I kept the same name. My son Mark is the restaurant's general manager."

The business is now on solid ground, but the halting progression from athletics to cuisine didn't always follow a simple recipe.

"Back in my time, I never made enough money to put away," Tim revealed. "So I had to scramble to survive outside the game. You learn pretty quick that it's a lot easier inside the game... You might have a bad day, but you got a paycheque so you could survive. But in private business, if you have too many bad days, you just don't make it."

Tim also learned that the immediate presence of an NHL franchise can take the anonymity out of working in a crowd. "Knowing everybody in the city kind of helped me in whatever I did," he recalled. "I knew radio people and everybody in the television industry. All of a sudden the team left and things changed a bit. The first year or so it seemed like business was as usual. But then ... business got a little tougher. It's a tough industry anyway, never mind the contacts. So I struggled a bit, but I was able to take a business that was failing a little and build it back up."

With his son watching over the sports bar, Tim has had time to pursue other adventures such as trading products in Panama's free zone. With connections in Scotland, he has been able to trade commodities such as Scotch whiskey and cigarettes that eventually end up in South America.

He has also developed an interest in the potentially lucrative business of salvaging sunken ships. "We read up on all the Spanish galleons that used to go to South America to pick up the taxes," Tim recounted. "They'd go from South America back up the coast by Guatemala and through British Honduras which is now Belize. And the second-largest barrier reef is right there off the coast. One after another, they'd hit some bad storms and get blown onto that reef."

Until recently, the Belizean government was unwilling to issue salvaging permits to bring back the lost treasures from its waters. But with the help of some local contacts, Tim has managed to soften them up. "I went down there and worked with the government through another couple of Belizeans and was able to get a permit to salvage those waters," he explained.

> *"We read up on all the Spanish galleons that used to go to South America... One after another they'd get blown on to that reef... [I] was able to get a permit to salvage those waters."*
>
> Tim Ecclestone

"I had a backer and we were ready to go. I took the Turner [broadcasting] people down. They were going to do a documentary on the whole thing. But the Belizean government got greedy. So there was a standoff. It's going to cost us a lot of money to ... do something like this and we want our expenses back first. But the Belizean government doesn't want to do that. So we backed off."

Tim explained that salvaging expenses could exceed fifty percent of the treasure's value. If the government doesn't reimburse them off the top, they run the risk of earning nothing for their labours. So for now, he and his backers are waiting with the hope that the Belizean government will loosen up.

In the meantime, Tim bides his time on land reading about Spanish galleons and playing golf once a week with former NHLers Eric Vail and Willi Plett.

Edwards, Gary: *Played goal for St. Louis, Los Angeles, Cleveland, Minnesota, Edmonton and Pittsburgh between 1968 & 1982. Born: Toronto, Ontario, 1947.*

Back in 1968-69, Gary Edwards was riding the St. Louis Blues' bench as support for Jacques Plante and Glenn Hall. One night, Plante had to leave a game near the end of the first period. While Glenn Hall was getting dressed to replace him, Gary stole away his first four minutes of time on NHL ice. Stan Mikita delivered the opening shot which Gary grabbed and tucked away as his most memorable moment in hockey.

From that time forward, his role in the NHL had been cast as the reliable backup who would roam the league providing insurance to teams in need of coverage. During the course of his fourteen-year career, he served nine different professional teams. Moving from city to city, however, did little to prepare him for a stationary life of nine to five.

"It was difficult to figure out what I really wanted to do," he admitted of his transition out of hockey. "After retiring, you give something your best shot... But you're almost afraid to say, 'Hey, this isn't really what I want,' because if you ever had that attitude while you were playing, then you were finished. I think that was the biggest part of the adjustment because you start by wasting a lot of time trying things out.

"My son is a sophomore in college and these kids are told that, 'By the time you're thirty, you should have gone through at least three job changes while you find your way.' So my thirty-four-to-forty was the same as some young fella twenty-two-to-twenty-eight. It was a bit difficult because you're anxious to choose a business and get on with it. You think, 'Heck, I've been doing hockey for ten, twelve years. Why can't I chose a business and get at it for another ten or twelve years'?"

But true to the college predictions, Gary fell right in with the profile of a man in search of meaningful work. After leaving the Pittsburgh Penguins in 1982, he resettled in Culver City, California where he got into selling insurance. "I don't want to be nasty to other insurance agents out there," he confided, "but it broke down to the fact that I couldn't tell enough lies ... just to make everything fit. I'm not very fond of insurance."

With full custody of his values, he then moved to Thousand Oaks to serve as a manager with a retail chain called "Big Five Sporting Goods". Seven years of long hours and arduous labour, however, stood like and interminable fence between him and his family. The sporting goods and the fence had to go!

Gary switched to selling windows as a construction agent until the industry became stagnant during the recession of the late eighties. He bailed out and, in 1990, made a successful landing in his current line of work with Barlow Painting, a commercial and residential paint-contracting business. "I have not been unbusy in the last four years," he remarked. "We have contracts with four different condominium complexes. We've done projects with the city government and the school districts. I do do some painting but I'm more or less in a semi-supervisory role."

To keep sanity in hand, Gary used to spend his leisure time on the golf course—that is, until his son became a serious volleyball player. He then took up the cause himself, helping to coordinate Junior Olympic tournaments across the continent. "I do the paperwork and make sure the money is paid out at the right time so that the kids have an opportunity to go to these tournaments," he related.

Nickname: *Scoop*

"It was given to me by a guy named Donny Grisebrecht when we played together with the Kansas City Blues," Gary recollected. "It happened in the lobby of a motel in Oklahoma City. The guys were there talking and one of them had a newspaper. They asked a question and I gave the answer over the shoulder. One of them said, 'What the hell, you got all the scoops?' So I got the name 'Scoop' as in a reporter who gets a scoop. It stayed with me everyplace I've been."

Edwards, Roy: *Played goal for Detroit and Pittsburgh from 1967-1974. Born: Seneca Township, Ontario, 1937.*

Standing only 5'8" and 166 pounds, Roy Edwards needed an agile mind and quick hands to cover all the gaps between the pipes. A member of the old school, he preferred the stand-up approach of forcing the shooter to make the first move. He was also quite mobile in his ability to clear pucks away from his net.

Roy first entered the pro ranks in 1958 as a member of the Chicago Blackhawks' farm system where he underwent a nine-year apprenticeship. It was not until league expansion doubled the demand for netminders in 1967 that he finally caught a break with the Detroit Red Wings. He shared duties with Roger Crozier and then Jim Rutherford before joining Les Binkley in Pittsburgh. One year later, Roy returned to Detroit where he closed out his career.

While enduring the uncertainty of life as a major- and minor-league goaltender, Roy found peace of mind from the secure notion that his second career was on a map with a definite destination. He had picked up valuable skills in home repair and cabinetry from his father and brother and had worked for the latter during the off-season.

By the time Roy put his goal pads to rest in 1974, he was primed and ready to head back home to Caledonia, Ontario where he established Roy Edwards Home Repair, a business which he ran until his retirement in 1993.

As a product of an older era, Roy first hit the ice at a time when a goaltender's face was still essential equipment. In such a vulnerable state, he sustained more than his share of serious head injuries. In recent years, the damage caused by repeated concussions has resulted in some loss of memory. A special tribute was held recently in honour of Roy that was attended by representatives of the NHL, including his nephew, former Sabres' goaltender Donny Edwards.

More recently, Roy and Don were honoured at a celebrity dinner and golf tounament sponsored by the New York Rangers' alumni. During the festivities the two kindred backstoppers were inducted into the Caledonia Hall of Fame, and a scholarship bearing their names was unveiled to benefit local high-school students.

At present, Roy spends his leisure time building and flying remote-control airplanes. He also constructs model-train layouts featuring various combinations of mountains, tunnels, trees and stations.

He and his wife, Mary, a librarian, have raised two daughters and are enjoying three grandchildren who are, as Roy puts it, the joy of his life.

Captain Jack Egers of the Kitchener-Waterloo Fire Department

Egers, Jack: *Played right wing for the New York Rangers, St.Louis and Washington from 1969-1976. Born: Sudbury, Ontario, 1949.*

Jack Egers was known to his teammates as "Smokey" because of his speedy, blistering slapshot which he used in 1969-70 to top the Central Hockey League in goals and assists. His numbers soon caught the attention of the New York Rangers who promptly summoned him to Madison Square Gardens where he saw limited action over the next two years. It was not until he joined the St. Louis Blues in 1971-72, however, that his big gun began to fire real bullets. Skating on left wing in the company of Mike Murphy and Garry Unger, Jack accumulated ninety-eight points in two seasons.

He went on to perform duty for the Washington Capitals before injuries forced him

to toss in the towel by 1976. Jack described his departure from hockey as a rocky descent from the lofty limelight to the hard surface of the earth.

His landing, needless to say, was far from soft. His agent, who managed such players as Garry Howatt, Bob Nystrom and Ron Greschner, embezzled money which he lost at the race track in 1976. In the end, his agent did some time while Jack left the NHL with some hard feelings and no money. When he and his wife, Wendy, returned to her hometown of Kitchener, Ontario, they couldn't even afford to buy their own home.

Jack's first move was to get into selling real estate for three-and-a-half years. "I wasn't very good at it," he quipped. "Then I got into the life-insurance business, but I wasn't very good at that either."

At about the same time, he coached two junior-B clubs, the Waterloo Siskins and the Kitchener Rangers. "I thought I might try to get a foothold in coaching, but it didn't work out," he added.

At age thirty-four, Jack's odyssey of trial and error finally ended when he was hired by the Kitchener-Waterloo Fire Department. He responded well to the collective concept of the department. "Teamwork! That's number one," he said. "That's exactly what firefighting's all about. If you have six guys on the ice, you're always covering each other's backs. The only difference I can draw is that firefighting is one hundred times more important than hockey because you're dealing with life and death."

Jack's dedication to his work brought him a promotion to the rank of captain in 1995. "A captain is basically in charge of four or five men at a fire scene or any emergency scene," he explained. "It's added responsibility for decision making. I guess the major consideration especially at fire scenes is, 'What is the safety of the men you're in charge of?' You want to make sure you're making the right decision ... and a lot of the time it's under stress."

Jack has also been president of the Kitchener Professional Firefighters' Association since 1991. His job is to preside over the collective agreement and the constitution. "If somebody gets their ass in a sling, you represent them and make sure that they're treated fairly," he remarked.

On the leisure front, Jack is an avid fisherman who also enjoys hunting and golfing. He and Wendy have raised a son and a daughter and recently became grandparents. They presently make their home in Waterloo, Ontario.

Ehman, Gerry: *Played right wing for Boston, Detroit, Toronto, Oakland and California between 1957 & 1971. Born: Cudworth, Saskatchewan, 1932.*

Gerry Ehman is best remembered as the minor-league journeyman who became a star for Punch Imlach's Toronto Maple Leafs during the playoffs of 1959. On a line with Billy Harris and Frank Mahovlich, Gerry surpassed himself by scoring six goals and seven assists in twelve games. Reality eventually set in, however, as he returned to the minors before having the good fortune to rejoin the Leafs in time for their Stanley Cup victory of 1964.

Gerry remained a part of Toronto's farm system until being traded to the Oakland Seals in 1967. It was with the Seals that his experience paid dividends for a team that needed all the collateral it could get. He tallied 155 points in four seasons before retiring to become a scout.

From the vantage point of today, there are few seasoned observers of the game who have sifted through the upside and the dark side of the hockey business like Gerry Ehman. He has earned his right to an opinion.

"If there's one thing that we should have changed, it was the idea of drafting players so young," he asserted with conviction. "Since we've had the underaged draft, there have been many, many players that were rushed in too soon and couldn't handle it. Then they fell by the wayside. Certainly nobody can say that those guys were all bad players. I think that there's just too much pressure, too much strain on them at an early age. But when you sign a player who's still playing junior and you reward him with today's

money, how can you then turn around and say, 'Sorry Mac, you've got to go to the minors yet'?"

But regardless of the money, Gerry remains a strong advocate for ensuring that such young prospects are sufficiently ripe before being ushered into the majors. To support his point, he cited numerous examples of NHL players in their mid-twenties who've done their time in the minors and are now coming into their own on physical, psychological and emotional levels.

When he retired from the California Golden Seals back in 1971, Gerry had an interest in coaching but opted for scouting first as a way to evaluate life among the ranks of management. He spent his first three years with Al Arbour in St. Louis and then moved over to the Islanders from 1975 onwards.

Gerry never made the transition into coaching. He observed that big money had tainted the attitude of the league and many of its players. Being grounded in the original-six values of team loyalty and a few dollars earned for a hard day's work, he felt more comfortable dealing with today's players from the stands rather than from behind the bench. And besides, he likes scouting.

"The job itself has always been interesting," he stressed. "Every day is a different adventure. And even though there are a lot of people in the same building, it isn't like you swap gossip stories about players. You try to do your own work with your organization. You get together, evaluate and hope that things turn out."

After serving as the Islanders' director of scouting for sixteen years, Gerry has spent the last few seasons as their pro scout. His future, unlike his past, remains unclear however. "I'll play it year by year now," he asserted. "I feel I'm contributing and it's interesting work. But it doesn't mean you can't branch into something else or a different phase of the game."

Gerry loves to spend holidays at his cottage on a Saskatchewan lake where he fishes, golfs, relaxes and, above all, avoids travelling.

He and his wife, Loraine, have raised three sons and a daughter and currently make their home in Saskatoon.

Nicknames: *Tex; Dad*

"I've been called 'Tex' for a long, long time," Gerry recalled. "Mainly because I was from Western Canada.

"And when I was in Oakland in my last years, they called me 'Dad' because I was going on thirty-eight years old and still playing. I think it

was either Earl Ingarfield or Bill Hicke who hung that one on me."

Nickname Challenge #7

Rico

"Roger Crozier gave me the nickname. I said, 'Why are you calling me Rico?' And he says, 'You remind me of a Puerto Rican playboy.' So I just laughed! There was no way that I looked Puerto Rican! I guess I was wearing a pair of fancy shoes or something. So from that point on, I was 'Rico'."

Who is he?

Clues

a. He played left wing for Buffalo and Los Angeles from 1971-1982.

b. He was a first-team all-star in 1974 & 1975.

If your shot was deflected wide, see page 285.

Engblom, Brian: *Played defense for Montreal, Washington, Los Angeles, Buffalo and Calgary from 1977-1987. Born: Winnipeg, Manitoba, 1955.*

"Live television is really quite amazing," Brian Engblom affirmed of his experience as a colour analyst for ESPN. "It's much more involved than you think. You have to learn the X's and O's of the business: how to get on and off the air. You have to get used to the producers talking into your ear, saying things like, 'Okay, in five seconds you're going to see a graphic and this is what it's about.' Meanwhile I'm still supposed to keep talking. It's very unnerving! I think that mothers would be really good at this because they're on the telephone and the kid's going, 'Mom, mom!' And she says, 'No, you can't have that!' She's having two conversations at once! It's the same kind of thing in broadcasting. Next time you watch somebody hosting a show and it looks like they're losing their train of thought, I'll bet you a thousand dollars that the producer has just jumped in his ear and is telling him something else. It throws you right off track."

Brian first started his career in hockey as an eighteen-year-old student at the University of Wisconsin back in 1973. Two years later he was drafted by the Montreal Canadiens and assigned to the Nova Scotia Voyageurs where he won the Eddie Shore Award as the top defenseman in the American Hockey League.

In 1977, he was promoted to Montreal where, as a rearguard, he was rarely flashy but always consistent. At 6'2" and 190 pounds, he was the little guy amongst massive Canadien blueliners like Serge Savard, Rod Langway, Larry Robinson and Guy Lapointe. He stuck to the basics in his own zone and was rewarded with two Stanley Cups within his first two seasons.

By the early eighties, however, Brian's career swerved headlong into the trade winds as he served four different teams in as many years.

While with Calgary in 1987, he underwent surgery to remove bone spurs in his neck—an injury which ultimately forced him out of the game. On the threshold of a major change, he then retreated to his home in Los Angeles to relax, heal and contemplate his next move.

A recurrent theme that remained in the wings, persistently washing over his mind since youth, lead Brian to conclude that his ensuing course needed to be outside the world of hockey. "I'd been involved with the game my entire life," he reported. "You come across so many people that say, 'Pro sports is not real life—you can't do that forever!' So when I retired, I was ready to step away from the game."

For the next three years he tried his hand as a salesman, first for an import company and then for Merrill Lynch in Los Angeles. One of the principal assets he gained through his excursion into "real life" was a renewed appreciation for the hockey world from which he had come.

"There are so many people out there who don't know how to work together," he affirmed. "I learned that stuff when I was nine. For these people, it's a whole new concept. So I thought, 'If this is what it's like in the business world, I tell you, there's nothing wrong with hockey players or sports people in general.' That's why I got back into hockey with renewed enthusiasm."

When a position as a radio colour analyst for the Los Angeles Kings was offered, Brian was poised to reenter an old world in a new way.

After several years of radio, he branched out, picking up additional work on television with ESPN. "I happened to be in the right place at the right time!" he exclaimed. "The radio thing worked and the ESPN thing just fell out of the sky!"

Brian left the Kings to work full-time with ESPN in 1995. "I do sideline reporting on ESPN-1 games, their main network and I do colour commentary on ESPN-2 games, their other network," he explained. His schedule has him working in any NHL city on the continent.

Erickson, Aut: *Played defense for Boston, Chicago, Toronto and Oakland between 1959 & 1970. Born: Lethbridge, Alberta, 1938.*

"When you work for the airline I work for," Aut Erickson attested of his association with America West Airlines, "I can commute for free! So it's easier to live here in Palm Springs and fly into Los Angeles every day than to fight that L.A. traffic!"

Aut had a short-lived brush with boredom while living life as a retiree in Phoenix, Arizona in 1992. Through his son, he got an offer to work for America West Airlines. Later, he transferred to L.A. where he presently works as a cargo manager at the Los Angeles International Airport.

He's been reticent, however, to redecorate his office or plan for a gold watch. "I'm probably going to retire again within the next two years tops and get back to having some fun again," he affirmed.

Aut's NHL career got underway back in 1959 with the Boston Bruins. During the decade that followed, he bounced around between the majors and the minors making stops in Chicago, Toronto, where he won a Cup in 1967, and Oakland. When he left the Seals in 1970, he went to play two seasons with the Phoenix Roadrunners of the Western Hockey League. He stayed on for another two years as a coach before making his return to the NHL.

"I went with the New York Islanders for two seasons as the assistant general manager," Aut recalled. "Earl Ingarfield and I coached part of the first year when Phil Goyette was replaced. Earl was the coach and I was the assistant—but they never really did give us titles. We both just coached."

In 1974, Aut left pro hockey for good, returning to his home in Phoenix in order to run his real-estate business. After a couple of years of pitching properties, he went into retirement for fifteen years. "I did some consulting and built some houses," he added, "but basically I was retired." That is until his brush with boredom got him into the airline business.

For leisure, Aut enjoys golfing and spending

time up north. "Earl Ingarfield and I spend summers together in Whitefish, Montana," he noted. "That's just below the Alberta-Montana border. It's a mountainous community just beside Glacier National Park. We've been going there since we were kids."

Aut and his wife had four children of their own although they actually raised six kids in total. "My wife's parents were killed very early in life," he recalled. "I raised their two daughters as well. So there were actually two boys and four girls." He and his wife are presently enjoying their thirteen grandchildren and life in the California desert.

Fairbairn, Bill: *Played right wing for the New York Rangers, Minnesota and St. Louis from 1968-1979. Born: Brandon, Manitoba, 1947.*

Bill Fairbairn was a tenacious, two-way player who made a steady habit of giving opponents a one-way ride straight into the boards. As a junior, he was known as "Bulldog"—a name that followed him to the NHL. In New York, he joined forces with Dave Balon and Steve Vickers to form the "Bulldog Line"—a trio of relentless checkers. "I used the boards a lot, grinding it up and down one side," he explained. "I stayed on my wing and used the boards as a sort of cushion you might say. It was a pretty hard cushion, but a cushion nonetheless."

Whenever Bill stepped out onto his right-wing lane, he knew what to expect and how to respond. By the time he took his final strides for the St. Louis Blues in 1979, however, his prospects in the outside world did not look nearly as predictable. He promptly retreated to his hometown of Brandon, Manitoba to chart a new path.

"I didn't know where to start," he recounted. "So I took a course and got into real estate. But I didn't like it, so I quit after two years."

From the outside in, Bill thought the sporting-goods business looked like a better bet, so he hooked up with a local store for the next three years while he learned the trade. He then struck out on his own, setting up The Hockey Hut, a sporting-goods store specializing in hockey equipment. "The economy was tough," he admitted. "There was plenty of competition, so I had to close down after a year and a half." He retained ownership of the building, though, and continues to lease the premises to a local business.

With an income on the side, Bill in now free to pursue his newest career objective: to land a job as a hockey scout. But the trail has run cold since his departure from the NHL. A scan of the league's personnel rosters quickly confirms that few people from his era still occupy positions of authority. Nevertheless, he continues to strive for his goal with the same spirit as the "Bulldogs" of his day.

And as the NHL's brain trust has changed, so too has its on-ice merchandise. "It's more an offensive than defensive game now," he stated. "Back when I played, a big year would be thirty goals and now it's ... up to fifty. I think that has a lot to do with the money. You get paid for scoring goals. Back then, you got paid for scoring goals but you got paid for defensive play too. There was no big separation like there is in today's pay scale.

"I don't think they look too much at plus-minus anymore. If you score sixty goals and are minus forty, I still think you're going to get paid for sixty. But in my way of thinking, you're not really doing the job. Because if you score sixty and you're on for forty [against], that's only twenty."

Bill also talked about changes in positional play: "When I played, I was a right winger and was expected to stay on the right side going up and down, up and down. You did your job just like the left wingers while the centres roamed. When more Europeans came into the league, it became a more European game with criss-crossing and pick plays. That was just coming in when I left. Thank goodness, because I didn't understand a lot of it then (laughs). That could account for a lot of the goals that are being scored too because there are a lot of defensive mistakes made when they're [criss-crossing]."

Bill stays active these days playing oldtimers' hockey, snowshoeing and cross-country skiing. He plans to make the odd trip over to Ontario to join in with the New York Rangers' alumni in some of their charity outings on the ice and the golf course.

He and his wife, Lloydene, have two daughters and a son and continue to make their home in Brandon, Manitoba.

⸺⟨⟩⸺

Favell, Doug: *Played goal for Philadelphia, Toronto and Colorado from 1967-1979. Born: St. Catharines, Ontario, 1945.*

Doug Favell did not possess the raw talent and skill of his former goaltending partner, Bernie Parent; but according to his ex-coach, Vic Stasiuk, Doug was steeped to his elbows in character, an essential ingredient that sustained him through almost 400 career NHL games.

Since retiring from the Colorado Rockies in 1979, he has continued to keep one foot in hockey while holding the other on a gas pedal.

Doug accepted an offer from head coach

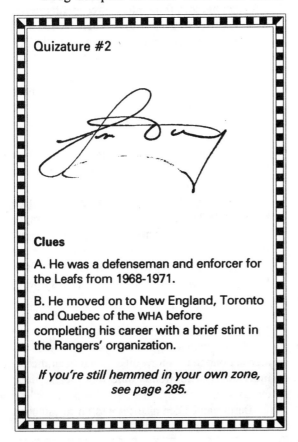

Quizature #2

Clues

A. He was a defenseman and enforcer for the Leafs from 1968-1971.

B. He moved on to New England, Toronto and Quebec of the WHA before completing his career with a brief stint in the Rangers' organization.

If you're still hemmed in your own zone, see page 285.

Marshall Johnston to work as an assistant at Denver University for the 1980-81 season. He then experienced the world of broadcasting as a radio and television colour analyst for the Colorado Flames of the Central Hockey League until 1983.

He also began to devote more time to his other passion—the automobile. "I maintained a summer home in St. Catharines where my neighbour owned Performance Car Company," Doug recounted. "He was doing a lot of importing and exporting. I always kind of wheeled and dealed with cars myself: I had exotic cars, Corvettes and so on. So he showed me how to get into the business. It was a natural. I bought a couple of cars in Edmonton and wheeled them down to Denver—so I learned as I went along."

He continued to develop his auto wholesale and importing business in Denver until 1985, at which point, he converted the business into a family operation and moved it to St. Catharines under the name "International Gallery of Cars".

These days Doug officially resides in Buffalo as an American citizen but commutes over to St. Catharines regularly to participate in the operation of the family enterprise. His responsibilities involve travelling to auctions to acquire virtually any kind of car—except for the more exotic, antique types. "You have to really know what you're doing with those cars or you'll get burned," he warned. He often bids on batches of used cars sold off by auto leasers and then resells them.

In response to his penchant for sports, Doug became an assistant coach at Brock University in St. Catharines while also managing and coaching a junior-B club called the Thorold Blackhawks. He held both posts until he became a goaltending coach for the Buffalo Sabres between 1987 and 1991.

Doug's current excursions into hockey involve three local oldtimers' leagues. He no longer plays goal, opting instead to pursue the glory of playing a forward position. "I don't like working out with weights and that stuff," he explained. "By playing hockey, I keep in shape, have fun and enjoy the comradery."

Bernie Federko
President & General Manager
Saint Louis Vipers Professional In-line Hockey Club
Member, Roller Hockey International

1819 Clarkson Road, Suite 301, Chesterfield, MO 63017

FAX (314) 530-7777

Federko, Bernie: *Played centre for St. Louis and Detroit from 1976-1990. Born: Foam Lake, Saskatchewan, 1956.*

Bernie Federko never won a major award during his fourteen seasons in the NHL—there simply weren't enough trophies to go around. By the time Wayne Gretzky and Mario Lemieux had put their padlocks on the hardware, all a tier-two superstar like Bernie could do was pat himself on the back. But behind the fanfare, he quietly went about his trade, exercising one of the more fertile of the playmakers' minds. During his 1,091 career games, he feathered passes to the tune of 827 assists and 1,231 total points.

Bernie is now thoroughly retired from professional hockey—but he still approaches his life like a centreman cruising in the slot, ready to score. "You have to find an opportunity," he asserted. "And when you get that opportunity, you've got to make something happen for yourself."

Since leaving the Detroit Red Wings in 1990, Bernie has not been wanting for scoring chances. He has his hand in four different businesses; he has done colour analysis for hockey games in the NHL and the IHL; he serves on occasion as a marketing consultant; and he is raising a family.

That is not to say that there wasn't an adjustment period when he left professional hockey. "If you could, you'd play hockey forever if it wasn't for wear and tear," he noted. "But the deal is, when you're done, you're done. There is life after hockey—but it's a big transition because you're used to being catered to... I played fourteen years and that's all I did. That was my career.

And when you're playing, you're always thinking, 'What am I going to do when I'm finished?' But you always put it off. You say, 'Ah something will come up,' and then it gets closer and closer to the end. Really, I don't think you're ever prepared... Then it becomes a completely different ball game because now you're out there in the real world."

Bernie had the good fortune to have made enough money during his playing career that he was not under pressure to make big money in a short period of time. He also had established some fruitful connections within the St. Louis community where he returned in 1990.

"When I announced my retirement, I got a call from one of the TV stations, KMLV channel four, which is a CBS affiliate," he recalled. "They asked me to join their sports department as a hockey analyst for all the Blues' home games for the '90-91 and the '91-92 seasons."

Bernie thoroughly enjoyed his new job although his shift from interviewee to interviewer took some getting used to. "When I was being interviewed all the time, it was very candid," he admitted. "I could just go with the flow. [Then] all of a sudden, I was the one in charge of asking the questions and analyzing the situation. I think I became a little more nervous ... especially when I was standing there looking at the camera. I became more aware that this was my job."

After two seasons behind the camera, Bernie left KMLV when the station downsized their hockey coverage.

In the meantime, he hooked up with close friend Dale Turvey, a specialist in the insurance industry. "He just wanted me to get involved," Bernie recalled. "So I went out and got an insurance license. I spend a lot of time with Dale. We travel around meeting people—he's showing me the ropes."

Bernie went to work for Dale's business, National Association Consultants. Their service involves providing benefits for various associations that in turn offer group insurance to individuals who would otherwise be on their own.

Bernie and Dale also teamed up to establish

Turvey & Federko Benefit Group which specializes in marketing a trust fund used to pay for Workers' Compensation on behalf of retailers across the state of Missouri.

As a sideline, Bernie went into partnership with his brothers by purchasing the Canadian manufacturing and distribution rights for a type of plastic flooring used for roller hockey surfaces. They operate under the name "Sports Court of Canada". Although Bernie maintains a small outlet in St. Louis, the Canadian market remains their central focus. "It's actually booming right now," he confided. "My brother, Kenny, is setting up a distribution network across Canada. So we're pretty excited about that."

At the same time, Bernie keeps his hand in the local hockey scene. In 1993, he and some partners established the St. Louis Vipers roller-hockey team. Bernie served as coach and general manager for their first two seasons and is now the club's president. His primary focus is marketing, fundraising and player recruitment.

For leisure, Bernie swings into action with a charity golf tournament held every Monday in the St. Louis area. Any other time he has is devoted to his wife, Bernadette, and the raising of their three children. His sons play hockey, so Bernie usually spends every other weekend on the road, attending various tournaments.

Ferguson, George: *Played centre for Toronto, Pittsburgh and Minnesota from 1972-1984. Born: Trenton, Ontario, 1952.*

For George Ferguson, the contemplation of his twelve seasons in the majors is a source of satisfaction equivalent to a warm bath that never cools. His longevity was sustained by his willingness to recognize his own limits. He was not overly gifted offensively, but he knew his way around both ends of the rink, and that made him the dependable sort who could put colour back into a coach's grey hair.

As he was practical on ice, George was also practical in his view of life after hockey. "I think a lot of the players who had a hard time were the ones that played prior to the seventies," he observed. "They lived year to year for hockey and I can understand that—it took so much of their time. That's what they had from childhood to look forward to. I guess they pretty much thought that it was going to be their lives."

George, on the other hand, was the product of a generation with a stronger vision for the future. "When I retired in '84, I already knew I had something else to go to or I probably wouldn't have retired," he admitted. "I could have gone to the minors for a bit and been called back and maybe squeezed in two or three more years. But I already knew what I was going to do, so the transition wasn't hard."

George had had a line on a sales position with Scole Engineering Company, a manufacturer of medical equipment. Any apprehensions he might have had about leaving the NHL were summarily dispelled by the well-planned blueprint that lined his pocket. Before his skate blades were dry, he was on his way to Culver City, California for a year's training on product lines and sales techniques.

He then resettled in Pittsburgh to assume his post as a regional sales manager, overseeing the company's operations in the Eastern United States. "It's very, very different obviously from playing hockey," he remarked. "Now it's a Monday to Friday job, it's not quite as exciting I'd say. I think one of the things you miss in hockey is the comradery and the travel—not that it's glitzy or glamorous like most people think. It's different. You're around a bunch of guys all the time. You have your high points and low points and there were many that you'd go through in a year."

In addition to his day job, George has been active as president of the Pittsburgh Penguins' alumni association for the past seven years. Their work embraces the cause of supporting various hospitals and minor-league hockey programmes in the Pittsburgh area.

He and his wife, Candace Ann, are raising a son who is presently the beneficiary of his father's coaching on a local mite-level hockey team.

George has also maintained an annual golf

tournament in his hometown of Trenton, Ontario since 1991. "We help to raise money for a cancer camp in Willington, Ontario," he explained with pride. "All of the money raised goes right to the camp. It's also fun to see the players and people you often don't get to see."

Nickname: *Chief*

"In Toronto a lot of times I was called 'Chief', mostly because I had George Armstrong's old #10," he reported.

Flaman, Fernie: *Played defense for Boston and Toronto from 1944-1961. Born: Dysart, Saskatchewan, 1927.*

Fernie Flaman did not sport the menacing facial features that characterized some of the NHL's tougher customers. He was, however, usually at the head of the check-out line when it came to abrasive, hard-nosed, bone-crunching play. He was a deadly combination of David *and* Goliath. He could beat his opponents with his heady play and smooth skating—or, if his simmering ire reached the boiling point, he could just plain beat the daylights out of most challengers. Either way, it was all part of Fernie Flaman's game.

The story began for eight-year-old Ferdinand on the outdoor rinks of his native Regina, Saskatchewan. His skill progressed in tandem with an imagination that became untethered by the radio tidings of Foster Hewitt. Organized hockey soon followed and brought with it an omen of things to come. "In Regina," he explained, "we had four pee-wee teams: the Maple Leafs, the Canadiens, the Americans and the Rangers. And a funny thing happened—I think it was fate really. Since we played ahead of the senior games, we got our roster listed in the programme. Next to every name, in brackets, was the name of the guy you corresponded with in the National Hockey League. Like I was #12 and in brackets, my name was 'Babe Pratt'. And as it happened, years later, I was in Hershey in 1946 when the Bruins called me up to replace the real Babe Pratt who was at the end of his career. Isn't that something? That actually happened!"

Fernie first sampled NHL ice for a brief stint near the end of World War II. He had been skating for the Boston Olympics when a call came through to join the Bruins who were short on personnel. "We were in New York and I was playing wing at the time," he recounted. "This was my first NHL game ever. The coach, Dit Clapper, leaned forward and said, 'Whatever you do son, don't cut into the middle!' and I says, 'Why not?' He said, 'There's a guy out there named Bucko McDonald and he loves you guys.' So not thinking about anything, I caught a pass, cut in the middle and then all I saw were blinking lights. Bucko laid me flat out! So that was my introduction to the big leagues."

Fernie eventually came to his senses and by 1946 became a Bruin regular until being traded to the Toronto Maple Leafs during the early fifties. When he rejoined the Bruins in 1954, his leadership skills began to emerge. At the start of the following season, he was awarded the captain's *C*, a responsibility he embraced until his final game in 1961.

Although he then relinquished his title to Don McKenney, the assumption of leadership remained central to Fernie's career in hockey, which after fifty-three seasons, has yet to end.

After Boston, he was dispatched to Providence of the American Hockey League as a player-coach for two years and then as the team's coach-manager for an additional two seasons.

A year prior to the NHL's first major expansion, Fernie joined the Los Angeles Blades of the Western Hockey League as their coach and manager. "We were trying to get the NHL franchise for L.A.," he recounted. "I was with the Tony Owen group. Tony was the husband of actress Donna Reed."

Fernie's group lost out on their bid for the Los Angeles franchise, so he moved on to Fort Worth of the Central Hockey League where he spent two seasons coaching the Detroit Red Wings' affiliate.

During the 1968-69 season, he served as a pro scout for the Boston Bruins before settling in as head coach of Northeastern University's hockey team—a division-one, NCAA school. "It was a little difficult at the beginning because the team I'd inherited didn't have very many division-one players," he explained. "I was alone so I didn't get out to see the kids except during Christmas break. Then finally, Don McKenney came in as my assistant to handle recruiting. From then on, we did pretty well."

Fernie ran the show for twenty years before acceding to life in a soft chair amongst the sports pages. He'd hardly settled in, however, when New Jersey Devils' owner Lou Lamoriello rustled him up and signed him on as a special-assignment scout. "I go down to Albany to work with the River Rats of the American Hockey League," he reported. "I'll spend say five days skating and talking with the players and going on bus rides to get their confidence up and to let them know what's ahead. You know these kids hear the coach talking every day of the week—and after a while, they don't always listen. So when you get someone new coming in, who's been through all the wars, it can really help."

Fleming, Reggie: *Played left wing for Montreal, Chicago, Boston, the New York Rangers, Philadelphia, Buffalo (NHL) and Chicago (WHA) between 1959 & 1974. Born: Montreal, Quebec, 1936.*

Reggie Fleming was a colourful, combustible enforcer whose job was to uphold the unwritten rules of player etiquette. Opponents who behaved and misbehaved alike, were kept in line by means of fisticuffs, elbows and intimidating play. He wasn't a particularly big man, but he used his large reservoir of fearlessness and guile to raise himself up to the level of his larger adversaries. And through all the battles, even in retirement, he never lost his sense of humour.

"I tell people I joined the PGA," he quipped. "You know what that stands for? 'The Professional Guests Association'!" He was referring to the frequent invitations he now receives to attend golf tournaments and various charitable functions in the Chicago area. The fans still remember the old guy and he willingly lends

his name and presence to support their local causes.

Even while employed by the Rangers, Bruins and Flyers over the years, Reggie always returned to Chicago during the off-season to work for various companies. "When I retired, I found a business of my own," he recalled. "It's what we call the ad-specialty business. We'll go to companies and sell them promotional items like pens, key chains and t-shirts. It's something like Alex Delvecchio's doing only I'm not as big as he is."

Reggie works out of his home under the name "RF Industries". Through his extensive collection of catalogues, he can obtain virtually any item suitable for promotional purposes. Once the items are acquired, he arranges to have them embellished with logos, slogans and company names. "Whatever the customer is looking for I can provide," he asserted. "I sell calendars, coffee mugs, golf balls, golf shirts, belt buckles and coasters."

In addition to his membership with the "PGA", Reggie spends his spare time enjoying horses. "My daughter's an equestrian rider so I go out and watch her," he proudly noted. "I follow horse racing too. Living close to the race track, I've made some friends out there. During the summer, I go to the track in the morning to watch some of the trainers training their horses and listen to some good stories."

And as he combs over the varied roles of his past, Reggie's voice betrays its warmest modulation for his experience of fatherhood. Along the way, he has raised a son who became a graphic artist and a daughter who is a chartered accountant. "I'm pretty proud of both of them," he confided. "You know, it's not bad for a run-down hockey player. I have two kids who went to college and graduated—and like me, they're both single and smart!"

Fogolin Sr., Lidio (Lee): *Played defense for Detroit and Chicago from 1948-1956. Born: Fort William, Ontario, 1926.*

"For every day you're happy and on top of the world," Lee Fogolin observed of life in the NHL, "there are days when you cry." The tone of his voice and the words he chose were like the blending of a war correspondent and a poet as he described the battles and the people that had crossed the stage of his career on ice.

In his day, Lee was a rock-solid rearguard who toiled for Chicago and Detroit for eight original-six seasons. When he retired in 1956, he went west to join the Calgary Stampeders, a farm team of the Chicago Blackhawks. "I was a player-coach, which as far as I'm concerned never works out," he noted. "How can you correct a guy for making a mistake when possibly two shifts from now, you're going to make the same mistake yourself? You can't tell them in one breath how lousy they are and they're not worth what they're getting; then, in another few minutes, tell them how good they are and that they should knock the heck out of the opposition."

Lee completed his first season with the Stampeders and returned home to Port Arthur, Ontario with a suitcase in one hand and ambivalence in the other. It was then that he took to conversing with his brother-in-law about his future in hockey. "They were talking expansion," Lee recalled. "But I couldn't see it. At the time Rudy Pilous was in Chicago and Frankie Eddolls was in Buffalo. I said, 'God knows when I'll get a chance [at another coaching job]!' So I made up my mind to go into business with my brother-in-law."

"We started with a little corner store. Then we expanded it into a mini-supermarket plus we put up an Esso service station."

He kept his hand in hockey by coaching a local senior-league club called the Port Arthur Bearcats. The team was a hot item in town and he found the heat was good for business.

> *"For every day you're happy and on top of the world, there are days when you cry."*
>
> Lee Fogolin Sr.

Lee fuelled cars and stocked pantries for twenty-three years before leaving his Esso operation to work at his cousin's steel company. But he soon found that the hard edge of the steel business was not to his liking—and that was all the motivation he needed to make a quick lane change.

While perusing the local classified ads, Lee noticed a golf course for sale. It caught his interest and in partnership with his daughter and son-in-law, he purchased the Centennial Golf Course in Thunder Bay. He's still at it today although old hockey injuries to his elbows prevent him from swinging the clubs. He's at the course every day, though, overseeing the operation and enjoying the people.

Forty years now lie between Lee and his time on NHL ice. "Winning the Stanley Cup in 1950 was exciting," he recalled. "But to me, every game was exciting. It was a challenge and I enjoyed every minute. You must remember that when I played there were only six teams and a total of thirty defensemen. So it was quite an achievement to have made it."

Nickname: *Lee*

"When I played junior back in those days, they changed everything, even your name!" Lee exclaimed. "They didn't like Lidio, so they said, 'We'll call you Lee.' And I said, 'Fine! Who cares'!"

Fonteyne, Val: *Played left wing for Detroit, the New York Rangers, Pittsburgh (NHL), Alberta and Edmonton (WHA) from 1959-1974. Born: Wetaskiwin, Alberta, 1933.*

Val Fonteyne was a small, fleet-footed winger who specialized in penalty killing and defensive play. He exercised his role with efficiency and consistency—and all with little fanfare. He was a quiet man who went about his business for nineteen professional seasons before receding into a modest career with the Wetaskiwin post office.

His life in the NHL, by contrast, had been subject to the capricious gales of training camps, trades and travel. As a kind of sandbag of stability, Val and his family had always remained anchored in his hometown of Wetaskiwin, Alberta. His eventual jump to Edmonton of the WHA finally brought him home for a taste of working in his own backyard.

The flavour was sweet, so in 1975, he jumped at an opportunity to drive a delivery truck for the local post office, a position he maintained until his retirement in 1994. "It was just an ordinary job, but it was fine by me," he admitted, speaking of his second profession. "I guess I could have tried something else—I had a couple of chances at scouting but I decided to stay put. My family was growing up at the time and working for the post office was stable and provided a reasonable living.

"I didn't know what to expect but it worked out fine," he continued. "It's a small place and I knew quite a few of the guys that worked at the post office as a result of living here."

At present, Val enjoys spending his time ice fishing during the winter and gardening during the summer. "A friend of mine has a farm just a couple of miles out," he related. "I go out there and put in a bunch of stuff and then I end up giving it away to people. You could go down to the farmers' market and stock up for a heck of a lot cheaper but I enjoy doing it."

Val and his wife, Anna, have raised two boys and two girls and are currently very taken with their two grandchildren. "I don't know that we'll want to be away too long," he stated. "It's nice to hang around the two of them."

Nickname: *Val*

"My full name is Valere," he pointed out. "I think it's a Belgian name and people could never pronounce it the right way. They'd call me Valerie or whatever. So I preferred Val."

Nickname Challenge #8

Meatball

"When I played in Chicago, one of my favourite meals was spaghetti and meatballs. This one night, I remember there were three or four of us out for dinner, including Burt Olmstead and Bep Guidolin. I guess I must have eaten quite a few meatballs because Bep said, 'You're going to eat so damn many of them, you're going to look like a meatball!' So that's where the name started."

Who is he?

Clues

a. He played centre for Chicago and Detroit from 1947-1958.

b. He scored 356 career points and won two Stanley Cups with the Detroit Red Wings.

c. His initials are M.P.

If you were called for highsticking, see page 285.

"If I had inherited a farm, that wouldn't be as much pleasure as me working my ass off, getting things paid for and feeling good." — Lou Fontinato

Fontinato, Lou: *Played defense for the New York Rangers and Montreal from 1954-1963. Born: Guelph, Ontario, 1932.*

"Farming!" Lou Fontinato said with authority, "It's my livelihood, my everything and it doesn't bother me a bit. I'm not one for vacations, I've got everything here. A nice home, land, cattle..."

Lou developed his love for rural life during his early days in Guelph, Ontario. "Our house was right in the city," he said. "But we had six acres just outside of town. My dad did some dust-bowl gardening. He kept a horse to do a bit of work and to deliver the vegetables to the market and around the street. We kept a cow because we needed milk for the six children in my family. So you get the smell of farming in you."

Lou's other passion was hockey. While the fields were at rest, he was at play, cutting a swath of ice off any eligible pond or rink. He progressed through the ranks to the Guelph

Biltmore Madhatters and on to the NHL where his hard checks, lightning fists and chicanery quickly made him the league's premier badman. He played with a lion's heart and Manhattan fans adored him. He lasted seven illustrious seasons with the Rangers before being traded to Montreal where a serious injury ended his career in 1963. "You had to play a bit of hockey to afford the farm," he said. "If I'd played today, I'd own all of Alberta! But I hold no regrets about money. I mean making the National League and making a little money to buy a farm. That's enough isn't it? No matter how low we were paid, it was a start. If you weren't playing hockey, what the hell would you be doing? Maybe working at International Malleable Iron? My dad raised six children working there. Coming from Italy, they'd split an egg in four in order to eat. So him coming to Canada, getting a job and raising a good family was certainly an accomplishment and he did it through hard work—same as myself. If I had inherited a farm, that wouldn't be as much pleasure as me working my ass off, getting things paid for and feeling good."

Lou bought his first spread outside of Guelph in 1959. Whenever the last puck was going to drop, he had his tractor idling and ready to roll. A headlong crash into the boards, however, almost put a nix to his plans. He lay on the ice, his neck broken and his future immobilized. He implored his doctors to patch him up well enough to lift a bail of hay. They got the job done and Lou has been out on the pastures ever since.

In fact, it's a rare day when Lou Fontinato doesn't rise with the sun. "I had the flu once over the last thirty years and missed my feeding rounds," he said. "That's it! Otherwise, I feed the cattle every day. My vacation is going west to buy cattle. I've done that about ten times over the years."

Lou takes pride and satisfaction in all he has built. His foothold in life is one step higher than his father reached. Each generation builds on the one before. "You only hope the third and fourth generations don't piss it all away," Lou exclaimed with a gusher of laughs. "I'm not bragging or complaining but you wouldn't have what I've got sitting in a goddamn rocking chair. Sure it took a lot of hard work and dedication. That's where hockey comes in handy. It teaches you discipline. With six teams, if you didn't cut your hair as short as they wanted, they'd get someone else... You had to do what you were told and with lots of hustle (laughs)."

Foster, Dwight: *Played centre for Boston, Colorado, New Jersey and Detroit from 1977-1987. Born: Toronto, Ontario, 1957.*

Dwight Foster's primary on-ice attributes were his great physical strength, leadership skills and ability to influence events at both ends of the rink. During his final season of junior hockey with the Kitchener Rangers, he piled up 143 points in sixty-four games to lead the Ontario Hockey Association in scoring. He moved on to the Boston Bruins in 1977 where he missed most of his rookie campaign with a damaged left knee. It was not until 1980-81 that he managed to skate through an injury-free season, racking up a personal-best twenty-four goals and twenty-eight assists. Over the six seasons that followed, he played for Colorado, New Jersey, Detroit and then returned to Boston to close out his career in 1987.

"I miss it extremely," Dwight revealed of his departure from the NHL. "The competitiveness is the big thing. I'm a physical person—I guess that's why I get into my work so aggressively. I think maybe it fills some of that void. It's quite a change. And if you don't have something to throw yourself at, the same way you did with your sport, problems usually crop up because you don't have anything to focus your attention on."

"Of course a lot of sports players have large egos," he admitted. "It comes with the territory. I think that that can also create some problems when you get out of the game, if you're not prepared. I mean it is quite a transition period

Foster, Glotzhober & Associates

Dwight A. Foster
President

24100 Southfield Road, Suite 310
Southfield, Michigan 48075
fax (810) 552-1360

when you're thirty, thirty-five and you're winding down out of something. Other people at that point in their careers are just getting going because they can do their line of work to an older age."

The transition may have been challenging, but Dwight did not find himself lacking for ventures onto which he could unleash his energies. Before entering pro hockey, he had already probed the anatomy of the business world while working with his father's automotive business in Kitchener, Ontario.

Later, as a Detroit Red Wing, he engaged his knowledge of mufflers and ledgers to set up his own insurance-investment company. Today, he operates the insurance arm of his business under the name of "Consolidated Benefit Plans, Incorporated" and his investment management company as "Foster, Glotzhober and Associates". "Right now my business includes both corporate and individual investments," he explained. "We do corporate benefits, high-net-worth individuals and pension plans."

As a respected consultant, Dwight also uses his connections to raise venture capital on behalf of a number

Dwight Foster

of public companies. Furthermore, in conjunction with some partners, he owns Fawne Development Corporation, which is mainly focused on the development of thousands of acres of land near Daytona, Florida. The project includes the construction of hotels, malls, amphitheatres and an entertainment complex.

A master of time management, Dwight still manages to nurture a fulfilling home life. He and his wife, Mary Anne, are raising three boys and a girl at their home in Detroit. Two of their sons play travel hockey which keeps Dad on the road from St. Louis to Sault Ste. Marie.

In the recent past, he has also served as president of the Detroit Red Wings' alumni association. The position has often drawn him out onto the golf course and ice in support of local charities.

Fox, Greg: *Played defense for Atlanta, Chicago and Pittsburgh from 1977-1985. Born: Port McNeil, British Columbia, 1953.*

Greg Fox entered the NHL after a four-year apprenticeship at the University of Michigan. He joined the Atlanta Flames in 1977 and embarked on an eight-year career as a physical blueliner whose forte was riding shotgun in his own zone. In 1979, he and Tom Lysiak were sent to Chicago where Greg experienced his best years before retiring as a Pittsburgh Penguin in 1985.

Although he'd been six years removed from Atlanta, Greg still had the city in his soul. "The main attraction was my wife," he said with a chuckle. "She's originally from the city and she wanted to settle back there."

"The transition was pretty smooth," he observed of his departure from the game. "There was really never any hardship along the way. I took my real-estate course and hit the ground running. I jumped right in with both feet."

Greg spent the next four years showing homes and closing deals. "It was very helpful as an experience," he remarked. "I learned about what's involved in purchasing homes and properties for personal investments. But with real estate, it just didn't seem like there was a lot of permanence. You never knew from one day or one year to the next, where your next meal would be coming from."

Greg preferred a more reliable, long-term plan and Domino's Pizza was taking orders. "Going with Domino's meant the opportunity to own my own business down the road," he said.

"They train you from the ground up.

"I started as a unit manager in training, learning how to actually run a pizza store. I went on to supervise a group of eight stores. From there I used my real-estate background to get into their real-estate division—opening new stores, closing others and renegotiating leases for the Eastern U.S. Then I got back into operations as a general manager of over seventy-five stores across Georgia."

"...I've put in a lot of long hours making pizzas, delivering them, cleaning the toilets..."

Greg Fox

Greg's ultimate objective, however, was to man his own garrison. "I was always keeping my eyes open for a good franchise opportunity," he explained. Four Domino's stores came available in Cape Cod, Massachusetts, so he bought the whole bundle.

"I love it," he said exuberantly. "There's nobody looking over your shoulder, telling you what to do. You make all the decisions. Running a pizza store is like running a well-oiled team. But it hasn't all been easy. Cape Cod's a real vacation area and we're extremely busy in the summertime. We took the stores over in April of 1996 and just never had enough people throughout the summer to keep them all going. Let me tell you, I've put in a lot of long hours making pizzas, delivering them, cleaning the toilets... You've got to wear all the hats to stay afloat (laughs)."

Cape Cod and pizzas now seem like half a world away from the life he once lead as a hockey player and yet, Greg's perspective remains alive. "I'm very proud that I played in the NHL as long as I did," he declared. "I enjoyed it. It was definitely just a phase in my life and life goes on. You just keep moving ahead. After my last year, I let it go—I didn't dwell on it. I mean, you've still got to put food on the table. So you just go out and hustle. Fortunately, a lot of the things I've chosen have turned out pretty well."

Fox, Jim: *Played right wing for Los Angeles between 1980 & 1990. Born: Coniston, Ontario, 1960.*

In 1979-80, Jim Fox treated the Ottawa 67's to 166 points in only fifty-two games. He lead all scorers in the Ontario Hockey Association that season and was scooped up by the Los Angeles Kings for the start of the following campaign. Standing a stalky 5'8" and 185 pounds, he built his game around quick, heads-up play, raking in 301 career assists over his nine seasons with the Kings. In 1990, he decided to retire and approached the impending change with the same steady strides he used to power himself on ice.

"I think that there's a lot made of athletes' career transitions," he remarked. "At times though, I think it's really less melodramatic than they make it out to be. There is an adjustment no doubt, but ordinary people go through it too. So it's not like athletes are the only ones."

Having been a single-city man during his time in the NHL, Jim was a logical choice to represent the Kings in the community—which he did via the team's community relations department. "I was responsible for arranging appearances for Kings' players and VIPs; creating and operating fundraisers within the community; handling fan mail; making sure that people writing to the Kings got proper information ... really anything to do with the public presentation of the Kings that was not a hockey game," he explained.

Jim attributes much of the large scope and volume of his job to the arrival of "The Great One". "Before Wayne Gretzky was a King there wasn't even a department," he pointed out. "But his arrival obviously created a lot of interest in the team."

In 1991, Jim ventured out from behind his desk to work as a colour analyst for Kings' games broadcast on the Prime Sports Network, a television network serving the Western United States and Hawaii. With no previous experience, he bravely took the producer's cue and a mike in hand. "It was a big adjustment," he admitted. "I think there were a lot of preconceived notions that it would be very simple to go up and describe the game to people. In my case, I was certainly

not a natural. It took awhile to understand the technical aspects of TV and everything else that goes into a broadcast that isn't apparent to the viewer. But each time out I gained more experience and became more comfortable..."

After several years of working in public relations and broadcasting, Jim found that they both required full-time attention. So, heeding the sway of the airwaves, he decided to focus exclusively on his career as a colour analyst. In addition to Kings' games, he now also covers roller hockey for ESPN during the summer.

And to conform to their West-Coast obligations, he and his wife, Susie, spend their leisure time in Southern California style, taking in the sunshine at the beach, golfing and exploring wine country. "We dabble in a little bit of wine tasting," he added. "We've been up to visit the Napa, Sonoma and San Jose wineries."

Gadsby, Bill: *Played defense for Chicago, the New York Rangers and Detroit from 1946-1966. Born: Calgary, Alberta, 1927.*

Hall of Famer Bill Gadsby was a versatile and selfless defenseman who could quarterback the quick rush up ice, direct pinpoint passes and effectively hurl himself into the path of threatening adversaries. He was fearless in his willingness to stand in the barrel of the canon, catch the ball and live with the consequences of stitches, contusions and broken bones. With sufficient gain, he believed, it was worth the

pain.

After twenty rugged years, Bill retired from the Detroit Red Wings at the close of the 1965-66 season. He had had plans to open a golfing range in Edmonton, Alberta until his partner died suddenly and the range had to be sold for estate purposes.

Shortly thereafter, he returned to Detroit for a stint as coach of the Red Wings. Experiencing success early in his second season, he was suddenly dismissed by Wings' owner Bruce Norris without the provision of a meaningful explanation.

With disenchantment in mind and hard feelings in hand, Bill left hockey to do public-relations work for the John Curran Crane Company until 1982.

Anticipating a transition to the metric system in the United States, he then ventured into business for himself, investing in a metric nuts-and-bolts distributorship. The endeavour was short-lived and costly, however, as a result of stiff competition and the fact that the metric system never really caught on.

Still brimming with resiliency, he went on to develop a hockey school in Southfield, Michigan called "Bill Gadsby Hockey Schools, Inc." in 1983. Edna, Bill's wife, explained: "We've had boys' and girls' hockey schools plus adult schools for the last ten, fifteen years. We're down to only two hockey schools now because we're kind of phasing out. Bill will be seventy on the eighth of August and he's been a very busy person since his hockey retirement. We are operating his twelfth-annual, adult hockey school right now and for the first time, we're going to have one in Windsor, [Ontario]."

Bill Gadsby
CHICAGO BLACK HAWKS

But if septuagenarians are supposed to slow down, then Bill is in serious violation. His most recent escapade has him joining his partner, John Gibson, in the establishment of Bill Gadsby's Golf Training Center in Howell, Michigan. The centre got off to an auspicious start when Bill noticed that his playing number with the Wings, #4, was the basis for the address number of the facility, 4444 East Grand River. "I couldn't believe it!" he exclaimed. "That number has come up in my life all the time. I go check in a coat during the wintertime and it's number four or check the car and it's forty-four on the ticket. I had four daughters and then we bought this place with the number 4444. It's amazing how the number has come up in my life. It's a good omen because all of the rest of it has turned out well!"

For recreation, he and Edna have spent a lot of time travelling in recent years. "We visited England and Norway in 1993; cruised the Caribbean East and West three times and spent five weeks in Maui in '93, '94 and '95," he said. "We also visit Florida three to four times each winter where I enjoy golfing and deep-sea fishing. Somebody has to do these things!"

Between trips, Bill finds time to keep tabs on today's NHL. "It's a lot more wide open with too much stick work and crosschecking," he noted. "The talent pool is too thin as well, so I pick and choose the games I'll watch. It makes sense when you figure that there are only thirteen quality goaltenders in a league with twenty-six teams!"

Bill and Edna have raised four daughters over the years and relish watching their seven

grandsons play hockey. They currently make their home in the Detroit suburb of Southfield, Michigan.

Gardner, Cal: *Played centre for the New York Rangers, Toronto, Chicago and Boston from 1945-1957. Born: Transcona, Manitoba, 1924.*

In 1944, the New York Rangers were into their third-straight season at the bottom of the standings. General manager Lester Patrick was on the lookout for young talent that could spirit his team up the ranks. His hopes were kindled by three radiant lads who, as Ranger property, were searing a path through the Eastern Hockey League with atomic force. Church Russell, René Trudel and Cal Gardner became known as the "Atomic Line". They were summoned to raise the Rangers' fortunes midway through the 1944-45 season. As a collective, however, their impact was minimal and only Cal Gardner survived beyond three seasons.

As a smooth-skating, rangy centreman, Cal sustained himself for an additional nine years on the basis of teamsmanship and dependability at both ends of the rink.

He experienced his most successful campaign during his third year with the Toronto Maple Leafs in 1950-51. He finished the regular season tied for tenth spot in league scoring with fifty-one points. During the ensuing playoffs, he was on the ice when Leafs' defenseman Bill Barilko beat Canadiens' goalie Gerry McNeil in overtime of game five to claim the Stanley Cup. It was Cal's second and final chance to hold the grand prize.

After a brief stint with Chicago, he closed out his career with the Boston Bruins in 1957. As a loyal Leaf and faithful Bruin, he then found himself divided between the prospects of staying in Boston or returning to his home base in Toronto.

"I had worked for an American transport company in the off-season called 'Denver, Chicago Trucking'," he reported. "I worked for them out of the Toronto area. Later, I started to do colour [radio] for Bruins' games in Boston—so I was combining both for a couple of years! I flew to Boston and different places for the games. Most of the time I would leave at four o'clock in the afternoon of the workday. I'd get to the destination at about 5:30 and then I'd go from there right to the rink."

Several years of experiencing life as a tale of two cities led Cal to make a full-time transition to Toronto—although not without some regrets. "I say we should have just quit everything here and moved to Boston," he concluded. "My two kids could have gone to Harvard. But they went to St. Mike's here so they made out all right..."

Through his connections with Foster and Bill Hewitt, Cal then threw his voice into the ring as a colour analyst for Leafs' games presented on radio station CKFH in Toronto. He still kept his day job with Denver, Chicago Trucking which involved coordinating the movement of Denver's goods on the Canadian side of the U.S. border.

Eventually, he left the trucking business and became an ad salesman with CKFH. The station's sale in 1981, however, precipitated a change of locale and style as he signed on with CHOO, a country-music station near Oshawa. Retirement from all forms of labour ultimately came in 1984.

These days, Cal breaks out the clubs for about fifteen celebrity golf tournaments across Ontario each summer. He also enjoys watching his grandson, who at 6'5" and 210 pounds, plays hockey for the London Knights of the Ontario Hockey Association.

Cal and his wife, Mary, currently live in the Leaside section of Toronto. They have five grandchildren complements of their two sons, Dave and Paul, who like their father, also played in the NHL.

Nicknames: *Ginger; Torchy; Pearly*

"When I first came to the Rangers in '45, they called me 'Ginger' because of my red hair," Cal recalled.

"In Toronto, Danny Lewicki called me 'Torchy' because it looked as though my red hair

was lit up like a torch.

"In Boston they had the 'Gallery Gods'. They were a bunch of people up in the centre-ice area on the one side in the Gardens. They got ahold of my middle name, Pearly, which came from my mother, Pearl. If I scored a goal or an assist, they'd always say, 'Way to go Pearly!' I'd have liked to have hidden under the bench. I didn't like it."

Gavin, Stewart: *Played left & right wing for Toronto, Hartford and Minnesota from 1980-1993. Born: Ottawa, Ontario, 1960.*

Early on in his pro career, Stew Gavin had decided that when his time was up in the NHL, he wanted to be the first to see it coming, and by his own choice, bow out with dignity.

When the Minnesota North Stars moved to Dallas in 1993, Stew felt it was time to play his hand. "So I packed it in, but it was very tough that year," he recounted. "You feel like you're standing in the middle of the highway. The bus is pulling out—the lights are just getting dimmer and dimmer and you're looking around, searching."

Stew had an interest in management so he began to pay his dues as a pro scout for the Dallas Stars. "It was a mild form of torture, having to sit up in the box and watch the people I knew ... watch the game I love to play and ... be on the outside," he lamented. "For the first time in my career I didn't have any emotion! For the first time in my life I was going to rinks not really caring with my usual passion as to who I wanted to win."

To evade the doldrums' grasp, Stew attempted a comeback with the Leafs at the start of the 1994-95 season. As a result of the lockout, however, there was no push to sign him. "I toiled a little bit for the Sharks' farm team in Kansas City and a little bit in Minneapolis where I was living at the time and then I just packed it in for good," he recalled.

Although his comeback was short-lived, his return to the ice brought a sense of closure that culled the unrest from leaving the game.

Nickname Challenge #9

Johnny Rotten

"During my first year with the Leafs, Ron Wilson, who is the coach of Washington, and I broke into the league at the same time. And in those days, it was a big thing to give guys haircuts as an initiation. Well, they cut our hair like punk rockers. They just cut hunks off of our heads! They called me 'Johnny Rotten' and they called Ron 'Sid Vicious'."

Who is he?

Clues

a. He played right wing for Toronto, Quebec and Hartford from 1977-1989.

b. He was the Leafs' first round pick in 1977.

c. He usually sported a red moustache and wore #10 with the Leafs.

If there were too many men on the ice, see page 285.

As well, some sage advice from an old pro helped secure Stew's footing on the treacherous path of transition. "A lot of guys think they want to own their own business," Stew remarked. "I was talking to Darryl Sittler and he said, 'Hey, whatever you do when you get out, don't go spend your money in a business venture. Keep your money and work for someone else. Learn before you put your money out'."

With clear resolve, Stew returned to Toronto where he landed on Bay Street with a financial-services company called "Corporate Planning Associates". "I'd had an interest in finance, managing money, stocks and different types of investments," he explained. "I think that stems from my days with the Leafs when ... I took a chartered financial-planner course through correspondence."

Now well on his way, Stew's experience in hockey has nurtured his knowledge of business to the extent that the latter reaches up to parallel the former. "I loved playing the game," he reported. "And when you look back at all the things you had to do to overcome the obstacles, to get to where you wanted to be, you had to love it! If you didn't, you would have never overcome those obstacles. It would have been too easy to turn back and I think in business, it's the same way. I love what I'm doing now. Looking back at hockey, being a players' rep and being involved in collective-bargaining negotiations, understanding about pension plans... All these things relate well to the business world."

Stew also plans to complement his work with what was formerly a diversionary sideline: his pilot's license which he obtained in 1985. "I try to use it now for leisure and as a business tool," he added. "You can reach out a little farther for the people you service. I also have a farm just outside of Pembroke that my brother helps me with. As a hobby, we've planted about 25,000 seedlings over the past five years." Stew pointed out that with his plane, he can be in Pembroke in an hour thus avoiding a four-hour car trip.

Stew's wife, Phyllis Ellis, is an accomplished athlete in her own right. She played for Canada's national field-hockey team from 1978 to 1985 and competed in the 1984 Olympics. Married in 1986, the couple has two children and currently make their home in Toronto.

Giacomin, Eddie: *Played goal for the New York Rangers and Detroit from 1965-1978. Born: Sudbury, Ontario, 1939.*

The setting was post World War II amidst the deep snow, long winters and frozen lakes of Sudbury, Ontario. Young Eddie Giacomin was seized by the excitement of becoming a goaltender. The source of his vision did not emanate from a cereal box with Turk Broda's likeness stamped on its back; instead, Eddie found all the inspiration he needed watching his older brother, Rollie Giacomin, strap on the pads and hit the ice.

"It was because of my brother really that I got into the game as a goalie because I used to go everywhere that he played," Eddie recalled. "I watched him very closely. And anytime he wasn't using the equipment, I would put it on, whether it was too big or not—it didn't matter.

"So I have to be indebted to him because anytime there was a decision to be made on who was going to play tonight, if we happened to have a game on the same night, he'd say, 'You play' and so I'm the guy who used the equipment a lot of the time.

"My brother was as good as many, many goalies—but I don't think he ever got the chance to go. There was a guy in Sudbury who wouldn't let him try out for other teams. I felt it was unfair because I thought he was as good as me, maybe even better!—we'll never know."

At the suggestion of two Giacomins between the pipes of the NHL, Eddie fondly quipped: "We would have always argued over who would have gotten the equipment!"

In the end, Rollie stayed behind in Sudbury while Eddie went on to become a fan favourite at Madison Square Gardens. For over a decade, he blocked shots and incited ravenous fans to chant the familiar war cry: "Eddie! Eddie! Eddie!"

During the 1975-76 campaign, however, news broke of his trade to the Detroit Red Wings.

Red Storey: *Still Calling The Shots*

Red Storey talks about the four principles of a good life, refereeing, Clarence Campbell and life after the NHL.

The Formative Years: Doing the right thing in the world, that's my goal. It's the way I was raised. I had a wonderful mother. Absolutely the greatest! We were raised in a very, very poor and broken home. No money! But we had four rules in our house:

- It doesn't cost any money to be neat and clean.
- It doesn't cost any money to be honest.
- It doesn't cost any money to have manners.
- And if you don't own it, don't touch it!

Born To Be A Referee: Actually, I'd never even thought of refereeing. But I was injured so much, I had to quit all sports. I had a total breakdown of my legs. So one day I got a call asking me if I'd like to referee hockey. My first game was a major-junior game in the Montreal Forum. I didn't even know the rules or what referees were supposed to wear!

That same year they asked me to referee lacrosse. And I said, "I've never refereed before." And they said, "We didn't ask you that. We asked you if you'd like to!" I accepted because in my heart, I think people are lucky if they are able to do the things they were born to do. I think I was born to be in the entertainment world—whether it was playing, refereeing or on the banquet circuit. With refereeing, I had a funny feeling that that's where I belonged. After my first night I figured, "Boy, I belong out here!"

Before long the schools phoned me and asked if I'd like to referee football. I said, "I've never refereed football." They said, "We didn't ask you that. We asked you if you'd like to!" So I took a crack at that and, son of a gun, it just seemed like I was born to be there.

Breaking The Big League Ice: I was in Toronto and the game wasn't thirty seconds old when I blew my whistle. Bobby Hassard of the Leafs came over and said, "What the hell was that all about Red?" And I says, "I didn't have no reason to blow!" He says, "What do we do now?" I said, "We drop the puck and we get the game going!" I always admitted if I was wrong.

Leaving The League In Scoring: I started in 1950 and I told them what to do with their job by 1959 (laughs). The league president, Mr. Campbell, had made some ridiculous statements in the papers. If I'd have accepted them as being true then I would have had a hard time convincing my kids that their dad had any guts. So I quit to lead my own life.

I took the course that if I was going to raise my family properly, I couldn't accept what was said by Mr. Campbell in the papers. All I asked for was a public apology in every paper he was quoted in and he refused to do it. So I told them what to do with their job.

Turning Up The Heat: Well Campbell made up his mind he was going to force me back into the NHL by starving me to death. He had me barred from the Canadian Football League. He had me barred for ten years from *Hockey Night In Canada.* He tried to get me fired from

Seagrams. He said that Red was too stupid to know how to feed his family and he'd be back in his office begging for his job back. But he didn't realize who he was talking to.

From Hockey To Seagrams: I always had a summer job because when you come out of poverty, you don't want to stop the money coming in. I sold cars in the summer for a long time. Then in '58, I was offered a job with Seagrams. I worked in sales and PR. Whatever they needed doing between the company and the public, I was there. I worked for Seagrams for twenty-five years. It was a perfect job for me because at that time I was doing thirty-two radio shows a week in Montreal and I was doing the banquet circuit.

"My talks are basically all on humour. I mean people don't pay money to sit down and cry!"

"There's more fun every day with people than there is in watching water and sand!"

Charity: I would say that about seventy-five percent of my life is spent on charity work—one way or another, whether it's with the Legends of Hockey or doing charity banquets. Now that's a privilege. That's a reward. People say, "You work too hard!" I say, "No, it's not work, it's a reward!" I think that anybody who has the opportunity to do it and doesn't is cheating the world and themselves.

Family: I have two sons, two grandsons and I'll be a great grandfather next month. We're all the same—workaholics. That might be the worst sin we have (laughs). I was married twice. My first wife passed away in '81 from cancer, and then I got very, very lucky six-and-a-half years ago and wound up with the best thing in my life. We know her as "Bunny"—just like a rabbit.

Pastimes: I've got no hobbies. I've got no time for hobbies. My hobbies are being out on the ice or being out on the golf course or being on my feet at a banquet. That's my life and I enjoy it. The last real hobby we had was in 1986. I was honoured at a banquet. They gave me two tickets to Hawaii. My wife and I went and it was so boring for both of us, it almost caused us to split up. There's more fun every day with people than there is in watching sand and water!

Red Storey was an NHL referee from 1950-59. He was born in Barrie, Ontario in 1918.

"My move from New York wasn't a very happy one," he admitted. "To have to leave New York after all those years!"

Eddie lasted only a couple of seasons with the Wings before calling it a career. But his marriage to the city of Detroit carried a more lengthy commitment than to his profession in hockey.

"I promised my kids that I'd stay in Detroit till their college days were over," he emphasized. "So while they were going to high school and college, I had to be doing something."

That "something" was Eddie Giacomin's Sports Den—a tavern which he owned and operated in the Motor City for the next seven years. "I always thought it would be nice to be on the other side of running a place," he related. "It certainly was a lot more than I thought. There's a lot more that you as a patron don't see.

"I did everything from being the janitor to closing the doors at the end of the night. You had to be a hands-on person in order to be successful in that business. You wouldn't do very well as an owner-absentee—they'd steal you blind!"

In 1985, Eddie received an invitation from Rangers' general manager Phil Esposito to serve as the team's goaltending coach. "It was the nicest thing to happen when Esposito called me," he remarked. "It was an out for me because really, by that time, I'd had my feed of the restaurant business. My place held 100 people, so there was a lot of work to be done to keep the place filled all the time. I was able to sell my place, get back to New York and put that restaurant behind me."

Espo was eager to have Eddie's expertise and winning tradition back with the organization. Eddie eventually found the arrangement to be problematic, however, since Espo had never sought approval from the

> *"I wanted to get on with my life as Ed Giacomin the person instead of Ed Giacomin the former hockey star."*
>
> *Eddie Giacomin*

various head coaches under whom Eddie had to serve. As Ted Sator, Tom Webster and Michel Bergeron came and went, Eddie never got a clear signal that he fit into their plans. He just kept to himself doing his job in the best way he knew how.

When Roger Neilson arrived in 1989, he insisted on bringing in his own people and it was clear that Eddie wasn't one of them. So he left quietly, joining Rod Gilbert as a goodwill representative for the Rangers in the local community where he attended alumni functions and held hockey clinics for kids.

In 1989, Phil Esposito successfully lobbied the Rangers' management to retire Eddie's #1. "He didn't get the credit he was due when I was in New York," Eddie admitted. "It was Esposito who took the initiative to see it through. I'm indebted to him for the rest of my life.

"There's only been one other Ranger player to ever have his number retired, that was Rod Gilbert. So to be only the second one in sixty, seventy years was unheard of!

"And when I started to see the banner with my number being raised to the rafters, it was very emotional. I had a flashback of all the things I'd done and of all the people who helped to make it possible."

Eddie later left the Rangers' organization after completing two years of public relations work. He had finally grown weary of the hockey business and retired to pre-expansion Florida where he knew he could leave the world of hockey behind—at least for a while. "I wanted to get on with my life as Ed Giacomin the person instead of Ed Giacomin the former hockey star," he asserted.

A portion of his fame, however, followed him south to Fort Myers. He loves to golf and his house is situated right on the course. While out playing as a foursome one day, his partner, after having spent the afternoon in Eddie's company, pointed to his house and said, "There's a famous guy who lives there!" Eddie replied, "You don't say!"

The present tense for Eddie Giacomin is now based firmly on an uncompromising foundation of values and simple life choices. The cornerstone of his pursuit involves spending five months each year in Montana, building log cabins for Yellowstone Traditions. He travels to different ranch sites as a foreman and labourer to erect log buildings out of local trees and recycled wood.

"You're dealing with the natural elements—the trees, the forests," he stressed. "When you're cutting one of them down, taking the bark off and putting them into a home—it's something special! It's completely different from buying lumber from a mill. There's a lot of *you* being put into the wood, into the building and therefore, it's a lot more unique, a lot more satisfying. It's time consuming, but it's worth every minute of it. You're putting your soul into it and you can take a lot of pride when it's all done!

"What happens today is that people come to do a job, but they don't take pride in their work. A lot of these people are here today and gone tomorrow. They couldn't care less! The pride is gone and that's why we've had so many problems in the country today. And sports seems to be headed that way as well.

"You've got your superstars going from team to team to team! God almighty, it's hard to believe! I look at a guy who has been sincere, staying with a club for fifteen years—I say that's a star! I mean why didn't Paul Coffey stay in Edmonton, play there for twenty years and be proud of the city where they won five, six, seven Stanley Cups? But no, he just keeps moving around and so there's no loyalty, there's no pride. And how many sweaters do you want your children to buy of Wayne Gretzky? That's mind boggling to me!"

As autumn draws the building season to a close each year and the cold winds descend on the North, Eddie's thoughts turn to his brother, Rollie, who made sacrifices all those years ago.

The two have maintained a solid relationship over the decades. "Even today it remains that way," Eddie stated proudly. "I look at it this way—it's payback time! And what better way to do it than to give Rollie an opportunity to leave the good old North with all the snow and stay with me. Last year he spent five months down here and he enjoys it."

Gillies, Clark: *Played left wing for the New York Islanders and Buffalo from 1974-1988. Born: Moose Jaw, Saskatchewan, 1954.*

Prior to the advent of the seventies, the more massive men of the NHL were usually fearsome at close quarters while resembling pylons on open ice. Clark Gillies was an early example of a new generation of weighty, mobile men who could play the big game on a respectable set of wheels. While Bossy and Trottier worked their give-and-go, Clark was in the wings doing the rugged clean-up work—all while piling up his own stock of offensive numbers that, by career's end, totaled 791 points.

He was voted a first-team all-star in 1977-78. The following season he scored a personal-best thirty-five goals and fifty-six assists. He was also selected as the NHL All-Star squad's MVP during the Soviet Challenge Cup series in 1979.

After twelve seasons and four Stanley Cup victories with the New York Islanders, Clark spent two years sporting a Buffalo Sabre jersey until injuries closed the door on his career.

"I wasn't sure if I wanted to retire," he admitted. "My knee wasn't in very good shape when I finished. There were some tears in both the cruciate ligaments and I didn't want to go through any major surgery. So I said to myself, 'Well, fourteen years, four Stanley Cups and a whole list of accomplishments along the way. Why don't you just hang it up and look for something else to do'?"

Knowing what direction to pursue, however, presented Clark with a dilemma. "You know, retirement is not a fun thing to deal with," he asserted. "You can ask anybody who has played a professional sport or anybody that's done anything for as long as I played hockey. All of a sudden, at age thirty-five, I had to try and figure out what to do with the rest of my life. I really had no idea what I wanted to do. So it was a tough transition."

Clark decided to take a year off to hang loose and relax. He hooked up with an oldtimers' team that included the likes of Darryl Sittler, Butch Goring, Steve Shutt and Bob Bourne. "We played all over Northern Canada: on Indian reserves, up in the Yukon territories, in Nova Scotia and New Brunswick," he recounted. "We played forty games. I started to feel pretty good. I was actually trying to see if I could get somebody to pick me up for the playoffs. But that was kind of a pipe dream and so I thought, 'Just forget about it and move on'."

A turning point came for Clark while watching daytime television. "I'm sitting there riding the stationary bike, watching *Sally Jesse Rafael* at 10:30 in the morning, while everyone else was out doing some sort of constructive work," he confided with humour. "And I said to myself, 'Boy, you better figure out what the heck you're going to do with the rest of your life because you can't be doing this forever'!"

Clark first considered options that would allow him and his family to remain in the

> *"I'm sitting there riding the stationary bike, watching Sally Jesse Rafael at 10:30 in the morning ... And I said to myself, 'Boy, you better figure out what the heck you're going to do with the rest of your life because you can't be doing this forever'!"*
>
> **Clark Gillies**

Buffalo area, a place he had grown to like. He looked into setting up a construction company or a sporting-goods store, but neither venture felt quite right.

He then got in touch with an old friend, Joe Duerr, who had sung the national anthems at Islanders' games for fifteen years. "He was in the securities business working as a manager at Smith, Barney," Clark recalled. "Joe said, 'Why don't you come back to Long Island and get registered in the securities industry and give it a shot'?"

So he moved in with Joe Duerr for eight months, got himself licensed and then set up shop with his family on Long Island in 1990.

After spending a couple of years at Smith, Barney and an additional year and a half at Prudential Securities, Clark and Joe became partners and branched out on their own. "When you're working for a large firm," Clark admitted of his earlier experience, "they have products that they're pushing and they really shove them down a broker's throat. With this operation, the products that we sell are the ones we *choose* to sell. One of our selling points is that we do what's best for the client, not what's best for the firm."

Doing business through Raymond James Financial, Clark and Joe have been able to expand their operation to include offices in Long Island and Florida. "It's been a great move," Clark emphasized. "Our business is growing and it looks like it's going to be great for many years to come."

Clark spends a lot of his spare time playing golf. As a two handicapper, he is enjoying his membership in the Celebrity Golf Association which is comprised of celebrities from the worlds of sports and entertainment. Popularity for their tournaments is on the rise as are the financial prizes to be won. Clark will soon be in

Lake Tahoe to vie for a first prize of $75,000. "On the last day," he predicted, "we'll get crowds of 35-40,000 people. They line the fairways and they take their lives in their hands, because we're not professional golfers. We do have a tendency to hit them a little bit..."

Clark refers to his domestic experience as "kind of a normal family life". He and his wife, Pam, have three daughters, four dogs and a bird. They all continue to make their home on Long Island.

⸺⟨≡≡≡⟩⸺

Goegan, Pete: *Played defense for Detroit, the New York Rangers and Minnesota from 1957-1968. Born: Fort William, Ontario, 1934.*

Pete Goegan was one of the more rugged, surly defenseman of his day and, whether on or off the ice, he always worked with a piece of lumber in his hands.

He started with a hockey stick as a young lad and soon afterwards his uncle hooked him up with a hammer and a two-by-four.

"Oh my God!" Pete exclaimed of his second career. "I worked at carpentry all my life! My uncle owned a construction business. That's where I learned my trade."

While playing in the NHL, Pete continued to work for his uncle, building houses and apartments in Fort William and Port Arthur, Ontario. "Every time I came home, I went to work during the summers," he recounted. "I usually went at it from May till almost the end of August. I'd take a week off and then go back to training camp."

After Pete took his last drive for the Minnesota North Stars in 1968, he returned to Fort William to set up his own construction business. He worked on his own for four to five years before hooking up with Headway Corporation. With Headway, he constructed apartments and houses throughout the Thunder Bay area for the next eighteen years.

In 1990, Pete was forced to retire because of a bad back and hip. Disgruntled about being forced to the sidelines, he admitted, "It's boring. There's too much time and nothing to do!"

As a diversion from the lingering pace of retirement, Pete enjoys visiting friends and attending local hockey games featuring the Thunder Bay Senators. He also keeps tabs on today's NHL. "Oh my God," he laughed. "Well, they're all better hockey players today. But when we played, nobody was buddy buddy. Everybody's buddy, buddy today. In my day we

Nickname Challenge #10

Granny

"I got the name during my first game in the NHL at the age of seventeen. It was an exhibition match in Maple Leaf Gardens. They made an error on the player roster—my name was announced as '#22 Granny ———'. Well, the guys had a howl of a laugh, like Dennis Hull and Jim Pappin! To this day, anytime Dennis Hull sees me, he says 'Granny' with a squeaky voice."

Who is he?

Clues

a. He played right wing for Chicago and New Jersey from 1974-1984.

b. He shares the record for the most points scored by a Blackhawk in one game: seven, which he notched on February 3, 1982.

If you're still short-handed, see page 285.

wouldn't talk to the opposing players. If we saw them in a bar after the game, they sat in their own section and we sat in our own and that was it! We never mingled. Today it's a different story."

Glenn Goldup singles out his good buddy, Dick Redmond, whom he undressed along with Tony Esposito to score for the Kings.

Goldup, Glenn: *Played right wing for Montreal and Los Angeles from 1973-1981. Born: St. Catharines, Ontario, 1953.*

In the world of hockey, making it to the NHL is equivalent to a mountain climber who sees a peak, scales its foothills and faces its natural barriers with love, determination and hard work. Once on top, the climber savours the view until one day, he realizes the inevitable: going down is inseparable from coming up.

Glenn Goldup made it to the top of his profession in hockey, he relished the view and eight years later, he too had to grapple with coming back down.

"You leave the game always saying, 'Jeez, did I leave too soon? Should I have done this better?' There's lots of second guessing going on," he confided. "So you really don't concentrate fully on what you're trying to accomplish in your next career. It takes a few years to kind of get your head adjusted."

Glenn described the initial descent as nothing short of dreadful. "Obviously it had a huge impact on my life. It was almost depressing for

the first two years," he recalled. "The only highlight was when somebody would remember your playing days and would make a comment about it. But for the most part, especially out looking for a job, you went from people chasing you down arena hallways for your autograph to people telling you in their office that basically you didn't have the right skills to do anything for them. And that's a 180° turn in terms of your effect on people. So it was very, very tough to take... You go from so much high regard and high respect to almost nothing and that can create quite the havoc in your life."

Glenn persevered and eventually hooked up with Kristofoam Industries based in Concord, Ontario. "We designed and dealt with goaltending gear," he explained. "We imported foams from England and Europe and worked them into the equipment.

"I was at Kristofoam for five years and into my third year, I started making really good money. The sales end and knowing how to deal with people became easier and easier. The whole thing just settled into a nice comfortable role. I started to develop a little pride in what I was doing again. And I was gaining some self-esteem back."

Glenn stayed with his niche in marketing and sales, but eventually jumped ship to the Toronto Argonauts of the Canadian Football League where he worked for the next three years. He was responsible for putting together sponsorship packages for corporations associated with Argonaut events.

During his tenure with the Argos, the team was purchased by the consortium of Bruce McNall, John Candy and Wayne Gretzky. "We won the Grey Cup in '91," Glenn recalled. "I actually have a picture of John [Candy] and I holding the Grey Cup. It's one of my prize possessions. People see that and say, 'That's unbelievable'!"

Later, Glenn used his well-honed skills in the field of sports marketing to strike out on his own, establishing Abraxas Marketing Services. He promoted such products as the Montreal Expos' game-day programme and the Toronto Blue

Jays' play book. He also organized a tour package of the Hockey Hall of Fame on behalf of minor hockey.

"I ran Abraxas for two years," he recounted. "But in the middle of the second year, baseball and hockey went on strike. All the properties that I was selling were baseball and hockey related. So I was one of those victims hit indirectly by the strikes—and afterwards, I just couldn't recover."

Fortunately, Glenn got a shot at being an account executive with FAN 590, an AM sports radio station in Toronto. It's a position he still occupies today. "Now I'm selling advertising on the FAN and it's a really good fit," he remarked. "I sell more based on sizzle than on numbers because I have the know-how to sell excitement in association with professional sports as opposed to using straight numbers to say here's what you can get for your dollar."

It's been fifteen years now since Glenn made his descent from the NHL. His love for the game, however, has never waned. "I still think it's the greatest game on earth," he exclaimed. "There's not another game that even compares to hockey. The only unfortunate thing is that we've got a guy like Bettman in there who, in my opinion, is trying to take aggressiveness out of a game that thrives on aggression... I mean every guy who straps on a pair of skates knows he's going out there and is going to take a risk. I think that's part of the love of the game. If you aren't paying attention during one shift, somebody's going to clean you and you know, that's kind of exciting. But for some reason, they're trying to take all the rough and tough out of the game and I can't buy into that philosophy in any way!

"But the players [today] are stronger and faster. They also have a good training regime. We used to eat steak the day of a game. What a joke that was! I mean we didn't ever have proper nutrition. I often think back and say to myself, 'Man, if I could have had a plate of spaghetti and gone to play the game, I probably could have been a lot quicker and more agile.' Nowadays the nutritionists say, 'Eat your protein the night before and then have a few carbohydrates the day of the game'—which makes perfect sense when

John Candy and Glenn Goldup savour the Toronto Argonauts' Grey Cup victory of 1991

you understand nutrition. We'd all be sitting in there with steaks in our bellies before the game just trying to work it out."

In his free time, Glenn enjoys photography and playing a lot of golf. He also likes to pick rhythm-and-blues-style guitar. Before raising children, he travelled extensively and could be found twice a year down in the Bahamas soaking up the sun and the gambling.

Glenn married his wife, Wendy, in 1988. They are currently raising two daughters and make their home in Etobicoke, Ontario.

Nicknames: *Goldy; Jake*

Glenn had a coach who referred to taking it easy during practices as "to jake it". This coach claimed that Glenn would "jake it" during practices and go all out in the games.

"Goldy" is an abbreviated form of Goldup.

Goyette, Phil: *Played centre for Montreal, the New York Rangers, St. Louis and Buffalo from 1956-1972. Born: Lachine, Quebec, 1933.*

Ken Mosdell's departure from the Montreal Canadiens in 1956 created an opening for a centreman to skate in the wake of Jean Beliveau and Henri Richard. Head coach Toe Blake made the impeccable choice of a twenty-three-year-old Phil Goyette. He was a shrewd playmaker who could score, kill penalties and play a solid game of defense.

Phil and the Canadiens captured four straight Stanley Cups during his first four years in the league. By 1963, he was shipped off to New York where his popularity and offensive numbers continued to flourish. His most productive season, however, came with the St. Louis Blues in 1969-70 where he notched seventy-eight points and was rewarded with a Lady Byng Trophy for gentlemanly play.

Phil had a brief stint with the Buffalo Sabres before seeing his final NHL action with the New York Rangers in 1972. He was then ensnared in the only ill-starred venture of his career. He agreed to coach the New York Islanders during their inaugural season.

His move directly off the ice to behind the bench represented much more than a change in locale—it required a psychological shift and a steep ride on the learning curve.

"You had to more or less separate yourself from the players because you were now management," he explained. "You were ... in authority and you had to act accordingly. It was your job—you had no choice! You were there to put the players through their system and their training. In other words, you were on the other side of the fence."

But it didn't seem to matter which side of the fence Phil was on, the Islanders were four quarts low on talent and all the coaching in the world couldn't change that fact. After

> *"We must have been worth a trillion dollars in those days [with] Rocket Richard, Gordie Howe or Bobby Hull..."*
>
> *Phil Goyette*

compiling a record of six wins, thirty-eight losses and four ties, he was dismissed in favour of Earl Ingarfield.

Phil spoke candidly about his decision to jump into the coaching quicksand in the first place: "I guess they were stuck ... and I took the bait. There was no way you could win with an expansion team. So the guy to get rid of was the coach. That was their first year and they had lost all of their players to World Hockey [WHA]. I made the wrong move and that was it.

"It's like everything else in life. You make mistakes... To me I should not have gone directly into the NHL as a coach. I should have gone more or less with an organization and learned the ropes from the inside out. There's a lot of learning to be done."

Phil's sour stint with the Islanders left him more than ready to leave professional hockey. His one and only coaching experience ended up as incorrect postage on a package that otherwise represented a highly successful career.

His transition was greatly eased by the fact that he had maintained a job outside of hockey in Montreal since 1957. "I'm in the customs-brokerage business," he explained. "So I just went back to what I was originally doing. I've been there thirty-nine years now."

Phil's work involves soliciting new customers and serving existing ones who import and export materials to and from Canada. His company takes care of the red tape in getting products across the border on behalf of its clients.

Outside of his customs work, Phil played hockey with the Montreal Canadiens Oldtimers for many years until he felt he was old enough to hang up the blades for good. These days he prefers to stay in shape out on the golf course.

He also continues to follow the NHL as a spectator. And like all fans, he exercises his right to express his opinion: "Money-wise let's face it, it's gone out of whack as far as I'm concerned. And Joe Doe is the only guy who's paying for it. I can't see *anybody* being paid six million dollars per year! I don't say that they shouldn't be well paid. But the only way they're going to get that type of money is by raising the prices. There's twenty-six teams. Not all players can be superstars with half a million or a million dollars a year. No way! We must have been worth a trillion dollars in those days [with] Rocket Richard, Gordie Howe or Bobby Hull... We were grossly underpaid. But we lived in our time. So I have no knock on that."

Phil is also perplexed by the senseless brutality of the current era. "I find there's too much hooking, too much hitting from behind and too much hitting for no reason," he charged. "You know, a guy doesn't have the puck and there they are, trying to put him through the boards! And they're always hitting around the head—I don't see any glory in that."

Grant, Danny: *Played left wing for Montreal, Minnesota, Detroit and Los Angeles between 1965 & 1979. Born: Fredericton, New Brunswick, 1946.*

Hockey players from the East Coast of Canada usually swim upstream to the NHL. When their teammates learn of their origin, they are quickly christened with names like "Sockeye", "Sword Fish" or "Halibut". And like the salmon, most of these men hear a distant, primal call to return one day to their places of birth.

Danny Grant, a man with prodigious scoring sense, roamed the rinks of North America for fourteen seasons. Fredericton, New Brunswick, however, was always home. Every summer, he returned to create and sustain relationships that would serve as a social bedrock for his life.

"I had some great friends at Moosehead Breweries," he recalled. "I had been involved with them in a lot of activities during the summers. So I had a standing invitation to work for them whenever I decided to retire."

Two years before hanging up his skates, Danny had suffered a serious injury known as an anterior thigh rupture. "I missed about a year and a half," he admitted. "The injury really took its toll. I was never the same after that. So I decided that that was enough."

He returned home to Fredericton and accepted the offer from Moosehead to do provincial promotions and sales on their behalf.

"I was looking at about a five-year deal because the job involved a lot of travel and lots of weekend and evening work," he reported. "It was just like hockey, but they were such a great company and they treated me so well!

"I really wanted a regular nine-to-five job, however, so I could be home and do some things on weekends and at night like coaching hockey. After nine years with the brewery, an opportunity to go with the sports branch of the Department of Municipalities and Housing came up and I took it."

Danny is now a consultant for the department's fifty-seven sports organizations across the province. He uses his expertise to insure the effective operation of programmes ranging from gymnastics to hockey.

"It's great," he said of the experience. "It's altogether different from what my whole life has been. Regular hours, weekends off—it's the closest thing to normal I've ever had!"

He also squeezes in time to serve on the board of directors for the Fredericton Canadiens hockey club; to coach the University of New Brunswick hockey team; and to scout for the Halifax Mooseheads, a Quebec Major Junior-A team, which most recently he has elected to coach.

As Danny looked back over his life in hockey, a contentious battle ensued over which would be the number-one highlight of his career. In the end, Danny replied that his two trips to the All-Star Game and his fifty-goal season were narrowly edged out by the experience of his first NHL game. "I came up through the Montreal system," he recalled. "Just being a kid and breaking in with a team like that was great. Being in the dressing room with guys like Jean Beliveau, Henri Richard and Claude Provost—I think that is one thing I'll never forget!"

Danny spent most of his first two years of

play in the minors, but was rewarded with the opportunity to play one game with Montreal. "In those days, the Canadiens hadn't had a rookie make the team for five years!" he said with awe. "They had won four Stanley Cups in a row and had had teams in the minors that could beat half the NHL teams today! I know a lot of people wouldn't agree with that (laughs). But there were a whole lot of young guys coming along in their organization: Mickey Redmond, Serge Savard, Rogie Vachon, Carol Vadnais and Jacques Lemaire. When expansion came along, they just couldn't keep them all."

"So I'm pretty satisfied," he said of his time in the NHL. "There are some things I would have done differently. But hindsight is worth a million dollars. Anyone who plays in the National Hockey League, National Baseball or National Football, is at the pinnacle of what he does best."

Guidolin, Armand (Bep): *Played left wing for Boston, Detroit and Chicago between 1942 & 1952. Born: Thorold, Ontario, 1925.*

It wasn't a windfall, but when Bep Guidolin stepped out of the NHL and into the minors he began to rake in more cash than he'd previously known in the big leagues.

"In 1953," he recounted, "I played for the Ottawa Senators which was part of the Quebec League. Punch Imlach was coach of the Quebec Aces and they had Jean Beliveau at the time. Because of Beliveau's presence, there were big fan turnouts and lots of revenue at all the rinks. We played from September to May and were paid every week, so in the end, we made more money than we did in the NHL!"

A decade prior to his minor-league prosperity, a sixteen-year-old Bep Guidolin became the youngest player to ever hit NHL ice. He racked up 290 career points on behalf of the Bruins, Red Wings and Blackhawks before rounding out his career in the minors.

In 1957, Bep was hired as a player-coach of the senior-league Belleville McFarlands. Although his initial stint behind the bench was brief, the experience was to his liking.

By 1965, he had advanced to the Ontario Hockey Association as head coach of the Oshawa Generals. That year's edition featured Bobby Orr, Wayne Cashman and Danny O'Shea.

Bep then took a five-year hiatus from hockey to work for Molson Breweries until the excitement of coaching prevailed over his wavering plans for secure employment. An offer from the London Knights of the OHA broke the intertia and set him on a course back to the NHL. His next stop was the Boston Braves of the American Hockey League. 1971 marked the Braves' first year of existence. Bep imposed a rigourous conditioning programme on his charges and they responded to the tune of an East Division title.

His success did not escape the eye of Bruins' general manager Harry Sinden. When coach Tom Johnson and the Bruins struggled the following season, Bep was brought in to replace Johnson and to tighten down the hatch.

Under Bep's direction, the team continued to be a league powerhouse. They were again knocking on Lord Stanley's door during the 1973-74 playoffs, but were overpowered in the finals by the Philadelphia Flyers. The loss coupled with rising tensions between Bep and some of his players, resulted in his dismissal.

He then grabbed a fast turnpike out of town, heading west to coach the expansion Kansas City Scouts from 1975 to 1977. "I left in the middle of '77," he admitted. "The team was going belly up. In hindsight, it was a mistake not to complete the contract. Things like that can damage your reputation. People will say, 'He can't take losing.' If I'd stayed on, I think other doors might have opened."

Bep retreated to his home base in Barrie, Ontario. "I cooled it for a while and took it easy," he disclosed. "I got a little job, just to keep busy and get away from hockey."

He did, however, make a brief return to the arena, coaching in Brantford and Sudbury, where, as he put it, he kept his car motor on idle. After that, he called it quits for good, although not before having one last temptation laid in his path. He received an offer to coach Wayne

Gretzky and the Sault Ste. Marie Greyhounds. Bep could have been the only man to have coached both Bobby Orr and Wayne Gretzky before they entered the NHL. "But I refused," he recalled. "I got tired of jumping to too many clubs. So I said, 'No more'!"

These days, Bep enjoys observing the NHL at arms length. "The game hasn't changed much since our day," he maintains. "Bigger, faster, stronger: I don't buy that. They're bulldozers!"

Over the years, he and his wife, Eleanor, a former Ice Capades figure skater, have raised three girls and a boy.

For recreation, Bep enjoys golfing and spending lots of time with his nine grandchildren at his home in Barrie.

Hadfield, Vic: *Played left wing for the New York Rangers and Pittsburgh from 1961-1976. Born: Oakville, Ontario, 1940.*

In 1961, the New York Rangers' "Duke of the dukes," Lou Fontinato, was shipped to the Montreal Canadiens to make way for a new enforcer: twenty-one-year-old Vic Hadfield, a tough man with strong hands and a short fuse. Vic was well on his way to replacing "Leapin' Louie" as a league leader in penalty minutes when the two had a shoulder-to-shoulder encounter along the end boards of the rink. Lou fell to the ice with a career-ending broken neck while, ironically, Vic was left to forward the donnybrook tradition on his own.

And forward the cause he did, racking up over 360 penalty minutes during the next three seasons. By the mid-sixties, however, Vic's slapshot and puck-digging skills began to demand equal billing with the roughing and fisticuffs. As a more balanced player, his offensive numbers lifted him to fourth in league scoring with fifty goals in 1972.

He was rewarded with the team's captaincy in 1971, a position he occupied until he was traded to the Pittsburgh Penguins in 1974.

While Vic was developing his hockey career over the years, he was also nurturing his other love in life, the golf business. If we are to believe

him (which we don't), he learned it all in a very short time. "I started working at the Oakville Golf Club when I was only fourteen," he claimed. "That's only a couple of years ago."

In 1970, while still with the New York Rangers, he joined forces with Andy Bathgate to develop the Indian Wells Golf Club in Burlington, Ontario. The most contentious issue the two faced was whether to go private or public. A stalemate ensued which resulted in Andy's departure in 1976. Vic continued the operation as a private course until it was sold in 1985.

In the meantime, he finished off his NHL career with the Pittsburgh Penguins in 1976. "I missed the guys," he admitted of his transition out of hockey. "But I didn't miss playing because I'd ruined my knees. I knew I couldn't play, so I had to accept that fact."

After parting with Indian Wells, Vic obtained his securities license and spent the next two years selling large, metal storage containers used to haul cargo on ships.

But the cargo business had none of the flammable properties that could fire his interest like a club and a fairway could. So, he readily accepted an offer, to manage the Huntington Golf and Country Club, a private course in Woodbridge, Ontario.

But with a hankering to administer his own fate, he left Huntington in 1992 to set up his own establishment, the Vic Hadfield Golf Centre in Woodbridge. "We have two hundred grass tees, thirty astro-tee mats, two natural putting greens, a chipping green ... sand traps and miniature golf," he declared. "I don't just stand behind the counter either. I do a lot of the cutting and the improvements on a day-to-day basis. I really enjoy pulling out the tractor. That's really my leisure time. I guess I'm a little bit of a workaholic but ... I don't consider it work. I just really enjoy the people business, being creative and building something that we can be awful proud of."

Vic also keeps an open line on New York City by doing promotional and public relations work for Trecom Business Systems. "They do the new switches and boards for ... all the large telephone companies," he explained. He makes frequent trips down to New York City to entertain clients with dinner, a round of golf or a trip to Madison Square Gardens to see the Rangers or the Knicks play.

At present, Vic is helping to pilot the organization of a New York Rangers' alumni association to be based in Ontario. "Because there are so many ex-Rangers living in the Toronto area," he explained, "we didn't have enough people left in New York City to generate funds and do charity work." Their plan is to play golf, baseball and hockey across Ontario and elsewhere to benefit various charitable causes.

Hajt, Bill: *Played defense for Buffalo from 1973-1987. Born: Borden, Saskatchewan, 1951.*

A picture of rural Saskatchewan of the 1950's typically includes hockey, farming and strong family values. Bill Hajt's life remains a reflection of that picture.

After fourteen dependable seasons on the upside of the NHL's plus-minus scale, Bill retired from the Buffalo Sabres' blueline in 1987.

The knowledge he gained while growing up on his father's farm formed the basis for his second career as a grain merchant for Lackawanna Products. Working from his office in Buffalo, Bill arranges the purchase and shipment of grains and feed ingredients destined for the livestock and pet food industries in Canada and the United States.

But whatever fulfillment or constraints his work may impose, family, as a personal tradition, remains his top priority. "We're small town Saskatchewan people," he stressed. "It's certainly a lot different than Buffalo, New York and the NHL. So family ties are very, very important to us."

While striving to keep their links back home, he and his wife put a small-town touch on the bigger-city life of raising four kids. "I want to enjoy them while they're here," Bill emphasized. During the time his son, Chris, has been billeted in Guelph, playing for the Storm of the Ontario Hockey Association, Bill travels to the Royal City as often as twice a week to attend games. Their commitment has paid off—Chris was chosen thirty-second by the Edmonton Oilers in the 1996 NHL entry draft.

With the possibility of his son one day entering the NHL, Bill has become all too aware of how the sport of hockey is ultimately governed by the business of hockey.

"The basic game hasn't changed a whole lot, just the content, the size and the number of teams," he observed. "There's a lot more hype involved too. I think that there's more pressure on these kids now because of the type of money they're making. When I turned pro I made $16,000 a year. These kids make $600,000 a year!"

With the 1996 draft experience fresh in his mind, Bill reflected back on the sleepy selection process that marked his own entry into the NHL in 1973. "There may have been a sprinkling of guys there," he recalled. "They had it in a small room and it really wasn't a big deal at all. But it's big business now. They're very much in the public eye right from when they're kids. Even from before the time they're drafted. I never experienced the pressures growing up ... that my son has already experienced. I guess there's good and bad in it. It makes you grow up a little bit sooner, but it's also hard on the kids. There's a lot expected of them. They're still kids—only seventeen, eighteen years old. There's so much hype it can be a bit overwhelming if you don't have a level head."

Hall, Glenn: *Played goal for Detroit, Chicago and St. Louis between 1952 & 1971. Born: Humboldt, Saskatchewan, 1931.*

Glenn Hall was one of the finest, most durable goaltenders to ever appear in the NHL. He played a miraculous 552 consecutive games between 1955 and 1963. As an innovator, he used his quick reflexes and drop-V style to power his way to a Calder Trophy as the league's best rookie, a Conn Smythe Trophy as the MVP of the 1968 playoffs, three Vezina Trophies plus seven first-team all-star awards.

Glenn's entire pro career was played out on the big-city stages of Detroit, Chicago and St. Louis. His home life, by contrast, unfolded on the pastures of his farm in Stoney Plain, Alberta. Life between the pipes was hard on Glenn's nerves and Stoney Plain was his annual cure.

When he left St. Louis in 1971, Glenn had more time to devote to the operation of his farm although he didn't put hockey entirely out to pasture. "I coached the junior B's locally here for a couple of years," he recalled. "It was the Stoney Plain team of the Capital Junior Hockey League. It was a nice handy league... There wasn't much travelling involved."

He eventually returned to the NHL with the Colorado Rockies as a goaltending consultant. "I did basically just a week of training camp and that was the extent of it," he explained. Although his stay in Denver was brief, he did get a goal pad in the door.

His next stop was as goaltending coach for the Calgary Flames. "Cliff Fletcher called and I've been with them for the last twelve years," he related. "I've found it really enjoyable."

Being a man of soft words, Glenn encouraged his protégés to feel invited but never pushed. "I still figure I'm more of a cheerleader," Glenn remarked. "I've got definite ideas on what is correct and what is incorrect ... but I talk about certain goalkeepers and explain their approach. Then I let them make up their minds."

After more than forty years in the business, Glenn retired from the Flames at the end of the 1994-95 season. "I'm still following them quite closely," he commented. "I go down and see them

Glenn Hall   **Calder Trophy**

now and again."

As he sits in the stands, his eyes look past hockey's consumptive glamour to expose the old-fashioned chassis that, since day one, has carried the game from the pond to the satellite dish. "There's no generation gap," he asserted. "The only difference is the equipment. The forwards are still trying to do to these kids what they were trying to do to me. Now they try to hurt each other rather than take each other out of the play like they did in the old days. But it hasn't changed very much. They're still trying to do what they've been trying to do for a hundred years!"

At present, Glenn is enjoying the best of what his farm has to offer without the labour. "We've got it rented out so we're not working the fields," he explained. "I've got a few horses that we fool around with and I enjoy doing little things around the farm, things I *like* to do."

Over the years, he and his wife have raised two boys and two girls. "They all live close by," he added. "So the grandchildren are here an

116

awful lot."

Nicknames: *Goolie; Mr. Goalie*

"All the old guys call me 'Goolie'," Glenn noted. "You're dating yourself if you yell 'Goolie' at me. I really don't recall how I got it, whether it was through Litz or Skovie—it was certainly from that era. I know it was in Chicago because the word 'Goolie' was a kind of localism they used there.

" 'Mr. Goalie', I'm not sure how that one came about. It probably came through the media."

———✦———

Harris, Billy: *Played right wing for the New York Islanders, Los Angeles and Toronto from 1972-1984. Born: Toronto, Ontario, 1952.*

When Billy Harris was drafted first overall by the expansion New York Islanders in 1972, he had more hopes pinned on him than the proverbial donkey. On the strength of his league-leading performance in the Ontario Hockey Association, the Isles and their fans banked on at least one star, Billy, to ease the pain of their expansion blues.

He scored reasonably well through the thin of those early years, although his impact was not enough to save the hapless Islanders. Through judicious drafting, however, the club's fortunes gradually improved, allowing him to shift from the prolific scoring role to his true forte as a crafty checker and penalty killer. The Islanders eventually attained halcyon success while Billy rounded out his career in Los Angeles and Toronto.

When retirement finally came in 1984, he seized the line on a long-standing offer from a close buddy to return to Long Island. "I ended up going to work for Original Equipment Sales," he recalled. "We sold audio and electronic components to car manufacturers. When a lot of European companies like Range Rover, Pougeot and Alfa Romeo shipped their cars to North America, they put in an upgraded sound system to appeal to the American market. We supplied the radios, the speakers and sometimes, the alarm systems. These were installed here before the cars

went to the dealers."

Billy's role with O.E.S. involved public relations and travelling. He cited his trip to Milan as a humourous example of how "the customer's always right" can go wrong. "Alfa Romeo installed a real Mickey Mouse antenna in their cars," he related. "We put the radios in over here and they didn't get good reception. Well, I had to fly to the factory in Milan just to install an antenna to prove to the people in Italy that it wasn't the radio that was the problem!"

In 1988, he accepted an invitation offered by another close friend, John Blair, to work for Lackie's Marina based in Toronto. "I've always loved boats," Billy noted. "When we negotiated the deal I said, 'I don't really know a lot about boats.' And he said, 'You know more about boats than most of my salesmen!' It was a totally different field. It was tough because there was a lot of service involved. I mean nowadays these boats have got air conditioning, electrical systems ... and if a guy's got problems and he's spent between $400,000 and a million bucks, you've got to know what you're talking about!"

Billy was brought on board to manage Lackie's new dealership up in the Georgian Bay area. He stayed on for three years until another close friend, Doug Illman, approached him with an offer too tantalizing to resist.

"Dougie's originally from Ontario," Billy explained. "We met when I got traded from the Islanders to the Kings. We became good friends and sometimes we joked about opening up a [bar] if the right place came along. Well, an opportunity did come along." Conditions were attached however. The only way that Dougie would agree to the project was if Billy returned to Los Angeles to participate directly in the operation.

The two have worked together successfully since 1992, creating Harry O's, a popular night spot sporting Billy's nickname from his playing days. "We've sort of become one of the hottest bars in L.A.," he declared. "We serve pub food and we have live entertainment every night. We get the odd movie star coming in, but it's mostly hockey and sports orientated."

The popularity of Harry O's got a galactic lift by garnering the kind of publicity that money can't buy. The bar was mentioned in prominent situations such as on NBC's *Late Night with David Letterman*. "Kelsey Grammer was in *People* magazine," Billy recounted. "He mentioned that he had met his fiancé in Harry O's and they had become engaged. So we've been real fortunate."

Billy continues to hold out for the life of a West-Coast bachelor. He has gotten into skiing of late and enjoys making excursions to places like Hawaii and Mexico. Otherwise, he can be found where everyone knows his name: at Harry O's.

Nickname: *Harry O*

"I don't know if you remember a TV show that was popular back in the mid-seventies with David Janssen called Harry O," Billy asked. "On Long Island, I was known as 'Harry' and then that show became really popular, so they added the 'O' and I became 'Harry O'."

Harris, Billy: *Played centre for Toronto, Detroit, Oakland and Pittsburgh between 1955 & 1969. Born: Toronto, Ontario, 1935.*

Sampson had his hair and Billy Harris had his Maple Leaf jersey. Without it, as was the case in Detroit, Oakland and Pittsburgh, his playmaking powers and fluid skating tended to dwindle from the form he'd known on Gardens' ice—a place where he pegged all but fifty-eight of his 363 career points. Clearly, the hometown stage of Toronto brought out the best he had to offer.

He described his final two seasons in the NHL as long and unsuccessful—for himself personally as well as for the Oakland Seals and the Pittsburgh Penguins. "I've always admired people like Beliveau and Syl Apps," Billy asserted. "Both of them retired on Stanley Cup teams. I'd find that very difficult to do. But I had had two miserable seasons so it was easy for me to start thinking retirement."

And besides, hockey wasn't the only career option open to him. While with the Leafs, he

Is Billy Harris Related To Billy Harris?

William Edward Harris the younger speaks about himself and William Edward Harris the elder.

Billy Harris the younger and the elder were both born in Toronto; they both played for the Leafs; and they both had exactly the same names. Billy the younger played pee-wee hockey for the Shopsy's team which was indirectly part of the Maple Leafs' organization. "Everybody figured that the older Billy was my father, since we had the same name and we were with the same organization," Billy the younger recalled. "I used to watch him on TV all the time, so that's why I took his #15 as my number. But there's no relation between us whatsoever. I've met him and we joke about it because he gets phone calls for me sometimes and I get confused with him a lot... Dave Dryden called me once when he was trying to organize an oldtimers' game. He was going on and on and I said, 'Dave, do you know who the hell you're talking to? This is the younger Billy Harris, not the older one!' And he goes, 'Ah Jesus Murphy, I'm sorry Billy. How are you'?"

spent his evenings and summers accumulating credits at the University of Toronto. He gradually earned a B.A. in economics. "I was leaning towards teaching," he explained. "I had another profession in mind at the time, so it was very, very easy for me to actually make the decision to leave hockey."

A six- to eight-month hiatus, however, brought on a change of heart and a new job, as coach of the Hamilton Red Wings during the balance of the 1970-71 season. "I think every athlete wonders if they'd be good at coaching," he remarked. "So I had an opportunity to find out that I enjoyed it."

Although he had very little coaching experience behind him, Billy got an offer out of the blue to coach the Swedish National Team for the 1971-72 season. He then returned to North America and coached the next three years with the Ottawa Nationals and the Toronto Toros of the World Hockey Association.

But the sustained excitement of coaching failed to override Billy's desire to stand at the head of a class. So he completed his bachelor-of-education degree with the goal of combining both teaching and coaching. Laurentian University made the perfect alliance when they signed him to a three-year deal as both the school's hockey coach and a lecturer in the Sports Administration programme. "I'd say seventy-five to eighty percent of my responsibilities were teaching and I thoroughly enjoyed it," he reported.

Even so, when the university stalled on his contract renewal in 1980, Billy exercised his option to join the Edmonton Oilers as an assistant behind the bench. "It was two great years in Edmonton," he declared. "I saw all of Gretzky's ninety-two goals the second year. It was a fun time with so many young players. I

knew they were going to win Stanley Cups."

In spite of the team's success, Billy's contract with the Oilers was not renewed after the 1982 season. He spent the next few years making inquiries, but no NHL offers came to light. And the longer he was away from the game, the further he drifted until he just didn't miss it anymore. In 1984, he and his family moved back to Toronto where Billy embarked on his next career—as an entrepreneur.

"I became self-employed," he recounted. "I did a lot of speaking engagements. I put together a slide presentation and I wrote a book. I just had a lot of free time and when people know you have free time, some interesting projects pop up." His book, *The Glory Years: Memoirs of a Decade, 1955-1965,* featured a treasury of behind-the-scenes photos he had had the foresight to take during the Leafs' successful era of the early sixties.

These days, Billy's hockey interests are occupied by his presidency of the Leafs' alumni association as well as frequent appearances as a Maple Leaf oldtimer at charity events.

In his leisure time, he has evolved into an avid traveller. "My wife passed away almost six years ago and the kids are all grown up and out on their own," he recounted. "For so many years I was paying all the bills for six adults and then, all of a sudden, I only had myself to look after. It took a lot of the pressure off... So now I've been able to make these major trips."

Billy's adventures include a recent trip to the Orient where he visited Hong Kong, Japan, China, Malaysia, Indonesia and Singapore. In previous years, he travelled through the Middle East; backpacked for six weeks in Ireland; visited Sweden and lived in a tent for a month in Finland.

"I've been very fortunate to see a lot of the

world," he said. "But I think ... the more you travel, the more you see, the more you realize how big the world is and that it's impossible to see everything." Yet like his hockey career, Billy will no doubt continue to give it his best shot.

Nickname: *Hinky*

"I still get that from family, friends and former teammates," Billy said. "I grew up with an uncle and I was four years older than he was. The closest he could come to saying Billy was 'Hinky'. So it became my nickname around the house, then the neighbourhood, then public school, high school and then hockey."

———

Hart, Gerry: *Played defense for Detroit, the New York Islanders, Quebec and St. Louis from 1968-1983. Born: Flin Flon, Manitoba, 1948.*

Flin Flon, Manitoba is a community with people rich in character and a pristine environment with a fortune in trees, lakes, beavers and bears. While growing up amidst this backdrop of intangible wealth, Gerry Hart saw limited prospects for making a living. People played hockey and they worked in the local mine. If you weren't doing one then you'd probably do the other. It was a haunting reality that Gerry would never forget.

"When I was playing in Detroit, I suffered a ... border-line, career-ending injury," he related. "I had just turned twenty and I was out for about a year and a half. I had no education. I had chosen to play junior-A hockey in Flin Flon along with Bobby Clarke and Reggie Leach, but I had to sacrifice going to school to do it. When I got hurt in Detroit, the reality of possibly having to return to Flin Flon to work in the mine was not very appealing to me, to say the least. And the alarm kind of went off... I realized I had

Gerry W. Hart

(516) 232-3222
Ext. 200
Fax: 516-232-3228

HIDDEN POND PARK
660 Terry Road
Hauppauge, NY 11788

better start thinking of some alternatives. So as I continued to make my way back into playing hockey ... I made sure that in each and every city I paid attention to what was going on in the world of finance. I met a lot of influential business people that were very willing to provide advice and direction ... and I used that opportunity to gain ground in the financial world."

While skating for the New York Islanders in the late seventies, Gerry began to lay the groundwork for his post-playing career.

"I met a very successful attorney who was in the real-estate business," he recalled. "He took me under his wing and taught me a lot about investing and financing."

Gerry learned to leverage his NHL contract to borrow funds to buy property. He gradually built up a portfolio of rental and investment holdings in the New York area.

Towards the end of his NHL career while playing in St. Louis, he also obtained insurance credentials to diversify his options. Afterwards, he and a partner set up a New York-based company called "General Warranty" which specialized in marketing extended-warranty programmes to various auto dealers and manufacturers. Being a new concept at the time, General Warranty experienced a very high level of success. Eventually, however, insurance carriers began to suffer losses, so Gerry beat a well-timed path out of the business.

He was then free to channel all of his energies into the management of his property empire. But the virtue of good timing again compelled him to unload a number of his holdings—along with the adjoining debts—just before the market went soft in the late eighties. His clamouring instincts then took a lean towards building and development.

In late 1991, Gerry took over a recreational project that had failed in mid-flight. He saw the project through to its completion, creating a model for the recreational-facility business called "The Rinx".

"The cornerstone of the facility is two ice rinks," he explained. "Ice, like it is in most parts of North America, is in big demand. We continue to develop programmes around that. We also dovetailed with an existing swimming pool complex and we have subsequently taken over the management of that complex as well. So we have an Olympic swimming pool, diving pool and kiddy pool that allow us to run very successful summer camps. We have a summer sports programme that consists of a multitude of sports and disciplines for boys and girls ages six to sixteen. We also run ten weeks of hockey camp and we have a figure-skating camp.

"I think that we're on the cutting edge of something terrific. It's a prototype of a privatization project with the municipality where we're providing recreational opportunities for the community at a very affordable rate and at no cost to the taxpayer."

Other cities, having seen the success of Gerry's sports complex, are lining up to create similar facilities in their own communities. This has opened up the opportunity for him to serve as a consultant and to obtain equity in these new ventures.

For a contrast to his work, Gerry likes to get away to Manitoba for a minimum of three weeks each summer. "I love the outdoors and I love the North," he affirmed. "So much so that I've always maintained a summer cottage up there. I love to hike, fish and do wilderness trips. And I really appreciate the pristine environment that still exists up there."

As for home life, Gerry has a teenage son from his first marriage. His current wife, Rosemarie, is an attorney. Together, they make their home on Long Island and share many of the same interests including the Canadian wilds.

Nickname Challenge #11

The Haileybury Hurricane

"During the fifties, there was a big hurricane called 'Hazel' that missed Boston but hit Toronto pretty good. The very next night, we had a game against Detroit and I had one of my better games—I think I got three goals and three assists. I got five of them in one period! When the reporters wrote about the game the next day, they referred to me as the 'Haileybury Hurricane'. It's a wonder they called me that because Haileybury, my home town, is a big word. They didn't usually go for such big words, and I wasn't no Rocket Richard either!"

Who is he?

Clues

a. He played right wing for Boston and Detroit from 1951-1962.

b. He played a mean-spirited and tough game while garnering 344 career points and 812 penalty minutes.

c. His initials are L.L.

If you're over the glass and into the crowd, see page 285.

Hebenton, Andy: *Played right wing for the New York Rangers and Boston from 1955-1964. Born: Winnipeg, Manitoba, 1929.*

Through the thick and thin of nine NHL seasons, Andy Hebenton never missed a single game! With the passion of a child on Christmas Eve, he held firm to the goal he'd worked so hard to achieve. He'd spent five years patiently toiling in the minors, waiting for such a day as when Rangers' general manager Muzz Patrick rolled the dice and brought him to Broadway.

Andy had entered the NHL as a twenty-six-year-old rookie and proceeded to make Muzz Patrick's hunch look like a box-office sleeper. He racked up over 400 career points in 652 appearances and, in 1957, claimed a Lady Byng Trophy for good behaviour.

The Boston Bruins drafted Andy in 1963 for one final season before dispatching him to the Portland Buckaroos of the Western Hockey League. His rights were then traded to the Toronto Maple Leafs.

"I went to Toronto's training camp," he recalled, "and they sent me to my hometown of Victoria, British Columbia where I played two years with the Victoria Maple Leafs. The team folded, so I got traded back to Portland in '67 and played there until 1974. I thought I might try out with the World Hockey Association, but the phone didn't ring, so I thought, 'Ah, that's enough!' I didn't make much money, but we had a lot of fun, a lot of laughs and I met a lot of good guys."

Andy stayed on in Portland and with a partner, set up a cement business called "A & L Construction". "My partner was a foundation man and I was a flat man, doing driveways, sidewalks and patios," he explained.

Getting up to his elbows in cool, wet cement became second nature after a time—but Andy soon realized that his hands could adjust more readily than his mind. "For the first year, I found it really hard," he admitted. "Everybody talking to you was going to training camp. The junior hockey team came into town and you saw the young kids playing and that was pretty tough. But after a while I just kept moving along. It's hard for a guy to play hockey all those years ... taking things easy in the summer, to then go to work five days a week for the whole year. But I enjoyed it. The people here are very friendly so that made it a lot easier."

Andy and his partner stayed at it for the next twenty years until retirement came in 1994. Now, the toughest part of his day is to contain the excitement he feels for his new life. "It's great!" he exclaimed. "I don't have to get up at six or seven in the morning and put my work clothes on! I'm staying home and working around the house, so it's been a really great change for me. I try to get the yard in good shape and I try and hide away from my wife. She's always got one of those 'honey do' lists that she sticks in a jar every morning. She writes things down that need to be done and I've gotta start doing them. I'm about a month behind!"

Over the years, Andy and his wife, Gael, have raised two boys and three girls. One of their sons, Clay Hebenton, played goal for the Phoenix Roadrunners and the Houston Aeros of the World Hockey Association.

Nickname: *Spud*

"When I went to the New York Rangers, they used to call me 'Spud' because I loved to eat potatoes," Andy recounted. "Phil Watson was the coach there at the time and he'd get mad at me because I'd gain weight eating french fries and baked potatoes."

Henderson, Murray: *Played defense for Boston from 1944-1952. Born: Toronto, Ontario, 1921.*

Murray Henderson's mother was the oldest of the ten Conacher children, which made Murray the nephew of hockey legend Charlie Conacher.

In spite of his lineage to one of hockey's premier families, Murray remained modest in setting his own goals. By the outset of World War II, he had progressed up the ranks to the peak of his aspirations—a stint with the senior Toronto Marlboros.

But with the war on the rise, hockey was put

on hold in favour of the Air Force. Serving as a planning officer, he kept in shape by skating with the Airforce hockey team until word came of his father's death in 1944.

With a compassionate leave in hand, Murray returned to a sports world replete with opportunities. "The NHL was desperate for hockey players," he remarked. "Of course I think Boston was more desperate than any other team. So I got my foot in the door."

Since so many NHL-calibre men were still in the service, Murray got the jump on securing a job with the Bruins. By the time the next training camp came around in 1945, he had a year's experience under his belt and a secure position on the Bruins' blueline. "It was just a twist of fate," he concluded. "If it hadn't been for that, I'd have never been in the NHL."

Murray remained a steady fixture in Boston until his retirement in 1952. Hockey, however, continued to be a strong tradition in his life.

"One of the biggest pleasures for me after leaving hockey," he recalled, "was starting the NHL oldtimers in the mid-fifties.

"It started out as a game or two a month," he continued. "Then it got to be pretty well every Friday night. We had Wally Stanowski, Bob Goldham, Harry Watson, Cal Gardner, Ivan Irwin, Danny Lewicki, Gus Bodnar ... and John McCormack. We were quite proud of the fact that we raised a lot of money. And that was a time when a lot of towns were trying to scrape together enough money to put up new arenas."

Murray and his mates were the first to play oldtimers' hockey on a consistent basis and to use their outings as an instrument to raise funds for good causes. They started a trend that today, thanks to alumni associations across the continent, generates millions of dollars a year on behalf of minor-league hockey and charities.

At the end of the 1951-52 season, the Bruins' brain trust, Art Ross and Lester Patrick, decided that Murray could better serve

the organization as a player-coach for their affiliate team in Hershey. He had no coaching experience, but gave it his best shot for the next four seasons.

In 1956, he was offered a scouting job with the Bruins, but declined. "I had a young family," he explained. "I didn't want to be here one year and out on the West Coast the next. So we decided to settle in Toronto. I think that maybe I was a little bit happy to settle down somewhere on a permanent basis. I was looking forward to working and living in one place all the time."

> *"One of the biggest pleasures for me after leaving hockey was starting the NHL oldtimers in the mid-fifties."*
>
> *Murray Henderson*

So Murray became a sales rep with Adams Distillers, a subsidiary of Seagrams. His job was to twist the arms of liquor-store managers to carry Adam's line of products as well as to showcase their wares at banquets, weddings and sales meetings.

While out on the circuit, it soon became clear that Murray had a touch for the finer aspects of the persuasive arts. As a reward he was named Ontario Sales Manager for Adams and later, was promoted to Central Canada Sales Manager for Seagrams.

After thirteen years with the corporation, however, he was laid off during a company shakedown. He transferred his services to another distiller called the "William Mara Company", where he served as a sales rep until his retirement in 1987.

Murray stays close to home in Toronto these days. His daughter passed away recently and his wife is experiencing poor health. His travelling is limited to periodic visits to the Georgian Bay area to visit his son and two grandchildren.

As for leisure, he keeps it simple. "I do a little gardening, I walk the dog and do quite a bit of reading," he said of his daily regime.

Nickname: *Moe*

"When I first went to Boston, I teamed up with Dit Clapper, one of the greatest individuals both on and off the ice that I ever met," Murray recalled. "He said, 'Jeez, I can't keep calling you Murray. That's too long, too difficult. I've got to shorten that up somehow. From now on, it's Moe.' It was a term of convenience."

Jim Henry
B O S T O N   B R U I N S

Henry, Jim: *Played goal for the New York Rangers, Chicago and Boston between 1941 & 1955. Born: Winnipeg, Manitoba, 1920.*

Early in 1941, Jim Henry had proved himself to be a top-line backstopper for the senior-league Regina Rovers in Saskatchewan. Word of his talent travelled east to New York Rangers' general manager Frank Boucher who needed to replace an old favourite—goalie Davey Kerr. Young Jim stepped into the job at the start of the 1941-42 season and inhibited the opposition to the tune of a 2.98 goals-against average and helped secure a first-place finish for the team.

Future success looked more than immanent until Jim heard the call of the Canadian Armed Forces and enlisted in the midst of World War II. It was not until the war's end in 1945 that he returned to the Rangers as a rusty goaltender. He shared duties with newly acquired Chuck Rayner until his departure to Chicago in 1948.

Jim went on to perform valiantly for an anemic Blackhawks' club before seeing some of his most dynamic action as Boston's number-one goalkeeper.

By the mid-fifties, however, he felt like a road-weary soldier. Whether in hockey or the military, he'd been on the move since the late thirties. "I think I'd probably had enough," he declared, speaking of his decision to retire. "We packed up here and went down to play in the States every year. My youngster had to go to school. He'd start out up here and then he'd go to school in the States. Then we'd come back up [to Winnipeg] and he'd have to go to school here again. It was just too much monkeying and moving around. And it was hard on the wife too. She had to pack up everything. So ... we just got tired of it and decided to pack it in."

Fortunately, while still with the New York Rangers, Jim had already taken his post-playing career by the horns. "I ran a tourist camp called 'Hockey Haven' in Kenora, Ontario in partnership with Charlie Rayner," he recounted. "We bought it just after World War II in 1946."

The name of the camp, however, was not part of the original purchase—that came later. "Charlie and I ... got down there, made the deal and were working for a month when a brother-in-law of mine came down and said, 'You guys take a couple of days off.' So we went to Winnipeg with our wives. We came back and he had a sign up. He'd named the place 'Hockey Haven'. Early in the spring, while we were getting the camp ready for customers, quite a few guys like Neil Colville, Alex Shibicky and Alf Pike would come down and we'd kibitz around ... so it really was a hockey haven!

"We had fourteen rentals and a little bit of a store and of course Charlie's living quarters and mine. They were all housekeeping cabins—people came in and did their own cooking. We just supplied the laundry and the dishes. We had boats and motors for rent too, and a fish house for them to clean fish. In the early years, we didn't have power, so we used to have to carry ice around to put in ice boxes ... and then of course later on, when the power came through, we put in refrigerators."

But by 1968, Jim and Charlie had done all the laundry and dishes their wrinkled hands could handle. It was time to sell. "We'd been in it for twenty-two years and you know, we were fighting the weather all the time," Jim related. "I guess we'd just had enough of it (laughs)."

"...quite a few guys like Neil Colville, Alex Shibicky and Alf Pike would come down and we'd kibitz around ... so it really was a hockey haven!"

Jim Henry

He and his family packed up and returned to his native Winnipeg. Soon afterwards, he went to work as a service writer for National Toyota which later became Woodhaven Toyota.

"When people came in, I wrote up the work order for whatever they needed," Jim explained. "I would designate all the work out to the mechanics. I guess I was something similar to an assistant manager in the place. I was responsible for all the money coming in.

"I enjoyed it. I met a lot of people and friends. I haven't worked there for nine or ten years and people who were customers still walk past the house and stop to talk to me."

Jim retired from the car business in 1985. Since then, he has had plenty of time to enjoy the spirit of Hockey Haven without the toil.

He and his wife, who passed away in 1994, raised one son, now living in Kenora, Ontario. Jim makes frequent visits to see him and soak up the surroundings. "I spend lots of time in the summer on the lakes and I do ice fishing there as well," he related.

Jim also enjoys hunting and fishing in Manitoba with former New York Ranger defenseman Bob Chrystal.

Hergesheimer, Wally: *Played right wing for the New York Rangers and Chicago between 1951 & 1959. Born: Winnipeg, Manitoba, 1927.*

The odds against Wally Hergesheimer's success in hockey were as firmly stacked in place as sandbags are against a flood. At the start of his pro career in 1947, he stood 5'8" tall and weighed a mere 145 pounds. He was a slow skater and had lost the index and middle fingers of his right hand in a punch-press accident in 1944.

"When I made it to the NHL," he recounted, "it was something I never really expected. It was little Wally this and little Wally that—but that didn't bother me at all. I loved the game! I just kept going and that was it. Everything seemed to fall into place."

By 1951, he was voted the American Hockey League's most outstanding rookie. He was quickly summoned by the New York Rangers where he became a proficient goal scorer. Known as the "Garbage Collector", he developed a knack for angling his way into the goal crease to cash rebounds into goals.

After his departure from New York in 1959, Wally extended his career until the early sixties by playing for Buffalo of the American Hockey League, for the Calgary Stampeders and finally, for the Los Angeles Blades of the Western Hockey League.

"I had to give up," he admitted of his departure from hockey. "I was getting older and ... I had three kids. And you can't just lug the family around to different places. So I knew the time had come."

He returned to his hometown of Winnipeg, Manitoba where he went to work for the Manitoba Liquor Control Commission—a place he had grown to know during his off-seasons with the Rangers.

For the next twenty-three years, Wally served as an assistant manager for various liquor outlets around the city of Winnipeg. "I enjoyed it," he said of his work. "I didn't mind it at all."

Since his second retirement, he has evolved into an astute devotee in the art of enjoying family, friends and the odd round of golf.

He and his wife, Ruth, have raised a daughter and two sons who in turn, have introduced six grandchildren to the Hergesheimer clan.

Nicknames: *Hergie; Fingers*

"In 1944, I was working during the summer and I lost two fingers [index and middle] at the knuckle on my right hand," Wally said. "So when we used to kibitz around, everyone used to call me 'Fingers'. It was all in good fun. But it didn't stop me. Maybe it helped me, who knows."

 –

Hextall Jr., Bryan: *Played centre for the New York Rangers, Pittsburgh, Atlanta, Detroit and Minnesota between 1962 & 1976. Born: Winnipeg, Manitoba, 1941.*

If there were such thing as a dictionary of hockey, the word *Hextall* could be defined as follows:

> **Hex•tall** : *n. a multi-generational assembly of roughnecks committed to the use of sticks, fists, passion, chicanery and guts to win hockey games.*

Bryan Hextall Sr. led the three-generational tradition as one-third of the New York Rangers' "Roughneck Line" which ruffled feathers and jerseys across the NHL during the thirties and forties.

His sons, Bryan Jr. and later, Dennis, took notice and carried the Hextall institution into its second generation.

"I actually started skating for the first time in Madison Square Gardens when my dad was playing with the Rangers," Bryan Jr. recalled. "Then he retired shortly after that and we went back to the Prairies where Dad played senior hockey and coached the St. Boniface Canadiens to a Memorial Cup. I was about thirteen then—and that's what really got me going. It was then that I realized to what extent my dad had been a great hockey player—that he'd won the league scoring championship and that he'd won the Stanley Cup.

"But I'd always had a desire to play, regardless of what he'd done. And Dennis, my brother, was the same way. It was just built in."

With passion at his back, Bryan worked his way up the ranks until in 1962, he cracked the Rangers' line-up for a twenty-one-game stint. The reality of his achievement soon hit home as he found himself on the blueline of the old Madison Square Gardens, in the same spot his father had stood a generation earlier, looking across, face to face with the Montreal Canadiens.

"During the National Anthem," he recounted. "I saw that whole crew standing there: Jean Belivieau, Rocket Richard, Doug Harvey, Jacques Plante... And here I am, twenty years old and just out of junior. And as I looked at those guys, I thought, 'What am I doing here?' I'll never forget that as long as I live. It was an absolutely amazing feeling!"

His first round at the top, although brief, induced a big-league state of mind that sustained him through a six-year apprenticeship that followed in the minors.

His next taste of the National League came in 1968 with the Pittsburgh Penguins. There he established himself as a hard-nosed assailant who could score his share of goals and fight his share of fights. Over his four-and-a-half seasons with the Pens, he reached his peak, netting 177 points. But from then on, life as an aging journeyman took its usual nomadic turn with stops in Atlanta, Detroit and finally, Minnesota.

"The North Stars put me on waivers near the end of the year," he recalled. "But nobody picked me up. And since I still had another year on my contract, I did some scouting for them and then, that was the end of the line. I just wanted a change. I had offers to stay in hockey, but I took the other road."

His alternative route lead straight back home to his prairie hunting lodge where nothing could stand between him and his passion. "I'm a real avid hunter," he affirmed. "I hadn't been able to do it for a number of years because of hockey—you're always away at training camp in the fall. Another major factor for settling down was that Ronny, my son, was at an age where I wanted him to stay in Brandon to get a good opportunity to play—and it worked out very well. Our whole family—Dennis, Ronny, my dad—we

Nickname Challenge #12

Mr. Clean

"I was with the Montreal Canadiens then. As you know, in the original six we travelled by train all the time and sometimes we'd have to drive all night. On our way to Chicago one time, we had the car all to ourselves. So I took my shirt and tie off and I had my t-shirt on. Now there was this commercial at the time for the cleanser Mr. Clean. Now I don't have a ring in my ear, but with my t-shirt on, my crew cut and my arms folded with flexed muscles, Henri Richard started calling me 'Mr. Clean'. Then in Chicago, just as I started putting my foot on the ice for the warm-up, the organist started playing the Mr. Clean music!"

Who is he?

Clues

a. He played left wing for Montreal, Chicago, Boston, the New York Rangers, Philadelphia and Buffalo in the NHL plus Chicago in the WHA between 1959 & 1974.

b. He always played it tough, racking up 1,728 career penalty minutes.

c. His initials are R.F.

If your pass was intercepted, see page 285.

have a great desire to succeed. And Ronny's got two boys coming along. Young Brett is eight and he's a dandy little player—he just loves the game."

With no hindrance of regret, Bryan then accepted an offer to work as a sales rep for Molson Breweries in Manitoba. "It was basically public relations," he explained. "I'd go to hockey banquets, sponsor golf tournaments and sponsor teams ... on behalf of Molson."

And with a background in hunting, he naturally got Molson involved with Ducks Unlimited. "It was right up my alley," he declared. "Ducks Unlimited is for the preservation of ducks, geese and wildlife ... by trying to maintain waterways and marshes instead of allowing farmers to dry everything up. It's sponsored by donations and fundraising dinners. I got Molson involved. We had a special series of decoys made every year and raffled them off at Ducks Unlimited dinners. It worked out well for Molson and for Ducks Unlimited."

Bryan quit his job with the brewery in 1988 and resettled in Victoria, British Columbia. "I'm basically semi-retired," he explained with satisfaction. "My wife and I purchased a tea house called 'Adrienne's Tea Garden' on Mattick's Farm in Cordova Bay. She's been running that for the last eight years. I do a lot of the behind-the-scenes work, but I also have a lot of time to do what I want, which is hunting, fishing and golfing. I'm doing it all."

It was a brainstorm of practical reasoning that lead Bryan to pursue his present lifestyle. "I think that too many people have to work too long," he observed. "By the time they stop working ... they can't do the things they could do when they were in their late forties and early fifties. But unfortunately that's the way our society is today.

"And fortunately, I never had any real serious injuries during my career. I'm fifty-six, but I'm like a thirty-five-year-old. I go up into the mountains to shoot sheep and I walk six miles every day—I'm very fortunate!"

Hicke, Bill: *Played right wing for Montreal, the New York Rangers, Oakland, Pittsburgh (NHL) and Alberta (WHA) from 1959-1973. Born: Regina, Saskatchewan, 1938.*

When Bill Hicke played hockey, it must have been for the love of the game because it wasn't for the love of money.

"When I quit hockey, I had two homes, two new cars and maybe twenty, twenty-five thousand dollars in the bank," he recounted. "I just didn't have enough money (laughs). I had to go to work.

"For the athletes today, the transition must be quite a bit more difficult. When you make a million bucks and then you go home and get a job for forty thousand bucks, it's pretty hard to compare. I think that it's going to get worse rather than better for these players because although they make twenty times more than we did, [there's] the cost of living. They have the big Lincolns and the big houses."

Bill didn't get down to earning any serious money until after he retired from the Alberta Oilers in 1973. "I was a bronchial asthmatic and I just couldn't play," he explained. "I had another year in my contract with Edmonton. I told Bill Hunter that I couldn't play and he then offered me the coaching job. But unfortunately, he didn't offer me any money. So I just decided it was the end for me."

Bill returned to his native Regina with the urge to get into business for himself. "I got into the sporting-goods business almost by luck," he related. "We had a hockey school going in Regina and we always dealt through Kyle Sporting Goods. Bill and Gus Kyle owned the place. Bill was the colour man in St. Louie but he had passed away playing oldtimers' hockey. So Mrs. Kyle asked me if I'd be interested in buying it. I didn't have that kind of money, but I worked with her for a year. And after nine months, I decided I could do very well in the sporting-goods business. That's when I bought Kyle Sporting Goods."

From the moment he made that decision, Bill set a pattern in motion of being in the right place at the right time. The enterprise flourished under his direction. "The year I worked for her, we did $345.000," he declared. "In three years, I was doing over a million dollars [a year]. The last few years we ... were averaging about a million, nine gross! It was very, very successful for me."

Bill attributed his good fortune to a flawless blend of timing and locale. "It's a funny story," he recalled. "I went to the bank to get a loan. Not knowing very much about business, I went to three banks before the Toronto Dominion finally gave me a loan. The Royal Bank said, 'Buy the business but don't buy the building.' Then the TD manager there said buying the building was a good deal. Eight years later the Royal Bank expanded. They tried to buy my building and I wouldn't sell to them! Then I finally had to sell because the government expropriated me and built a shopping centre there. I had paid $45,000 for the building and they paid me $475,000. So I was making money hand over fist!"

Between frequent trips to the bank, Bill also managed to squeeze in some gamely fun as co-owner and GM of his former junior club, the Regina Pats. After a decade on top he sold his shares in 1995.

Retirement is now Bill's door pass to a storehouse of special interests: playing golf, riding horses and restoring antique cars.

He got started on the latter hobby during his junior days with the Pats. He took a motor mechanics course and was given permission to build a car within the context of the

128

programme. "I built a '29 Model-A roadster hot-rod," he fondly recalled. "Then I just got hooked on cars. I was pretty handy with my hands. Mechanically I'm excellent. In fact I might even be a mechanic if it wasn't for grease. I hate dirty hands.

"I still have a 1926 Model-T that I bought in 1959. I have a '62 Rolls Royce, a '55 T-Bird and a '66 Pontiac 2+2. It's a silly hobby because you can only drive one at a time."

Between the golf clubs, the saddle and the Model-T, Bill still lends an eye to the NHL. "This is the first year that I can remember that I didn't watch a whole game in the Stanley Cup [playoffs]," he reported. "I just got mad. I feel sorry for the referees because the rules are there. The problem we have is that referees have a tendency to use their own discretion. And nowhere in the rule book does it say 'a deliberate trip'. Tripping is tripping. Holding is holding. The problem is that they let a little bit go in the first period. The second period they call maybe a little bit less and the third period a guy could have a gun! I can't see somebody spending seven million dollars for an offensive-minded hockey player who has tons of God-given skills and then allowing a $500,000 hockey player to hold him all night! The game has changed so much that if a guy can't put the puck in the ocean, they call him a checker or a minor leaguer."

Bill and his wife, Lee Anne, now savour a lifestyle that straddles the green of the North and the warmth of the South. Summers are reserved for Regina while winters are eluded at their getaway in Scottsdale, Arizona.

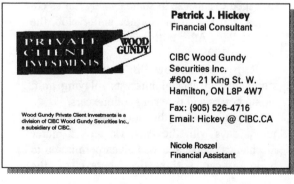

Hickey, Pat: *Played left wing for Toronto (WHA), the New York Rangers, Colorado, Toronto, Quebec and St. Louis (NHL) from 1973-1985. Born: Brantford, Ontario, 1953.*

Pat Hickey was quoted by the Hamilton Spectator as saying, "I was a student of every organization I was in. My whole career has been a lesson in economics and corporate finance." Add entrepreneurial gumption to the mix and it becomes clear that Pat is a self-made, life-long learner.

While he was playing junior hockey for the Hamilton Red Wings, he enrolled himself at McMaster University on the side and got a year of economics under his belt before moving on to the pro ranks.

Pat entered the World Hockey Association as a first-round draft pick of the Toronto Toros in 1973. By age twenty, he was arousing fans with his quick acceleration and long locks of blond hair that tailed in the breeze.

Two seasons later, he jumped to the NHL's New York Rangers where he played all three forward positions, snagging a career-high seventy-three points in 1977-78.

As his NHL career was winding down in the early eighties, Pat spent his summers learning a new trade with Bear, Stearns & Company, a brokerage firm for big banks in New York City.

On retiring from the St. Louis Blues, he entered a full-time training programme with the Wall St. brokerage company of Drexel Burnham Lambert. Pat commented that the learning process was so engaging that his conversion from athlete to broker slipped easily and quietly under the bridge.

The following year, he stepped up to the position of Vice President of Institutional Sales at Daiwa Securities in New York City. To balance his ascension in the business world, Pat used the weight of philanthropy to keep his feet on the ground. Reaching into the heart of the community, he founded a New York City after-school programme called "Ice Hockey in Harlem," a project aimed at providing Harlem children with positive life experiences and hockey skills. This programme allowed the kids to rub elbows with role models such as Wayne Gretzky, Ron Duguay, John Tonelli and Pat himself.

Two factors collided to precipitate Pat's eventual departure from Wall Street and his return to the world of hockey: The financial markets were moving into a steady downward cycle and, Bruce McNall had entered the NHL.

McNall and the Los Angeles Kings hired Pat to run their American Hockey League affiliate, the New Haven Nighthawks. The appointment marked the beginning of a long and mutually beneficial relationship between Pat and the AHL. In addition to serving as the Nighthawks' general manager, he spent five years as a league governor. In 1992, he was recognized as "Executive of the Year" by the American Hockey League.

With still more to come, he took on three partners and established the Hamilton Canucks, a new AHL club affiliated with the Vancouver Canucks. Serving as CEO, Pat sought to use his marketing expertise to accomplish what the AHL had failed to accomplish in St. Catharines and in Newmarket years earlier. In terms of corporate and fan response, his expectations were fulfilled. During their second season, however, local politicians had fixated on obtaining an NHL franchise to the extent that they failed to support Pat and his efforts. So he sold eighty percent of his interests to a couple of Toronto businessmen who in turn, moved the club to Syracuse, New York in 1994.

Pat has since reentered the world of business, and presently occupies a position as a financial consultant for Wood Gundy Private Client Investments, based in Hamilton, Ontario.

He and his wife, Deborah, a professional figure skater, also obtained the Canadian rights to the Plié Power Workshop. This programme was first developed by gold medalist and skating pioneer John Currie. It was designed to integrate the fundamental movements of dance and ballet into the art of figure skating. Deborah travels from Halifax to Vancouver teaching and marketing the Plié programme.

On the domestic front, Pat and Deborah are raising a daughter and two sons at their home in Ancaster, Ontario. Although Pat enjoys golfing and playing Mr. Fix-it around the house, he observed that "at this stage, being there for the kids and their activities is my hobby: horse riding lessons, minor hockey, swimming lessons and figure skating."

Hiller, Dutch: *Played left wing for the New York Rangers, Detroit, Boston and Montreal from 1937-1946. Born: Kitchener, Ontario, 1915.*

After thirty years of service to Los Angeles Wholesale Drugs, Dutch Hiller retired in 1980. His employer decreed that he leave in June while Dutch insisted on leaving six months earlier. As he always did, Dutch stayed true to his word and left on his own terms. The company retaliated by docking a percentage of his pension. His response showed that same old spark that had sustained his NHL career all those years ago. To his employer he warned: "I'll make you pay—I'll live a little longer!"

"I'll make you pay—I'll live a little longer!"

> Dutch Hiller

Dutch entered the NHL with the New York Rangers in 1937-38—and he was determined to stay there! "During my day there were some who were better and some who were worse," he affirmed with the squint of one eye. "But I'll tell you, no matter how big, tough or mean a guy was, he wasn't getting past me." His hurricane speed made certain of that and soon became his calling card as fans wondered whether his blades ever actually touched the ice. Dutch and the boys sped their way to a Stanley Cup in 1940 before the trade winds began to howl. He was moved to Detroit, Boston, Montreal, back to New York and then returned to Montreal—all within a span of four years.

Before the end of the 1945-46 season, he had had plans to call it quits. "My legs were still good." he recounted. "But I said, 'I've had ten years as a professional and two Cups. I've never been hurt seriously and I can't see across the ice. Get out when the getting's good'!"

Dutch was referring to his failing eyesight that descended like an ill-timed scoring drought. "I used to fill in on a baseball team and I never struck out," he recalled. "I'd always get a piece of the ball. But all of a sudden I started to strike out. So I had my eyes tested and sure enough, I put on the glasses and started to hit again.

"Well, I tried the glasses in hockey. Now, I was about 5'8" and I was just about the height of shoulders and elbows. I got the rims of the glasses shoved into my [face] and about eighteen stitches. So I decided to take the glasses off and play half blind."

That idea didn't work well, so he tried on a pioneer's version of contact lenses. "They were the old kind where you had a bubble and a

Eighty-two-year-old Dutch Hiller bent for a round of snooker

suction cup that fit over the whole eye," he explained. "They didn't move with your eye like the new types do. I tried them for a couple of years, but it didn't work out either." The trial was soon laid to rest, but those lenses still live on as an historical display at the museum of optometry in Calfornia.

With the contacts as the last straw, Dutch turned his sights towards retirement. But before he could execute his plan, his rights were traded to Toronto at the end of the 1945-46 season. Conn Smythe wanted to keep a supply of experienced men in Pittsburgh as insurance in case his youth movement with the Leafs didn't work out. Dutch agreed to put in one season in exchange for getting his amateur card back.

In 1947, with card in hand, he retired from professional hockey and returned to his hometown of Kitchener, Ontario where life was full of promise. He then quickly stepped into a job as manager of Rockway Golf Course—a post that left him free to coach the Stratford Khroellers of the Ontario Hockey Association, a team that featured a sixteen-year-old George Armstrong. Dutch also coached, managed and captained the Kitchener Dutchmen of the Ontario Senior Hockey League.

All was well for about a year until his wife became ill. "The doctor said, 'If you want your wife around, you better move to Arizona or California'," he recollected. "I had figured on staying in Kitchener for the rest of my life. I had everything there just the way I wanted it."

His wife had a rheumatic heart condition and required a warm, dry climate to survive. So together, they made a whole new start, eventually settling in Los Angeles. The move helped his wife's condition although in the end, it wasn't enough. "She lived five years longer than they expected," he related. "But she died at fifty."

When Dutch first arrived in California, he spent two seasons coaching the Los Angeles Monarchs of the Western Hockey League. Near the end of his second year, the team's owner openly criticized him in front of the players. Dutch didn't agree with the owner's handling of the situation and resigned.

After a brief stint with Hartman Tool & Engineering, he then settled in for the long haul with Los Angeles Wholesale Drugs in 1950. "I did everything in the business from stock clerk, to buying, receiving, shipping ... everything there was to do."

He would often work till ten at night, putting his best foot forward for the company. When he eventually became a salesman, however, he changed his approach. "I'd just start to make some money," he complained. "Then they'd cut my territory. They would bring somebody else in and then they expected me to build my territory up again. So when they started the monkey business, why I said, 'I'll give you eight hours and that's all I'll give you'!"

In 1969, Dutch married his second wife who, coincidentally, hailed from the Kitchener area. When a mutual friend described the former hockey player to her, she said she used to "boo" him whenever he came to Toronto to play against her beloved Leafs. In spite of the antipathy, they hit it off very well.

When Dutch retired in 1980, he and his wife returned to Canada to be near her two sons. They settled in Richmond Hill, Ontario for several happy years before she developed Alzheimer's disease and had to be institutionalized. Dutch still keeps a close eye on her.

These days he lives on his own. "I've been alone for six or seven years. But that's life," he concluded. "That's the way it goes. I said, 'How lucky can you be? I've had two good wives'."

Dutch spends his leisure time like a leaf in the wind. "I don't like to sit around too much!" he asserted. "I'll get something to eat, do a bit of putting in the livingroom and I even take some swings with my chipping iron just along side the coffee table. After that it's coffee with my friends and a round of snooker downstairs."

In parting, Dutch explained the secret of his health and well being: "I always live by the Golden Rule—'Do unto others as you would have them do unto you'—except of course when it came to hockey. Then it was the rule of retaliation. You don't let anybody beat you down!"

"I always lived by the Golden Rule—'Do unto others as you would have them do unto you'—except of course when it came to hockey! Then it was the rule of retaliation. You don't let anybody beat you down."

Dutch Hiller

Nickname: *Dutch*

"There was a PR man who worked for the New York Rangers by the name of Jersey Jones," Dutch recalled. "He asked me to come into his office one morning and he said, 'We can't go for that name Wilbert!' I was on what they called the 'Roughneck Line' with Phil Watson and Bryan Hextall. I guess he figured the name didn't suit our style. And since I was from the Kitchener area which is German and Dutch, he said, 'We'll tag you with "Dutch".' And it stuck."

Hillier, Randy: *Played defense for Boston, Pittsburgh, the New York Islanders and Buffalo from 1981-1992. Born: Toronto, Ontario, 1960.*

Randy Hillier performed his brand of rugged, stay-at-home defense for eleven seasons, stopping up goal creases like a cork in a pricey bottle of wine. He made the rounds with Boston, Pittsburgh, New York and Buffalo before deciding it was time for a change. "Physically, I still felt like I could play, but mentally, I was pretty exhausted," he acknowledged.

Buffalo had bought out his contract in 1992, so the moment was ripe to try something new—like playing hockey in Klagenfurt, Austria. Although unaware, Randy, his wife Heather and their two daughters were about to embark on an experience that would add new colours to the lens through which they view their lives.

"After playing in the National Hockey League for so many years, the hockey was almost secondary compared to the cultural experience," he declared. "That really was for me the essence of the trip. I always wanted to play a year or so in Europe to ease out of my playing career."

"The residents of Klagenfurt were just good, plain, hard working people," he continued. "The town I was in worked nine to five. Weekends, everything closed at noon and didn't open up until Monday morning. They took two- or three-hour breaks in the afternoon every workday."

Within the value system of the Klagenfurt people, Randy found something more than a postcard to take back home. "The money and the commercialism is so much greater over here [North America]," he concluded. "And sometimes I think we get caught up in it. In Klagenfurt, family, friends and taking care of themselves seemed to be more of a priority than having the nicest car or the biggest house."

After completing one season in Austria, Randy returned to his home base in Pittsburgh to pursue a career in financial services. While still toiling in the NHL, he had put in a few summers learning his trade at Luttner Financial Group Ltd.

In 1993, with his playing days complete, he set up shop with Luttner as a full-time personal, business and estate planner.

"In this business, it takes a long time to develop relationships and to develop a clientele," he explained. "You need to stick in it three or four years before you can really get going. The process we take people through is very time consuming. We're selling estate planning, so you could go two, three, four months with a client before you actually sell him something... I'm just over that three-year period now. My clientele is really starting to build, so, it's been a great move for me."

Although he works in an environment with time lines and deadlines, he still has a lifeline tied to the aspect of his own value system that was tempered by the people of Klagenfurt. On the outside, he may look like just another runner in the race, but somewhere on the inside, in spite of worldly demands, he slips away to a mental mountain in Austria.

Away from the office, Randy coaches a local high-school varsity hockey team. He also participates in local sports celebrity events for worthy causes. There are not enough former Penguin players in the area to sustain a regular alumni team, so he and a handful of other former Penguins join in with local media people and former Steeler players like Jack Lambert and Tunch Ilkin to form a celebrity hockey team which raises money for charity.

Hillman, Larry: *Played defense for Detroit, Boston, Toronto, Minnesota, Montreal, Philadelphia, Los Angeles, Buffalo (NHL), Cleveland and Winnipeg (WHA) from 1954-1976. Born: Kirkland Lake, Ontario, 1937.*

In 1975, Larry Hillman was into his twenty-second consecutive season as a professional hockey player. He wasn't far off the possibility of catching Gordie Howe for the ultimate badge of longevity. It was something he'd at least thought about. But then a contract dispute knocked Larry out of the game like a career-ending injury.

"The problem was that I was making $60,000 a year. Winnipeg was tied in for forty of it and Cleveland for twenty," he explained. "Cleveland

was going under, so Winnipeg was going to get stuck for the sixty if they kept me. They figured it would probably be cheaper just to give me back to Cleveland. But my contract had said that I could not be traded without my written consent, which I wouldn't give. Why would I want to go back to Cleveland who was going under? Winnipeg was still flourishing. So I had to bring a lawsuit on them."

Larry lost the first round, so he filed an appeal which meant he had to sit out for six months, waiting for the proceedings to begin. In the meantime, he got an offer to play for the Calgary Cowboys but was forced to decline because of his dispute with Winnipeg. So he signed on instead as the Cowboys' assistant coach and completed the 1975-76 season behind the bench.

In the spring of 1976, Larry won his appeal. In a surprising turn, he then received an offer from the Jets to be their head coach. He signed a two-year deal, and in his first season, won the Avco Cup with the help of Bobby Hull, Ted Green, Anders Hedberg and Ulf Nilsson.

Going into year two, however, the Jets lost fifteen of their twenty-five starters to the NHL. They also opened the season without a general manager.

Word came in December that John Ferguson would fill the general manager's role. In the interim, Larry did his best to keep the team on track and experienced a fair degree of success. But two months before the end of the season he was fired. "Ferguson wanted to bring in his buddy, Tom McVie," Larry explained.

Larry entertained other coaching offers, but opted instead to leave professional hockey in favour of operating a tourist camp.

"When I was still in Winnipeg," he recounted, "I had bought into a fairly big camp in Manitoba. It was a 200 air-mile fly-in camp... But after I was fired, I didn't have the same feeling for the city, so I sold my percentage to my partners."

Larry took a real-estate course in St. Catharines, Ontario in order to facilitate his ability to purchase a camp somewhere in the province.

He eventually settled on Hillman's Birchway Lodge on Long Lake near Englehart, Ontario in 1981. "It was a small-scale tourist camp," he observed. "There were five housekeeping cottages that I ran from the May 24th weekend until the moose hunt was over in October. Half of our guests were from the States. We'd get the odd hockey player out too. If I had Shackie [Eddie Shack] out there, I'd have to have a beer in his hand and a steak cooking raw!"

Not long after Larry opened his camp, he was beset by a rare disease called Guillain-Barré syndrome. "It can paralyze you right down to where you can only blink your eyelashes and it can kill you," he declared. "It goes to a peak ... and then it just reverses itself. But it's a slow procedure coming back down."

Larry believes that good physical conditioning played a big role in his recovery. He received two weeks of treatment in Toronto and underwent two months of rehab in Kirkland Lake. He eventually attained about a ninety-nine percent recovery.

Larry sold Birchway in June of 1996 after fifteen years of operation.

Even without the lodge, he still manages to keep busy. He has been a director for the Englehart Chamber of Commerce for the past eight years. He runs a hockey camp every August and attends an annual skate-a-thon for Easter Seals in Sudbury. For the past five years, he has helped a thousand kids take a thirty-mile train ride with Santa Claus, featuring entertainers and bags of goodies at the end for each child.

As for his career, Larry is considering options that range from dabbling in real estate to reentering the world of coaching professional hockey.

While discussing the perils of coaching athletes of the nineties, he couldn't resist comparing attitudes of players from his era versus those found in today's game. "In our day, we were much more dedicated," he declared. "I think there are a lot more good-time-Charlie guys playing today. They think about negotiating their contracts first and what type of car they're driving second.

"In sports in the old days, women were probably number one. We couldn't afford big, fancy cars and when we negotiated the next contract, they told us how much they were going to give us and that was that!"

Larry and his wife, Elizabeth, have one daughter and currently make their home in a three-story, A-frame house in the village of Charleton, Ontario.

Nickname: *Morley*

"Johnny Bucyk and I were both playing for Detroit in 1956," Larry recalled. "The Red Wings had bought us all new suitcases after our Stanley Cup win the year before. We put our initials on them, and mine was L.M.H. One day Johnny said, 'What the hell does that *M* stand for?' 'It's Morley, my grandfather's name,' I said.

"So a year went by and Bucyk got traded to Boston for Terry Sawchuk and I end up going to Boston too. Now we had a Larry Leach, a Larry Regan and Larry Hillman there. Milt Schmidt would yell, 'Larry!' You didn't know if it was a forward, a defenseman or in between. Somebody would jump over the boards or sometimes two guys would jump. So Milt Schmidt said, 'Who the hell has got a nickname?' Bucyk stood up and said, 'Morley does!' That's how it originated. Then when I played with my brother, Wayne, in Philly whose nickname was 'Mooner', we became known as 'Mooner and Morley'."

Hollett, Bill (Flash): *Played defense for Toronto, Ottawa, Boston and Detroit from 1933-1946. Born: North Sydney, Nova Scotia, 1912.*

The White Star liner *Titanic* was born onto the open sea on April 10, 1912. The Royal Mail Steamer was well out in the North Atlantic by April 13, when Flash Hollett was born.

Weighing 1,200 tons and held together by three million rivets, the *Titanic* appeared invincible. Flash, on the other hand, weighed about eight pounds and could neither float nor walk.

The *Titanic* was built to outlast Flash and his generation. By April 14, however, an iceberg ripped into her hull, sending the steel giant to the bottom of the Atlantic. At the time, Flash was only a day into his own maiden voyage with an ocean of icebergs to face during the course of his life. But in contrast to the *Titanic*, he is still seaworthy.

Flash leaned back in his chair at the Sheridan Villa rest home where he now resides and made a showcase of his dauntless sense of humour and durability.

"I was seventeen years old in 1929 when the stock market crashed," he recounted. "I had no idea I was going to be a professional athlete at the time. My brother had gotten me a job at Murray Printing at the corner of Queen and Spadina in Toronto. My job was to pour lead into containers, break it up when it got cold and then put the pieces into the type machine. It was very interesting but I didn't have any protective equipment on, so I got sick with lung trouble. I spent the whole winter in the hospital recuperating from lead poisoning. The doctors used a device similar to an apple corer to drain the fluid from my lungs. It got to the point where I would shake all over whenever I saw them coming near me with that thing! They even took out a piece of my rib to make it easier. When I finally got out of the hospital, I couldn't play baseball or hockey for about a year because the guys I used to skate around were skating around me!"

In his weakened state, Flash was unable to make the Ontario Hockey Association, so he joined a local junior church team and played lacrosse with Lionel Conacher during the warm months.

"While I was playing lacrosse," Flash related, "Conn Smythe said, 'If you can play hockey like you play lacrosse, we could use you in the International Hockey League next winter! In the meantime, I'll give you a thousand dollars to play lacrosse and a thousand dollars to come to our training camp to see if you can make the minor leagues.' I didn't have a job, so it was fortunate I played good lacrosse!"

During his training camp with the Leafs in 1933, Flash spotted King Clancy looking the wrong way and flattened him like a floorboard. "The guys were ribbing King because he got

...the way he used to spin a puck.

nailed by a rookie," Flash relayed with a laugh. "But that kind of thing never got him down. After practice he asked me where I would be spending the season. I told him I didn't know and he said, 'Don't worry, I'll put in a word to make sure you get on in Buffalo.' That's the kind of guy King was—150 pounds, all heart and a real prince!"

Flash joined Buffalo of the IHL to start the season. "There were only nine players on the team counting me!" he exclaimed. "The coach said, 'You're going to have to put in a lot of time. If after a month we're not in last place, I'll be satisfied.' At the end of that month, I had

eight goals and we were at the top of the league! Then Ace Bailey's career was ended when he got knocked into a comma by Eddie Shore. So Smythe brought me back to the Leafs and put me with Hap Day for three weeks while Red Horner was serving a suspension. Then Smythe said that Buck Boucher, the coach of the Ottawa Senators, wanted me, so I spent the

Flash Hollett spinning yarns...

remainder of the season there. Smythe threw in an extra 500 bucks."

Flash returned to the Leafs in 1934—but he had yet to be formally accepted by the boys. "If you came up as a rookie, look out because you had to join the club!" he stated with a wary tone. "They put you through an initiation. They got me while we were on the train one night. I was sitting in the smoking room and I didn't suspect anything. But as they came by the door, I heard them whisper, 'Let's go and *get* him!' So I ran up about two cars before they caught me. Big Charlie Conacher, Hap Day and King Clancy were the ring leaders in all these things. They brought me back and said, 'Where's his locker?' They were going to get my hat and cut it into the shape of a tradesman's hat. Somebody said, 'There's his locker over there!' But it wasn't mine, it belonged to Hec Kilrea! So they got Hec's hat, cut it and Charlie wore it."

The ringleaders didn't take missing the

mark lightly, however. Flash's rite of admission would have to exact a larger toll. "They sat around saying, 'Who's the strongest player on the team'?" he recalled. "They'd pretend to argue and put money out to bet. Then they'd say, 'All right, we'll prove it right here and now!' They'd picked two strong guys and had them lay down on the floor. Then they'd say, 'What do you weigh, Flash?' Of course whatever I said, they made damn sure it was the perfect weight they were looking for. So they told me to get down between them—with my arms underneath them of course—and my feet were locked under their feet. Then they took my pants down and dumped a pail of ice on me!"

Flash was now an NHL regular with a few irregular habits that added scope to his vocation. After healing from his bout with lead poisoning years earlier, he had attempted to return to the print shop, but was refused admission by the shop's management who feared for his health.

Instead, he turned to his former school teacher, Mr. Brown, for help. "I said, 'Could you give me a reference so I can try for a job at the Toronto Standard Stock Exchange?' He gave me a swell write-up and I got the job," Flash recounted. "I worked on the exchange floor for three years and for three different brokers. I'd answer the phone, send out mail, I'd do everything—at eight bucks a week! So I developed quite a background in the brokerage business. In fact, I was studying all the time I was playing hockey. When I was in Boston, I used to read the *Wall Street Journal* every day. At one point, I borrowed a book on mining from the University of Toronto and studied drill holes—how lead, zinc and copper had to be a certain width to be commercially viable. I got to where if I could see a drill hole in a newspaper or in *The Northern Miner*, I could tell if they

> *"...I bought Golden Manitou at forty-three cents per share and I sold it at about $4.50. I made 12,000 bucks! I said, 'Okay Florence, away we go'."*
>
> *Flash Hollett*

were hitting these ore bodies. I bought Steep Rock shares at seventy cents and sold them at seven bucks! That was my first killing."

By 1945, the winds of retirement began to blow in Flash's direction. His wife, Florence, had grown tired of big-city life and was no longer willing to accompany him to Detroit during the season. Instead, she waited out the winter at their fruit farm in Clarkson, Ontario with their two children.

Flash had also begun to rub against the abrasive general manager of the Red Wings, Jack Adams. "I was making $6,500 a year in Detroit," Flash complained. "Adams said I could only have a $500 raise because there was a league restriction. But I knew that wasn't true because I knew Eddie Shore was getting $10,000 a year. So I was pretty mad about the way Adams was treating me."

Flash got word that Rangers' president Frank Boucher was attempting to secure his services in New York—the offer: double the salary and an opportunity to be Boucher's right-hand man. But again, Florence was unwilling to take on a life under the lights of New York City. Putting his family first, Flash declined his New York option and said *adios* to Jack Adams and the NHL.

"For the next four years, I lived off of the fruit farm," he recollected. "I used to raise little chickens by letting them run around the orchards. Then at four o'clock in the morning, I'd be off to the St. Lawrence Market in Toronto, selling my apples, pears, peaches and chickens. We survived—I don't know how, but we did."

In 1953, Flash received a call from Joe Primeau who, at the time, was head coach of the Toronto Marlboros. "He said, 'Conn Smythe wants you to come down and help us with the Marlies'," Flash relayed. "They had George Armstrong, Danny Lewicki, Hugh

(From left to right) The author, Flash Hollett and former Canadiens' defenseman Glen Harmon

Bolton—we had a wonderful team. They were twenty-one years old and I was forty-one. I hadn't done anything other than skate on the river in Port Credit. But I said okay. They gave me $250 a week and I needed it. So I went down and the rest is history."

Eventually, the Leafs offered him a coaching position in Pittsburgh. "I was working as a broker for Harold Playfair & Company," he explained. "I was doing all right, so I didn't want to do anything to spoil it by leaving home."

Instead, he made a commitment to remain in the brokerage business. Playfair eventually merged with Andras, Hatch & Heatherington where he served as a junior partner until his retirement in 1977.

As Flash experienced monetary prosperity, he put his fruit-farming days and rattling glass behind him. "The farm was right on the crossroads of the railroad tracks," he complained. "We got sick of trying to listen to the TV with the trains going 'Boo-ooh!!' They used their horns in those days. So I bought Golden Manitou at forty-three cents per share

and I sold it at about $4.50. I made 12,000 bucks! I said, 'Okay Florence, away we go.' She found a house down by the lake in Port Credit—a dandy place. We didn't change our way of living outside of getting a nice home. I just kept doubling and doubling the investments till I had my first heart attack and by then, I had a good pile put away!"

Flash's cardiac troubles flared up while playing basketball at age sixty-five. "We'd won four-straight games," he declared. "I finally said, 'Can you put a guy in my place? I can't go anymore.' They said, 'Like hell we will! You're staying here till we lose!' We had more fun than a picnic. At the end, I had a breakaway. I got under the basket and faked... A guy went over top of me and I put it in and I thought, 'Oh Jeez, I'm dead!—but seven heart attacks later, I'm still here!"

Today, at age eighty-five, Flash remains a vibrant archive of his era. In spite of health problems that could single-handedly maintain a doctor's practice, Flash is a survivor and, to use his own words—he's a real gentleman and a swell guy.

138

Horvath, Bronco: *Played centre for the New York Rangers, Montreal, Boston, Chicago, Toronto and Minnesota between 1955 & 1968. Born: Port Colbourne, Ontario, 1930.*

As a twenty-five-year-old rookie, Bronco Horvath hit NHL ice packing a playmaker's mind and a clean, accurate shot—neither of which seemed apparent during his first two seasons at the top. He came up empty with the Rangers and Canadiens and was subsequently shipped to Boston where he fell into the perfect mix.

Bronco was united with Vic Stasiuk and Johnny Bucyk to form the high-powered "Uke Line," a trio that clicked like a finely-tuned engine. Over the next four years, Bronco netted 215 regular season points. In 1959-60, he lost the league's scoring race to Bobby Hull by a single point.

The following year, however, the "Ukes" were disbanded and Bronco's scoring touch fell into decline. He was traded to Chicago and then returned to New York.

Near the end of the 1962-63 season, his playing rights were traded by the Rangers to the Toronto Maple Leafs. Punch Imlach promptly sent him down to play for Rochester of the American Hockey League.

By early 1968, he was playing for the Leafs' affiliate in Tulsa, Oklahoma under head coach Johnny McClelland. Bronco had just broken his thumb in three places. "I was getting two needles every period just to keep playing!" he exclaimed.

At that time, Bill Masterton of the Minnesota North Stars had just died as a result of an on-ice accident. The North Stars were in need of players and so Minnesota's general manager, Wren Blair, negotiated a deal with Punch Imlach and Joe Crozier. They secured Bronco's services for all games except those played against the Leafs.

With a broken thumb and determination in hand, Bronco left Tulsa for Minnesota. He was still receiving needles between periods. "I remember watching Moose Vasko almost pass out at the sight of one of those needles," he related with a laugh. It may seem funny now, but at the time it was a clear indication of his determination to succeed in his second coming to

the NHL.

After fourteen games with the North Stars, Bronco felt good about his contribution to the team. He also suspects that Crozier and Imlach felt the same way. Imlach promptly called Wren Blair and said he wanted Bronco back to play in Rochester. "Crozier and Imlach were playing games," Bronco recalled. "They said they wanted five players and $50,000 dollars for me!"

Unwilling to meet the Leafs' demands, the North Stars were forced to return Bronco to Rochester. "I could have had a good life in Minnesota," he lamented.

By the end of the following season, he decided to pack it in, having lost interest in playing professional hockey.

He changed course and embarked on a new career in coaching, putting in a year with the London Knights of the Ontario Hockey Association before hooking up with the Cape Cod Cubs, a Boston Bruins' affiliate. With Johnny Crawford in the wings as general manager, Bronco applied himself to a long career of player development. "Nick Fotiu was my prodigy," he declared proudly.

Bronco has since retired from the Cubs and is taking his life at a slower pace these days. Although golf was his primary hobby, arthritis now prevents him from holding a club.

He and his wife, Dolly, continue to make their home in Cape Cod, Massachusetts. Over the years, they have raised a son and a daughter who in turn, have added three grandchildren to the clan.

Howatt, Garry: *Played left wing for the New York Islanders, Hartford and New Jersey from 1972-1984. Born: Grand Center, Alberta, 1952.*

Known as "Toy Tiger" during his days with the New York Islanders, Garry Howatt was trouble's twin brother. There were no dark alleys in the NHL upon which he feared to tread. And although he stood only 5'9" and 175 pounds, he waged effective battle against any willing foe who lurked the league. As retribution, he received 2,125 career penalty minutes or roughly thirty-five hours of game time to contemplate his deeds.

Along the way, Garry had the good fortune to partake in two of the Islanders' four Stanley Cup victories before being dispatched to the Hartford Whalers. There, he racked up a personal-high fifty points and 242 penalty minutes in one season. He then concluded his career under a dark cloud of the New Jersey Devils in 1983-84.

"I'm not happy with what I accomplished in the NHL, because I felt that I could have played at least another three years," he related. "I mean I'd asked to be traded from the Islanders when they didn't want me to ask. And then I was a frigin free agent in Hartford when they'd offered me a real good contract and wanted me to be their team captain. But I made the mistake of listening to a couple of former teammates that were then with the Devils who said, 'Come on over here!' So I did, but I had a problem with the Devils' organization. But hey, that's life. I should have listened to my wife. She was the one who said we shouldn't leave the Island when I did. And then she said we shouldn't leave Hartford when I did. So if I would have listened to her the first time, then who knows, I might have been with the Islanders, coaching or whatever. But it worked out for the best, and now—my wife thinks she's the boss!"

Since leaving hockey, Garry's decision-making powers have made a full recovery. His

> *"Well I never really liked anybody telling me what to do."*
>
> Garry Howatt

first test run came when he spotted a thirty-six-acre tract of commercial property in Mount Freedom, New Jersey. His instincts, his wife and his partner said, 'Buy!' and prosperity has been quick to follow. "I don't think it was much of a risk," he said of his initial outlay. "It was just a good piece of property. My wife and myself are here all the time and it's been a lot of fun to watch it grow over the last fourteen years."

"Originally," he continued, "the place had a thirty-five-year-old driving range on it, a little pitch-and-putt par three and a miniature golf course."

Since making the initial purchase, he and his wife, Karen, have worked steadfastly to rebuild all the original facilities and add new features as well. They christened the place "Mount Freedom Golf".

"Now I've got a big driving range, batting cages, a nine-hole pitch-and-putt par-three course, a miniature golf course and a snack-bar centre," he declared. "The old house here was over a hundred years old. I lived in it for the first five years. Then I built the bottom into a big snack bar and I'm going to redo the top into apartments."

Garry's work at Mount Freedom involves eight solid months of intense work with little time to do anything but service the facility. The upside, however, is he's now his own boss.

"Well I never really liked anybody telling me what to do," he quipped with a laugh. "So I like it. If anybody screws up, it's my fault. I've got nobody else to blame. And I'm not going to an office every morning. I wore suits for twelve, fourteen years playing hockey. Now I put in about fifteen hours a day, but if I've got to go somewhere, I just go!"

Such pressing priorities take him to West Point Academy to watch his son play hockey; to Connecticut or New York to play oldtimers' hockey; and best of all, to check in on a second investment with a driving range that is ringing in the cash in Commack, Long Island.

Howell, Harry: *Played defense for the New York Rangers, Oakland, California, Los Angeles (NHL), the New York Raiders, the New Jersey Knights, San Diego and Calgary (WHA) from 1952-1976. Born: Hamilton, Ontario, 1932.*

During his twenty-fourth season in professional hockey, forty-three-year-old Harry Howell tipped his dusty hat to Mother Time and made his final ride for the Calgary Cowboys of the World Hockey Association in 1976.

It marked the end of a distinguished career that began back in 1952 when, as a Guelph Biltmore Madhatter, he was summoned by Rangers' general manager Frank Boucher to give his club a tune-up. Harry joined the team's blueline corps and quickly evolved into one of the league's top defensive defensemen. In 1967, he was named as a first-team all-star and awarded the James Norris Trophy as the NHL's top rearguard.

After seventeen reliable seasons in New York, he then took on the frontier towns of Oakland and Los Angeles before rounding out his on-ice career in the WHA.

As an elite member of the order of longevity, Harry's knowledge and experience had rendered him a desirable candidate for the management side of hockey. Bill McCreary of the Cleveland Barons took notice and wasted little time in procuring his services as an assistant general manager.

But halfway through his first season, Bill McCreary was fired. So Harry got the nod as the club's general manager for the next two years.

"Then I moved to Minnesota as a result of the Cleveland-Minnesota merger," he recalled. "Lou Nanne was already a GM there, so I coached for a short stint before becoming chief scout for the Stars for the next ten years."

In 1987, however, Lou Nanne was replaced by Jack Ferreira as the team's new general manager. "He got rid of everybody and brought in his own people," Harry explained of his departure from Minnesota.

He then went straight from the North Stars' organization to his present position as pro scout

"To me, getting into the Hall of Fame was my Stanley Cup—and I went in with a couple of half-decent players in Bobby Orr and Henri Richard."

Harry Howell

for the Edmonton Oilers. "Nowadays, I cover the western NHL teams and the IHL," he noted. "Although I used to cover the East and West divisions of the NHL."

But as league expansion extended its reach over time, he was gradually enveloped by more teams and more personnel than any one man could hope to cover. The Oilers agreed and brought in fresh troops. "Pete Mahovlich, who coached the Cape Breton Oilers in '94-95, is now the pro scout for the East Coast," Harry reported with relief.

"Basically we scout teams that are farm clubs for the NHL teams. We rate all the minor-league players and [decide] which ones we would prefer in case a deal were to come up or a player were to become a free agent.

"We have our own little code that we use. If we really desire a player, he would be a 'one'. If we don't like a player he would be a 'six'. If we're lucky enough to get a 'one' in a trade then we take him right way. In between, it'll be a discussion."

As a senior observer and participant in the NHL since 1952, Harry is of course acutely aware of how hockey has evolved over the years. "It's a completely different game [today]," he concluded. "When I was there, we had sixteen-man rosters during the fifties and early sixties. We had 110 or 115 players in the whole National Hockey League. Now twenty-six teams times twenty players plus all your farm teams means the opportunity is there for a lot more people to play. They are taking advantage of it because if you do happen to make the National League, you're set for life. The carrot's out there—everybody has a chance! It wouldn't be bad being sixteen years old again!"

The pinnacle of Harry's post-playing career came with his induction into the Hockey Hall of Fame in 1979. "That was very, very exciting!" he exclaimed. "I had never won a Stanley Cup as a player. And of course you talk to anybody and that's the ultimate thrill in hockey... To me, getting into the Hall of Fame *was* my Stanley Cup—and I went in with a couple of half-decent players in Bobby Orr and Henri Richard. Part of my speech was that I wished I'd played with them instead of against them throughout my whole career. But it was a thrill! There still aren't that many people in the Hall of Fame. There are a heck of a lot more people with their names on the Stanley Cup than are in the Hall... That's one way of looking at how important it is."

Today, Harry's choice of an engaging workout takes him onto the charity golf circuit where he enjoys old friends and a hearty whack at the ball. "I'm not very good," he admitted, "but I like the walking and the fresh air." He also enjoys relaxing at his cottage during the off-season.

He and his wife, Marilyn, have raised a daughter and a son, the latter of whom died as a result of an accident in 1976. They have two grandchildren who live only ten minutes away from their Hamilton home, much to Harry's pleasure.

Ingarfield, Earl: *Played centre for the New York Rangers, Pittsburgh, Oakland and California from 1958-1971. Born: Lethbridge, Alberta, 1934.*

Earl Ingarfield played his hockey with the heart and consistency of a blue-collar man. He'd show up for work with a lunch pail and stick, punch in at the time clock and hit the ice—no fanfare, just an honest night's work. He first checked in at Madison Square Gardens in 1958, a time when Ranger on-ice fortunes were in danger of bankruptcy. He added some solvency to the line-up, especially when flanked by Andy Bathgate and Dean Prentice.

Although never prolific in any aspect of his game, Earl was a quality skater who possessed a respectable shot that, during the course of thirteen seasons with New York, Pittsburgh and Oakland, brought home 405 career points.

His steadiness as a player and as a person can be traced directly to his home life, which, no matter where he was stationed as a player, was always firmly anchored in his native Lethbridge, Alberta.

Retirement from the California Golden Seals in 1971, however, forced Earl to abandon his tradition. He'd signed on as head coach of the Regina Pats junior team, a move which required him to take up residence in Saskatchewan while his family remained in Lethbridge.

One season of separation, though, was more than enough for the Ingarfields. "My wife and family weren't interested in moving," he recounted. "We still had a young daughter and we were just building a new home." So at the end of the season Earl and the Pats parted ways.

The following year offered up a ground-floor post as a scout with the newly formed New York Islanders. The job allowed him to do his work while remaining based in Lethbridge. But halfway through their first campaign, Phil Goyette was fired as head coach and Earl was brought in to salvage the season. Having rallied Islander fortunes, he was invited to lead his charges on a permanent but dubious basis—an offer he wisely refused, preferring the cool solitude of life as a scout.

After two additional campaigns which included his involvement in the acquisition of Bryan Trottier, Earl traded scouting for the excitement of his own venture in his own backyard. The arrival of the Lethbridge Broncos of the Western Hockey League spelled opportunity—to which he responded by purchasing the team and serving as the club's assistant GM and coach for two-and-a-half seasons.

Nickname Challenge #13

Pie Face

"There used to be a chocolate bar in Canada quite a few years ago. It was kind of round in the shape of a puck and it was called 'Pie Face'. The logo had a little, wee body with a larger head. Gerry Melnyk said, 'Gee, you look like that *Pie Face*.' So that's how it started. Of course I had a lot of other nicknames—'Short Ass', 'Stumpy' and 'Mickey Rooney'. When you're short, they pick on you."

Who is he?

Clues

a. He played right wing for Chicago, Detroit, the New York Rangers and Boston of the NHL and Philadelphia, Vancouver, Minnesota, Cincinnati and New England of the WHA between 1958 & 1979.

b. He won two Stanley Cups with the Boston Bruins.

If your puck is still frozen,
see page 285.

By then he was ready for a break and a local radio station provided the perfect escape. He signed on as a sales manager and spent the next five years courting regional advertising.

But Earl and hockey are like a gem in a ring—the one is the setting for the other. And as such he resumed his scouting career with the New York Islanders in 1982. These days, his primary focus is on the three major-junior leagues, the U.S. high schools and colleges and occasionally, the National League itself.

Earl's main source of diversion during the off-season is to hit the fairways with his wife, Grace, for a round of golf.

He and Grace have raised two daughters and one son, Earl Jr., who had a brief stint in the NHL with Calgary and Detroit.

***

Irvine, Ted: *Played left wing for Boston, Los Angeles, the New York Rangers and St. Louis between 1963 & 1977. Born: Winnipeg, Manitoba, 1944.*

When Ted Irvine was on top of his game, his 6'2", 195-pound frame was subject to a burst of energy that set hard skating, heavy checking, occasional fighting and streaks of scoring in motion. He was a role player who could rival a miner when it came to digging in corners and staking claims against opposing wingers.

Off ice, Ted practised a different brand of dynamism in maintaining a long-standing commitment to the well-being of his native Winnipeg, Manitoba. When retirement came in St. Louis in 1977, there was little question that Winnipeg would continue to be his power spot.

He did, however, run into some surprises as he launched his second career. "When I quit hockey to go into the business world, I thought it would be an easy transition," he admitted. "But then I found it took a lot more education and a lot more discipline than I realized. It was not at all what I expected... I found that leaving the game and going into the financial-planning world was tough ... I just didn't have the education. I was three, four, five years behind everybody else. I was still living like an ... athlete, still spending like an athlete, and my ego was still like an athlete's. It took me a long time to get everything in sync..."

To bring himself up to par, Ted began an intensive period of study in the field of business. The challenge, however, was to know when he had crossed the threshold of knowledge he needed to put himself on a level with his peers.

"There's a Gretzky, a Messier and then there's an Irvine," he remarked. "You know what your order is and you've got a role to play. In the business world, I've always checked: 'Is there anybody else doing this? Am I doing it the right way?' Somebody said just last week, 'Forget about comparing yourself with everybody else. Go do your thing—you're good at it. You can't keep worrying about what everybody else is doing!' And in sports, I never did. With New York, my role was to be on the checking line. I knew that was my role so I didn't have to be a Jean Ratelle or a Vic Hadfield or Rod Gilbert. In the business world ... you should be doing what your strength is and take satisfaction from it..."

As part of his initial training, Ted secured an insurance license as the basis for founding Ted Irvine Financial Services. At present, retirement planning provides the central core of his business. He helps NHLers like the Sutter brothers, Kelly Kisio, and Joe Sakic as well as members of the local community to build their portfolios using products like mutual funds and guaranteed investment certificates.

Ted also became associated with the Special Olympics movement early on in his professional hockey career. During his first years with the project, he had observed some resistance to accepting the potential of special-needs children. This intrigued him, so on retiring from the NHL, he teamed up with a local teacher named Dan Johnson and together they launched the new Manitoba chapter.

"We started from scratch," Ted declared. "I

"That's why there's so much oldtimers' hockey ... that's one time in your life that you were king of the castle!"

Ted Irvine

remember having the kids run up and down the school hallway because they didn't know how to run in a straight line. Now ... the kids lift weights, speed skate, play soccer and baseball. It's been one of the greatest thrills of my life to be a part of the whole thing."

Ted also works with the Winners' Foundation, an organization designed to educate athletes about drug and alcohol abuse.

"We've been invited into a lot of different dressing rooms to talk to kids about the effects of alcohol and drugs on an athlete and how it sneaks up on you," he explained. "The one asset we have is that, being former players, we bring a certain comradery. No matter what age they are, we know what's going on in the dressing room. You know what's going on in the player's head... We talk about the moulding of a young hockey player, how it starts at such an early age. They're the king of the castle. They can do no wrong and they're infallible. That's what we do to young people. Aunts and uncles, grammas and grampas, moms and dads, brothers and sisters put these kids on a pedestal and [they] get a little bit of a mislead on life.

"What we say to young people is, 'You've been under a lot of pressure without anybody knowing it. You can't react to certain things because you've got a role to play...' I just know that when the athletes go home at night, whether they have had a good game or a bad game ... they're now alone with their own minds. It becomes very lonely for them sometimes. So we try to tell them, 'We know what you've gone through... You are a different type person. But we also know that you're going through some fears and hurts and pains ... that sometimes you don't know how to express. You can do it in the dressing room sometimes but you can't do it with other people.'

"That's why there's so much oldtimers' hockey. It's called comradery. It's called getting in the dressing room and reliving the past. It's very difficult to explain that feeling. Women call it male bonding. 'How come you guys sit in the dressing room till one o'clock in the morning and tell stories from twenty years ago about who scored the goal?' they ask. Because that's one time in your life that you were king of the castle!"

Ted has also had his hand and voice in the broadcasting business as a colour analyst for local radio and television on behalf of the now-departed Winnipeg Jets.

Away from Winnipeg and the office, his love is boating in Washington state. Having been bitten by the rugged beauty of the place, he and his wife, Bonnie, bought a home in Sudden Valley as well as a 30' power cruiser. They spend a lot of their time cruising the American San Juans and exploring the islands. They also enjoy the tranquility of their lake home and the frequent visitations of deer, geese and ducks.

Joyal, Ed: *Played centre for Detroit, Toronto, Los Angeles, Philadelphia (NHL), Alberta and Edmonton (WHA) between 1962 & 1976. Born: Edmonton, Alberta, 1940.*

Ed Joyal grew up in a land where icicles, frozen fingers and tundra toes were indistinguishable. The time was the mid-forties. The site was the small town of St. Albert, a tad north-west of Edmonton, Alberta.

"We lived right alongside the river," he recollected. "When I was about five or six years old, my mother used to put my brothers' skates on me while they were in school. It was downhill to the river and they had iced it over. So you could put the skates on in the house and just coast down onto the ice. My mother would push me down there and I'd stay on the river practically all day. She'd say, 'Make sure you come back home before your brothers get in so they don't find out you're using their skates!' I spent a lot of time when I was younger on those rivers and ponds."

Ed followed a continuum from rivers to ponds to rinks and eventually to the NHL. He was into his second season with the Detroit Red Wings in

1963-64. By April of that year, the Wings were embroiled in a disagreement with the Maple Leafs over who had a right to hoist the Cup. Game five started with the series deadlocked. The match was knotted at one-all when Ed Joyal picked up the puck on his opposite wing. A quick glance at Johnny Bower in net, a glance back at the puck and Ed proceeded to slide a life-long memory past Johnny's agile feet. "I just let go with a wrist shot," he proudly recounted. "It went right along the ice and just happened to catch the corner. I don't think Johnny was ready for the shot. I'd scored the winning goal in the Gardens. The game was on television with my friends watching. I loved it!"

There was never a more gratifying moment in his career. He had brought the Wings to within one victory of seizing the Stanley Cup—but unfortunately for Ed, it was as close as he'd ever get. The Leafs took the next two games and the championship.

Ed eventually settled in with the Los Angeles Kings where he put up his most prolific offensive numbers during the late sixties and early seventies. After a brief stint in Philadelphia, he then jumped to the World Hockey Association where he rounded out his career in the service of the Edmonton Oilers in 1976. Fourteen seasons of professional hockey was enough. "You get the feeling that the game may be passing you by," he quipped with a laugh.

"I met my wife, Dori, while I was in L.A.," he continued. "I took her up to Edmonton during my four years with the Oilers. She didn't like the cold and neither did I, so when I retired, we headed to San Diego. When I played for the Kings, I used to go down there with some of the guys and I really liked the place.

"When we first started out, Dori got her real-estate license while I baby-sat our boy. Then I got my license while Dori baby-sat for a while. Eventually we started doing real estate together. Now she does most of the selling while I do the stuff in the background."

During the course of their long career in the business, they acquired a home with a large residential lot on the edge of a canyon in the La

Mesa area of San Diego. The property is graced by fifteen lime and thirty avocado trees along with the house and gardens.

Ed and Dori also invested money in various income properties in the area. Over the ensuing years, they've sold some while renting others as an extra source of income.

"We owned two four-plexes down by the ocean," Ed explained. "But there are a lot of wild people down there... If you don't get the right people in, you can really get hurt. We made a couple of mistakes along the way and we paid for it, so we eventually sold them. I didn't particularly like going down there and kicking people out. You never know what they're going to do when you tell them to leave."

Ed spends his spare time playing oldtimers' hockey in a local over-thirty league. "I also like rollerblading two or three times a week," he added. "And I tend to the trees and the gardens as well."

Nickname: *The Jet*

While playing for the Los Angeles Kings, team owner Jack Kent Cooke referred to Ed as "The Jet". "He thought I was a fast skater," Ed related.

Juzda, Bill: *Played defense for the New York Rangers and Toronto between 1940 & 1952. Born: Winnipeg, Manitoba, 1920.*

"I was with the New York Rangers after the war," Bill Juzda recollected, speaking of his return to the NHL after several years in the Air Force. "We signed our contract in Winnipeg but didn't realize that the cost of living in New York was higher. We talked to Lester Patrick about it, but he said, 'You signed it, that's it!' Then while we were playing the Wings in Detroit, we talked to a union man named Murphy. A reporter had seen us and the next day's headlines read: 'Rangers Talking Union.' Lester Patrick promptly awarded us all a $500 cost-of-living bonus with the understanding that there was to be no more union talk. So what do you make of that?"

One thing that Bill himself didn't "make of

that" was a whole lot of cash. "We didn't earn enough money as players to take the summers off," he reported.

To make ends meet, he nurtured a second career with the railway—a line of work that would willingly bend to the seasonal terms of professional hockey.

The origin of his intrigue for boxcars and engines can be easily traced to the boyhood haunts where those mammoth machines of ultimate affect rumbled past his home.

"I didn't live very far from the railroad tracks," he recounted. "You'd just go up the street near the CPR station in Winnipeg and there they were! And of course when I was a kid, I'd see one of those big engines going by and I naturally wanted to become an engineer."

As a young man, Bill took the first step towards his goal by becoming what was known as a wiper. For the curious wage of 32¼ cents an hour, his job was to keep the engines glistening. "They used to have those steam engines for passenger trains," he explained. "And to make them look real shiny, you had to squirt oil on them and polish the engines, the cabs and the tender.

"Then from a wiper you went on to be a fireman—this is when you had to shovel coal, which was hard work! But later, they brought in automatic stokers and after that ... oil burners. So you didn't have to shovel any more coal."

After five years of sweat and polish, Bill finally climbed aboard as a full-fledged engineer. At about the same time, he also entered the NHL as a full-fledged blueliner. The irony was that when winters came and he hit the ice, it was often difficult to distinguish which of the two professions he was engaged in. Running into the extended hip of his 5'8", 203-pound body was not unlike a head-on encounter with a train.

He was able to maintain his dual career until the end of the 1952-53 season after having spent one season in the American Hockey League with Pittsburgh. "At that point, I devoted my full-time energy to working as an engineer," he explained.

Bill rode the 132-mile stretch of rail between Winnipeg and Brandon, Manitoba for the

Canadian Pacific Railway over the next twenty-seven years. And as he modestly describes it, the work was pretty straight forward. "You'd get on the engine and away you'd go," he stated. "And then away you'd come back." In 1980, at age sixty, he finally decided it was time to take life at an easier pace.

Since then, he has spent his time curling during the winter and golfing during the summer. As well, he and his wife, Beryl, take pleasure in slipping away from their home in Winnipeg to spend time at their cottage on a lake—a getaway enjoyed by their two sons and four grandchildren as well.

Nickname: *The Beast*

"When I was with the New York Rangers, I used to grab ahold of Edgar Laprade or Tony Leswick and squeeze, leaving purple marks on them," Bill recalled. "They would yell back, 'You damn beast!' I guess I didn't know my own strength."

Keenan, Larry: *Played left wing for Toronto, St. Louis, Buffalo and Philadelphia between 1961 & 1972. Born: North Bay, Ontario, 1940.*

According to Larry Keenan, about thirty percent of the players of his day had sufficient star status to garner multi-year contracts and a good night's sleep. The other seventy percent were what he called fringe players on edge—and Larry counted himself among them.

"Outside of my first year of pro, I signed all one-year contracts and I was never signed before I went to training camp," he recounted. "There was a lot of pressure on you... But I think being used to going to bed at night, not knowing if you're going to be traded or where you're going to be the next day ... probably helps you cope with the pressures outside of hockey once you get into business."

Larry's ascent towards the pro ranks gained its first real momentum as he played junior at St. Michael's College in the late fifties. He then donned a Maple Leaf jersey for two games in 1960-61 before being consigned to the minors where he remained until the league expansion of

1967 made journeymen a desirable commodity. The fledgling St. Louis Blues were quick to capitalize on Larry's experience, opening the door to his most sustained period of productivity. He then rounded out his NHL career with Buffalo and finally, Philadelphia in 1972.

From the Flyers, he went on to harness two additional seasons with their farm team, the Richmond Robins of the American Hockey League. Under the wiley guidance of head coach Johnny "Iron Man" Wilson, Larry enjoyed a rewarding time until injuries forced an end to his career.

He then resettled in his hometown of North Bay, Ontario where he and a partner set up a fitness-club business. The next four years would be replete with lessons hard learned. Tensions grew as the partnership failed to gel and, unlike today, the general public had yet to be seized with an obsession for fitness. Without the necessary clientele base, they were forced to shut down.

"The experience wasn't that great," he admitted. "I lost a few dollars... Today or even ten years later, I would have done things a lot differently ... if I'd been able to survive."

Larry followed up with a job as a sales rep and public-relations man for Pepsi-Cola Garland Beverages in North Bay for a number of years.

Then, in 1991, he created his own coffee-supply business called "K-Koffee Services". "I supply coffee to businesses, offices and to whoever wants it," he explained. "I have drip machines and I sell coffee to restaurants too."

Being his own boss—the second time around—has been much more to Larry's liking. Hard work and long hours now roll off his back like a duck in charge of his own pond.

He and his wife, Lois, have raised two sons and a daughter. One son, Cory Keenan, played for the Kitchener Rangers of the OHA and was on the Memorial Cup all-star team with Eric Lindros. He was drafted by the Hartford Whalers but elected instead to go to university. He presently plays hockey in Europe.

For the last ten years, Larry has spent his spare time coaching a local triple-A midget team. He also finds pleasure in golfing, fishing and working around the yard.

Nickname: *Kiss*

"The name that I had and is still used around North Bay is 'Kiss'," Larry said. "I used to eat *Kiss* candies a lot and so it stuck."

Kennedy, Forbes: *Played centre for Chicago, Detroit, Boston, Philadelphia and Toronto between 1956 & 1969. Born: Dorchester, New Brunswick, 1935.*

Twenty-one-year-old Forbes Kennedy saw his first NHL action as a Chicago Black Hawk in 1956. Ice shavings flew as he hit the ice like a bulldozer with faulty brakes. He banged and bashed his way around the end boards of every rink in the league, taking on foes of any size or disposition.

Such intense physical contact, however, gradually took its toll over the years. By 1969, he still had a competitive mind, but his body was bruised and failing.

"I had had two operations on my knee," he revealed. "That's why I quit. I couldn't play anymore."

After leaving the Toronto Maple Leafs at the end of the 1969 season, Forbes embarked on a string of consecutive coaching assignments that remains unbroken to this day. He coached teams in Corner Brook, Newfoundland; Cap-Bolle, New Brunswick; Winston-Salem, South Carolina; Richmond, Virginia; and Summerside, Prince Edward Island.

He has occupied his present post as coach of the Charlottetown A&S Scrap Metal Abbies since 1984. "At one time we had five kids from our team in the OHA," he declared with pride. "In one year we lost four top players. But that's what we're here for. We like to see the kids go away and do well. We never hold them back."

Now well established in Charlottetown, Forbes spends his summers working for the Charlottetown Recreation Department. Being in the vicinity of so many sports fields has allowed him to coach minor-league baseball for the past fifteen years. These days, at age sixty-two, he has reduced his workload to preparing and maintaining all the baseball diamonds and

soccer fields in the city. During the rest of the year, he turns his attention to coaching the Abbies.

Sadly, his wife, Marie, passed away in 1989 after a battle with cancer. Together, they had raised two sons and two daughters.

Today, Forbes spends his recreation time slicing up the fairways. "I'm no good at it!" he exclaimed with laughter. "I like it ... but I don't care what my score is as long as I get out and play!"

Nickname Challenge #14

Tuna

"I got the name while I was playing in Minnesota. Players with Maritime roots are usually associated with fish, so they called me 'Tuna'."

Who is he?

Clues

a. He played left wing for Montreal, Minnesota, Detroit and Los Angeles between 1965 & 1979.

b. He won the Calder Trophy as rookie of the year in 1969.

If you were unable to split the defense, see page 285.

Klukay, Joe: *Played left wing for Toronto and Boston from 1946-1956. Born: Sault Ste. Marie, Ontario, 1922.*

Red Wing iron man
Joe Klukay

Joe Klukay was a quintessential role player with a likeable personality who became a welcome addition to the 1946 edition of the Toronto Maple Leafs. His were the very qualities that helped the club's chemistry to a Stanley Cup mix—a balance that sustained the Leafs to four championships in five years.

When teamed with Nick Metz, he was peerless in the art of penalty killing. He also made a solid and consistent third-line winger in the company of Max Bentley.

By 1955, at age thirty-three, Joe had slowed a step and began to see his numbers decline. Eighteen games into the schedule, he was approached by Leafs' general manager Hap Day, who said, "Joe, if you go down to Pittsburgh and play, there may be a coaching job there for you." With his interest piqued, he joined the Hornets until, much to his surprise, the team folded forcing him to host other offers.

He initially considered settling in Toronto to take a run at the art of sales. "I tried it there," he recounted. "But I couldn't sell anything. And that gave me a little nudge to get the hell out of there."

Joe later received a job offer from Tony Wisne, the owner of Progressive Tool and Die based in Detroit. Wisne had recently purchased the Windsor Bulldogs, a senior-league club in the Ontario Hockey Association. Joe took the opportunity to join the team as a player and also to learn the tool-and-die trade at the same time.

The following year, Wisne sold the Bulldogs. Joe, however, continued skating for the team until 1962 when they won the Allen Cup with Harry Watson as head coach. The next season, Joe assumed the club's helm as they joined the International Hockey League. "But things were tentative as far as salaries were concerned," he explained. "We only lasted about another month in the league and then we folded up. That was my coaching tenure."

And as the Bulldogs finally went, so did Joe's career in hockey. He gathered up his memories and moved on to a new life as a full-time man at Progressive Tool and Die. "I've always been a machine operator," he stated. "There were a few opportunities to have moved into sales, but I don't think I could sell..."

"...I couldn't sell anything. And that gave me a little nudge to get the hell out of there."

Joe Klukay

After forty years with the company and at age seventy-five, Joe is still manning his machine. "Well I'll tell you that the big thing is the hospitalization," he remarked. "I work at an average of two maybe three days a week. I give [Wisne] whatever hours I want. He keeps me on as a full-time employee and that's with all the benefits. So I can't ask for anything more than that. He's treated me fabulously!"

As a diversion, Joe enjoys golf, fishing and hunting. He and his wife, Francis, live in Southfield, Michigan which also allows him to don the blades as an honourary member of the Detroit Red Wing oldtimers' team. "Last year we played twenty-eight games for charity," he declared. "So it's not like I'm just seeing guys at funerals and weddings. We see each other a couple of times a week."

He also keeps a close eye on today's NHL. "I enjoy watching it," he said. "There's a multitude of good hockey players. The only thing that turns me off is this crosschecking across the back of the neck and the kidneys. I can't remember ever being subject to anything like that. Maybe once a year. But this seems to go on quite a bit now. Somebody's going to get seriously injured or paralyzed, I'm sure, because that's a vital area to be taking a stick to. And a lot of those sticks are now aluminum."

Korab, Jerry: *Played defense for Chicago, Vancouver, Buffalo and Los Angeles from 1970-1985. Born: Sault Ste. Marie, Ontario, 1948.*

Putting an exclamation point to the end of Jerry Korab's career was preceded by a flurry of question marks, "sort of's" and "maybe's".

Jerry had hung up the blades at the end of the 1982-83 season. He returned to his home in Chicago with plans to take a year off and reflect on his new career path. But a funny thing happened on the way to the stadium.

While attending a Blackhawks' game in December of 1983, he became a wanted man. "I was sitting in the sky box with all the press guys," he recounted. "As I'm going through there, I bumped into Jack Davidson who was the assistant general manager of the Blackhawks. He said, 'Would you be interested in coaching in Milwaukee?' which was Chicago's farm team at that time. They wanted me to go down to coach and play. Meanwhile, the game goes on and after the second period, I bump into Joe Crozier who was, at that time, the assistant coach for the Buffalo Sabres. He asked me what I'd been doing. Had I been skating and of course I said, 'Yeah, I'm staying in shape (laughs).' And he said, 'Scotty Bowman wants to see you after the game.' And I said, 'You've got to be kidding!' And he said, 'No, we're thinking about bringing you back to Buffalo to play.' So I went from not having a job to two job offers in one night just because I went to a hockey game!"

Jerry was keen to rejoin the NHL, so he accepted Buffalo's bid and came out of retirement to complete the 1983-84 campaign.

The following season, he was not invited back to the Sabres' training camp. So he retired again and returned to his home in Chicago with plans to take a year off to reflect on his new career path.

Then, another funny thing happened to him on the way to the stadium. Early in the 1984-85 season, Craig Hartsburg of the Minnesota North Stars had broken his ankle and the team found itself in the market for an experienced blueliner who could steady their young defense. Lou Nanne, the North Stars' general manager, invited Jerry to join the club immediately.

"I thought, 'Oh God, this is great. It's an even better opportunity than I had the year before'," he related. "I figured with Minnesota I could probably end up getting a couple of years. They wanted me within a day and I said, 'Well, I have to go home and talk to my wife about it.' And obviously it didn't matter what she said, I was going anyway ... even if she said no!"

Jerry signed his new contract just after the waiver draft, so he had to go on twenty-four-hour waiver in order to get passed by the league. He'd been practising with the team for three days and was settling in quite nicely. But somewhere deep down in his shin guards, he had an uneasy feeling.

"We were waiting and waiting. It was five minutes to twelve," he recounted. "We got a phone call. Guess who it was from? Scotty Bowman! Now the last team I expected to pick me up was Buffalo because they'd just let me go the year before. So Scotty Bowman picked me up at five minutes to twelve and I said, 'You've gotta be kidding me!' Now I've got all my friends calling me from Buffalo going, 'Jesus Christ, you're coming back again. We just got rid of you'!"

Jerry finished the 1984-85 campaign with the Sabres and then retired for keeps. In retrospect, he figures that Scotty's machinations probably cost him an extra big-league season as a North Star.

His on-ice plans were nixed, but a warm trail of contacts beckoned him in Buffalo. He stuck around for an additional year to work for the

Sabres' Public Relations Department. He hosted a post-game show called *Kong's Corner* where he interviewed the night's first star for about five minutes. He also did colour analysis for Sabres' broadcasts.

Public relations work, however, was not enough to engage the full breadth of his interests. So, as the season closed, he pulled up stakes in favour of Chicago where he could retreat to renovate his home and evaluate his hazy options.

"I was in limbo," he confessed. "I sent out a lot of resumes to Coca-Cola, Pepsi and the beer companies—the usual jobs that a hockey player would get into."

"I was in limbo. I sent out a lot of resumes to Coca-Cola, Pepsi and the beer companies—the usual jobs that a hockey player would get into."

Jerry Korab

But before Jerry received any replies, his job search was cut short by a friend with know-how to share about the packaging business. "I sat down with him," he recalled, "and he started going through all the different items that I could buy from a manufacturer and resell. And I said, 'Forget it. It would take me twenty years to learn all this stuff'!"

On the surface his logic gave a definite "no", but his straggling insight whispered "maybe", until the verdict was overturned. Within the two months that followed, he was selling tape to every team in the NHL. Inevitably, people began to request other packaging items, and before he knew it, Jerry had his own business up and running under the name "Korab Inc".

Ten years later, he has progressed from learning the ropes to tying the knots of the packaging field. "I can supply almost anything from A to Z," he asserted with confidence.

Jerry and his wife, Mary Ann, raised one son and have remained settled in Chicago. Recreation time means regular dates on the fairways and greens plus a semi-solid skate with the Blackhawk oldtimers every Friday afternoon.

Koroll, Cliff: *Played right wing for Chicago from 1969-1980. Born: Canora, Saskatchewan, 1946.*

Cliff Koroll and Keith Magnuson were like two feathers in a Blackhawks' head dress. Throughout their careers, the two made a habit of being at the same place at the same time.

Both men played hockey for the University of Denver in the late sixties; both were drafted by the Chicago Blackhawks, joining the team in 1969; and both players retired from Chicago during the 1979-80 campaign.

It seemed fitting then that the two teamed up to coach the Hawks for the 1980-81 season—Keith as head coach and Cliff as an assistant.

But their concurrent paths finally diverged, at the point of the 1981-82 season when Keith Magnuson was fired. Cliff, by contrast, survived the purge to prosper under the regimes of Bob Pulford and Orval Tessier. He also put in a season as head coach of the Milwaukee Admirals, the Blackhawks' affiliate in the International Hockey League.

In 1987, however, Bob Murdoch came in as Chicago's newest head coach. He came armed with his own set of assistants, so Cliff grabbed his chance to join the front office where he could pursue his interest in the management side of the game.

"I did a little bit of everything: sales, marketing, public relations and community relations," he explained.

He stayed at it until the end of the 1988-89 season when the winds of change turned into a bad breeze. "Mike Keenan was brought in and that's when I decided it was time to pursue another career," he asserted. "There wasn't any light at the end of the tunnel with him coming in... The way the deal was set up, [Keenan] was going to coach and then ... become the general manager. There weren't going to be any opportunities for advancement under those circumstances."

Cliff's reality check lead him to a reluctant

resignation. As the club's pillar of continuity over two preceding decades, his departure was, to say the least, anticlimactic. "I was twenty-one years in professional hockey, all with the same team," he remarked. "I was never traded, nor was I ever fired. I counted my blessings and figured it was time to move on."

"I was twenty-one years in professional hockey ... I was never traded, nor was I ever fired. I counted my blessings and figured it was time to move on."

Cliff Koroll

And move he did, putting countless vocational miles between himself and his sport. He hooked up with McClement Sales Company, a food supplier to the McDonald's restaurant chain based in Chicago. "We controlled about six suppliers to McDonald's: all the sauces ... condiments ... salad dressing, strawberry jam and grape preserves," he explained. "We were responsible for the production, distribution and pricing."

Being his first venture outside of hockey, Cliff had some adjusting on his hands, although he was better able to cope having earned a college degree in years past. "In my rookie year, there were four of us who came out of college hockey," he recollected. "There was Keith Magnuson, Jim Wiste and myself out of Denver and Tony Esposito out of Michigan. We broke the barrier."

After five years with McClement, Cliff moved to another McDonald's supplier, Cargill Inc. "Cargill is the largest privately held company in North America," he declared. "They're heavy into grain, raw materials, raw ingredients and commodity items. I'm manager of customer service and logistics. So my responsibility is to be sure the customers get what they want, when they want it. I oversee about five or six plants in the U.S. that produce [oil and shortening] for McDonald's."

He is also entirely responsible for the company's export business to McDonald's restaurants throughout the world. To that end, he makes frequent trips to places like China, Israel, Saudi Arabia, Oman, Kuwait, Egypt, India and South America.

Out on the front lines Cliff aims for global consistency. His work is on the mark when "the Big Mac sandwich you buy in Toronto is the same as the one you buy in Chicago and is the same as the one you buy in Beijing."

But despite the encompassing scope of his job, there remains more to Cliff's life than condiments and travel. He and his wife, Lynnay, are absorbed with raising two sons and a daughter. And when spare time does call, he spends it wisely, flying an airplane with friends, playing hockey with the Blackhawks' alumni team and helping out with Ronald McDonald children's charities.

Kurtenbach, Orland: *Played centre for the New York Rangers, Boston, Toronto and Vancouver between 1960 & 1974. Born: Cudworth, Saskatchewan, 1936.*

Orland Kurtenbach's impact as a player was as much determined by his presence as by his actions. He was a charismatic, imposing figure who could play tough, fight hard and in his later years, instill poise and assurance in the minds of younger teammates.

It was with these qualities in mind that the expansion Vancouver Canucks made Orland their first team captain in 1970. He responded by potting a personal-high 108 points in his first two seasons and quickly established himself as a role model in both the eyes of his teammates and the club's management.

By 1974, Orland's character was still intact, but his well-travelled blades were worn out. His usefulness to the organization, however, was far from complete. In recognition of his leadership qualities, the Canucks quickly employed him in the capacity of player development.

He spent the 1974-75 season coaching the Canucks' farm club in Seattle. He then moved on to Tulsa where he coached a club stocked with players from the Canucks and the Atlanta Flames.

But midway through the 1976-77 season, Canucks' head coach Phil Maloney was fired thus clearing the way for Orlands's ascent to the top.

Once established, he then enticed his long-time friend and former teammate, Arnie Brown, to join him as an assistant to start the 1977-78 campaign. The Canucks' lineup, however, was a quart or two low on talent. After struggling to a third place finish with a record of twenty wins, forty losses, and seventeen ties, Orland and Arnie were fired.

Following seventeen years of NHL service, Orland felt ready to pack away his hockey past and move forward into the world of business.

He obtained his license and became an insurance broker dealing in general and commercial insurance. He's still at it today, although he has kept other kettles on the fire.

His connection with hockey has been sustained by coaching a junior-A team in Richmond, British Columbia. He also developed a golf driving range which he ran in White Rock, a community just north of the Washington state border in British Columbia. He sold the operation in 1993.

At home, he and his wife, Laurel, have raised four daughters and two sons and presently reside in White Rock. Orland passes his spare time enjoying a round of golf and playing hockey with the Vancouver Canucks' oldtimers. "We have a very strong alumni out here," he declared with a great sense of pride. "It's the oldest alumni ... in the NHL. It was developed back in the forties and fifties, so our alumni was around long before they started the present ones. We play twelve to twenty games a year around the province for charity. [The money] usually goes to minor hockey. We also fund close to ten kids now from the B.C. Junior Hockey League with full, four-year scholarships at about $2,000 a piece."

Jerry Toppazzini, Leo Labine and Walt Tkaczuk out at River Valley Golf & Country Club in St. Marys, Ontario

Labine, Leo: *Played right wing for Boston and Detroit from 1951-1962. Born: Haileybury, Ontario, 1931.*

For Leo Labine, the official NHL rule book was little more than a list of bad habits to be avoided. An early pioneer of "trash talk", he used every trick, foul or tool available to terrorize and needle his opposition. He had an above-average scoring touch and a ferocious sense of team spirit that was not unlike his spiritual cousin, "Terrible" Ted Lindsay.

The intense battles were put on hold during the off-season while Leo returned each summer to North Bay, Ontario to serve as a representative for a local automotive company. "I was just getting paid to show up," he declared of his responsibilities. He kept himself in the public eye on behalf of his employer, playing fastball for a team sponsored by the company.

During the last five years of his career in the NHL, he worked as a rep for Carling Breweries in the North Bay region. Having sports-celebrity representation, as was evident to Leo, gave the breweries the distinctions that were seldom found in their own bottles. "There's not a helluva lot of difference what with all the beer anyway—only the labels!" he remarked. "So we always had some special events for fishing and hunting that we could use to promote our products."

Leo also discovered that it's a small world when you're working in promotions as an NHL player. "We only had six teams and everyplace you went, people knew you," he recounted. "A lot of them liked you or hated you! They were either Montreal fans or Toronto fans and seeing me from Boston, they were walking kind of a tight line. In a lot of cases they didn't have a helluva lot of use for you!"

After he put in his last shift with the Detroit Red Wings in 1962, he devoted his full-time energies to doing promotional work for Carling.

Ten years later, Carling and O'Keefe downsized as a result of their amalgamation and without much seniority, Leo was sent packing.

He then hooked up with a trucking firm called "Husband Transport". He performed similar promotional work for Husband as he had done for Carling years earlier.

He carried on in the same capacity working for Star Transport up until his retirement in early 1994.

These days, Leo enjoys participating in charity golf tournaments organized by the NHL Players' Association. He and his wife also love to travel across the province visiting with family and friends. They continue to make their home in North Bay, Ontario.

Lambert, Yvon: *Played left wing for Montreal and Buffalo from 1972-1982. Born: Drummondville, Quebec, 1950.*

Near the end of his career, Yvon Lambert became known as *Ti-gris*, which means "a little grey" because he had a touch of grey hair. Today, as he glides up the ice, he looks more distinguished than ever with what is now a complete mane of silver.

After eight-plus solid seasons, five Stanley Cup victories, and 415 regular-season points with the Montreal Canadiens, Yvon moved on to the Buffalo Sabres where he closed out his career in 1982. He then accepted an offer to become an assistant coach under Mike Keenan who, at the time, was in charge of the Rochester Americans of the American Hockey League.

In his second season, Yvon shifted his role by suiting up as a player-coach under newly hired Joe Crozier. When Crozier fell ill in November of that year, Yvon got the call to assume the head coaching position.

With sufficient success and experience under his belt, he received an invitation from Scotty Bowman to coach Rochester for an additional season. But with Montreal on his mind, Yvon refused the deal.

"Serge Savard offered me the head coach's position with the Montreal Junior Canadiens in Verdun," he recalled. He signed a two-year contract but resigned by the end of the first season. The going was too tough—he decided that the time had come to get out of pro hockey.

Starting in 1985, Yvon purchased a couple of restaurants and embarked on a long and gradual process of learning the food-service business from the inside out.

Eight years later, he sold both of his establishments and became manager of the *Bistro du Forum*, a restaurant in the old Montreal Forum. With the Canadiens' transition to a new stadium on the drawing board, he knew that the changes were coming that would affect his position.

"Serge Savard and Réjean Houle opened doors for me getting in with Molson in the transition to the new Centre," Yvon acknowledged. He now serves as an assistant manager of the new restaurant in the Molson Centre. He has also joined the ranks of Rocket Richard, Henri Richard and Guy Lafleur by serving as an ambassador for Molson-O'Keefe, making promotional appearances at banquets and golf tournaments throughout the province of Quebec.

Married for twenty-four years, Yvon and his wife, Sandra, raised two daughters and continue to make their home in the Montreal area. Yvon also helps to raise money for charitable causes by touring with The Greatest Legends of Hockey oldtimers' club.

GT Lane Financial Group, Inc.

A Financial Advising Firm

Gordon T. Lane
President

5239 Lightfoot Path
Columbia, Maryland 21044   Fax: 410.992.5115

Lane, Gordie: *Played defense for Washington and the New York Islanders from 1975-1985. Born: Brandon, Manitoba, 1953.*

Gord Lane's NHL career can be evenly split into two distinctive halves: five-and-a-half seasons at or near the bottom of the Norris Division on one side, and four Stanley Cups on the other.

It all began with the Washington Capitals in the mid-seventies. Heavy goal-crease traffic was a hallmark of the talent-shy Caps. It was up to the likes of rugged Gord Lane to limit the damage by controlling riff-raff with whatever means were available. He did so to the tune of over 600 penalty minutes before he ascended to the heavens of the New York Islanders in 1979-80.

Gord stepped into a powerful Islanders' line-up just in time to start a run on four-straight league championships.

It put a thrilling finale to his ten years in pro hockey. But when the curtains finally did come down, he went back stage, figuratively speaking, only to find that he'd neglected to write act two.

"I hadn't pursued any other career," he recalled. "So I had to fall back on the hockey industry."

To that end, he returned to his native Brandon, Manitoba to coach the Wheat Kings of the Western League for the final three months of the 1985-86 season. He then received an offer from Islanders' general manager Bill Torrey to coach their affiliate, the Springfield Indians of the American Hockey League. Gord served as a player-coach during his first year and as head coach for the 1987-88 season.

"Then I left," he reported. "I realized during that final season that coaching ... wasn't my calling."

To lift his employability to an even keel, he returned to school and secured a degree in accounting. "I entered the private sector and worked with firms here [in Maryland]," he related. "But I think the freedom I had as an athlete prevented me from being comfortable with the constraints of nine to five. Sitting at the same desk, day in and day out, doing the same stuff—it was very hard."

In patented form, Gord harnessed his frustrations and distilled them into creative fuel—the force of which was used to shape his new expedition.

"When I was playing," he remarked, "we always thought that we would play forever and so personally, I didn't manage my affairs. I had an accountant who received my paycheque and sent me living expenses. I didn't learn how to be a businessman till I was sent out into the real world—and it was really a hard experience. So I took my experience as a hockey player and the experience I had gained in the world of business and designed a financial-planning strategy for professional athletes."

The finished product came in the form of G.T. Lane Financial Group Inc., an advisory firm designed to give financial guidance to athletes in the United States and Canada. His clients usually come from the worlds of football, baseball, women's tennis and hockey.

"If I can get ahold of a kid who's twenty, twenty-one, with the money they're making now," he explained, "I can take advantage of very conservative investment strategies, make sure they learn how to invest their money, how to pay their bills, and about business itself. Then they should be set by the time they're through."

The problem with the industry as Gord sees it, is that there are too many agents who simply baby-sit their clients. They control everything until the athlete's career is finished and then they disappear, leaving their clients to flounder for one to five years until they figure out how the system works.

Gord's mission has been to challenge and empower these athletes to take charge of their lives while they're still on top and there's money in the bank.

Away from the office, Gord is a spirited family man. Along with his wife, Kathy, he has a quest to do for their two teenage daughters what he seeks to do for athletes—to nourish, empower and educate. "I suppose they're my major hobby," he declared, "just watching them grow up and mature." Gord, Kathy and the girls make their home just outside Washington, D.C. in the state of Maryland.

Langelle, Pete: *Played centre for Toronto from 1938-1942. Born: Winnipeg, Manitoba, 1917.*

When Pete Langelle speaks of his time in the NHL, his words describe events while his spirit recreates an era that only the oldest amongst us might remember. "In 1938, I was playing in Syracuse," he recalled of his stylish arrival into the big leagues. "I got the word that the Leafs needed me right away. My instructions were to meet Conn Smythe in Buffalo because in those days, there were no trains running between Buffalo and Toronto. I didn't even have time to pack any clothes! I met Mr. Smythe and we were chauffeured to Toronto in his Cadillac! I explained to him that I had to get back to Syracuse as soon as possible to pick up my clothes, but Mr. Smythe said, 'Buy some clothes on me'."

As he settled in with the boys, Pete found himself as the exception to some traditional rules—and although puzzled, he wasn't complaining. "Your number was an indication of your standing with the club," he explained. "Players 1-12 were on a protected list—they were untouchable. For some reason, I got #11 when I first arrived with the Leafs. Having numbers one through twelve meant privileges such as getting the lower berth on the train and that you couldn't be initiated. I remember Roy Conacher yelling for my initiation. But I got out of it by reminding them of my train berth and my number."

Pete was drafted into the army in 1942,

Pete Langelle and Hap Day at Leafs' training camp in St. Catharines, Ontario circa 1942

although not before leaving the NHL in the same Cadillac style with which he had arrived. This was the year that the Leafs made their famous comeback from 0-3 in the finals against the Detroit Red Wings to claim the Stanley Cup. Pete scored the Leafs' second goal in game seven—the actual game winner.

Shortly thereafter, he found himself as a member of the Canadian Air Force stationed in England. "We were sent for political reasons," he explained. "There was a public outcry over hockey players not doing their part. There were quite a few pro hockey players over there. We'd play a game once a week with guys like Roy Conacher. We even played ten games in Wembley Stadium."

Pete left the Air Force in 1947 and embarked on a hockey comeback. "Conn Smythe had no place for me in Toronto, so I played for four years in Pittsburgh of the AHL," he recounted.

He then retired from hockey and returned home to Winnipeg, Manitoba. "I worked as a rep for Shea's Brewery, a Manitoba brewery which was bought out by Labatts in '54," he reported. "I travelled for seventeen years on my circuit between Dauphin and Churchill." In all, Pete represented the brewery for thirty years before retiring in 1982.

Since then, he and his wife pursued their penchant for travelling, taking in such places as Alaska, the Yukon, Germany and the Canadian Maritimes.

Pete has lived on his own in Winnipeg since his wife passed away in 1995. She is survived by Pete, a son, a daughter and four grandchildren.

Laprade, Edgar: *Played centre for the New York Rangers from 1945-1955. Born: Mine Center, Ontario, 1919.*

Edgar Laprade could handle a stick the way a crafty politician could handle words. He was a fluid skater who could weave a creative web of dekes and passes that dazzled and entertained New York's long-suffering fans.

By the end of his first season with the Rangers in 1945-46, he had notched thirty-four points and claimed the Calder Trophy as the league's brightest rookie.

Being small in stature at 5'8" and 157 pounds, Edgar preferred a clean style of play. He went unpenalized in three of his ten NHL seasons and was awarded the Lady Byng Trophy in 1950.

During the off-seasons, he made a point of returning each summer to his home in Fort William-Port Arthur, Ontario to work at a local sporting-goods store. Finding virtue in the trade, he put plans on the board to buy into the store for the day when hockey was done.

Getting out of the NHL, however, proved more difficult than getting in. "No one liked the idea of me retiring," he recalled. "I guess they figured I had one or two more good years in me. Frank Boucher would say, 'We're okay. We'll grant you your release. But so and so won't.'

Then I'd phone them and they'd say, 'Oh no, we're all right. It's so and so.' So I got the run around. It took me two years for them to finally decide to let me go."

When that day came in 1955, Edgar left the New York Rangers and switched from wearing skates to selling them. He teamed up with former pro baseball player Guy Perciante and operated Perciante & Laprade Sporting Goods for the next thirty years.

"It was a wonderful experience," Edgar declared. "I just learned by working and going away to the different sporting-goods shows. We could really pick up some good, new stuff. There were also a lot of nice people who came into the store over the years—sportsmen, fishermen, you name it. We handled a lot of the sporting goods for soccer, football, hockey and we were very big in hunting and guns."

While still with the Rangers in 1950, Edgar was enticed to throw his hat into the ring of municipal politics in Fort William-Port Arthur, known today as Thunder Bay.

"The future mayor got together with some of us who ran as a group," he recounted. "The incumbents weren't too popular so they were trying to get them out, and they were successful. They had asked me to run—that's the only reason I did! I wasn't particularly interested in politics at the time."

But once he got a taste of the process he had a change of heart. "I enjoyed it very much because I like to be able to accomplish things," he remarked. "When I saw some of the things I worked for like the Marina park which was very successful, it was satisfying. So I was busy and enjoyed every minute of it."

He stayed on as an alderman until the mid-seventies when he made an unsuccessful bid for the mayor's office. He then retired from political life for good.

In 1985, Edgar sold his sporting-goods business although, as an investment, he retained ownership of the commercial block where his store was situated.

Once retired, he and his wife travelled extensively until she passed away a few years ago.

Since then, he has stayed close to home except for the odd visit to Mesa, Arizona to see his daughter. "I don't feel the need to travel a lot," he remarked. "I like the four seasons and the Thunder Bay winters."

As for the NHL, he watches the odd playoff game but otherwise rarely follows the sport. "If I can't play, I don't watch," he exclaimed. "I get frustrated—I'm not a very good spectator."

Edgar continues to relish acknowledgments from the past though. He still receives a few requests for his autograph every month from fans in New York City who remember his exploits from the old days. He also received the ultimate post-playing honour of being inducted into the Hockey Hall of Fame in 1993.

Nickname: *Beaver*

While with the New York Rangers, Edgar was considered to be an eager beaver when it came to hard work.

Larson, Reed: *Played defense for Detroit, Boston, Edmonton, the New York Islanders, Minnesota and Buffalo from 1976-1990. Born: Minneapolis, Minnesota, 1956.*

It takes only a few minutes in the presence of Reed Larson to realize that although he has aged physically, his mind remains a youthful storehouse of humour, stories and anecdotes that could stretch any CD-ROM beyond its limit.

Now to activate a CD, you have to press a button. Getting Reed to share his antics from the past requires no effort at all.

"Do you remember a restaurant called 'Grapes' owned by Ian Turnbull?" he asked. "We were in there after a game one time. We all had our trench coats and were having a few beers. There was Paul Woods, Dennis Polonich and Greg Smith. This guy comes in and says, 'You guys are the Red Wings' and he starts giving us a hard time. Dennis Polonich said, 'Why don't you sit down if you're such a big man and see if you can drink with us?' So we had this complete stranger sitting at the table with us and Polonich started ordering shots of Peppermint Schnapps.

Only Dennis was drinking water and this guy had *real* Schnapps!

"It gets to be about ten or twelve shots and ... we're losin' him minute by minute. His speech is slurring and he's drooling and he's trying to keep up. It's his pride.

"Meanwhile, I'm smoking a big cigar and I'm flicking my ashes into the pocket of this guy's trench coat. Polonich is getting him mad, saying he's not man enough and this guy is just hurtin'. Now his pocket starts smoking and going on fire. Polonich hollers at him and everybody throws their beers [at it] because the coat's on fire. Now we weren't always this mean, but the guy was a loud mouth. And you've got to remember now, I was probably twenty-two at the time."

"I miss that million-dollar stuff!"

Reed Larson

As an NHL defenseman, Reed Larson was productive in all categories, compiling 696 career points and 1,454 penalty minutes on behalf of six different teams.

He left the Minnesota North Stars at the end of the 1988-89 season in favour of sampling an Italian brand of hockey. He lasted most of the following season but in response to the urging of his coach, Barry Smith, he returned to the NHL to help the Buffalo Sabres in their run for the playoffs. He played only one game and then retired from the majors for good.

Reed then continued his course in Italy for four more seasons, playing in Alleghe, Milan and Aosta. "It's where France, Italy and Switzerland all come together," he said of Aosta. "I skied Mount Blanc and the Mattahorn. It was unbelievable!"

From the present-day perspective of maturity, he reflected back on his European experience: "I was glad I was in my late thirties when I did it. I think if I would have been in my young twenties, I probably would have just played hockey and chased girls."

Nickname Challenge #15

King Kong

He played his first game for the Blackhawks in 1970. As a rookie, he had not been out on the ice yet when a brawl broke out against the Boston Bruins. "I paired up with Derek Sanderson and I won," he bragged. Later, Derek mentioned to a reporter that his opponent was as big as a gorilla, like King Kong. Next day's newspapers referred to him as 'King Kong ——' and the name stuck. These days our subject is known to his close friends as "Kong".

Who is he?

Clues

a. He played defense for Chicago, Vancouver, Buffalo and Los Angeles from 1970-1985.

b. He stands 6'3" and weighs 218 pounds.

If you're still hemmed in your own zone, see page 285.

In the spring of 1994, Reed finally surrendered to the call of family and the urge for stability. "I might have stayed over there playing or coaching," he remarked, "but my kids, at the time, were young and I just decided to get on with my career here in Minneapolis."

As an opening volley, he recouped his old job as a loan officer at Bell Mortgage—a post he'd held during his off-seasons in the NHL. He disliked the work but preferred the toil to the sound of the wolf at his door.

Partial relief came soon, however, with an offer to join the Minnesota Moose of the IHL. He did his best to juggle both the Moose and Bell, but the Moose were short on money and Bell was short on interest, so in the end he left them both.

To fill the void, he eventually hooked up with Excel Telecommunications based in Dallas. In addition to standard phone services, they provide pagers, cellular systems and home alarms. "Unless you're living in a cave," he warned, "telecommunications is the new frontier. I've been doing it for fourteen months and it's incredible!"

The Excel system is based on multi-level marketing in the style of Amway or Mary Kay. "All you do is gather and maintain customers on the service," he exclaimed. "This is going to blow my NHL career away if it keeps going the way it is! And I miss that million-dollar stuff!"

Reed dedicates his leisure time to playing charity golf, water-skiing, boating and fishing.

Divorced in 1990, he has stayed in close proximity to his daughter and son in Minneapolis. "They're five or ten minutes from me, so I can see them whenever I want."

Nicknames: *Otis; Gabby*

"In Detroit, a couple of guys would call me Otis," Reed said. "It's not fair, I don't want to advertise it! Do you remember Andy from Mayberry? I used to call my best friend 'Guber' and he'd call me 'Otis'. I can't tell you who he was or he'd kill me! But once in a while we'd get out on the road, drinking pretty good. And that's what got us started with the names.

"I got called 'Gabby' sometimes too. As you can probably tell, I talk quite a bit."

Lefley, Chuck: *Played left wing for Montreal and St. Louis between 1970 & 1981. Born: Winnipeg Manitoba, 1950.*

Imagine the story of a retired hockey player who returns to his father's farm to devote his life to raising cattle and grain. While the modern world spirals onward, life on his farm remains embedded in the simple customs of the past. There may be some truth to this image for the average hobby farmer, but for a serious farmer like Chuck Lefley, the traditional farm of the past exists only in our minds and in quaint portraits hung on grandmother's wall.

"Just about everything we use has got a computer in it to help us get the right amount of this on and the right amount of that." he observed. "So we've come a long way from when you saw the guy pulling the plow with two horses."

Chuck grew up working on his father's farm in Grosse Isle, Manitoba, about twenty miles outside of Winnipeg. And as Lou Fontinato puts it, Chuck got the smell of farming into his system. He and his younger brother bought the family farm in 1978 and have been running it ever since.

Over time, they have gradually expanded their operation by purchasing more land and adding new ventures. "We have about fifteen hundred acres now. But in this day and age, it's not as big as it sounds," Chuck remarked.

"We're doing what we began doing," he added. "Growing wheat, canola, flax, barley and oats. We vary what we grow each year according the what we think the market is going to do."

And a marketplace crystal ball is another tool to be kept in the modern farmer's work chest. "You have to start learning how to be a stockbroker," he asserted. "We've all got to become market players ... with the futures prices on the grain."

In recent years, Chuck has diversified his operation by adding a cow-calf programme to the mix.

As for the focus of his spare time, nothing has changed. "I still do all the things I used to do," he

Chuck Lefley enjoying some quality time with his daughter in Grosse Isle, Manitoba

reported. "In the summertime, we play baseball and I golf as much as I can with Ab McDonald."

Through the winter, Chuck serves as a caretaker for the arena just down the road in the town of Warren. It's there that he plays oldtimers' hockey once a week with the locals.

It's a world far removed from his days as a left winger with the Canadiens and Blues where he once scored a personal, season-high forty-three goals and forty-two assists.

Today, Chuck rarely gets out with any of his NHL comrades. He did, however, spend a five-year period during the eighties playing with the Montreal Oldtimers. "I played with the Rocket, Henri and Jean Guy Talbot," he recollected. "I enjoyed the bus rides more than the hockey games. They were so much fun. The stories really, really expand over time. Stories that, twenty years ago, were only little ones are now just hilarious—they've been boosted up a bit!"

Chuck married his wife, Sandy, a year after he retired from hockey. They are raising one daughter who was born in 1987. "Being forty-six," he added, "I don't plan on having any more."

160

SENTINEL

Life Management Corp.

BOB LEITER
Insurance Services

800 - 330 St. Mary Avenue
Winnipeg, MB

Life Ins. Disability   R.R.S.P.

Leiter, Bob: *Played centre for Boston, Pittsburgh, Atlanta (NHL) and Calgary (WHA) between 1962 & 1976. Born: Winnipeg, Manitoba, 1941.*

A product of the Winnipeg Braves juniors and Kingston of the Eastern pro league, Bob Leiter attained NHL status via the Boston Bruins where he performed spot duty off and on during the sixties. He was then dispatched to the minors before resurfacing with the Pittsburgh Penguins in 1971. His robust and effective two-way style of play brought him increased ice time and higher offensive numbers.

General manager Cliff Fletcher took notice and plucked Bob from the NHL expansion draft to help with his newly formed Atlanta Flames. The mix had all the right ingredients: Bob's bright red Flames' jersey was just the right fit. The Omni ice was just the right temperature. By season's end he had accumulated a personal-high twenty-six goals and thirty-four assists.

He remained with the Flames until 1975 when he jumped to the World Hockey Association's Calgary Cowboys. Fifty-three games later, Bob stepped off a precipice and into retirement.

"I don't know whether you just think it's never going to end or what; but I certainly wasn't prepared for when hockey was over," he admitted. "It took a few years to get my head on straight. I think you're like a kid coming out of school at twenty-three, only you're thirty-five."

Bob found himself experimenting with different career options in an effort to find his mark. "The real world was a lot different than I thought as far as working was concerned!" he confided.

He tried his hand at selling real estate, working as a salesman for a dairy and selling office furniture. He also purchased a sporting-goods store along the way and ended up in some financial difficulty.

Finally, in 1983, he ventured into the insurance business and hasn't looked back since. He established a brokerage company called "Sentinal Life Management Corporation" which is based in Winnipeg. There he serves as a middleman between insurance companies such as Equitable Life and Great West Life and the general public, offering a variety of insurance services. Today, he's still prospering at his trade.

"I don't know whether you just think it's never going to end or what; but I certainly wasn't prepared for when hockey was over."

Bob Leiter

From his current vantage point, Bob sees his life's journey on the upside of a two-sided coin. "The transition was hard, but having had the opportunity to play ... I would never trade it," he remarked. "I mean they can't take it away from you—that's something I'll always have. It's a skill that not many people in the world possess. I mean a lot of people have just stayed at regular jobs and worked for thirty, forty years ... pension often in good shape, financially secure. But having had the best of both [the hockey and business worlds], I really don't have any regrets. It was fun and a good career."

He and his wife, Judy, have raised a son and a daughter and presently reside in Gimli, Manitoba. Bob finds pleasure in taking walks with his wife, playing a little recreational hockey and coaching a local senior team. He also coordinates and runs the Gimli Hockey School for four weeks every August.

Lindsay, Ted: *Played left wing for Detroit and Chicago between 1944 & 1965. Born: Renfrew, Ontario, 1925.*

Ted Lindsay survived in the NHL by adhering to two basic principles: play it tough and play it honest. Every cell in his body was geared to score if he could shoot, to hit whatever moved and, regardless of the company, to speak his mind.

In the mid-fifties, he began to question the degree of control that team owners exercised over their charges. His rough calculations indicated that although the gate receipts were generating handsome sums of money, the players themselves were getting more stitches than dollars.

Ted moved ahead of his time by initiating a drive to form a players' union. Like the team captain he was, he carried his on-ice demeanor into the boardrooms of the NHL and created a stir.

"I remember Johnny Wilson on the radio one night talking about Ted," his wife, Joanne, recalled. "And he said that Ted was probably the best captain that he'd ever had—that he took care of his players. He defended them. He was right in there mixing it up all the time and looking out for their best interests. And that was the main reason he tried to start the Players' Association... But he wasn't doing it for himself or for Gordie Howe or for the premier players. He was doing it for the fringe players because they were just so mistreated—he couldn't stand to see it."

The team owners knew, however, that Ted couldn't do it alone, so they keyed in on undermining his support amongst the other players. In spite of some heated battles, the owners successfully isolated him and managed to quell the union fire before it spread into lost revenues.

Shortly thereafter, Ted was dispatched to Chicago by Wings' general manager Jack Adams, as some say, to punish him for his actions.

The owners won that first round, but Ted had turned the hardened soil of subservience and planted a seed that would eventually grow to maturity.

During his three years in Chicago, he kept his home, family and business interests in Detroit.

**Ted Lindsay – Detroit
First Team All-Star**

Eventually, the logistics of being based in two different cities became too much, so he called it quits in 1960.

Upon retirement, he was snapped up by the management of a television station in Windsor, Ontario to fill a half-hour slot. He hosted his own sports-interview show immediately preceding *Hockey Night in Canada.*

He also kept the rust off his blades by working out with the Detroit Red Wings during some of their practices.

In 1964, at age thirty-nine, Ted was asked by Wings' general manager Sid Abel to rejoin the club. The disbelief expressed around the league at the thought of a man of Ted's age trying to keep up in the NHL was probably enough in itself to spur his return. Add to that the chance to be resurrected and finally laid to rest in a Red Wing jersey and the offer became too tantalizing for him to refuse.

He completed the 1964-65 season, garnering a pugnacious 173 penalty minutes and then laid his playing career to rest for good.

In the ensuing years, Ted went into business with his former teammate, Marty Pavelich. They operated Lindsay and Pavelich, a plastic-injection moulding company that produced materials for the automotive industry.

"They eventually sold the business to a company called 'Chivas'," Joanne noted. "Marty and Ted then went to work for them. They got out of running the nuts and bolts of it and they were just as happy."

In 1977, Ted made an ironic return to the Red Wings' fold as the club's general manager. He now held the very seat used by Jack Adams to jettison him to Siberia all those years before.

Through a flurry of transactions, Ted was able to take the worst team in the NHL and levy them up to second place in the Norris Division within one season. He was subsequently selected as the NHL's Executive of the Year by *The Hockey News*.

By 1980, however, the Wings were back in the cellar and Ted was dismissed. His departure marked the end of his career in the NHL.

He returned to his work in the automotive business only to find that his trail of contacts had cooled in his absence. "He was really in tough shape for a couple of years trying to get himself back together again," Joanne remarked. "He had lost so many contacts. Certainly his name did help to get him back in the door though. But then you have to plant these little acorns to have them come out and be big oaks about three or four years down the line."

Ted is now seventy-two years old and still working full-time selling original auto equipment such as ashtrays, overhead lights and steering wheels to the big auto makers.

In 1991, some belated recognition came his way with the bestowal of two honours: his #7 jersey was retired into the rafters of Joe Louis Arena and, he was asked by the NHL to serve as one of four official "Ambassadors of Hockey", in celebration of the league's seventy-fifth anniversary.

At home, he and Joanne have raised one son and two daughters who in turn have brought four grandchildren into the Lindsay clan.

Ted spends his off-time coaching his grandson's hockey team. He also keeps himself in shape by rollerblading around the streets of Rochester Hills during the summer and by playing recreational hockey during the winter.

Nickname: *Terrible*

"I can show you articles from back in the forties and fifties where he *was* terrible!" Joanne exclaimed. "He was always in trouble and he just had a mouth that wouldn't stop.

"He came to win and that's the only reason he put his skates on. He played with a ferocity. I was just reading something from one of the Detroit players that said, 'Ted was a bastard, but if he was your bastard, you were lucky'."

> *"I was just reading something from one of the Detroit players that said, 'Ted was a bastard, but if he was your bastard, you were lucky'."*
>
> Joanne Lindsay

Lonsberry, Ross: *Played left wing for Boston, Los Angeles, Philadelphia and Pittsburgh from 1966-1981. Born: Humboldt, Saskatchewan, 1947.*

The span of a continent and two decades now lie between Ross Lonsberry and his moment in the Flyers' sun with Lord Stanley in hand. And yet even today, under the California sun, the sound of the name Lonsberry still flows like a open-ice pass.

"I'll run into people from Philly out here that say, 'Holy [Jeez], you mean you're Ross Lonsberry?' It's just hard to believe that it was twenty years ago and people still have that fondness in their hearts for the Flyers," he remarked. "It really makes what we did something special."

The main event unfolded in 1973-74—the

year the Philadelphia Flyers became the first expansion team to win a Stanley Cup. Head coach Fred Shero had some plum pickings in Bobby Clarke, Bill Barber and Bernie Parent, and yet from their midst, it was Ross whom Shero described as his most valuable player.

As his opponents knew well, to play against Ross Lonsberry was to *know* Ross Lonsberry. He was in their faces so closely they could hear his nostrils flare. He could backcheck, forecheck and exact his pound of goals and assists year in and year out.

Ross eventually found his way to the Pittsburgh Penguins where he spent three seasons before retirement finally loomed in 1981. To stave off the inevitable, he put out feelers with the hope of being grabbed by another team. In the meantime, while attending a wedding out in California, he received a job offer to work as an insurance broker for a company handling accounts for the Los Angeles Kings and Lakers.

With no bite forthcoming from the NHL, Ross packed up and resettled in Southern California. Acquiring a brokerage license, he then embarked on the steep incline of life as a rookie insurance salesman.

"When I played [hockey], I did what I had to do," he reported. "People didn't bother me—they knew they'd get an effort out of me. So I kind of said, 'You leave me alone and I'll leave you alone.' Then all of a sudden, I wasn't the honoured guest. I was just some other guy on the street coming in the door to offer a product to a buyer. And to me somebody who sold was always humble. You're humbling yourself—you're asking for something and I never was a very good asker."

Like learning a backhand shot, Ross persisted until asking and selling became second nature. In hockey, the toughest barrier was negotiating some space in the slot from an opposing defenseman. In sales, the barrier was more intangible. "Insurance people unfortunately are probably a rung above a used-car salesman as far as popularity with people goes," he noted. "There are so many scam insurance deals out there that they become wary of the insurance agent. So I

think the trust factor, the ability to come across as being forthright and honest, is the biggest sales tool you need."

Initially, Ross dabbled with life insurance, which drew him in close to his own apprehensions. "When I first got into the business, there was a fear factor," he admitted. "I was always a professional in what I did. Now all of a sudden, I'm getting into something I didn't really know anything about. I had no problem sitting down with the players, it was the players' agents and attorneys who scared the hell out of me. I'm a believer in life insurance, but it's a real hard sell and that's just not my make-up."

To find relief, Ross changed his theme to property-casualty insurance which offers coverage for dwelling damage and for third-party liability such as being sued by people who fall and injure themselves on your property. Today, he is still in the game, working for Alliance Insurance Services in the San Fernando Valley.

Unlike most Californians, Ross spends his spare time playing oldtimers' hockey. "I play in an over-thirty league out here, which is about twenty years too young for me!" he quipped with a laugh. "I don't do much to stay in shape, but it's a lot of fun."

His greatest love though is reserved for fishing. "I go probably ten, twelve times a year," he declared. "I'll get on a little kick and just take off every once in a while and put my chair at the side of the lake and sit there. It's just a way to relax and get away."

He and his wife, Wahnita, have raised two daughters and a son. The two have taken up residence in Santa Clarita, California, a community about forty-five miles north of Los Angeles. Living close by are three young granddaughters who love nothing more than to terrorize Grandpa while he speaks on the phone.

Nickname: *Rosco*

"I probably got it while I was playing junior hockey," Ross recollected. "It didn't really mean anything. It was just a derivative of Ross."

Lorentz, Jim: *Played centre for Boston, St. Louis, the New York Rangers and Buffalo from 1968-1978. Born: Waterloo, Ontario, 1947.*

During the mid-sixties, Jim Lorentz made a big splash in Oklahoma City as a scoring champ and rookie of the year in the Central Hockey League. The sparks that flew were observed as far as Boston where he cracked the Bruins' line-up in 1969. The following season, he settled in as a fourth-line centre behind Phil Esposito, Derek Sanderson and Fred Stanfield, and by May of that year, was in possession of his one and only Stanley Cup.

From there he made brief stops in St. Louis and New York before hitting full stride wearing the Sabres' blue and gold in 1972. Over the next seven seasons, he evolved into a reliable centreman adding 134 goals and 197 assists to the league's score sheets.

By 1978, however, retirement loomed like a taxi waiting in the wings. But with options galore in his own backyard, Jim felt little if any angst about where to go from the ice level up.

"I could have gone on to Detroit," he reported. "But I'd lost my desire to compete at that level, so I retired."

He went on instead to become head coach of the Buffalo Junior Sabres and the job was to his liking. He coached for several more years at the local level before the reality of the profession struck home. "I could have pursued coaching extensively," he stressed. "But it would have meant moving around which I didn't want to do."

Luckily, Jim had stoked the fires of a third career using another of his natural aptitudes—an ability to communicate effectively in both written and spoken media.

Over time, he established himself as a free-lance writer, publishing numerous articles in outdoor magazines on the subject of his expertise—fly fishing. He also shared and continues to impart his techniques at fishing clinics he sponsors in the Buffalo area.

He also attained publication of some short stories in the hard-sell market of fiction. His story lines are drawn from his own life experiences and sometimes incorporate a supernatural twist.

But writing aside, the art of speech remains his formost calling. His first break came in 1980 with a chance to be a radio colour analyst for Sabres' home games. Part-time soon became full-time as the buzz of the airwaves aroused his spirit. "I'd do a half-hour pregame show, colour commentary, intermissions and a half-hour post-game show," he explained. "I'd do six or seven interviews per night!" Multiply that by eighty outings per season and it becomes evident that he enjoyed talking to the tune of over 500 interviews per year!

Jim eventually gravitated from the singular dimension of radio to the broader spectrum of television—and his persona has related well to the camera ever since. Along the way, he also set the standard as the first former player to call the play-by-play of an NHL game. Although others have received credit in more recent times, Jim was the first to perform the feat, doing a series of Sabres' games earlier in the 1990's.

Lorimer, Bob: *Played defense for the New York Islanders, Colorado and New Jersey from 1976-1986. Born: Toronto, Ontario, 1953.*

As a defenseman, Bob Lorimer's job was to cover the fundamentals of his own zone. Guys

Bob Lorimer

like Denis Potvin could worry about goals and assists; Bob, on the other hand, would handle killing penalties, clearing slots and using his speed and agility to carry the puck up ice.

It was a balance that worked well as every Islander seemed to fit into place. By 1980, the team was well en route to claiming four-straight Stanley Cups. Bob had the good fortune to be in on the first two victories before moving on to Colorado and New Jersey, where he saw his final action in 1986.

The entire span of his decade-long career had unfolded in the United States. When it came time to pack up the gear, however, there was just enough Canadian spin on his life to pull out the tender roots and draw him back home.

"When I retired," he related, "we had considered staying in New Jersey. I had a job offer there, but my wife had a job in Toronto, so we decided to return to [Canada]."

Setting themselves up in Aurora, Ontario, his wife, Sheila, went to work as a special education teacher for the Scarborough Board of Education.

Meanwhile, Bob followed through on plans to set up a local trucking business with his cousin. But as their project moved from the drawing board to the street, his desire got lost on the planning-room floor. Despite their initial success, he left the trucks and his cousin to revisit the world of finance.

Bob's tie with managing money had begun back in Jersey while weaving his future with Goldman, Sachs, an investment firm on Wall Street. As a personable sort with a knack for numbers, he soon realized that the next best thrill to clearing a goal crease was clearing a profit.

"I joined Prudential Corporation as an account executive," he explained of his post-trucking career. "I work on the pension side." More specifically, he makes pension arrangements for the employees of Prudential's client companies. Reports from his peers indicate that he has become very successful and effective at his work. "Things have changed a bit though," he added. "Prudential was bought out by London Life about two months ago. I'm basically doing the same things but under a different banner."

In his spare time, Bob is an avid golfer and skier with the connections to pursue his hobbies in style. His brother has a place in Whistler, British Columbia, a skier's haven equivalent to the gambler's Monte Carlo.

And as he slides down a slope or approaches a green, hockey recedes to occasional memories about goals achieved and the mystery that once enshrouded the game. "When I was growing up," he recounted, "you used to only be able to watch the Leafs' games from the second period on, so the NHL had this mystique. You always wondered what went on behind the scenes. But I think everybody is inundated now with analysis and so

many games, so I don't think the game holds the same mystique that it once did. When I was young, it was an unbelievable event to go to Maple Leaf Gardens. But I get the sense that kids today don't get that same awe because they can watch games on TV as easily as going down to the rink.

"But as for myself, I'm proud of what happened during my time in the NHL. I was just what they call a plumber, but I enjoyed it. It was a goal of mine to play there and so I look back with very fond memories."

Nickname: *Vladimir*

"I had a number of names over the years, but my teammates with the New York Islanders called me 'Vladimir' after I played in the Isvestia tournament in Moscow," Bob recounted.

Lund, Pentti: *Played right wing for the New York Rangers and Boston from 1948-1953. Born: Helsinki, Finland, 1925.*

There is little question that the face of today's NHL has been irrevocably changed by the impact of helmets, visors, insurance companies, agents and big-money contracts.

Conditions have improved greatly for today's players by comparison with their counterparts of the original six. But perhaps amidst all of the protection and security that comes with caution and tight regulations, the modern player has lost at least some of that reckless, inspirational abandon that made their predecessors into legends instead of millionaires.

By today's standards, Pentti Lund's loss of an eye while playing for Boston in 1951, would have dictated the end of his career—if not by decree of armchair sensibility then certainly by decree of his team's insurance company. But Pentti was a product of the old era, so his decision to stay with the NHL came from his heart rather than his agent.

"I'd go out on the ice with one eye and it wasn't a pleasant experience at the end," he admitted, "although I played with the Bruins for the '52 portion of the '51-52 season and I made the team again for the following year."

In spite of the limitation, he managed to notch another eight goals and nine assists before leaving the NHL. "I don't think the Bruins wanted a one-eyed player, so they sold my

contract to Victoria," he surmised.

Pentti's stay in Victoria was short and spelled the end of his career in professional hockey. As a reinstated amateur, he then joined the Sault Ste. Marie Greyhounds where he took part in an early effort to develop a visor. "They brought in a fellow from Toronto who had something cooked up," he recounted. "He tried to make it work but it fogged up all the time."

By 1955, Pentti retired his murky visor and himself for good, believing once again that the Greyhounds didn't want a one-eyed player either. He undertook a brief stint as a restaurateur before becoming a sheet-metal salesman until 1958.

With his options on the wane in the Sault, he then resettled at his home base in Port Arthur and sold real estate and cars until 1962. But his niche continued to elude him until he got a call from the publisher of the *Fort William Times Journal*. "He called me into his office," Pentti recalled. "I think he was dangling a carrot in front of me. He asked me if I knew of anyone for their sports department and I said, 'Well how would I do?' That's where it started."

Pentti became their sports editor in 1965 and remained as such until his retirement in 1990. "When I look back," he speculated, "I think that none of this would have happened if that eye injury hadn't shortened my playing career in that fashion. If I had gone to a newspaper and asked to be hired, I would not have been—I didn't know how to change the ribbon in a typewriter! But they were willing to let me stumble about for the first year or two."

And while out on his beat, he couldn't help but notice that his big-league history gave him an edge in the hard-bitten setting of locker rooms and hallway scrums. "A lot of coaches give some rookie reporters a hard time," he explained. "But I had a leg up because I had a sports background. Life turned out beautifully for me."

Nickname: *Penny*

"My first name is Pentti," he said. "When I was growing up playing junior hockey, most people would skip the t's and go with 'Penny'. So after a while it stuck."

Nickname Challenge #16

Batman

"During the '76 playoffs against Philly, a bat got into the Auditorium. It was swooping in at ice level and players were swinging their sticks at it. In the second period I took a swing and killed it. The game, being covered by the CBC, had extensive coverage and letters poured in from animal activists. To this day people remind me of the act."

Who is he?

Clues

a. He played centre for Boston, St. Louis, the New York Rangers and Buffalo from 1968-1978.

b. He is the first former NHL player to have ever done play-by-play for NHL games.

c. His initials are J.L.

If your shot was tipped wide,
see page 285.

Lysiak, Tom: *Played centre for Atlanta and Chicago from 1973-1986. Born: High Prairie, Alberta, 1953.*

Through the eyes of four-year-old Tom Lysiak, the inhabitants of his native High Prairie, Alberta engaged in peculiar winter rites. He was fascinated to see people sliding what appeared to be a kitchen kettle along the ice while others frantically swept its path with brooms only to have the kettle collide with other pots, scrambling them in all directions. The ritual was of interest to young Tom, but its solemn pace could in no way compare with boys and men who used long sticks to chase what appeared to be a wafer of black licorice.

"I saw these guys dancing all around the ice ... and I said, 'Dang, I kind of like that. I'd like to play that game—it looks like fun'!" he recounted. "The next thing you knew, I had a pair of skates on and I was doing the same thing."

Tom continued to play hockey for the pure love of the game. Thoughts of the National Hockey League were limited to airwaves, pictures and headlines.

"Between the farming activities and me working and fooling around with my buddies, there wasn't a whole bunch of NHL that I got to watch," he recalled. "Frank Mahovlich was the biggest star we had because if you drank so much hot chocolate, you got a picture of him... He was my biggest man! Bobby Hull wasn't much because he didn't have the hot-chocolate deal."

It wasn't until Tom won the Western Canadian Hockey League scoring championship two years in a row, matching Bobby Clarke's feat, that he began to recognize the degree of his own talent and that the NHL was a possibility.

> *"I mean what do you think my chances were of ever meeting Boom Boom Geoffrion without being drafted? I was drafted and ten minutes later I was shaking his hand... Frank Mahovlich was something back then, but all of sudden, Boom Boom—man I'm living!"*
>
> Tom Lysiak

In the spring of 1973, his career began to unfold. While attending the NHL entry draft, he heard the New York Islanders make Denis Potvin the first overall choice. Next up were the Atlanta Flames who promptly announced: "Tom Lysiak!"

"I remember sitting there in Montreal and my name was called. I'd been drafted!" he declared. "Anybody can get lucky and score a hat trick. But to get drafted—that was my biggest highlight. Then the guys who owned, managed and coached the teams came up and shook my hand. I mean what do you think my chances were of ever meeting Boom Boom Geoffrion without being drafted? I was drafted and ten minutes later, I was shaking his hand. You don't think that's a highlight? I remember one night when I was supposed to be checking Gretzky and I scored a hat trick. That didn't even come close to being drafted and shaking Boom Boom's hand. Frank Mahovlich was something back then, but all of sudden, Boom Boom—man I'm living!"

Tom got more than just a taste of life in the NHL when he suited up for the Atlanta Flames in 1973. He also caught a sniff of that rural Georgia air—and he liked its sweet smell. From then on, no matter how far he would stray, his future was cast in the mould of a southern country gentleman.

He purchased a hunting camp out in the sticks which he used as a retreat for many years. "When I got traded to Chicago, I had no ties left in Atlanta other than my friends," he explained. "I needed a place to live during the off-season, so I moved out to my hunting camp."

By 1986, Tom was experiencing back problems and decided to leave while he was ahead of the game. "I quit before I got kicked and that makes a big difference," he asserted. "I never forced management to ever make a decision. I never stole anybody's limelight.

"I didn't want to be one of those guys they say is hanging on by apron strings just to keep playing. This I'm not embarrassed to say—most of the people who end up hanging around shouldn't be hanging around. They should be out of there. But I guess if you kiss enough ass you can get a job. I didn't care if I had to sleep in a trailer, I wasn't going to be one of those guys. They're just trying to keep everybody happy. But one thing I've learned in life is you can't keep everybody happy. You have to step on toes... But I tell you what, they do have a lot more money than I have."

Tom and his wife, Delta, retreated to their rural camp in Georgia where they lived for four months until they purchased their present home, a forty-acre spread in Social Circle, a town about forty minutes east of Atlanta.

"We've got a four-and-a-half-acre lake out front and lots of parrots, swans, dogs and fish," he related. His relaxed air, by contrast, made it hard to believe that this was the same man who had scored 906 points in thirteen seasons of rough-and-tumble hockey.

As for his new livelihood, Tom founded his own business called "Monarch Landscaping" which services local residential and commercial properties. He also reaps the benefits of some real-estate investments on the side which supplement his income.

Back at the ranch, he has a third enterprise on the go—raising tri-colour horses known as paints. "I raise them for enjoyment and for sale," he explained.

Tom reserves his leisure time for deer hunting and fishing. He also makes periodic trips up to Canada to do some salmon fishing and to visit with family.

His wife recently took a five-year leave of absence from her job with Delta Airlines. Their aim is to spend more time with their ten-year-old daughter, Jesse, and to enjoy life's simpler pleasures in the Georgia wilds.

Fleming Mackell / wing

Mackell, Fleming: *Played centre for Toronto and Boston from 1947-1960. Born, Montreal, Quebec, 1929.*

The Mackell family's Stanley Cup tradition first began in 1920 when Jack Mackell hoisted the Cup on behalf of the Ottawa Senators. His relationship with son Fleming, however, has often been overlooked even by the National Hockey League itself. "The NHL spelled his name wrong [McKell]!" Fleming revealed. "I pointed that out to Brian O'Neil, but they never corrected it."

The NHL's *Official Guide & Record Book* lists Jack and Fleming on separate pages of the retired players index. Fleming would one day like to see his name reunited with that of his father's.

"I may be wrong," he wagered, "but I'm pretty sure there aren't [many] father-sons who both won two Stanley Cups.

"My father won the Cup again in 1921. But he only played a few years because there was no money in hockey—not that there was much when I played either! So he became a lithographer and moved to Montreal."

It was on the outdoor rinks around the city that Fleming began to develop his own career in hockey—and quite independently of his father. "I never saw him play," Fleming admitted. "I never knew he played hockey really. He had a job and he worked hard, so he didn't interfere at all."

By age fifteen, Fleming was playing in the Quebec Junior Hockey League. He then attended St. Michael's College in Ontario where he was groomed to join the ranks of the Toronto Maple Leafs at age eighteen.

It was while playing for the Leafs that he won his two Stanley Cups before settling in as a career Boston Bruin for eight-and-half seasons.

"Near the end in Boston," he divulged, "the management and I weren't seeing eye to eye. I had a big family and the thought of moving to another NHL city didn't sit that well. The Bruins' management approached me with the idea of coaching Quebec in the American Hockey League. I thought the coaching end would be good, but it never worked out. I put in two years with Quebec, which was a mistake when I look back, because I had to leave my family anyway. I could have played two more years in the NHL. New York and Detroit both wanted me. Really I should have let them trade me."

But instead Fleming opted for the more civilian existence of owning and operating a Texaco service station in his hometown of Montreal. "I just got into it by chance," he remarked. "I was looking for something to do. I didn't know a lot about the business, so I took Texaco's training course."

After three years of filling tanks and selling tires, however, Fleming concluded that it was more lucrative to sell cars than fix them.

> *"I made more money in the auto business than I ever made playing pro hockey! ... I was a Grandmaster Salesman five different times! ... For me, getting someone into the right car—boy, it was like scoring a goal."*
>
> *Fleming Mackell*

"I knew the owner of Harland Pontiac-Buick at D'Or Val," he related. "I just went in one day and they hired me. I didn't do very well at first—it was always a challenge! But I gradually learned the business and financially, I did very well. In fact, I made more money in the auto business than I ever made playing pro hockey! And the perks in those days were fantastic! I had an automobile no charge, repairs no charge and I had insurance ... no charge. I was a Grandmaster Salesman five different times! It's an award given by General Motors to a couple of hundred salesmen across Canada. You had to sell quite a few cars to win the award. For me, getting someone into the right car—boy, it was like scoring a goal (laughs)!"

After twenty-seven years of fun, Fleming retired from the auto-sales business in 1992 and has since resettled in Knowlton, a small tourist town in the Eastern Townships of Quebec. It is there that he enjoys riding long distances on his twelve-speed bike and playing tennis. "It's on Brome Lake," he noted. "It's where Brome Lake duck comes from. I used to stay in a cabin owned by Bob Berry's father on the other side of the lake. So moving out here wasn't done out of the blue."

With the precision of hindsight, Fleming pondered his achievements in the NHL: "To me the high points were winning the Stanley Cup, making the first all-star team and leading the playoffs in scoring in '57-58. I had nineteen points during those playoffs! I set a record playing against New York—fourteen points in six games! We scored twenty-six goals and I was in on fourteen of them. You know, Gretzky's great, but I don't remember him doing that—maybe he did—but at that time, to get fifty percent of your team's goals was quite an achievement."

MacMillan, Billy: *Played right wing for Toronto, Atlanta and the New York Islanders from 1970-1977. Born: Charlottetown, Prince Edward Island, 1943.*

Billy MacMillan's formative years in hockey were steeped in the tradition of Canada's National Team which, in the sixties, was under the aegis of Father David Bauer. Billy would have represented his country in the 1968 Olympics if it weren't for an ill-timed broken wrist.

Known as "Yakie" by his teammates because of his admiration for a Russian player named Yakushev, Billy graduated to the NHL in 1970-71. He joined the Toronto Maple Leafs and turned heads, scoring a personal-best twenty-two goals and nineteen assists during his rookie campaign.

Injuries the following season, however, undermined his momentum. The promising form he had initially exhibited receded, leaving in its wake a role player who put up modest numbers on behalf of the Atlanta Flames and New York Islanders until 1977.

From an on-ice roster, he then moved up into the ranks of management—a graceful step at a time. "I was eased into retirement kind of softly," he observed.

His first gentle stride came as a shift from Long Island to Fort Worth where he played and coached his charges to a league championship.

"It was a great experience," he declared. It was also inevitably a humbling experience. "As a player, you think you know it all," he acknowledged. "But you find out how little you know about the game when you start coaching."

In 1979, Billy promised Islanders' head coach Al Arbour that he'd join the parent club as an assistant, but only until they had claimed a Stanley Cup. His car had hardly cooled by the time the deed was done, but nevertheless, he stayed true to his word. As a glutton for danger, he moved on to Denver to replace Don Cherry as head coach of the teetering Rockies.

The following season, he dove in even deeper as the club's vice president and general manager. When the insolvent franchise came tumbling down, he was thrown clear through the team's transition to New Jersey where he became the Devil's first head coach and GM. The move back East and the new labels, however, did nothing to change the hapless content of their on-ice product. Billy pulled on all the stops with little effect. In the end he was rewarded with a pink slip and an enlightened resolve to pursue hockey on a smaller and more intimate scale.

Retreating to his home of Charlottetown, he coached the Charlottetown Islanders before settling in as head coach of the University of Prince Edward Island's hockey team. "It was enjoyable and it was different," he noticed. "College kids are not as serious as professionals, but I think perhaps they have more fun."

After seven stable seasons at the University, Billy finally closed out his hockey career in 1995.

Since that time, he and simplicity have been fast friends. After living on a farm throughout his playing and coaching careers, he and his wife, Marjorie, recently purchased a Cape Cod-style home in Cornwall that requires less maintenance. "I'm interested in doing some things I've never done before," he asserted. One such pastime is bird watching on his property. "I guess as you get a little older, you become interested in the things around you rather than being hyper and go, go, go," he concluded. "They often say that the university years are the best days of your life, but I think the best days of one's life are now."

Although he's retired from coaching in the formal sense of the word, Billy is still a keen observer of the sport. "I enjoy going to the games and watching rather than being under the gun," he remarked. "I still coach though. I mean you're always thinking about the next move, especially in the playoffs. I think the NHL playoffs are great. So much is put into them and they're playing for less money than they make in the regular season. How do you figure it?"

As for his livelihood, Billy seems happy to labour at an easygoing pace. "I manage a liquor store here, and I'm quite content," he stated.

Magnuson, Keith: *Played defense for Chicago from 1969 to 1979. Born: Saskatoon, Saskatchewan, 1947.*

"I can honestly say that I played every night," Keith Magnuson asserted in defining the spirit of his game. "I didn't play my best every night, but I always *tried* to give my best. When I went out on the ice, I went out to create a situation, whether it was physical or defensive. Billy Reay, our coach, used to say, 'None against!'—the number-one aim was to keep the puck out of the net even if you had to stop it with your head or your teeth!"

Keith lent every part of his body to the cause of 'None against'. But ten years of wear and tear took a big toll. "I had been hurt quite a bit throughout my career," he confided. "I remember going into the 1979 regular season. We were playing Boston and I had an elbow that was hurting me a lot. I also had a brace on my back and my knee. Terry Ruskowski got into a fight with Terry O'Reilly and I happened to grab ahold of Stan Jonathan. He said, 'Do you want to go?' I'd never been *asked* if I wanted to go... I said to myself, 'Am I hesitating here?' We fought that night. It wasn't a big fight, but I thought maybe I'd lost my pride and zest for the game—not that fighting was all of my game. But I certainly believed in being energetic, physical and putting 110% into everything I did... So that night, I went up to see Bob Pulford and said, 'I'm out of here'!"

Keith stepped behind the bench and put his work ethic to use as an assistant coach for the duration of the 1979-80 season. He then replaced Eddie Johnston as head coach for the start of the 1980-81 campaign and lasted until 1982. "It was tough," he admitted. "Especially since eighty percent of the players were my

> *"We give away ... scholarships every year and each one is equal to $2,000 a year over four years. We choose three or four boys and we say, 'Hey, it's not just hockey, it's what you do in the community—it's what you do academically'."*
>
> **Keith Magnuson**

former teammates. It's like in any business, it's rare to keep managers in the same area where they developed. And really, I didn't have any experience as a coach ... but we did some good things... In looking back, if I could change anything, I think I would have spent a year in the minors before coaching in the NHL."

Keith's sudden departure from the Blackhawks, however, did not leave him dangling at a loose end. Being a graduate of the University of Denver, he had already done some clear thinking about his career in the bigger picture. Through company president Bill O'Rourke, Keith had joined forces with Joyce Beverages, a Chicago-based bottler and distiller after his first season in the NHL. During the next twelve years, he developed a parallel career, establishing contacts and learning all facets of the soft-drink industry.

By 1984, Bill O'Rourke had moved on to the Coca-Cola Corporation. Keith had remained with Joyce Beverages, anticipating the promise of upward mobility. When opportunities were slow to materialize, he entertained an offer from O'Rourke to join Coca-Cola. "He came to visit me and my wife, Cindy, at our house just after lunch one day," Keith recounted. "He came with his selling shoes on because he didn't leave until the next morning! He stayed until we agreed that I was going to join his company. He wouldn't take no for an answer!"

Today, Coca-Cola is still home for Keith who serves as director of chain sales in the Chicago area. "Each chain is a group of three or more stores," he explained. "We handle thirty different chains including Walmart and Target." His responsibilities include supervising and directing the administration of the chains in his region.

He also keeps a busy agenda outside of his

principal career. He sits on the board of the Amateur Hockey Association of Illinois, plus he coordinates the Future Stars programme in association with Coca-Cola. Future Stars is a programme designed to promote the development of hockey skills amongst young players across the United States.

One of Keith's larger responsibilities is his role as president of the Chicago Blackhawks' alumni association. "We're a not-for-profit organization," he declared with a sense of accomplishment. "We have about eighty former players and about two hundred businessmen involved. Our board has Stan Mikita, Cliff Koroll and Jack Fitzsimmons as our secretary. We give away three or four scholarships every year and each one is equal to $2,000 a year over four years. These scholarships are given to the most deserving hockey players in Illinois. We choose three or four boys and we say, 'Hey, it's not just hockey, it's what you do in the community—it's what you do academically'. Hockey is only the fourth item that is considered in the process of choosing the players. Hockey is important, but I don't think it's as important as total character development. So we're very proud of the whole association."

As Keith helps today's generation of players establish their careers in hockey, he can reflect proudly on his own contribution to the validation of college hockey programmes. "My four years in Denver were special to me because we won two national championships," he recollected. "I played with people like Cliff Koroll, Jim Wiste, Craig Patrick ... guys I will never forget because of the championships we won. We showed that, at the time, college hockey was on the move and that those players could play in the NHL.

"From there, walking into Chicago and being on a team with Bobby Hull and Stan Mikita—a young Canadian couldn't be more thrilled to be in that kind of dressing-room atmosphere!"

Keith savours spending free time on the golf course although he emphasized that his main priority is his devotion to family. He, Cindy and the kids reside in the Chicago suburb of Lake Forest, Illinois. Their son, Kevin, plays hockey

and their daughter, Molly, plays tennis; so Keith and Cindy have plenty to do just keeping pace with their children's schedules.

Mahovlich, Pete: *Played centre for Detroit, Montreal and Pittsburgh from 1965-1981. Born: Timmins, Ontario, 1946.*

Known as "The Little M", 6'5" Pete Mahovlich could have stood amongst the clouds and not have escaped the shorter shadow of his illustrious brother, "The Big M"—Frank Mahovlich.

But in his own right, Pete was an accomplished major leaguer who could kill penalties and backcheck with the finest of the NHL. His effective stickhandling, playmaking and rushing skills netted him 845 career points over sixteen seasons.

It's hard to believe that as a towering centre in Detroit, he went virtually unnoticed until he was obtained by the Montreal Canadiens in 1969. Sharing the line-up with brother Frank, the Mahovlichs helped power the Canadiens to two Stanley Cup victories.

By the late seventies, Pete had moved on to the Pittsburgh Penguins for a couple of seasons before seeing his final action in Detroit.

He left the Red Wings in 1981 to spend one additional year with the Adirondack Wings before his contract was bought out. In his transition off the ice at age thirty-five, he keenly missed some of the characteristics and values that defined his era.

"When you think that thirty out of thirty-five years, you've been going to the rink with people ... and then all of a sudden you stop," he remarked. "Of course you're going to miss some of the things about the game, like the comradeship that you develop with different teammates.

"I don't think they have it today because there's so much movement of players—you know, free agency and so on. Agents are dictating to players that you can get your best deal here ... or there. What ever happened to 'Jeez, I like playing in this city. I'd rather stay here even if I have to make less money'?"

It was at the start of the 1983-84 season that Pete picked up the thread of his career in hockey, working as a colour analyst for the New Jersey Devils. "I was fortunate enough to work with Mike Emrick. Mike was tremendous," Pete observed. "He really brought me along and gave me some good advice."

Pete enjoyed broadcasting, but found its passive nature to be a pale second to the exhilarating affect of life behind the bench. So, he hit the road for Toledo, Ohio to coach in the International Hockey League.

Once there, it became evident that his experience in the National League combined with years of teaching at hockey schools left him well-equipped as the social worker-psychologist-tactician that today's modern coaches are required to be. Initial success was in the palm of his hand until his stint with the club was eclipsed by reasons beyond his control. "I was to go back for the following season," he recalled, "but when the owner of the team passed away in the summertime, the team disbanded."

With prospects scarce for coaching, Pete then renewed his relationship with Phil Esposito who, at that time, was general manager of the New York Rangers. "We had played together with Team Canada in the Russian series," Pete emphasized. "So Phil and I got along extremely well."

Pete came on board as a special-assignment scout for the Rangers. It soon became clear, however, that shopping for talent took more than eyes and a souvenir programme. "I never really appreciated what the scouts had to go through," he admitted. "It's a tough process. You can do all the right things to make a decision but if the player stops developing for whatever reason, you can certainly make a big mistake—and a lot of mistakes have been made. A good friend of mine who scouted for a number of years [Bill Dineen] said to me, 'You know you don't have to be right all the time. As a matter of fact, if you could be right fifty-five percent of the time, you're ahead of the game.'

You get about eight or nine draft picks. Out of those eight or nine, if you can get two of them every year to play in the National Hockey League, you're doing a great job!"

But Pete found scouting as uncertain as coaching. And as the September turnstiles made their annual shuffle, he was sent out to lead Ranger farm hands in Denver. "I look at the team I had there," he recounted. "Tony Granato, Mike Richter, Mark Tinordi, Mark Jansens, Kevin Miller and Paul Broten. To see a lot of them now playing in the National Hockey League is fun!"

All remained steadfast in Denver and New York until 1988 when Phil Esposito was fired by the Rangers' organization. And as the captain went, so did his crew, including Pete.

In an effort to elude the dispiriting jolt of jobs given and taken away, he retreated to his home in Glens Falls, New York to open a restaurant of his own called "Mahov's". "We had worked at it very hard," he recalled. "Things looked like they might be successful... But about six months later, there were a tremendous number of layoffs in the area from the pulp-and-paper industry. As a result, we never could get enough volume to really make it a success. So we decided to close it down after three years."

With no other options in the wings, Pete hit the road again the following year to coach for a season in Fort Worth, Texas where he'd played earlier in his career.

He was then approached by the Montreal Canadiens to join Dick Irvin as a radio colour analyst. "My wife and I talked about it," he said of his decision to leave Texas. "We thought that the exposure at the National Hockey League level would be more beneficial, even though it was something other than coaching."

Their plan worked. The following spring, Pete got an offer from Glen Sather to join the Edmonton Oilers' organization as head coach of the Cape Breton Oilers.

From there he was summoned to share pro-scouting duties with an over-worked Harry Howell at the start of the 1995-96 season. "It's a little different than the amateur side," Pete observed. "With pro scouting, you're more involved with the trade talks which is great because you have more immediate impact on an organization."

Pete remained with the Oilers until a reunion with Phil Esposito brought him to Tampa Bay as a pro scout in 1997. "Right now I'm not looking for anything else," he stated. "I think this is the area I'm best suited for."

Fortunately for the Lightning, he takes scouting more seriously than household maintenance: "I play a lot of golf," he quipped. "It's either that or doing yard work. But the way I do yard work is to call the lawn-care people."

Up in Toronto, Pete has two sons and a daughter from a previous marriage. He and his current wife, Elise, share a home overlooking Lake George in Bolton Landing, New York. "The one blessing I have is a wife who has been very supportive," he said. "It hasn't mattered what I do or where I go. She says, 'Let's go. Let's do it'!"

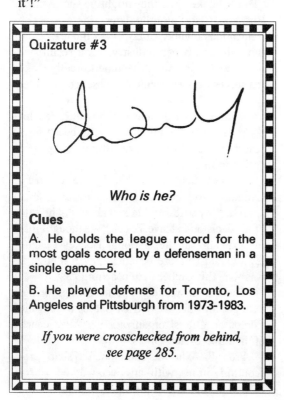

Quizature #3

Who is he?

Clues

A. He holds the league record for the most goals scored by a defenseman in a single game—5.

B. He played defense for Toronto, Los Angeles and Pittsburgh from 1973-1983.

If you were crosschecked from behind, see page 285.

Manery, Randy: *Played defense for Detroit, Atlanta and Los Angeles from 1970-1980. Born: Leamington, Ontario, 1949.*

The 1972 NHL expansion draft gave Randy Manery and the Atlanta Flames just what they both needed. For Randy, it meant a chance to expand his career beyond the confines of the minor leagues where he'd been detained by the Detroit Red Wings for two years. The fledgling Flames, on the other hand, were the beneficiaries of the Wings' oversight as Randy quickly emerged as a steady, intelligent blueliner—just what the expansion doctor ordered.

For the next five seasons, he was a dependable fixture in the Flames' goal crease as well as on the point during power plays.

In the late seventies, he was shipped to the warm climes of Los Angeles where he stayed the course until his retirement in 1980. But the lure of the hot sun and fast pace of Southern California held little attraction for him once his hockey days were over. He still had Georgia on his mind.

Upon resettling in Atlanta, Randy propelled himself into a series of small-business ventures such as dry-cleaning stores, a small construction company and a Baskin Robbins ice-cream shop. "We ran some of these at the same time," he reported.

In 1990, Randy completely shifted his career focus from small business to global business. "I'm working for a Christian organization called the 'Haggai Institute'," he explained. "We bring Third World Christian leaders in to advance their leadership skills so in turn, they can take these skills back to their own countries."

He went on to explain that the Haggai Institute is committed to maintaining a learning atmosphere that is as compatible as possible with the home environments of their clients. Therefore, rather than running the risk of exposing their invitees to culture shock, the Haggai Institute holds all of its training sessions in Singapore and Maui.

Randy works in the fundraising department. Although based in Atlanta, he frequently travels to Singapore and Maui to deliver lectures on fundraising techniques. "I'm growing and enjoying my work," he asserted. "It's very fulfilling."

His wife, Linda, is the manager of a real-estate office. Together, they are raising a teenage daughter and son. For leisure, Randy spends time supporting his son's interest in hockey. He also has a seat on the board of the Georgia Amateur Hockey Association.

Maniago, Cesare: *Played goal for Toronto, Montreal, the New York Rangers, Minnesota and Vancouver between 1960 & 1978. Born: Trail, British Columbia, 1939.*

Cesare Maniago reached the threshold of the NHL like a knight held back from the Round Table for want of enough chairs.

In Toronto, he picked up seven games and a 2.57 goals-against average as a backup to Johnny Bower, the 1961 Vezina Trophy man. Exit Cesare to the minors.

The following season, he was drafted by the Montreal Canadiens who had Jacques Plante, the 1962 Vezina Trophy man. Exit Cesare to the minors again.

By 1965, he had caught a break with the New York Rangers only to discover that the principal goal-crease resident was future Hall of Famer Eddie Giacomin.

It was not until Cesare was drafted by the Minnesota North Stars in 1967 that his status as a front-line goaltender was finally assured. Standing an exceptionally tall 6'3", his game was defined by acrobatic moves, quick reflexes and emphasis on playing the angles.

He sustained his quality of life in the NHL and afterwards through hard work and in part by adhering to the principle that a well-placed decision today makes for a better existence tomorrow. If life were a big kitchen he would have said, in all likelihood, that you've got to shop before you can cook.

Cesare made one of his well-placed decisions while still playing in the big leagues. He applied his summers to working as an estimator for his brother's construction company, an experience

MANIAGO SPORTS

CESARE MANIAGO
PRESIDENT

4455 ALASKA STREET
BURNABY, B.C. V5C 5T3
FAX: (604) 294-8038

that would later prove invaluable in preparing him for his post-hockey career.

Towards the end of his stay in Minnesota in 1976, he got into the wholesale sporting-goods business with the help of an experienced friend. One of their product lines was Northland hockey sticks, produced in Minnesota.

When the North Stars announced their intention to trade him, he invoked another well-placed decision, exercising the contractual right to approve his new destination. He chose the Vancouver Canucks' goal crease as his new home where he could be close to family.

In making the move, Cesare brought the Northland line of hockey sticks with him to Western Canada. While he was tending goal he also tended to his future by establishing a Canadian foothold for his business.

But a year and a half after having entered the sporting goods field, his partner died suddenly of a stroke. With an aim to keep the business afloat, Cesare had to purchase the entire operation and manage it himself.

When he finally left his playing career in 1978, he was able to turn his full-time attention to running what by then was called "Maniago Sports Ltd". He has remained there since and is prospering. "We've expanded tremendously!" he declared. "We have one line we're distributing all over Canada."

Cesare returned to the NHL as a goaltending coach for the Vancouver Canucks in the late eighties. "It was not an employment situation," he emphasized. "I was just lending a helping hand."

Having been close to the league in recent

years, he remains positive in comparing today's game to that of his own era. "I see a twenty-five percent betterment of the game itself," he affirmed. "The skill level has increased by at least twenty-five percent. So naturally I think the game is a lot quicker than it was when I played.

"And a lot of people ask about the salaries. I don't belittle the players if they can get that kind of money. Good for them! It's supply and demand. If management and ownership are still willing to pay the big dollars, so be it. It's no different than any business for that matter. The only unfortunate thing is the poor average Joe out there who would like to go to an NHL game but can't afford it. It puts that individual out of reach

of the game as far as seeing it in person. That's the only sad aspect that I see right now."

Cesare devoted his recreational time to playing oldtimers' hockey until he broke his hip blocking a shot during a game in 1994. It took three pins to bolt him back together, so these days he prefers to make golf his primary focus.

He and his wife, Mavis, have raised three daughters and reside in West Vancouver, British Columbia.

Mann, Jimmy: *Played right wing for Winnipeg, Quebec and Pittsburgh between 1979 & 1988. Born: Montreal, Quebec, 1959.*

For Jimmy Mann, like most human beings, making it in the NHL required sacrifices and a deep commitment to his sport.

Now, nine years later and retired—little has changed for the rugged right winger. He still leads a life that requires a deep commitment to hockey although some of the sacrifices are noticeably absent.

Playing an eighty-game schedule with The Greatest Legends of Hockey tour, Jimmy pointed out with tongue in cheek that life on the oldtimers' circuit is tough. "It's different from the pros," he joked. "With the Legends, if you're caught in your room before four a.m., you get fined!"

Jimmy's hockey life today is a far cry from his combative entry into the majors with Winnipeg in 1979. By the close of his rookie campaign he had racked up 287 penalty minutes and looked most at home in close quarters with the NHL's villains and riff-raff.

Shortly after he retired from the Pittsburgh Penguins as a result of injuries in 1989, he was approached by Legend's team captain Jean Guy Talbot to join the tour. Since then, he and his sense of humour have blended in nicely with the usual oldtimers' antics. And with all the practice, he now throws a better pie than any punch he ever threw in the NHL.

"I'm busier now in sports than I was as a player in the NHL!" he stressed. "I spend six-and-a-half months a year on the road. We play

Nickname Challenge #17

Little Beaver

"When I was in Detroit, the guys were joking around giving each other names. I guess because of my size, they named me after a midget wrestler who was well known at the time in Montreal named 'Little Beaver'."

Who is he?

Clues
a. The Los Angeles Kings retired his #16.
b. He was awarded the Art Ross Trophy as the league's leading scorer in 1980.

If that failed to click,
see page 285.

from coast to coast [in Canada], in the Yukon, Alaska, Seattle and Portland. We've had sellouts everywhere! We had to add a second game in Halifax because of the great attendance. They make it fun for the family with laser shows, dancers and so on."

The players also make it fun for themselves. While touring on the West Coast, Jimmy and some of his mates slipped away on a side excursion. "Playing with the Legends offers a lot of flexibility," he observed. "Last year we played two games in Whitehorse. At the reception after the first game, we were able to get a few guys to go fishing with us. We also met another guy there who owns a helicopter. So I got ahold of Guy Lafleur, René Robert, Jean Guy Talbot and Mario Faubert. We went the next morning really early. I went with the first crew. The second crew had two policemen, Jean Guy and Guy Lafleur who flew the helicopter because he has his license. So we went about an hour north of Whitehorse. It was one of the most beautiful things you'd want to see. We were flying over mountain rams and caribou. It was just unbelievable. Once we were there at the lake, we caught Arctic Grayling and cooked it right on the shore. We spent almost the whole day there, and then Guy flew the helicopter back."

Jimmy also joins the boys of summer for a charity softball tour. "We play thirty-five games a year with former pro ball players like Bill Lee, Rodney Scott, Bert Campaneras and Sparky Lyle as well as with Jean Guy Talbot and Steve Shutt," he declared. "We go coast to coast during all of August."

On the home front, Jimmy's wife, Barbara Paquin, has a travel agency in Trois Rivières. They have also built up an investment portfolio of apartment blocks that Jimmy manages and services himself.

He and Barbara are currently raising a son and a daughter. For leisure, Jimmy enjoys bow hunting in places like Colorado and Northern Quebec. "I've arranged with Tiger Williams for a B.C. hunt coming up later this year," he related. "I used to fight with the Tiger during our playing days, but we get on just fine now."

Nicknames: *Jethro; Jumbo Shrimp*

"When I was a kid they used to call me 'Jethro' because I ate so much," Jimmy recalled. "When I was with the Winnipeg Jets, I used to eat those jumbo-shrimp cocktails. So Dale Hawerchuk, Brian Mullen and Scott Arniel gave me the name 'Jumbo Shrimp'."

Marcotte, Don: *Played left wing for Boston between 1965 & 1982. Born: Asbestos, Quebec, 1947.*

With fifteen seasons notched on his stick and countless miles logged en route to countless rinks and hotels, Don Marcotte found that family was often limited to the people who wore the same jersey as he did.

In 1982, he skated his final shift for the Boston Bruins, and with his decision to retire came an opportunity to make up for lost ground on the home front. "I took a couple of years off just to get back with the family," he explained. "Once the season started, you were on the road all the time. I was home maybe one, two or three days a week at the most. And when I did come home, it was during the week when the kids were in school. Then by the weekend we were gone again. So you never really saw anybody which was tough on the family."

After two years of strengthening family bonds, Don was ready to make a new career move. Coaching, as is often the case, seemed like a natural extension to his career as a player, so he gave it a shot. "I did a little coaching up in Manchester, New Hampshire," he reported. "Just to see what it was like."

It took only a short while for him to determine that coaching wasn't his calling. "The game has changed a lot," he remarked. "I tried stuff that I knew could work, but you just couldn't get the kids to do it. All they wanted to do was score goals."

Attitudes had apparently come a long way since the days when an eighteen-year-old Don Marcotte gave the biblical Job a run at the league lead in patience. Don spent his first four seasons with the Bruins, *making* himself useful as a utility man. He played all three forward positions on all three of the club's lines. He dished out honest, bone-jarring checks and killed penalties like a hound dog. And through the trials of making it to the top—he never complained.

So the notion of keeping close company with one-dimensional, goal-hungry kids was not to his liking. He left Manchester and instead turned his focus back to the familiar ground of Boston where a new opportunity was unfolding.

Milt Schmidt, who at the time had been the manager of the Boston Madison Square Garden Club, located in the old Boston Gardens, needed some help running the show. So he invited Don to join the club's management team.

During the next couple of years, he worked as Milt's assistant, learning the ropes and how to tie the knots.

"It was something I'd never really done before," he admitted. "I started dealing with just under 600 members all the time: ordering tickets, coming in for hockey games, serving food and drinks... So it was something new I had to learn."

After Don's second year with the Garden Club, Milt Schmidt decided to pull back into semi-retirement. Since then, Don has taken charge of the helm with Milt as his right winger.

When asked why the Boston Madison Square Garden Club had a rival rink in its name, Don elaborated: "The club first started in 1928 when the Gardens first opened up. It was part of a chain. I think the first club was in New York. So Boston [adopted] New York's name except they added Boston in front of it."

"It's a private membership," he continued. "You have to know members before you can get in because members have to pick up the application form to co-sign and sponsor you. It's a pretty close family. Everybody knows everybody in here. So it's been a nice experience for the last eight to ten years."

Don devotes much of his spare time to

playing hockey, golf and softball for charitable events sponsored by the Boston Bruins' alumni. He and his wife, Helen, have raised two daughters and a son over the years and reside in a suburb of Boston.

Marshall, Don: *Played left wing for Montreal, the New York Rangers, Buffalo and Toronto between 1951 & 1972. Born: Verdun, Quebec, 1932.*

During the early fifties, Montreal Canadiens' general manager Frank Selke Sr. faced a necessary changing of the guard amongst his charges as the heroes of the forties began to fade, making way for a plethora of fresh names and faces to lead the Canadiens into a new decade.

From the incredible vein of candidates available, Selke gradually introduced a youth movement comprised of Dickie Moore, Jacques Plante, Henri Richard, Claude Provost and Boom Boom Geoffrion.

Slotting himself edge-wise amongst such

talent was left winger Don Marshall—a highly competent role player who could skate, shoot, pass and kill penalties among the better men of the league.

He made himself a valuable commodity to the Canadiens and later the Rangers, Sabres and Leafs by doing effective clean-up work and in the process, securing five Stanley Cup victories and 612 career points to boot.

Effective work on ice, however, failed to liberate most players of Don's generation from toiling at mandatory off-season employment.

"While I was still playing, I worked in the summertime for a firm in Montreal ... called 'Premier Industrial Sales'," he related. "We were selling mechanical power-transmission products for conveyers, bucket elevators and really, any type of machine. We sold them to mines and different industries around Montreal."

When Don retired from the Toronto Maple Leafs in 1972, he turned his full-time attention to working as a sales rep for Premier where he spent most of the following eight years. He also put in a brief appearance with a similar company called "Syncro Drive" before retiring with a capital *R* in 1980.

Since then, he and his wife, Betty, have set up shop in Stuart, Florida. With sunshine in large supply he is able to play plenty of golf all year round.

They also like to take in the best of the North. "We go back up there in the summertime to visit my daughter, south of Montreal," Don reported. "We also have a home in the mountains west of Plattsburg, New York. We do a lot of work up there ... the whole ball of wax, landscaping, repairs, maintenance. It sits empty for eight months and for four months it needs a lot of work. When I'm there I also like to golf and do a little sailing."

Don and Betty have raised three girls and a boy who have since brought along five grandchildren. "We visit them in Vancouver. They're really a pleasure," Don emphasized. "I like to get out and ski with them. My wife said if she'd known they were so much fun, she'd have skipped the in-between part."

Martin, Pit: *Played centre for Detroit, Boston, Chicago and Vancouver between 1961 & 1979. Born: Noranda, Quebec, 1943.*

Pit Martin was a crafty, hard-working centreman who won the Bill Masterton Trophy for sportsmanship and dedication in 1971. He saw his first NHL action with the Detroit Red Wings and Boston Bruins before being swept into a blockbuster trade that sent Phil Esposito and Ken Hodge to Boston and left Pit to fill their skates in Chicago. It was an order so tall that it sometimes obscured his contribution and significance to the Blackhawks' organization. But through his scrappiness and determination, he remained undaunted in racking up 867 career points by the time he retired from the Vancouver Canucks in 1979.

"I don't want to overgeneralize but some people seemed to have a certain jealousy like, 'You were a big star, you should be able to take care of yourself'!"

Pit Martin

He then returned to his home in St. Clair Beach, Ontario to face what amounted to a difficult transition. "I prepared a resume and made it known in the community that I was looking for work," he recounted. "But at age thirty-five, even as a graduate from McMaster University and bilingual, I was offered nothing other than an insurance job. I don't want to overgeneralize but some people seemed to have a certain jealousy like, 'You were a big star, you should be able to take care of yourself!' So I had to make it on my own."

Pit's first step was to spend a couple of seasons doing colour commentary for the French CBC and for *Hockey Night in Canada* with Bob Cole and Danny Galevin.

He then got his life-insurance qualifications and accepted an offer from a close friend to work for Prudential Assurance. "I gave it a go but I wasn't suited for it," he admitted. "Saying half truths ... having to mislead people to sell to them

... a certain dishonesty was required. So I got out."

Instead of towing an inflexible company line, Pit aimed his sights at self-employment. Setting up shop in Windsor, Ontario, he opened a restaurant-bar called "Pit Martins". He described it as a semi-successful operation which he sold several years later.

Then, in 1986, he bought an existing business called "Windsor Pool Service", which he currently operates. "I keep it small enough for my own comfort," he declared. "I have no real ambition to make it big."

Having obtained his pilot's license years earlier, Pit used to spend his spare time in the skies until 1994 when he sold his airplane. These days he prefers keeping his feet on the ground at the golf course.

Martin, Rick: *Played left wing for Buffalo and Los Angeles from 1971-1982. Born: Verdun, Quebec, 1951.*

When Rick Martin unleashed a shot on goal, it was never a vague generality in search of a lucky bounce. On the contrary, he was extremely specific in directing pucks to the destinations of his choice—over outstretched gloves, inside corners or through open five-holes.

He achieved the feat 408 times during his career, mostly in the company of his "French Connection" line mates, René Robert and Gilbert Perreault.

Rick was twice named as a first-team all-star and appeared headed for Hall of Fame numbers when a serious knee injury cut his playing days short. His career was dead by 1982 although it wasn't laid to rest for years to come.

"I ended up having a lawsuit filed against the NHL and the Sabres," he recounted. "That wasn't resolved for about twelve years! It was a tough choice to make, but I was told there's no way that the injury I sustained should have ended my career! So I guess I had to stand up for what I felt was right or wrong. It just took a lot longer than I thought. So when I stopped playing, I kind of got put into limbo. If I hadn't been in litigation,

(KML)   **Rick Martin**

Kieffer, Martin Limited
a computer consulting company

Fax 655-2389   101 Treehaven Lane
                               Elma, NY 14059

I probably would have liked to pursue something in hockey—it's something that's in your blood. It's something that would have been a natural transition if I could have stayed in the game—but it wasn't an option."

Instead, Rick returned to his home in Buffalo to sort out his remaining options. Through a friend he eventually got into selling tax-sheltered investments until 1986 when the market dried up as a result of government legislation. Rick had purchased some gold shelters and mining products of his own before the collapse. Through his deepened involvement, he ended up going to Africa on behalf of a mining company called "Eden Rock".

"They had some properties in the Ivory Coast that they wanted to start developing," he explained. "I went over there with mining engineers and did some drill programmes. It's a Third World country so things were a lot different. The most striking thing is the poverty; but then right next to the poverty there's this immense wealth. We had a crew of about fifty or sixty people working for us, mostly native ... and some people from the government. It was a great experience—I met some neat people. To this day, I still get letters from over there saying, 'Can we come over? We'll come and take care of your house. I can bring my sister and myself. I'll take care of your grounds and she can cook'."

Rick had an option to stay on in the Ivory Coast for another two years. But family considerations and an offer from a friend to work in the computer-consulting business held more timely, long-term prospects. "I told him I didn't know anything about computers but he said it was more a marketing-sales job, so I took it," Rick reported.

It was there he remained until his boss resigned and asked him to join forces in setting up their own company called "Keiffer, Martin Ltd." in 1994. "I came in on Friday and resigned too," Rick related. "By Sunday we were sitting in his kitchen and we'd started our own (laughs). We started out with one employee and we're currently in the mid-thirties as far as employees go. We're a contracting firm that supplies analysts for corporations that need temporary services. Obviously with all the downsizing and rightsizing that is taking place, there's a big need for the type of resources we provide." With business flourishing, Rick is looking to expand into the Toronto market in the near future.

At home in the suburbs of Buffalo, he and his wife, Martha, are immersed in the adventures of raising three sons. As for hobbies, Rick likes to golf and fish out on Lake Ontario and Lake Erie. And although his knee is still sensitive to skating, he recently started playing about five or six oldtimers' games each year.

———❦———

Martin, Terry: *Played left wing for Buffalo, Quebec, Toronto, Edmonton and Minnesota from 1975-1985. Born: Barrie, Ontario, 1955.*

Throughout his career as a player and as a coach, Terry Martin has donned a variety of jerseys and stood behind many benches. Each new assignment brings with it a shift of loyalty and focus. And yet anytime he gets near Carlton Street in Toronto, he is reminded of a deeper fidelity he has carried since youth that is not easily cast aside.

"I always had really good relations with the Toronto organization," Terry confided. "When it comes down to it, I have a bigger place in my heart for Toronto than any other team."

A product of the London Knights of the Ontario Hockey Association, Terry caught his first break in the NHL with the Buffalo Sabres where he performed journeyman's duties for four seasons. It was not until he joined the Toronto Maple Leafs, however, that his speed and hard-

hitting style began to etch their mark on the league's score sheets. During his four years with the Leafs, he tallied 138 points.

In 1984, Terry was dealt to Edmonton and then to Minnesota before bowing out of the big leagues to spend his final season playing for Springfield of the American Hockey League.

"When it comes down to it, I have a bigger place in my heart for Toronto than any other team."

Terry Martin

He then returned to the Leafs' organization where he embarked on the first stage of his second career. "My long-term goal was to get into coaching," he reported. He hooked up with the Leafs' minor-league affiliate in New Market, Ontario as an assistant to head coach Paul Gardner.

Using his new foothold as a catalyst, Terry stepped up to head coach of the Toronto Marlboros for the following two seasons. He described his role as a great opportunity to gain valuable experience.

When the Marlies were sold to Hamilton in 1990, he was reinstated in the American Hockey League as an assistant coach with the Rochester Americans for the next six seasons. "We made it to the Calder Cup finals three of the six years I was there," he reported.

Terry made his return to the NHL for the start of the 1995-96 season as an assistant coach to Ted Nolan of the Buffalo Sabres. He spent most of his time up in the press box during games, watching for patterns or details to emerge that might not have been as apparent to the coaching staff down at ice level. "It's two different perspectives of the game," he remarked. "When you're down at ice level, you're right there where the action is, and everything happens so quick. Whereas up top things happen a little slower and you can see things developing."

Terry is taking on a new assignment for the 1996-97 season. "I'm pro scouting for the Sabres this year," he explained. "I'm doing all of the NHL, all of the American League and all of the International League. I'm doing a lot of travelling but I'm not going on the road for any extensive periods of time. Larry [Carriere] feels that if you ... go on the road for too long and you see too many games you start to go a little punchy!"

Away from the rink, Terry derives great pleasure from golfing. "I love it more and more as the years go by," he asserted. He and his wife, Nancy, have one daughter and reside in Buffalo, New York.

Maruk, Dennis: *Played centre for California, Cleveland, Minnesota and Washington from 1975-1989. Born: Toronto, Ontario, 1955.*

Dennis Maruk played hockey like a compact car that slips down side streets and tiny lanes to stay ahead of the crowd. Although small in stature, he was a quick and powerful skater who could break a game open on a small stretch of unencumbered ice. He once scored five short-handed goals during his rookie campaign with the California Golden Seals in 1975-76.

He saved his most prolific numbers, however, for the Washington Capitals where in 1980-81, he broke the fifty-goal barrier only to better himself the following season with sixty goals and seventy-six assists.

After calling it a career with Minnesota in 1988, Dennis decided to stay on with the North Stars' organization to work in their sales and marketing department.

He cleared the path in advance by taking a series of business and sales courses. But he also saw that in addition to facts and figures, he needed to explore the human diversity of life outside the often hard-edged world of business and sports. To that end, he volunteered at hospitals and community events wherever he played professionally—and was rewarded with a more balanced set of interpersonal skills.

"The transition of going into the business field with the North Stars was smooth," he recounted. "When I got into the offices to talk with the decision makers, they wanted to talk

hockey. So I'd combine my business sense with my experience in hockey and next thing you know, I'd end up getting the sale."

A year and a half down the line though, the team's ownership fell into the hands of the controversial Norm Green—known for his unsettling impact on the franchise. To avoid tumbling at the owner's whim, Dennis packed his bag of sales skills and moved on.

After a brief search, he landed at his present job with Creative Concepts in Marketing where he arranges to have company logos and messages placed on items ranging from mugs to ball caps to coasters and pencils. "I thought I could use my sales skills and also have a lot of fun," he remarked of his new position. "I wanted to have some flexibility. I didn't want to have to sit down in an office and look at machines for eight hours! I wanted to be out and about with people."

Having an adaptable schedule with Creative Concepts has also allowed Dennis time to slip away for rounds of golf, tennis, fishing and, during the winter months, to coach a high-school hockey team in the town of Chaska, Minnesota.

And although the North Stars have left the Twin Cities, at least in his heart, he still harbours a special place for the NHL. "My first five or six years were probably my best times in the league because of the love of the game from all the players," he recollected. "It was a team-like, family-orientated game. Everybody loved to play and to play for one another. I think nowadays it's more of a business—not just in hockey, but in all sports. I think the money aspect has taken away from the importance of the game itself."

Dennis also observed that some of today's players talk about how much money they make and then as an afterthought, they'll add that perhaps someday they will win a Stanley Cup. "I played fourteen years and I think about that every day!" he emphasized with conviction. "It doesn't ever leave you."

Dennis and his wife, Joni, a nurse at the local hospital, currently make their home in Eden Prairie, Minnesota where they are raising a daughter and a son plus an adopted daughter of Korean heritage.

McCreary, Keith: *Played right wing for Montreal, Pittsburgh and Atlanta between 1964 & 1975. Born: Sundridge, Ontario, 1940.*

Keith McCreary was one of the hardest working NHL forwards of his day. He was drafted by the expansion Pittsburgh Penguins in 1967 and immediately made his mark as a diligent, two-way man with a one-track mind for making the opposition earn whatever it could get.

In 1972, he was snared by the expansion Atlanta Flames who had an eye on his leadership potential and infectious work ethic. He was appointed straightway to the team's captaincy and remained as such throughout his tenure with the Flames.

By 1975, Keith had begun to entertain overtures from the World Hockey Association. His league rights were owned by the Calgary Cowboys whose brain trust, comprised of Joe Crozier and team owner Jerry Patterson, approached Keith in an effort to entice him to join the club. "But they didn't have enough money to offer," Keith asserted. "Joe Crozier, however, convinced me to try out ten days late. Within no time I was assistant coach, running practices and negotiating contracts—and all while not having a contract of my own! I gave an ultimatum for a resolution of the situation, but it didn't happen, so I left. It was not a very professional organization."

With an eye to his future, Keith had already obtained a license to sell insurance. After settling into his home base in Bolton, Ontario, he hooked up with Sun Life Insurance in the fall of 1975 and opened the valves on his second career.

"It was terribly difficult for a long period of time," he admitted of his transition off ice. "I had no experience at all in being regulated the way the business world is—at the office at eight

"It wasn't long before requests came from people saying, 'Why don't you consider running in the next election'?"

Keith McCreary

o'clock, working full days. Even just to manage and set up an office properly was all new to me."

But with the help of an effective support team, Keith outlasted his untutored status to become a well-groomed professional with polish in all the right places.

He also attributes his success to his ability to draw upon his past-life experiences. "I came from a background that wasn't strong financially," he recollected. "We had to work all the time to make things come together. And consequently, I think I carried good work ethics through hockey as well. It doesn't scare me to work six hours or ten hours or fifteen hours a day... I think that was helpful to me in the transition."

By 1978, Keith had mastered his office regime and, true to the instincts of a former team captain, he rejoined the fray of public life—this time as a Counsellor for Peel Region. "We had a couple of situations, one in particular, close to my home," he explained. "It was a zoning change that really piqued my interest—that got me involved in public meetings... It wasn't long before requests came from people saying, 'Why don't you consider running in the next election?' So I did some research ... and before I knew it, I was into it (laughs). I ran for the regional council. I was successful on the first go and that's where I stayed for ten years."

Meanwhile, Keith left Sun Life in the spring of 1982 and with a partner, set up an insurance and financial service which eventually settled under the name "McCreary & Associates".

"We're primarily into insurance planning and financial planning," he explained. "We do a lot of work with registered retirement savings funds, some corporate pension and corporate group benefits and a lot of high-end life insurance."

Keith McCreary

McCreary & Associates
—————— INSURANCE ——————
& FINANCIAL SERVICES

10 McEwan Drive, Bolton, Ont. L7E 1H1   Fax: 857-6917

Although he left his post as a Peel Region Counsellor in 1988, his life has been no less political in nature. In 1990 he was named the first and only president of the Professional Hockey Pensioners' Association, and as such, was asked to apply his public-relations savvy to assist the collective in supporting litigation against the NHL.

"At the onset, we had seven individuals [Bathgate, Howe, Hull, Stanley, Reise, Shack and Brewer] who brought an action against the National Hockey League and the club owners," Keith declared, describing the birth of the Association. "Now when the writ was brought down, those seven applicants had said, 'How are we going to fund this? We certainly don't want to be reaching into our pockets because we have no idea how long this is going to go on.'

"Carl Brewer was really the driving force that brought those people together and got their names on the action. He was lobbying me to get involved because ... I had done quite a number of fundraisers... So we started having golf tournaments, hockey games and card signings ... and I ended up orchestrating and organizing all those things.

"The action was asking a question about pension surplus monies... The courts had to decide if the money belonged to the players, the members of the pension plan or ... to the owners.

"The second part of our request was, 'If it belonged to the players, please give it back and give it back with interest.'

"The third part of the equation was, 'We'd like to recover our out-of-pocket costs as well.' We were awarded all three of those items."

Outside the office, political or otherwise, Keith is no less active. "I enjoy fishing in Ontario, B.C. and northern Quebec," he related. "I'm also into carpentry. I've built two homes since leaving hockey. I contracted, sub-contracted and did some work myself."

McKenney, Don: *Played centre for Boston, the New York Rangers, Toronto, Detroit and St. Louis between 1954 & 1968. Born: Smith Falls, Ontario, 1934.*

To hit a ball or slap a puck; to split the defense or slide at first; such were the dilemmas facing Don McKenney—a young man whose athletic promise exceeded the scope of any single sport.

During the early fifties, his sticksmanship was turning heads in the OHA as a member of the Barrie Flyers. But no sooner than spring had warmed the fields, he'd beat a shortstop's dash to the baselines where line drives and squeeze plays made for the sweet music of summer.

His swing of the bat had a quality pop that brought home offers from the Red Sox and Yankees to sign with their farm clubs. Although complimentary, Don knew his strongest options were waiting at the Boston Gardens where he joined the Bruins in 1954.

It was there that he soon established himself as a smooth skater and slick playmaker who could tread so lightly his adversaries often failed to notice his feathered passes leading to thunderous goals.

In 1964, Toronto Maple Leafs' coach and general manager Punch Imlach risked the wrath of critics by acquiring Don's services along with Andy Bathgate in exchange for a handful of players considered essential to the Leafs' chemistry. But when the playoffs rolled around, Don wasn't about to let his best shot at a championship slip by—simply put, he was stellar in notching four goals and eight assists. Don McKenney got his one and only Cup and the Leafs remained on top.

By 1965-66, his NHL career appeared to be headed in the same direction as the golden era of original-six hockey itself—towards a final resting place in our collective minds. He played out his final games of the season with Detroit and then retired.

When expansion came in 1967, however, he got one more crack at the big leagues with the St. Louis Blues. He put in forty games and extracted twenty-nine points before being dispatched to Providence of the American Hockey League. "I played another year and a half there. I lasted up until Christmas of '69 when I got hurt and retired again," he revealed.

This time, retirement took precedence over the erosive sway of second thoughts. And Don knew that to extend his life in hockey, he'd need to redefine his calling.

Fortunately, the process had been well underway since his days with the Bruins. "Doug Mohns and I ran the All Star Hockey School from 1961-1975," he related. "We ran sessions from the end of June through the end of August each year. Later on we ended up having two camps going on at the same time. Dougie ran one and I ran the other. We ended up with 565 kids all together!"

Don's prolonged association with the Boston community translated into an ample supply of friends, collegues and contacts—one of whom was his former teammate, Fernie Flaman.

As head coach of Northeastern University, Fernie was in dire need of an assistant to help bolster the school's resource-stricken hockey programme. Heeding the timely call, Don eased his way into the breach.

"When I retired from playing hockey completely, I went into Northeastern on a part-time basis," he recounted. "In those days, the freshmen couldn't play varsity. So I was in charge of them while Fernie coached the older kids."

By 1974, Northeastern's fortunes had risen in tandem with Don's increased attendance. As a full-time assistant and scout, he was responsible for enhancing the team's talent pool. Regular trips to Canada yielded a healthy crop of academically sound hockey players who in turn brought championship status to the school.

Don and Fernie worked their give-and-go for nineteen years until Don came down with front porch-fever—or so he assumed—in 1991.

"I took a year off and didn't do anything," he related. "I went deer hunting for the first time with my brother-in-law out of Ottawa. But then the Nordiques contacted me and asked me to do some scouting around New England in the colleges and high schools—so I went part-time with them."

In spite of the Nordiques' conversion to the Avalanche, Don continues to mind his East Coast affairs, unaffected by the rumblings of the NHL. Although he does serve up the occasional criticism.

"The game is a lot different today with so many teams," he remarked. "It's really watered-down—there aren't the rivalries that there were thirty years ago. We played each team fourteen times [a year], seven home and seven away. And especially with Toronto, Montreal, Boston and New York, we'd always play back-to-back games... Now, if you play a team once a year, where is the rivalry?"

Don and his wife, Margaret, currently reside in Braintree, Massachusetts where he devotes his spare time to playing golf and slipping out of town. "I have a cottage down on the Cape [Cod]," he said. "We spend most of our time down there in the summer. It's right on the water. I like to do a little bit of everything there. Our kids come down all the time—we have a lot of fun together!"

McKenzie, Johnny: *Played right wing for Chicago, Detroit, the New York Rangers, Boston (NHL), Philadelphia, Vancouver, Minnesota, Cincinnati and New England (WHA) between 1958 & 1979. Born: High River, Alberta, 1937.*

For a youthful John McKenzie, life was one big rodeo. Known as "Cowboy" to his friends, he spent his off-seasons roughing it as a rodeo rider in his native Alberta. His summers were reserved for roping calves and his winters for tying and branding his on-ice opponents.

Few NHL players were as effective as John McKenzie at needling his adversaries with roughhouse tactics accentuated by a goading smile.

Starting in the late fifties, John made the rounds with Chicago, Detroit and New York before finding his cosmic centre in Boston. He fit into the Bruins' game plan the way a groundhog fits into a garden replete with rows of mature carrots. The pickings were good with a harvest of two Stanley Cups.

He then jumped to the World Hockey Association where he toiled on behalf of five different clubs before retiring with 963 points to his credit.

During his twenty seasons in professional hockey, John beheld the ceaseless parade of trades, expansions, agents and bankers. By the time he retired in 1979, he'd tasted all the ins and outs of lacing up a pair of skates in the big leagues. And that knowledge, simmering in his mind, was beginning to show promise for the marketplace.

But in its hazy form, such mental merchandise would require a season of percolation to attain the right flavour. So, in the interim, he returned to the familiar ground of Boston to work... and wait. "I bought a home here in '70," he recollected. "Even though I went away to play hockey in different places, I always came back to Boston in the summertime. After you win a couple of Stanley Cups, it makes it pretty nice. It was twenty-five, twenty-six years ago now, and yet it was like yesterday! People still say, 'Hi Pie, how are ya doing?' Of course they can identify with us because we didn't wear the hats."

John found work initially as a salesman for a local building-materials company. For the next two years, he travelled a circuit of construction sites selling lumber and building supplies.

By then, his well-brewed ideas were ready to pour. "I got together with three or four gentlemen and we started a bank," he reported.

John launched his full-service bank with a view to giving it an extra twist. While still in professional hockey, he had observed that most of the players had the same basic financial needs. Under the umbrella of his bank, John proposed to assemble a board of directors of player agents who could work together to provide the best possible financial services for their clients. They could supply mortgages, car loans and investment packages specifically tailored to the needs of hockey players. And it would all be coordinated under one roof.

The idea was sound but some key participants liked nothing better than the sound of their own voices. "All of the agents were jealous of each other," he attested. "If I was an agent and you had player X and I had player B, I'd be nervous that you were going to talk to my guy and you'd be nervous that I was going to talk to and try to steal your guy."

Needless to say, the idea was undermined by a collective bad will. John's vision was ahead of its time. "The service I proposed is what they're doing now, twelve, fifteen years later," he remarked. "I hear some of the agents are talking about trying to get a group formed. They've kind of pulled in their horns a little bit and they're finally starting to talk to each other..."

Fortunately for John and his partners, the player-agent programme represented only one facet of their operation. They also conducted the usual business of most banks. "We were hooked into purchasing land and building condominiums," he explained. "Then that boom came here. Interest rates flew up and everything hit the proverbial fan."

The fan came in the form of the government's elimination of tax write-offs associated with investing in land development. The market quickly dried up and so did a number of banks, including John's in 1985.

When the dust and the dollar signs settled, John emerged as an auto salesman for BMW Gallery, located about twenty miles outside of Boston in the town of Norwood. He's still at it today, savouring his stylish drive to work every morning in one of the company cars. "Well BMW, it's the ultimate driving car," he sighed. "You meet a lot of nice people and everybody leaves here with a smile on their face when they drive away in a new BMW!"

John spends his leisure time playing hockey and slow-pitch baseball with the Bruins' alumni. "We keep busy all year round raising money for charities," he reported. "And the nice thing is we don't have to worry about curfews anymore. When we get to our age, we *have* to be in before one a.m. because we can't keep our eyes open."

Merrick, Wayne: *Played centre for St. Louis, California, Cleveland and the New York Islanders from 1972-1984. Born: Sarnia, Ontario, 1952.*

Wayne Merrick was a classic-style centreman who possessed excellent speed, smooth passing skills and a mind evenly split between seeking goals and preventing them. He put up his best offensive numbers as a St. Louis Blue and a California Golden Seal, although his greatest team achievements came while winning four Stanley Cups in Islanders' blue.

It has now been thirteen years since he made his final poke-check on Long Island. In 1984, he traded his stick in for a briefcase and readied himself for the pregame warm-up in the marketplace.

Today he speaks as a man well seasoned in the art of business. But if you listen carefully to the tone of his voice, you'll notice that it's still charged and ready for a breakaway the moment he receives a pass. He leaves the impression that if you could look into a window on the side of his head, you'd see a hockey player in there skating around his desk shooting pucks into wastepaper baskets.

But before Wayne could fully embrace the world of business, he had first to resolve the impact of hockey's demise. "When you're playing, you don't really think it's ever going to end," he divulged. "You think, 'I'll just keep working hard and I'll be here.' It sneaks up on you and then *boom*, 'What do I do?'

"You know, you're not really in the real world when you're playing hockey," he continued. "So when you get hit by the real world, it really jars you. You're used to getting a lot of things done for you. But suddenly you have to take care of yourself."

Fortunately Wayne had already begun to look out for himself towards the end of his playing days by taking some courses in business administration. "I wanted to get into business from the get go," he declared. "When I got rid of hockey, I owned a commercial and industrial air-filtration company. I was very interested in environmental pollution and air quality. We installed systems for welding smoke, oil smoke, any type of smoke. I was president of the company and was involved in the sales and management side. It was great work."

He also joined some partners in developing a health and racket club in New York. "I really enjoyed that! Being an athlete, it was on the top of my list," he emphasized. "It was an old grocery store at one time. We built it up from scratch—it was great to watch it grow. They've got indoor tennis and aerobics classes which are real big today."

Farther down the road, Wayne got an itch to move into the insurance business—which he did in 1992. Having discharged the necessary schooling, he signed on with Metropolitan Life Insurance Company in New York. "It was something I always wanted to do," he stated. "I wanted to get into the financial-services field."

Because of his previous experience with business operations, he felt that his insight could be used to help small-business owners obtain the man advantage. "I have empathy for owners who are a busy lot," he remarked. "They don't have the time to do a lot of the things that they really should be taking care of—like business insurance, retirement planning, group plans and group insurance."

In 1995, Wayne caught wind of an opening with Metropolitan Life in his hometown of Sarnia, Ontario—a desirable place on his familial itinerary. "We'd always been thinking about moving to Canada," he reported. "The last few years my son, Andrew, has been playing hockey up here and this is where our family is. It was an opportune time. I'm glad we made the move, it's worked out really well."

After an eighteen-year absence while on Long Island, Wayne found his return to the old and familiar grounds of London to be exciting and challenging. "It's scary! It's overwhelming to be honest with you," he confided. "The number of people who know you! I remember their faces and some of the names, but these people *all* remember me. Of course there's an upside too. It's nice to know people. These days I'm getting established. I'm getting Canadianized—it's a big step!"

Outside of the office, Wayne's priority is to spend time with family. He also loves to golf and is feverish to get back on the ice with some local hockey clubs where, just like the old days, the subject of pucks and gilded contracts can set his passion afire.

"Why is it that people are upset with the amount of money these NHLers are making??" he queried. "I'm happy they're doing it. I wish I was playing today! Pat Verbeek just signed a contract for two million dollars. Isn't that great? Why doesn't somebody write that? It doesn't take away from the way these guys play just because they're making money. They're there playing at that level because of the heart they have for the game. The money is there sure and they want it... But number one is that they play well.

"It affects the ticket prices I know. But you can see it on TV. People watch some of these movie stars make twenty million a year. Some will make twenty million a movie!"

Nickname: *Bone*

"When I get with hockey people, the guys say, 'Hey Bone, how are ya'?" Wayne reported. "When I was playing junior hockey in Ottawa, I was fairly lanky... So I got the nickname 'Bones'. I played there with Denis Potvin and when we went to the Islanders, he brought the name along. When the guys caught on to it they changed it to 'Merrick Bone' and then just 'Bone'. So I blame Denis Potvin for 'The Bone'!"

Nickname Challenge #18

Flipper

"I used to like to bounce or flip the puck around, so Davy Keon gave me the name 'Flipper'. If I was behind the net, I could flip it over the net like a lacrosse shot. If I was skating up the ice and my alleyways were cut off by a guy coming straight at me, I could flip the puck right up over his head."

Who is he?
Clues

a. He played defense for Toronto, the New York Rangers (NHL), New England, Toronto and Quebec (WHA) from 1968-1979.

b. During his rookie year, he once sparked a bench-clearing brawl between his Leafs and the Pittsburgh Penguins. He received a cheque for $100 from King Clancy for his spirited display.

c. His initials are J.D.

If you were called back on a two-line pass, see page 285.

Mohns, Doug: *Played defense and left wing for Boston, Chicago, Minnesota, Atlanta and Washington from 1953-1975. Born: Capreol, Ontario, 1933.*

Doug Mohns hails from Capreol, Ontario which was a divisional point for the Canadian National Railway. His father and two older brothers were all engineers. "So we're railroaders from way back," Doug remarked. And although he didn't fall directly in line with the tradition, Doug has been a railroader in his own way, being as strong, fast and durable as a railroad engine on skates.

He made his NHL debut in 1953, having made a direct jump from the Barrie Flyers of the Ontario Hockey Association. He quickly established himself as a versatile cornerstone of the Boston Bruins' blueline corps for the next eleven seasons before being traded to the Blackhawks in 1964.

In Chicago, Doug joined Kenny Wharram and Stan Mikita to continue the tradition of the "Scooter Line"—one of the league's most productive trios during the sixties.

In the early seventies, he returned to his defensive position in the service of Minnesota, Atlanta and finally, Washington.

Several years prior to calling it quits in 1975, Doug had been laying the groundwork for his next career move.

"Having played twenty-two years, in the latter stages of my career, I knew I couldn't last forever," he revealed. "It wasn't as if I had retired at thirty-six or thirty-five... I was forty-one! So I had invested in a construction company and I had also invested in a rehabilitation hospital. I had the option ... of going to one or the other.

"I was a silent partner in the construction company. But then I thought, well, it's not really the type of thing I prefer to do. So I leaned towards the hospital because I liked what they were doing... And as it turned out, it was just

> *"It certainly did my heart a lot of good to see the kind of work we were doing in helping people rehabilitate."*
>
> **Doug Mohns**

marvelous. It certainly did my heart a lot of good to see the kind of work we were doing in helping people rehabilitate."

Doug was one of nineteen limited partners who, along with three general partners, founded the New England Rehabilitation Hospital in Boston. In the ensuing years, they became the Advantage Health Corporation and set up approximately forty-nine different outlets along the Eastern Seaboard as far south as Florida.

"I was vice president in charge of human resources, wages, policies and procedures for everybody," he remarked. "I was also a member of senior management and the board of directors."

Doug sustained his second career with Advantage for nineteen years before retiring in 1994.

"You know retirement is quite an adjustment for me," he admitted about leaving the hospital business. "It's new waters and it's exciting. I actually took on a part-time job at Lexington Gardens. My hobby was always plants, flowers, shrubs and so on. I have a big place down on the cape. It's a three-story, fifteen-room, six-bedroom [home] right on the water and I have a big lot. I've spent an awful lot of time in the last twenty, twenty-five years doing work outside in the garden, so it fit in well with my interests. I worked a couple of days a week when the manager was off, but decided about two months ago to give it up. I thought, well, it's time for me to retire."

He also pulled back on his involvement with the Dianne De Vanna Center which he participated in founding in 1978. "We started by looking at an article in the newspaper one night," he related, speaking of the Center's beginning. "This young girl had been beaten to death at eleven years of age, Dianne De Vanna of Braintree, Massachusetts. And this one fellow wanted to buy a gravestone for her because the family didn't have any money. So we went to the meeting. We got so many responses and so much interest that we not only bought the gravestone, but we went on to get a twenty-four-hour hotline and we developed a centre. We really did a lot of good things for the community and for abused children."

Doug still sits on the Center's board of directors although he relinquished his position as president to Don McKenney's wife, Marg.

"I actually took on a part-time job at Lexington Gardens. My hobby was always plants, flowers, shrubs and so on."

Doug Mohns

These days, his primary focus is to sustain stalwart drives, flawless putts and plenty of travel with his wife, Tabor. "One of the things we like to do is bike," he emphasized. "We go on these organized tours all over the place. We've been to New Mexico, Arizona, California and of course the New England area. And we're heading to England next year. It's really well organized. We don't sleep in pup tents and we don't carry any bags. We stay in the best inns and hotels."

On the subject of the present-day NHL, Doug paused to consider the current changes that now enshroud the simple basics of old-time hockey. "They still use the puck. They still put it in the net and they still try and keep it out," he related. "But the game in itself has changed. I don't think it's as defensive minded. You know the coach used to emphasize that defense was at least as equally important as offense—and that's where my emphasis was most of my career. I focused a lot on defense even when I played on the famous 'Scooter' line in Chicago. It was definitely a two-way game. When you lost possession of the puck, you immediately went to your check. That's the way you were trained! I used to practise it all the time. *Click*! It would go into my head; 'the other side's got the puck.' Bang!—'You've got to get to your player.' But you and I know that today, you see an awful lot of open players out there and you see a lot more goals being scored as a result."

Monahan, Garry: *Played left wing for Montreal, Detroit, Los Angeles, Toronto and Vancouver from 1967-1979. Born: Barrie, Ontario, 1946.*

When the NHL held its first amateur draft in 1963, the Montreal Canadiens made Garry Monahan the first player ever chosen. With the Canadiens' talent pool swollen to its limit, however, Garry was destined to a career in the minors until he was rescued by the Detroit Red Wings in 1969.

By the following season, he had landed at Maple Leaf Gardens where his career finally took shape. He soon evolved into a dependable tradesman who was strong on defense and could play all three forward positions.

In 1975, he joined the Vancouver Canucks where he continued in the same vein for three-and-a-half years before returning to Toronto for one final major-league season.

He then closed out his NHL accounts and signed with the Saibu Corporation to play for their company team in Tokyo, Japan. "We had three great years there," Garry reported.

From 1979 to 1982, he and his family faced an exotic world as the exception to the cultural rule. "It was a bit of a shock to start," he revealed. "But we adjusted very quickly... We ended up loving it there. The kids went to an English-speaking school and my wife taught school there as well."

And although hockey was Garry's going concern, education continued to play a steady supporting role. During his time in the NHL, he had been chipping away at his university degree. He then set his sights on getting certified to teach high school. "I got one year [in] at Trent University in Peterborough while I played junior," he recollected. "Then I picked up the rest of my degree by extension courses and during the summertime and evenings when I was with the Leafs. I took half of my teaching certificate in Tokyo at Sofia University. Then I ... finished up at the U of T Faculty of Ed. in about '82."

Garry completed his practical teaching requirements, but upon graduation found himself tethered to a career that, after all, was not his calling.

So instead he and his family returned to Vancouver where he fell into a new line of work as a radio and television colour analyst for the Vancouver Canucks.

His move into the broadcast booth was exciting, but carried with it a test of personal conviction. "It was difficult at the start because I didn't like to be critical of players and management ... when they would make a mistake on the ice," he admitted. "But really that's the job of the analyst ... to call it as he sees it. So as difficult as it was, I had to get the confidence to do it. It took awhile to get, but after some time I think I had it."

In 1987, he became a part-time broadcaster to clear the way for his entry into the world of finance as a stockbroker. "My first day on the job was 'Black Monday'," he asserted with a dash of dark humour. "So it was a bit of a struggle! I kept my head above water. It would have been easier previous [to Black Monday] because the market was jumping around pretty good for a few years after that. It made it tough to learn..."

After four years of treading water with the markets, Garry changed hats by joining forces with his wife, Barbara, to sell residential real estate in West Vancouver.

"In real estate, you're your own boss," he emphasized. "You have to get up in the morning and make yourself go to work because nobody's telling you to... So you have to be a self-starter which I guess is sort of the same as with hockey."

And through their enterprises, he and Barbara have found prosperity in the lucrative markets of Vancouver. "I'm well known in the area and I have a good reputation," he added.

On the leisure front, Garry looks forward to a bit of skiing and playing golf—although he was quick to emphasize that he and his clubs do not always agree on where the ball is going.

Nickname: *Mondo*

"Paul Henderson made the name up," Garry related. "I don't know what it meant. I think it was a play on my last name."

Nickname Challenge # 19

Mr. Zero

"When I tried out with the Bruins, Tiny Thompson was the favourite. He'd been in Boston ten years. I was in Providence with their farm team for one year, and it was only forty miles away. So I used to go to a lot of games in Boston. I noticed that when the Bruins went on the ice, the fans would raise the roof. But that night, when I went on the ice, I could hear the people in the box seats breathing. So I said, 'If I have a bad night, I'll catch the next train out.' But I think I had six shutouts in seven games. Bill Cowley gave me the name, but he'd always say 'Zee'. The media added 'Zero'."

Who is he?

Clues

a. He played goal for Boston and Chicago between 1938 & 1950.

b. He won the Calder Trophy as rookie of the year and the Vezina Trophy as best goalie in 1939.

c. His initials are F.B.

If your puck is stuck on the mooring, see page 285.

Dickie Moore

Moore, Dickie: *Played right wing for Montreal, Toronto and St. Louis between 1951 & 1968. Born: Montreal, Quebec, 1931.*

Dickie Moore started out in life as the youngest of ten children. Growing up in such a bustling, competitive environment, his youthful needs were often overrun by the uneven distribution of sibling justice. As a result, he learned early in life that if he wanted butter on his bread he'd better learn to milk the cow. "I decided to empower myself," he stated. "To be resourceful and to treat people well."

This latter characteristic has been Dickie's trademark for years. Even when he and the Canadiens were on top of the world with five consecutive Cups in tow, he always had time for people. "I used to go out and play street hockey with some kids in the neighbourhood," he related. "There was an Oriental boy across the street who wanted to play goal. I used to practise my shot and he'd practise being a goalie. It reminded me of when I was young. We used to use frozen manure as goal posts!"

Forty years later, Dickie still leads the scoring race for treating people well. When the Montreal

Canadiens' alumni purchased a van for Dave Balon who is stricken with multiple sclerosis, Dickie showed up as a surprise guest to pay tribute to his former teammate. The emcee for the occasion was Bill Hicke who remembered Dickie from the early days. "He's a beautiful person," Bill declared. "When I first went to Montreal, almost two-thirds of the team were from Quebec. Eighty percent of them spoke French only, so Dickie took me in under his wing. He was good to everybody! He was a very underrated hockey player too. I mean he won the scoring race for two years with a cast on his hand!"

Dickie also believed that you need to shape you own destiny in this world, and to do that, you have to be well planned. While playing with the Canadiens, he always kept his eyes open for opportunities that, like cobblestones, he could collect and lay onto the path of his post-playing career.

"I tried to do business wherever I went," he recollected. "While travelling on the train, I'd be reading the want ads. The guys would say, 'What are you doing?' I'd say, 'I'm looking at businesses for sale.' I went into business even as a player. I wanted to live the same quality of life I enjoyed in hockey, so I bought my first Dairy Queen ice-cream shop in 1954. Then I added Arundel Golf Course which is twelve miles west of St. Cervite in the Laurentians."

In 1961, he set up an equipment rental outfit called "Dickie Moore's Rentall". "I ran it out of the back of a Dairy Queen I set up in Lachine," he explained. "A year later, I opened a proper location for the business."

Dickie eventually tried to establish a rental outlet in Scarborough, Ontario as well; but the enterprise didn't gel, so he decided to limit his focus to the Montreal area.

Before he finally retired from hockey, Dickie's career had come to a gradual halt while passing through several phases. After leaving Montreal in 1963, he resurfaced with the Toronto Maple Leafs for the 1964-65 season. He then retired, only to be enticed back to the NHL with the expansion St. Louis Blues in 1967.

"While playing my final season in St. Louis, I even did business there," he declared. "I proposed to supply equipment to Fluor Construction Company in Chicago. The guy didn't recognize my name. I said, 'Do you know Bobby Hull?' He said, 'Sure do!' I said, 'Well, I play in the same league against Bobby Hull.' I got an open order from them as a result. I learned about selling and how to name-drop. I guess Bobby got an assist on that one."

Dickie retired from professional hockey for good at the end of the 1967-68 season. He then devoted his full-time attention to directing his businesses. Today he remains front row and centre in running his two rental outlets in Montreal. He and his wife, Joan, lost their oldest son, Richard Jr., at the age of sixteen. Their surviving son and daughter work with Dickie in the rental business—a place of satisfaction not unlike the old Montreal Forum. "My hobby is my work," he asserted in closing. "I really enjoy it—especially all my years in hockey."

Mortson, Gus: *Played defense for Toronto, Chicago and Detroit from 1946-1959. Born: New Liskeard, Ontario, 1925.*

In 1946, general manager Conn Smythe took a chance by giving his Leafs a tune-up with a set of young spark plugs. Toronto fans were introduced to unfamiliar names like Klukay, Barilko and Meeker. Among the recruits were Jim Thomson and Gus Mortson who became known as "the Gold Dust Twins"—a name born from Gus's sideline as a northern prospector. Paired together on defense, the two helped reinstate Leafs' supremacy for years to come.

For his part, Gus was both a splendid skater who could lead the rush and a robust defender who could dish out shattering bodychecks. In all, he spent thirteen years in the NHL, claiming four Stanley Cups and a first-team all-star award in 1950.

After closing out his major-league career with the Detroit Red Wings in the late fifties, Gus attained the distinction of having helped set a Canadian fast-food phenomenon in motion. "I introduced pizza to Canada," he stated with pride. "I'm half Italian, so I'm qualified!"

Gus spent the 1959-60 season with Buffalo of the American Hockey League. While shopping in a local grocery store, his interest was piqued by a new and curious creation called "Freezer Queen Pizzas"—a product he noted for future reference. At the close of his season in Buffalo, he then retired from hockey to focus on a food-brokerage business he'd established in Oakville, Ontario.

"I had a couple of lines from the States that I was bringing in," he explained. "Then, after I retired in 1960, a broker from Buffalo phoned up and asked me to take over Freezer Queen, so I did—and it really took off!"

But for reasons beyond Gus's reach, Freezer Queen suddenly pulled out of the Canadian market after only three years of operation. Gus knew a breakaway when he saw one, so he and a partner set up their own pizza plant called "Mansion House Pizza", based in Toronto. Their company caught the right wave, churning out grocery-store pizzas by the truckload. By 1969, however, Gus had had his fill of pepperoni.

"I decided to sell out to my partner," he stated with a tinge of remorse. "Actually, I missed the boat. What I should have been doing was getting into the franchise business, but I didn't do that. So I missed a real opportunity. And that's the only thing I regret..."

Life after Mansion House lead him straight back to his native north where, through friends, he got a crack at managing a brokerage firm in Timmins, Ontario. Timing, however, was not at his side.

"I didn't like the brokerage business at all," he lamented. "It was a bad market at the time which didn't help make it any easier. So I was glad to get out..."

Six years of tracking mercurial stocks and bonds left Gus hankering to sell products of a more stout and grounded nature—like mining equipment and steel.

"Now I was into a business I

enjoyed—selling for Northern Allied Steel!" he affirmed. "Later, I got into selling conveyer systems to the mines as well."

Gus continued his wholesale ways until he experienced a brush with retirement in 1985. He narrowly escaped, however, and has since been supplying energy products such as natural gas and electricity to industries on behalf of Energy Advantage, based in Oakville.

Today, at age seventy-two, Gus has reduced his workload to make way for his weekly skating, his walks with his wife, Sheila and his occasional forays into the nostalgia of hockey's past.

"Hey listen!" he chirped, speaking of his baptism into the world of hockey. "Saturday night, Foster Hewitt, that's all we ever listened to! Everything was always Toronto against somebody else. We'd hear names like Apps, the Metz's, Gordie Drillon, Turk Broda and Johnny Mower in Detroit.

"And of course all the kids in Kirkland Lake played hockey. That was the thing to do in the wintertime. Prit near all our hockey was played on outdoor rinks except for one game a week indoors. Ted Lindsay and I played juvenile for the same team for five years. He was the same fiery guy except that he was smaller and couldn't enforce himself that much. But he was always a go-getter."

Moving up the line from his origins, Gus recalled the thrill of his first shift as a "Gold Dust Twin": "The first game I wore the blue and white was in Detroit. By the end of the first period, Thomson and I had yet to leave the bench. Hap Day didn't put us on the ice at all. I guess he was afraid to. Between periods, I remember [Conn] Smythe coming into the dressing room and saying, 'Hap, I'm paying these guys to play hockey, not sit on the bench!' So during the second period, we started to take our regular turn and we did all right—we got our start. I felt quite an emotional sense at the time and believe me, the adrenalin was running!"

Nickname: *Gus*

Gus entered the junior-hockey programme at St. Michael's College as James Mortson. "A priest there by the name of Father Malin was our team manager," Gus recollected. "He said, 'We'll call you Gus!'—and that was it."

Mulvey, Grant: *Played right wing for Chicago and New Jersey from 1974-1984. Born: Sudbury, Ontario, 1956.*

As one of the NHL's bigger men, Grant Mulvey knew how to use his size to an advantage. In the corners, he was a hard-working obstacle who, upon hitting open ice, could stickhandle and shoot with authority. In 1982, he tied a Blackhawks' team record by potting five goals and two assists in a single game.

Grant was equally dynamic in assessing his transition off ice in 1984. "As a pro hockey player," he declared, "you have a different chemical flowing in your body. In NHL retirement, you have to grab ahold of the line that made you a success as an athlete. If you start again from ground zero and you parallel these same qualities in whatever you pursue, success is inevitable. The transition out of the game is probably the most devastating thing a person can go through! You're twenty-seven facing a transition that most people face at age sixty to sixty-five. An older person is more apt to be ready for a change. But at twenty-seven—you want to keep playing but your time is up!"

When Grant's time was up in 1984, he left the Devils the way an arrow leaves a bow. "I retired from the NHL on Friday and I was at work on Monday in the field of commercial printing," he reported. "Since I was twenty years old, I've always worked during my summers in graphic arts.

"At about the same time I owned a restaurant. We worked really hard, had a lot of fun and made a lot of money!" he declared. He eventually sold the business and with two partners, started a new enterprise called "Taste of Chicago" within which they orchestrated twenty-seven community-fest parties over a three-year period

Grant had also had an itch to enter the white-collar world, so later, he started a distribution business for licensed sports products. "We couldn't get a card license, but we had a good product and distribution network," he explained. "In the end though, we just couldn't make enough money."

So he shed the distribution but retained the white collar while adding a few hats and a couple of partners to found the Chicago Wolves of the International Hockey League. He served in every aspect of the operation as the club's president, general manager and coach until his release in March of 1997.

And in addition to establishing and running the Midwest Elite Hockey School, Grant speaks to various youth-hockey groups in the Chicago area. "I tell the following story for the benefit of parents who might be tempted to yell at their kids," he related. "I ask the following questions:

- How many of you out there work in a structured environment?

- How many of you are around 5'10"?

- How many of you work with others who are 6'4"?

- If a dollar bill was tossed in the corner and everyone converges on it, who do you think will come away with the bill? (Most people inevitably think the 6'4" guy will and therefore aren't necessarily willing to try.)

Then I follow up with:

-Your child is about four-feet tall and yet you expect him to go in the corner and do the same thing. It takes courage and it's a level of courage that you yourself might not have! So think about that next time you're tempted to criticize your child's play."

When asked about his hobbies, Grant shrugged his shoulders and claimed to have none. "I'm the most boring guy," he contended. Simply put, he loves to play, manage, promote and talk hockey, anytime, anywhere.

Napier, Mark: *Played right wing for Toronto, Birmingham (WHA), Montreal, Minnesota, Edmonton and Buffalo (NHL) from 1975-1989. Born: Toronto, Ontario, 1957.*

Mark Napier was a speedy right winger, blessed with a great sense of balance and a hard, accurate shot. During his junior days as a Toronto Marlboro, he racked up 156 goals in three seasons. He then jumped to the World Hockey Association at age eighteen and notched 256 points in 242 games. He was a hot item ready to burn a path on Montreal Forum ice.

Although the points were harder to come by in the NHL, Mark continued to excite fans and score goals. He won his first Stanley Cup with the Canadiens in 1978-79 before seeing action in Minnesota, Edmonton—where he won his final Cup—and in the end, in Buffalo.

At the close of the 1988-89 season, Mark had two offers on his kitchen table. Return to the Sabres' camp in the fall without a contract or take up general manager Ron Chipperfield's offer to play for Bolzano in Italy.

"We always wanted to play in Europe," he recalled. So he and his wife, Jan, decided the time was right for a change. He cleaned out his locker in Buffalo and they packed their bags and passports for Italy.

"The first year was just a one-year deal," he recounted. "We were looking at it kind of like a paid vacation. But I had a good year and the team won the championship, so we ended up staying for three more years."

In his second season, he joined former Oilers' goaltender Jimmy Corsi in Varasi. For his final two seasons, he played under head coach Ted Sator in Milan alongside Tom Tilley and Roberto Romano.

Mark attributes his success in Italy to getting the kind of skating room that was hard

MARK NAPIER

Elite Cresting Inc.

167 Denison Street
Markham, Ont. L3R-1B5

to come by in the NHL. "It was great for me because they had the wide European rinks," he explained. "It was more of a skating and passing game which suited my style very well. Each team usually had two pretty solid lines and two or three solid defensemen. It wasn't the calibre of the NHL but it wasn't bad hockey either."

Over the span of three years, he also developed a working knowledge of Italian which made negotiating for necessities a little easier. "I only played two games a week, so I had lots of free time," he reported. "We'd get down to Rome and Venice and we'd go up into Switzerland and Austria. We did quite a bit of exploring."

By 1993, Mark was ready to retire from the nomadic life of professional hockey. So he and his family returned to Ontario to write a new chapter of their lives.

"What we really wanted to do was to settle down," he remarked. "And for us, Toronto was home. If I had decided to stay in the hockey business, then obviously there would have been a lot of travelling. Especially coaching—you're two years here and three years there. Our number-one priority was just to stay in one place. (At least until his appointment as head coach of the St. Michael's Majors of the OHA in May of 1997.) It wasn't easy at the time. There was a recession going on when we first got back, so there wasn't a lot out there. I spent about half a year looking around for something to do."

Mark eventually hooked up with a partner and established Elite Cresting based in Markham, Ontario. "We deal a lot with sporting-

goods stores," he explained. "For instance they will send us blank jerseys and we'll put crests, numbers and names on them. We also do team jackets and prepare marketing materials for company promotions."

In his spare time, Mark plays golf and is a devoted spectator of his kids' sports activities. "I coach my son's hockey team and my daughter's into golf," he related.

Neilson, Jim: *Played defense for the New York Rangers, California, Cleveland (NHL) and Edmonton (WHA) from 1962-1979. Born: Big River, Saskatchewan, 1941.*

Jim Neilson does not speak of his past life in sentimental terms. Whether describing his accomplishments as a family man or as a professional hockey player, he prefers to dodge the limelight which in its afterglow, exposes a man who deep down inside, is proud and knows his worth.

"Everybody goes to work for the city and digs a ditch. Nobody writes about them!" he contended. "So I wonder, what the hell do they want about me? I didn't do anything. I just played hockey—your average Joe player. I mean you want to talk to some guys who did something, won some Stanley Cups, scored four goals in a game!

"I was just part of the twenty guys and went about my business. There was no fanfare then. Why should there be any now? I don't miss what I never had."

Jim cleared the slot for the last time in 1979 during the Edmonton Oilers final season in the WHA. He then headed south to start a business.

"I started playing hockey in '62," he recollected, describing the origin of his second career. "I couldn't afford to golf in the summer because we never made enough [money] during the winter, so we had to work in the summer. Maybe ten years later, when I was making some coin, doing an appearance on the banquet circuit, I didn't have to work steady. So, I started golfing. At one point, I was a ten handicapper.

"When I finished hockey in 1980, myself and

four other guys bought a golf course in L.A. We lasted three years. Things were a little wrong internally—it just didn't work out. So when we got an offer from a Korean outfit, we took it and I came back home to Canada."

Over the years since then, Jim has applied his stick and his knowledge to a variety of endeavours.

"I play occasionally with a Native team called Sagkeeng," he reported. "It's out of Fort Alexander, just north of Winnipeg. I've been to tournaments in London, Paris, Lillehammer, France and Daytona. Our team holds bingos to raise money to attend these tournaments."

He also plays oldtimers' hockey with a team based in Winnipeg, joining Ab McDonald and Nick Mickoski on Thursday nights to have some fun and raise money for charity. "You've got to do something for exercise," he remarked, speaking of his participation. "You go have a couple of laughs for an hour and then go have a couple of beers..."

On occasion, Jim is also invited to do some work with Native groups. "I'll be doing a three-day conference at a Native symposium ... teaching hockey basically," he explained.

When he addresses such events he usually draws on themes close to home. "Respect your own ability, but be part of the whole scene and treat people the way you'd like to be treated," he advised, relaying the central focus of his talks. "I just keep it simple.

"I never grew up on a reserve. I grew up in an orphanage in Prince Albert... I've been around enough to know if people respect themselves, obviously they're going to start respecting other people. That's a good way to start things off. If you've got faith and respect for yourself, it's going to help you on your way to at least striving for what you're looking for. If you get there or you don't, you can keep your head up high and say, 'Well, maybe I have to go left instead of right ... a little curve in the road or maybe you do a little something else'.

"Like myself, I just played hockey. I had no vision of sugarplums in the NHL when I was a kid. I just kept playing and going up the ladder.

All of a sudden, one day I was looking at the Empire State Building. Somebody said, 'Did you dream of that?' I said, 'No, things just happen sometimes'."

Jim's pride slipped to the surface as he described his family which is comprised of a son and two daughters. "My son, David, plays with the Cape Breton Oilers," he declared. "I have a daughter who's a lawyer in Vancouver and my oldest ... is a mother in Toronto. They had a good mother! We got divorced, but my ex and I get along pretty well. We did a lot of things together. They'd attend all the games in New York and I'd take them up into Northern Saskatchewan to do some fishing. Now it's called quality time. In the long run it worked out well for the kids and I guess we can pat ourselves on the back once in a while."

When challenged to the effect that he's a more interesting person than he maintains, Jim embraced its likelihood with diminishing skepticism. "I guess I'm a stubborn Dane. There's lots of Danish blood in me, let alone aboriginal—so sometimes I sell myself short," he confessed. "You could call tomorrow and I'd probably start trying to brag to you. Like, 'I had a good career. I played with super guys. I played against the best in the world. I know I'm well respected for what I did ... in terms of figures and things like that'.

"In those days you were taught to be a good two-way player," he continued. "I learned to be a stay-at-home defenseman. I thought I did that pretty well... But I guess the ultimate is to win the Stanley Cup. All those years I was in the finals only once and Boston had a #4 somebody. I guess what I accomplished was that I was able to stay for a while... I didn't just have a cup of coffee. For just an old stay-at-home defenseman, not too flashy, I guess people like that are needed—a kind of trustworthy-type player. You're always there. I guess sticking around for a few years makes me feel a little good."

Nickname: *Chief*

" 'Chief'! What do you think it was? When you're native, it doesn't matter who you are, everybody's 'Chief'. It is just a term used by certain white guys who can't remember names. In the fifties there wasn't the racism that there is now. Back then everyone seemed to be comfortable. It wasn't meant to be racial. So I thought, 'Hey, they're just calling me "Chief". It's a nice nickname and I'm part native—so why not'?"

—⚬—

Nystrom, Bob: *Played right wing for the New York Islanders from 1972-1985. Born: Stockholm, Sweden, 1952.*

Under the feet of the right person, a setback can be perceived as a springboard upon which greater heights can be attained. Bob Nystrom did some springing of his own during the mid-seventies when it was discovered that his agent had been embezzling money which, instead of securing Bob's future, was used to secure wagers at the race track.

"Fortunately because of that bad turn of events, I met a gentleman who became my good friend, and I guess my guru, by the name of Eddie Bloomingfeld," Bob recollected. "And he said, 'Bob, you're going to have to work sooner or later. You better find something you like.' I would say that's probably the best advice I've ever gotten."

Taking the tip to heart, Bob used his summers to sample career options like hors d'oeuvres at a party. "I knew that unfortunately the money in those days wasn't going to give me enough of a nest egg to say, 'I quit. I want to just take it easy'," he reported. "So I worked with a bank. I worked for a sporting-goods company. I worked for a direct-marketing firm. I worked for a real-estate outfit and then I got into insurance consulting... And you know, that's why I looked forward to training camp every year," he revealed with a laugh. "I would recommend that to any player who feels that things are tough in hockey. It gives you a whole new outlook on playing the game."

While in his prime with the New York Islanders, Bob Nystrom was synonymous with rugged, inspirational play—particularly during playoff overtime games. Of his four sudden-death goals, he saved two of them for the Islanders' drive towards their first Stanley Cup in 1980. He set the stage during the semi-finals by scoring against Buffalo at 21:20 of post-regulation time. Then with the Islanders leading the Flyers three games to two in the finals, he scored seven minutes and eleven seconds into overtime to win the Cup. A frenzy ensued as he flew past the net to the end boards where he was assailed by his jubilant teammates.

Bob remained on Long Island throughout his career, netting 596 career points including eighty-three points in only 157 playoff games.

When an eye injury forced his early retirement in 1985, however, he began to ease himself out of hockey in stages. To start, he became the Islanders' assistant coach under Terry Simpson for two seasons.

> *"It's interesting because my first ... half a season as a coach, I was probably the biggest jerk that ever lived!"*
>
> **Bob Nystrom**

"It's interesting because my first ... half a season as a coach, I was probably the biggest jerk that ever lived!" he remarked. "Unfortunately when you move to the other side, you become extremely critical of the players. You take it as a personal insult when the team loses. It's disappointing to see that the players don't go 110 percent all the time. It took me about half a year and then I took some tapes out and watched myself play. I came to the realization that I was no bargain on plenty of nights either."

Bob eventually got an offer for a ticket out of town as head coach of the Islanders' farm club. But as much as he liked coaching, the notion of life on the road ran contrary to his stable, family lifestyle. Instead, he stayed on with the Islanders' organization in New York with one foot in and the other foot out.

"The team asked me to get involved in the marketing side, so I basically work two jobs now," he reported. "I work two-and-a-half days right here with the Islanders and I work two-and-a-half days with a company called 'KM Consulting'. There, I am the marketing director. We're an employee-benefit consulting firm—we work with companies here on Long Island and nationally to develop benefit programmes for their employees. It's been great! Ultimately, I'm going to have to make a decision here. It's becoming more and more difficult to split my time because the workload is becoming heavy. But I've got to say that I've had a real true love affair with the game and the Islanders have been gracious enough to allow me to maintain contact with them."

Since joining the Islanders' front office, Bob has handled marketing, rinkboard advertising, community relations and radio colour commentary for home games. And his debut behind the microphone was not unlike a first lesson in violin. "I was probably just terrible!" he quipped. "You know it takes a little time. It takes a little practice and knowledge to get your thought process going fast enough to fit into a ten-second segment. So it's been a lot of fun."

Bob spends his recreational time keeping his body in finely tuned form. "I'm a physical-fitness fanatic," he affirmed with enthusiasm. "I run two marathons and I do triathlon. I ran in the New York City Marathon... We get about 25,000 runners. I never knew what to expect because I thought it would thin out over the twenty-six miles. But I was running with a pack of about one hundred people at all times... And I don't run all that fast—I'm just a bulldozer."

Bob also makes a priority of spending time with his family. He and his wife, Michelle, are raising a son and a daughter. "I love watching my son play hockey and my daughter play basketball," he reported. "They basically take up a lot of the weekend. But I truly enjoy that."

O'Brien, Dennis: *Played defense for Minnesota, Colorado, Cleveland and Boston from 1970-1980. Born: Port Hope, Ontario, 1949.*

There were few noticeable distinctions between Dennis O'Brien the hockey player and Dennis O'Brien the man. On ice, he was a rugged, no-nonsense, stay-at-home defenseman who spent most of his career in Minnesota. Off ice, he was and is a down-to-earth, stay-at-home family man whose commitment to his loved ones was about to be put to the test.

The year was 1980—a time filled with changes and turmoil that would affect the O'Brien family's course for years to come.

"I went down on waivers," Dennis recalled. "So I would have had to stay in the minors and gamble on maybe somebody taking me later. If someone would have scooped me for a run at the playoffs, it would have been a year here and a year there. I was getting a little long in the tooth and it was time to hang them up. After playing that long upstairs, I didn't feel like riding buses and crap like that. I can remember how much energy I had when I was young and I wasn't about to be chasing the young guys around and putting up with all the garbage.

"So I made my decision. I phoned my wife and I told her, 'That's it! I'm going to end it. We'll sell the house and we're going to go back to Canada.' It was made that quick."

Dennis sold his house in Boston, but two days before leaving, his daughter, Kelly, contracted a virus that damaged her kidney to the extent of requiring a transplant. "We ended up staying a year longer. It was something that we just had no choice in," Dennis explained. "We had to hang in there till she got better. So once she was finished with the transplant, the doctor was happy and allowed the family to move home."

In the ensuing years, Kelly underwent two additional transplants and was to receive her fourth kidney. Dennis was very hopeful about her eventual recovery. But since our original interview, she passed away during the summer of 1996. In spite of the adversity, Kelly faced the challenges of her short life with dignity and

Nickname Challenge #20

The Duke of Paducah

"Back in my era, guys had to dress up. You didn't come down to practice with a jacket on. You came down with a suit, a shirt and a tie on. You know you didn't just look like you were off the boat. And it was kind of nice. So Annis Stukus, who used to play with the Winnipeg Blue Bombers, came down to Toronto to be a sports writer—and a good one. Since I took pride in being dressed up for the rink, he hung the name on me."

Who is he?

Clues

a. He played left wing for Toronto and Boston from 1946-1956.

b. He was born in Sault Ste. Marie, Ontario and notched 259 career points in the NHL.

c. His initials are J.K.

If you were poke checked on that one, see page 285.

strength.

Long before her passing, Dennis returned to his native Port Hope, Ontario where he was approached by two friends who worked for a local corrections facility. On their suggestion, he got hired as a supervisor at Brookside Youth Centre. He started out by being responsible for phase-one kids who were between the ages of twelve and fifteen. But in 1985, when their jurisdiction changed government ministries, Dennis became a corrections officer for kids over the age of sixteen.

"We're not in one big institution where you walk down halls and doors clink," he emphasized, speaking of his facility. "They're like big bungalow houses with eighteen bedrooms, so there's eighteen to nineteen boys per unit down one hall. They can come out of their rooms at any time—they're not locked in. So it's an easier setting for the kids.

"We organize everything. We get them up for breakfast. They do their chores. We take them to school and then when they're in school we do different things like some of us will stay in school in case there's trouble while some us have to be doing interviews."

Dennis stressed that he's grateful to be where he is. "I don't think I could work in the adult part of corrections," he remarked. "To go in every day and just open cell doors to let so many out—but when you're working with young teenagers, you know a lot of them want help. But their home life's been awful. Mom and Dad have been bad actors. They want to change and they're young enough to realize that if they get on the right track, that maybe they can make something out of their lives."

For recreation, Dennis is a member of a local golf club and takes pleasure in playing some oldtimers' hockey as well.

Thinking back on the NHL, he reflected on his perception that the stars of his day shone a little brighter than the luminaries of today. "I do know that we had some awfully gifted players in our time," he recollected. "I have a hard time picking them out on the ice right now. You do have your Pavel Bures. But we had an awful lot of guys who could do a lot of things with the puck, like your Gilbert Perreaults and Marcel Dionnes. But then again, Gretzky did amazing things for years and Lemieux's another one. I'm just wondering why our superstars seemed to shine so much more than the ones today. I don't know why that is. I wonder whether we as average players were maybe not as good as the average players today. It just seems that the average guys today get away with a lot more than we ever did."

Oliver, Murray: *Played centre for Detroit, Boston, Toronto and Minnesota between 1957 & 1975. Born: Hamilton, Ontario, 1937.*

Murray Oliver was as quick and smooth on skates as a finger passing through a candle's flame. He had a playmaker's mind and a knack around the net that, over sixteen seasons, brought home 753 career points. As a versatile and dependable performer, he became recognized as a premier penalty killer who played a clean, honest game.

During the earlier stages of his career, Murray and his peers typically negotiated their own contracts directly with their team's management. And for the most part, he discovered that the word "negotiation" was a polite term used by team owners to mean: "We're the only game in town, so take it or leave it!"

But gradually over the years, player agents came onto the scene and began, however slowly, to rearrange the furniture. Late in his career, Murray decided to try one on for size while negotiating his contract with the North Stars in 1975. The problem was, they hadn't quite gotten the bugs out yet. "When I quit in '75, I could have played a couple more years because I could still skate," he asserted. "But that's the only time I ever had an agent. We were trying for two years, but they only wanted to give me one year. Finally they said, 'The hell with it! You're done!' So I went looking for another job."

Murray dispensed with his agent and hooked up with the Northland hockey-stick company as a sales rep in the Minnesota area. "I handled the professionals for them—selling sticks, helmets, masks and that kind of stuff," he explained. "It turned out to be a good thing to get away from the game, to get out in the business world and see what the real world is ... like—to get some experience in selling and talking to people in different walks of life."

But after three years on the Northland sales circuit, he was well primed to rejoin the North Stars as an assistant under head coach Glen Sonmor. But Sonmor was replaced by Lorne Henning who came complete with his own staff—so Murray got the squeeze into amateur scouting.

"Then in 1988," he recalled, "when Herbie Brooks was here, Lou Nanne, the North Stars' general manager, quit because the game was driving him nuts. Jack Ferreira took over and wanted to have his own people here, so we all got let go."

Murray's tumble onto the open market, however, was cut short by Pat Quinn who brought him on board as a pro scout for the Vancouver Canucks. He is still with the club today, serving as director of pro scouting—a job that taps deeply into his forty years of major-league experience.

"You know what it takes to make it in your own heart," he remarked on the subject of judging talent. "You're not always 100% ... but I'm willing to bet that I'm right more times than I'm wrong as to whether a guy can play or not, and how good he's going to be... I don't think I know everything—I'm always willing to learn something and I do pick up things from other guys. But I think it's a basic instinct—you get to know what you're looking for and some things never change. Guys have to be able to skate. And then there's the intangibles: the skill levels, the goal scoring, toughness... You go to a game and you look at body language. Does a guy sulk when he gets taken off the ice? Does he slam the door when the head coach takes him off? There are all sorts of tricks, things that you look for..."

When Murray has a break from the road and time on his hands, he usually fills it with hammers, saws, or golf clubs. "I love to play golf and I'm a carpenter," he reported. "I took my apprenticeship when I was playing junior in Hamilton and became a journeyman that year. I worked for my uncle who had a construction company in Mount Hope. Then I turned pro so I haven't worked at the trade for a long time—but I'm still pretty handy around the house."

Over the years, he and his wife, Helen, have raised a son and a daughter and are now grandparents twice over. They make their home in Edina, Minnesota.

Nicknames: *MO; Muzz*

"When I first started playing junior hockey, the guys used to call me 'MO', after my initials," Murray said. "Then in Detroit, my first roommate was Alex Delvecchio. He started calling me 'Muzz' and that stuck with me ever since. He made the connection with Muzz Patrick in New York because we both had Murray as a first name."

Bert Olmstead

Olmstead, Burt: *Played left wing for Chicago, Montreal and Toronto from 1948-1962. Born: Scepter, Saskatchewan, 1926.*

As a professional hockey player, Burt Olmstead gave the best of his essence to his teammates, to his team and to the National Hockey League. In return, he and his peers received a smidgen of the league's revenues coupled with the promise of a pension that would hardly sustain grandma's penchant for tea and biscuits.

In the ensuing years, Burt witnessed players who fell on hard, financial and personal times. But the league offered little if any support.

As more of the story about the league's exploitation of its past players was revealed, his feelings of bitterness grew to the point where today, he has severed all ties with the NHL.

In fact, even a mention of what he considers to be the betrayal of himself and his generation, raises his wrath to such a height that it takes him a day or so to return to earth.

And although Burt has made his stand, he's never lost sight of the human side of the issue. When news broke that a dinner was to be held in honour of his former teammate, Dave Balon, who now suffers from multiple sclerosis, Burt took notice.

"There were 700 people at the dinner," said Bill Hicke, the evening's host. "But the biggest surprise was that Dickie Moore and Burt Olmstead showed up. It was just a fantastic tribute to Dave! The fact that they were there speaks for itself."

Bill also added some additional insight into the character of his former teammate: "Burt Olmstead! Nobody ever understood him because he was such a competitor. And he was so mean! But he's a tremendous human being. The fact that he was there was even more of a surprise because he doesn't associate too much with anything."

"I like him," Bill continued. "He was my coach in Oakland. The guys there just didn't understand him because he's a fierce competitor. I remember my first year in Montreal. We won the game five to one. The Rocket scored three goals against Chicago in the Stanley Cup playoffs. Burt went in the dressing room and the first guy he jumped on was the Rocket—told him he didn't play that good. He was a competitor!"

After all these years, Burt still hasn't lost his edge. He was a strong moral supporter of the Professional Hockey Pensioners' Association's bid to sue the NHL and many team owners over surplus pension money. For him, news of the Association's victory was like breaking free for an end-to-end rush capped by a bullet drive in the upper corner of the NHL's coffers.

In the wake of their success, Burt stated that a special induction category should be created for entry into the Hockey Hall of Fame that would allow the signatories of the lawsuit, Alan Stanley, Leo Reise Jr., Carl Brewer, Gordie Howe, Bobby Hull, Eddie Shack and Andy Bathgate to gain entry on the basis of their legal action alone. He also suggested that certain league builders already in the Hall should be removed to make more room.

Parisé, J.P.: *Played left wing for Boston, Toronto, Minnesota, the New York Islanders and Cleveland from 1965-1979. Born: Smooth Rock Falls, Ontario, 1941.*

As a hockey player, J.P. Parisé specialized in being backed into a corner by rival throngs. He could be waylaid along the boards by twenty bodies and still be the first to tunnel free with the puck. His ability to scramble at close quarters earned him 652 career points and a spot as the designated grinder for the 1972 edition of Team Canada—a team which is still making history.

And although he sported a number of team colours in his day, he spent more time in a North Stars' jersey than any other. The city of Bloomington, Minnesota had become his home and he wanted to keep it that way. Fortunately, he'd made friends along the way including North Stars' general manager Lou Nanne.

After threading his final pass for the Stars in 1979, J.P. was invited to stay on with the organization as a scout. "I basically started from scratch," he related. "Lou Nanne wanted me to

work at all levels. So I did some junior scouting, some special-assignment scouting and some pros for possible trades. Then the following year, I was an assistant coach with Glen Sonmor and Murray Oliver. My job again was to do some advanced scouting. I also worked with kids like Dino Ciccarelli on their shots and individual skills."

In 1982, J.P. spent a season coaching the North Stars' farm team in Salt Lake City before returning to the parent club to work as an assistant to a succession of head coaches that included Bill Mahoney, Lorne Henning, Glen Sonmor and Herb Brooks.

But with the arrival of Head coach Pierre Pagé and general manager Jack Ferreira in 1988, the decks were cleared for a whole new crew—and fortunately J.P. was more than ready to jump ship.

"I was already looking around because I knew that things were getting tough," he reported. "I wanted to get out of hockey because I wanted to spend some time with my kids. If you stay in the National Hockey League ... you're never home. And I didn't want to do that. So I said, 'I'm going to get out of this stuff. I'm going to get out of hockey.' It was a little scary because I'd never done anything else."

One of J.P.'s friends was president of Accordia Commercial Insurance Agency based in Minneapolis. "He asked me if I wanted to get involved in insurance," he recollected. "I said, 'I know absolutely nothing about insurance.' So my friend said, 'Here's what you do. You're going to see if you can get your license.' If you are able to do that, then your mind is working pretty good because it's tough. That consisted of a week of school, nine hours a day. They gave us all of this information and on the Saturday morning we went to write the exam. And so I did it—I got my license. Then I had to start from scratch because I had never really sold anything. It was trying at times, but I had a lot of support. Within two or three years, I was right on top of things! So I did pretty well."

J.P. stayed with Accordia until the summer of 1996 when an irresistible offer pried him loose to

204

direct the hockey operations of a private prep school called Shattuck-St. Mary's in Saribault, Minnesota.

One of his responsibilities is to use his sales savvy to recruit new students for their hockey programme. He contends that Shattuck has the edge over other schools because the state of Minnesota limits high-school hockey players to twenty-two games per year in an effort to support a stronger focus on academics. "It makes it more appealing at our school because our kids play fifty-five to sixty games a year," he declared. "And we travel all over. So we're sort of a rebel team! We're not very popular amongst the high-school coaches."

In addition, he serves as head coach of the school's bantam team while former NHLer Scott Bjugstad does honours with the midgets.

J.P.'s oldest son, Jordan, is attending Shattuck and playing hockey this season. His wife, Donna, and their youngest son, Zach, are remaining in Bloomington for an additional year before reuniting in Saribault when Zach becomes eligible to attend the school.

And although J.P.'s focus is devoted to minor hockey, he is still keenly aware of the NHL today. "I think that the 1972 series against the Russians really did wonders for the game of hockey," he emphasized. "The Russians really studied the game. Where as we basically played an up-and-down style, the Russians were going out in circles and skating all over, interchanging positions. It expanded things—it opened up our eyes!

"And around the same time, video came in so people could study hockey," he continued. "You could study power plays, penalty killing. You could look at games, break them down. Then one thought leads to another—coaches could become very, very creative.

"Also, when I retired, I think the bigger players really came into play—with the arrival of Clark Gillies. Before, if you were that size, you were sort of awkward and clumsy. And all of a sudden guys like Holmgren came along who were into the 6'2", 3", 4" [range]. These guys became just as agile and mobile as the little players and probably tougher and stronger. So I think hockey

has reached a wonderful level.

"I have a film called *Highlights of the North Stars From 1972-77*. I'm watching this and I'm saying, 'Holy cripes, we were kind of slow'!" J.P. quipped. "But unlike today, we were pretty well self-taught. Everything we learned we had to learn ourselves and we learned from each other."

Today, as J.P. pointed out, players are taught every detail of the game within an organized structure right from the start.

Park, Brad: *Played defense for the New York Rangers, Boston and Detroit from 1968-1985. Born: Toronto, Ontario, 1948.*

Brad Park was a gritty defenseman who had a flair for every aspect of his game. He was an honest sportsman who could fight well when he had to; clear pucks from his zone like a street sweeper; send opponents head-over-heals with his patented hip-thrust bodychecks; design plays like an architect; and shoot a low-flying point shot with pin-point accuracy.

If it weren't for Bobby Orr and Denis Potvin, Brad would have owned the James Norris Trophy as the league's top defenseman during the first half of his career. He was voted a runner-up six times but never took the prize.

He was, however, selected as a first-team all-star five times and was awarded the Masterton Trophy in 1984 for sportsmanship and dedication to hockey. He received his ultimate acknowledgment in 1988 when he was inducted into the Hockey Hall of Fame.

One of the personal strengths that carried Brad through his hockey career and beyond was his ability to remain highly focused on whatever unfolded in his midst. He was not the type who diffused his energy by attempting to be in two places at the same time. When he was on the ice, he played hockey and when it came time to retire, he retired. He didn't spend time looking over his shoulder regretting the past or second-guessing his choices.

After leaving the Red Wings in 1985, he returned to his home base in Boston to launch his new career as a colour analyst for ESPN in the

United States and for CTV in Canada. "I handled both networks for the first half of the '85-86 season," he recounted. "And then Mike Ilitch, the owner of the Red Wings, approached me to take over the Red Wings as head coach for the second half of the '85-86 season."

Under head coach Harry Neale, the Wings had compiled a record of eight wins, twenty-five losses and four ties. With the team mired in last place, Brad was brought in to stir up some silt at the bottom of the standings. By year's end, little had changed as the club continued to sit on the bedrock of their division.

"A political situation developed with Ilitch and GM Jim Devellano and I was fired in June," Brad revealed. "I had inherited a last-place team for three months. I kept them in the same place and was fired."

Brad then returned once again to Boston to focus on his home and his family. "I played general contractor for a while," he recounted. "We built a house that could accommodate my ... second-oldest son who has cerebral palsy and is in a wheelchair."

After a year of construction work, he turned his focus back to the world of business and making a living. While still in Detroit, Brad had purchased a couple of Little Ceasars Pizza shops. He retained ownership even after returning to Boston although he eventually sold them back to Mike Ilitch.

He then established a small, building-products company that supplied cabinets, appliances and hardware for building kitchens. He dabbled in the field for about two years before joining a friend in the computer-software business.

"A friend of mine from Toronto who was down here asked me if I'd give him a hand," he recounted. "He was dealing with computer products for companies that deal with employee-performance evaluation, a kind of human-resources software. So I found that to be interesting."

Brad did promotional work for his friend's software company until about 1990, when he was struck by an idea for a project of his own. While travelling in Quebec, he had seen a new concept

Brad Park

12 Hunt Road
Amesbury, MA 01913
(508) 388-5788

Located at Exit 54
On Route 495

called tube sledding. People were sliding on inner tubes down a large hill on lanes fashioned out of snow. He saw a potential for the sport in the Boston area, but found it difficult to obtain information on how to set up such an enterprise. So he spent two years researching, preparing a plan and pulling the necessary capital together to launch his project.

He and his partners eventually settled on a site in Amesbury, Massachusetts. Their plan was to develop a park with year-round activities. "We opened up with a driving range in the summer of 1992," he recounted. "Then we opened up the sledding in December. Now we move somewhere between forty to fifty thousand people through here in the winter and we employ over one hundred people..."

Amesbury Sports Park has continued to grow steadily since its opening. Miniature golf, go-carts, bumper boats and volleyball have sprouted up like mushrooms on a joy ride.

However, the addition of so many new attractions has meant hard work and long hours for their owner. "I'll do anything from working the track if we're shorthanded to setting the snow guns to make snow at two o'clock in the morning," Brad reported. "I'll be supervising the entire facility on a weekend, dealing with the public. I've never worked so hard for so long and for so little money in my whole life!"

Steady expansion has also meant a constant rolling over of capital to fund new developments. "The first few years, you're not making a whole bunch of money because you're paying off your

Art Skov:
Between A Puck & A Hard Goal Post

Art Skov speaks about comradery, respect and loving the Blackhawks and the Leafs with equal measure.

Starting Out Under The Wing Of Red Storey: Red Storey was like a father to me. He's one of the best referees that the NHL has ever had. The first game I had was in Chicago. Montreal was playing and I was working with George Hays and Red Storey, two of the oldest guys in the league. I'm in there as a young rookie and Rocket Richard and Doug Harvey were on the ice for that game. I don't know if I blew the whistle at all that night, my mouth was so wide open (laughs).

Between A Puck And A Hard Goal Post: I remember I had a game on a Saturday night in Toronto. Chicago was in town. My youngest boy was a Toronto fan and my oldest boy was a Chicago fan because he knew Glenn Hall and Bobby Hull quite well. So I was coming home the next day. I remember getting off the plane to hug my kids and they're both mad at me. And I said, "What the hell's wrong?" My oldest is mad because Chicago got beat and the other guy's mad because I gave Dave Keon his first penalty of the year sometime in January. I said to my wife, "What the hell am I doing home getting hell from the kids?"

Life After The NHL: I wanted to become a supervisor but there were no jobs available in the National Hockey League at the time. So I worked part-time with the junior referees in the Central Hockey League for a year. Then Bobby Frampton, the referee-in-chief of the World Hockey Association, asked me if I'd come and help him supervise the games. So I did that for three years until the league folded.

Life After The WHA: I worked part-time in a sports shop back here in Windsor. I did that just to keep myself busy for a while. We had a trophy business right in the shop. The boss wanted to get out of the trophy end of things, so I took it over and moved it across the street. We worked at that for about two years but it didn't pan out the way we thought, so I packed things in.

Then I wasn't doing much of anything for quite a while until Brian Lewis of the NHL invited me to join a training program for referees in the IHL, AHL and the East Coast League, but they eventually dropped the programme.

Flying With The Red Wings: Since then I haven't been doing too much of anything outside of being with the Red Wings' alumni association. We have a heck of a good time together. We do about twenty-eight games a year. All the money goes toward charity. We never get a penny out of it. All we ask for is a little get-together with a pizza and a beer after the game. You start telling stories—you know, like how great you were in your day. And after about three beers, you start believing everything you tell them. This is what keeps everybody close.

Today Versus Yesterday: I think that the pride the guys had playing the game and the respect they had for each other was central. They played hard. Don't get me wrong. If they wanted to hit somebody, they'd hit them with their bodies and knock them on the seat of their pants. But today, these kids go with sticks that are so damn high and they're getting away with so much. I just don't understand it. They go at each other seriously with their sticks and hurt each other. I mean I saw that with that [Claude] Lemieux hit on [Kris] Draper. I mean hitting

"Rocket Richard and Doug Harvey were on the ice for that game. I don't know if I blew the whistle at all that night, my mouth was so wide open."

"You start telling stories ... like how great you were in your day. And after about three beers, you start believing everything you tell them."

from behind like that was God awful.

About three days after that happened, I was out at a golf tournament and John Ferguson was there. And I says, "Johnny, I thought of you right away when I saw Lemieux hit this guy. What do you think?" And he said, "I'm so goddamn mad about that! Nobody did nothing!" And I says, "I tell you John, back in our day, if I was a linesman, I wouldn't want to try and stop you!" And he said, "No, I would have went right over top of you." And I said, "I know damn well you would have! I would have gone down the other end of the ice to check the net or some damn thing. I wouldn't have wanted to see nothing."

The Heart Of The Matter: Since I retired when I was fifty-five, I had a bypass operation. In fact I thank Jimmy Peters and the Red Wings' alumni group for catching this thing... We went down to Michigan State University to get checked over to see how healthy we were.

The reason we were checking was because of what happened to George Gee. He was with the Detroit oldtimers before I got to them. They were playing a game in Warren, Michigan. At the end of the first period, George came in, sat down and fell right over dead. He had a heart attack and died right there.

So Jimmy was real close with George and he said, "It's never going to happen again. We're going to make sure we're all healthy on the damn ice before we go out to play." So when we went down to Michigan State, the doctor found that I had a problem with the heart. So I had the operation before anything happened.

Art Skov was an NHL linesman and referee from 1956-1975. He was born in Wheatley, Ontario in 1928.

expenses," he admitted. "But once we get fully operational and get all of our equipment purchased, then things will start to turn around."

Brad spends his spare time far from the madding crowds of bumper boats and inner tubes. "Wherever I can go and the phone doesn't ring," he asserted. "The last few years I've been able to coach my boys in hockey during the winter and I really enjoy that. I've been able to play a little golf with them and we have a cottage. I enjoy it whenever I can get up there."

He and his wife, Gerry, have been raising four sons and a daughter. "We have kids in college and one out of college," he explained. "So they're ... growing up and whenever they get the chance, they come up and work here with me. It's great! As long as they're working for me, I don't have to give them an allowance!" he quipped.

John Peirson

Peirson, John: *Played right wing for Boston between 1946 & 1958. Born: Winnipeg, Manitoba, 1925.*

Although not overly large, John Peirson could play on the feisty side of the fence when the puck found its way into a back alley. He was also a capable defensive forward who had a sharpshooter's aim and a playmaker's brain in the proximity of the opposing net.

He played all of his eleven NHL seasons in Bruins' black and gold. All told, he tallied 352 career points in 554 games—a handsome total in its day.

Off ice, John had the good fortune to have married his future boss's daughter. When he began to see signs that his playing days were near an end in 1957, an offer came through from his father-in-law to work in the furniture business.

"You reach a point in your career where you realize you've lost half a step," he remarked, reminiscing on his decision to retire from hockey. "In those days with six teams, there weren't a lot of places to go. I had a job offer which I had to weigh against the possibility of making the team again or moving to another team ... and with four kids, that didn't make any sense."

So he took his final stride for the Bruins in

1958, opting instead to follow the more sure-footed path of the furniture business.

In the early stages of his second career, John learned the ins and outs of selling tables, sofas and chairs through an association with his father-in-law's factory in Cambridge, Massachusetts.

His transition out of the game and onto the sales circuit was virtually seamless, although the defining essence of hockey was hard to replace. "After you've been in sports for a length of time, say from midget, to bantam, to high school, to college and to the pros, you miss the excitement and the comradery between the teammates," he remarked. "But aside from that, I was really excited about my new job—so that took a lot of the sting out of not playing again."

John stayed on at the furniture factory until his father-in-law eventually sold the business. He then struck out on his own as an independent sales rep for a furniture company based in Hickory, North Carolina. These days, at age seventy-two, he's still going strong—covering all of New England and upstate New York.

"In the furniture business we're considered as

being high end ... in other words, more expensive than normal," he explained. "We're into period furniture of the eighteenth century—and in New England, it's fairly popular. The type of consumer we're targeted towards would be in the top five or ten percent of the earnings curve. And there are still lots of those kinds of people out there. I've built up a pretty good clientele over the years which I've enjoyed doing."

As for family and leisure, John and his wife, Barbara, raised two sons and two daughters. And when he has time off of the road, his number-one love is chipping and tapping golf balls with his former teammate, Paul Ronty.

Forty years now stand between John and his final game in the NHL. While reflecting on the evolution of professional sports over that time, he expressed concern about how big money has clouded the motivation and goals of today's athletes.

"I think the money has not done the game any good," he emphasized. "It hasn't done any sport any good. And despite what people say—that they want to end their career playing with a winner—they go where the money is. You can see it every day in the National Hockey League—people changing teams, and for what reason? For money! They mask it behind what they think is the ability of the team they're with to win the Stanley Cup or to be competitive, but in essence, they move for money.

"In my day, it was just the opposite because we weren't getting paid the kind of money that they are today. When you look at the first contract I ever signed in 1946, it was for forty-five hundred dollars. I thought that was pretty big money in those days!" he revealed with amusement. "I look at it today and I say, 'Wow ... how stupid!' But I'd have given my eyeteeth to play on a Stanley Cup winner.

"I don't blame the players. I think the system is the problem. If it's there, the players should go for it. But don't tell me you want to win a Stanley Cup!"

Pelyk, Mike: *Played defense for Toronto (NHL), Vancouver and Cincinnati (WHA) from 1967-1978. Born: Toronto, Ontario, 1947.*

Twenty-year-old rookie Mike Pelyk was expected to forego the customary year in the minors to facilitate his entry directly onto the Maple Leafs' stage in 1968—the year after Toronto's last Stanley Cup victory. Expectations were high and Mike's level of experience was low. Trial and error became his teacher as he suffered growing pains while the Leafs grew accustomed to the subterranean side of .500 hockey.

Mike Pelyk

It wasn't until 1973 that he had evolved into a frontline defender who could pot a few points and uproot the weeds from his crease—all just in time to jump to the World Hockey Association where he remained until 1976.

He then returned to Toronto for two additional years. And although his final NHL season is listed as 1977-78, he had actually signed a two-year deal with the Buffalo Sabres.

"I was thirty-one at the time," he related. "I'd been playing hockey for thirteen years. Scotty [Bowman] and Roger [Neilson] saw me as a sixth defenseman, penalty killer, assistant coach. I thought, I'm not really interested in coaching and I'm not getting any better ... maybe it's time to start looking at other things. I ended up quitting in training camp.

"I then came back to Toronto and started to work for a company owned by Peter Pocklington called 'Patrician Land Corporation'," Mike continued. "I basically went in there and said, 'Look, I can do the job! Just give me a chance.' I took the job initially for one thousand bucks a month. After three months I got a raise to two thousand dollars a month, and then I was on my way.

"I started there because I wanted to be in the real-estate business... We were trying to develop shopping centres across Ontario and upper New

York state. I was a jack-of-all-trades. I did marketing, development, leasing, public relations ... you name it."

And like a four-wheel drive, Mike was rolling from coast to coast. He left Patrician and stepped up to Burger King Canada, helping to develop new restaurant sites across the country for the next three years.

Then, when Wendy's International bought back the rights to Wendy's restaurants in Canada, they sought Mike's services for their new development team. "They recruited me out of Burger King to be director of real estate and franchises," he reported. "They had about seventy restaurants in Canada at the time. So the mandate was to build more restaurants and take some existing ones in certain areas where they were clustered and develop them into franchise markets."

Three years later Wendy's began to experience some tough times in the United States. Fearing that the instability might spread to Canada, Mike jumped ship to the Hudson's Bay Corporation as their director of real estate. Their holdings included The Bay, Zellers, Simpsons and Field department stores.

But, like a highly touted draft pick, Mike continued to catch the eye of the corporate scouts who secured his rights for the Loblaws group of companies in 1987. "They liked the work I'd done for them while I was still with The Bay," he remarked. "So they hired me to reorganize their whole real-estate function within the company."

Two years later, Mike moved his game to J.D.S. Investments. "It was a big development company building shopping centres and residential and office buildings," he recounted. "It had been a family-run business. But they brought a group of us in with a mandate to try and get it operating as a more professional company instead of a mom-and-pop place."

"I basically went in there and said, 'Look, I can do the job! Just give me a chance.' I took the job initially for one thousand bucks a month..."

Mike Pelyk

But a year and a half later, after the company changed hands, the new owner experienced debt problems and everyone, including Mike, was given walking papers.

With his career heaving about like that of a hockey coach, he then hooked up with Bramalea as a consultant. "I worked there for about six months," he related. "Then they made me the vice president of their industrial and business parks which was a big part of their portfolio."

Two years later, Mike branched out on his own as a consultant for a short while before connecting with his present employer, Oxford Development Group, Inc. "I'm head of retail leasing for Oxford," he explained. "We own and manage a portion of a portfolio of about twenty-seven million square feet that includes shopping centres, industrial parks and downtown office developments right across Canada and the U.S."

Away from the office, Mike approaches recreation with the same fearless panache he applies to his career. "I like to golf, play tennis, squash, work out, go to the theatre and play bridge," he asserted. "There isn't anything I won't try."

And as his corporate real estate has brought him knowledge and experience, his endeavour to raise children has advanced him on a slow, wending excursion towards wisdom. "First and foremost you want them to be happy," he pointed out. "And second of all, you want them to be successful. As long as they're happy with what they're doing, I'm happy. And I'll tell you, it took me a long while to come to that conclusion! I guess I'm like any parent... You always want your children to do better and to work a little harder than you did. Then you wake up one morning and realize that everybody's different. What makes them feel happy and successful aren't necessarily the things that do it for you."

"...we're going to meet to give away probably thirty, forty, fifty thousand dollars. We're having a ball! It's been peaches and apples really."—Jim Peters

Peters, Jim, Sr.: *Played right wing for Montreal, Boston, Detroit and Chicago from 1945-1954. Born:Verdun, Quebec, 1922.*

The year 1940 was an eventful one for Jim Peters. He'd just started his first year of pro hockey and life in the NHL was closer than the length of his stick. But then again, so was World War II. "I came back to Montreal in 1940 and went into the army for five years," he recalled. "And while I was gone, we had a set of twins, a boy and a girl."

When Jim returned from overseas in 1945, his priorities had quite naturally shifted from pro hockey to the welfare of his family. If he were to have entered the NHL at that point, he'd have required a real push. "I wanted to get a job and raise my family," he reported with a firm tone. "But the Montreal Canadiens said, 'You're playing for us!' I said, 'No I'm not!' They said, 'Yes you are!' I said, 'No I'm not! I'm not good enough!' And then I said, 'Well, if I'm playing, I guess I'm playing.' So that's how it all started."

Four years later, while playing for the Boston Bruins, Jim was traded to the Red Wings in exchange for Joe Carveth. For Jim, as he later described, it was the best thing that could have happened.

The city of Detroit proved to be so much more than just a place to play hockey. It offered a secure future. "I think Detroit has been really, really great to the athlete who wants to work outside of hockey," he remarked. "They give him an opportunity and if he works at it, he gets a little lucky and then he gets himself a job."

Jim was one such athlete who wanted to work. In 1950, he began to spend his summers in the service of the automotive industry. By the time hockey was laid to rest in 1954, he was raring to step into a full-time pair of sales shoes—which he did, representing a supplier of welding systems used to assemble sheet metal for car manufacturing. Jim is now seventy-five years old and after forty-seven years, he's still selling for the same company. "We do work for Ford, Chrysler and G.M.," he remarked. "We knock on the door and ask for an opportunity to bid on a job. Then we take it back to the plant and estimate it. If we're lucky then they'll give us a purchase order."

Jim admitted that, like a child in a toy store, the wonder of assembly lines and welding sparks has kept him coming back. "First you start out not knowing how a car is made," he recounted. "Then you go on an assembly line and see what they're doing and you get kind of amazed! Plus, you meet a lot of wonderful people."

In leisure as in work, Jim is the iron man of the Detroit Red Wings' alumni team, edging out Joe Klukay as the club's oldest member by one month. "I've been there from day one," he declared. "We go out and play for different charities which is wonderful. In fact, Monday we're going to meet to give away probably thirty, forty, fifty thousand dollars. We're having a ball! It's been peaches and apples really."

Over the years, he and his wife, Olive, raised two daughters and a son, Jim Jr., who like his father, also played in the NHL.

Jim and Olive remain settled in their home overlooking a lake in Pontiac, Michigan.

—⸺⸺⸺

Peters, Jim, Jr.: *Played centre for Detroit and Los Angeles between 1965 & 1975. Born: Montreal, Quebec, 1944.*

Jim Peters Jr. saw his first steady major-league action with the Detroit Red Wings starting in 1967. The following season he joined the Los Angeles Kings where he settled in for the duration of his NHL career as a defensive specialist.

He spent most of the 1974-75 season playing for the Kings' American Hockey League affiliate in Springfield. "The Kings brought me up just for

Jim Peters Jr.

a couple of games," he recounted. "So that was my final time of ever playing in the NHL."

Jim spent the following season playing for Fort Worth of the Western Hockey League before finally drawing the curtain on his pro career.

Heading out into the deserts of Arizona would hardly be the next anticipated move for a former hockey player. But as Jim soon discovered, cacti, sand and ice are not entirely incompatible. With the hope of one day coaching at the collegiate level, he jumped at the chance to lead a club team at Northern Arizona University in Flagstaff—all in exchange for free tuition.

Over the next four years he seized the opportunity to complete his bachelor's degree in education and then later, his Master's degree.

He then returned to Michigan to put his new training into action as a substitute teacher and to work for a golf course.

"At the end of that year," he recounted, "lo and behold, the Athletic Director at Northern Arizona called me and said, 'We're going to make this a varsity sport. We'd like you to come back and be their first coach'."

So Jim and his family put their winter gear in storage and headed back to the sun-baked desert. This time his position required extensive travelling to play games and recruit new prospects. It was only a matter of time until staring at the back of a Greyhound seat left him yearning for the stay-at-home life of a family man. Three years transpired before he finally resigned and headed east to resume his career in education.

His first outing was teaching grade-five geography and grade-eight history at a private day school in Birmingham, Michigan. "It was a real tough year for me," he related with angst. "I think the most difficult thing was being in the classroom for the very first time. History not being my major, I was automatically teaching something I was unfamiliar with. It was a very exclusive school with a lot of money—I just felt that there was a lot of pressure on me. I was up very late doing papers, finding that there just weren't enough hours in the day, trying to figure out what I could do in the classroom to make it more interesting. Battling twenty-four kids with discipline issues was really tough! It was a real shocker for me. I remember coming home in October and telling my wife, 'I can't go on! I can't go back.' But I stuck it out and made it through the year."

Jim made his escape from the world of classrooms on the tailwind of an offer from Rensselaer Polytechnical Institute in Troy, New York. He landed as an assistant coach to Mike Addesa. "I was basically the team's recruiter," Jim reported. "The most famous player I recruited during my three years there was Joe Juneau who is now with Washington."

But again, he found that the distance between himself and his family was expanding with every mile spent on the road. To seal the gap, he pounced on an offer to become an athletic director and hockey coach at a prep school called Vermont Academy.

Nine years later, he still holds the director's chair. His responsibilities include scheduling sporting events, arranging transportation, coaching hockey and golf and serving as a dorm parent.

Now thoroughly settled in his New England way of life, Jim looked back on the distant breach of leaving the NHL. "For me it was difficult," he admitted. "But it made it a lot easier knowing that at least I had the wisdom to keep pecking away, saying, 'I need to get an education'. Getting that bachelor's degree and getting that Master's degree certainly made the transition easier for me. But even today at my age, fifty-two, if I ever lost my job here, I really don't feel that I could do much of anything else. Hockey has been my life. And being an athletic director, I really learned as I went along. I guess I could do that at some other place. But for many hockey players, you almost have the feeling that that's all you can do."

For the past seven or eight years, Jim has also donated his time to teaching on behalf of Hockey Ministries International. He reserves the rest of his spare time to spend with his wife, Nancy, who is a part-time nurse at the school, and their sons, Jim III and Andy. They currently reside in the small town of Saxton's River, Vermont.

Nickname: *Pistol Pete*

"While we were playing in Los Angeles, Bill Flett named me 'Pistol Pete' after the basketball player Pete Maravich," Jim recalled.

Picard, Noel: *Played defense for Montreal, St. Louis and Atlanta between 1964 & 1973. Born: Montreal, Quebec, 1938.*

Noel Picard was an original St. Louis Blue. As such, he refined his rugged brand of defense in the presence of such legends as Glenn Hall and Dickie Moore. He also waged combat against a legion of greats lead by Bobby Orr who was the beneficiary of Noel's hook, launching Orr into his now immortalized horizontal leap after scoring in overtime to claim the Stanley Cup from the Blues in 1970.

When it came time to fold up his Atlanta Flame jersey in 1973, Noel stuck with tradition by continuing to keep prestigious company.

He returned to his home base in St. Louis to work as a television colour analyst with Dan Kelly whom he described as "the greatest hockey announcer I ever saw!" From 1974 to 1979, Noel added colour to the booming voice that came the closest to rivaling a slap shot. "He was great to work with," Noel emphasized. "And he was a big, big eater. He could eat all the time. But outside of that, he was a great guy."

With the rest of his time, he established a restaurant seventy miles south of St. Louis in Cuba, Missouri. He called the place "Noel Picard's Midway" and operated it for eight years.

At that point in time, he was recruited by Anheuser Busch Breweries to promote their products—in a less than conventional manner. Having gained experience with horses while growing up in rural Quebec, he was enlisted as a trainer for ten of the breweries' Kleidsdale horses. They moved from city to city in three large trucks. It's ironic that when he and his crew came to town they could whip up more attention and fanfare than an entire hockey team.

For the next eight years Noel marched his leviathan charges through parades in villages, towns and cities across Canada and the United States. "The work I was doing with the Kleidsdales was a prestige job," he emphasized. "It was like I was playing hockey again."

He and his horses eventually relocated to Fort Collins, Colorado where Anheuser had opened a new brewery. They set up a ranch facility right next door where he could continue to manage the Kleidsdales.

But after an additional four years of touring, Noel had finally had his fill of horseshoes and hooves. So he resigned from the brewery and shifted his focus to another skill he had learned in Quebec—building furniture. Having

Nickname Challenge #21

Knuckles

"When I first broke into the league, I fought a fair amount. I've got fairly big hands which, most of the time, were fairly bruised—so Brian Spencer nicknamed me 'Knuckles'. He also had a shorter version of it. He'd say, 'Hey "Knucks", how ya doing'?"

Who is he?

Clues

a. He played right wing for the New York Islanders from 1972-1985.

b. He scored four overtime playoff goals during his career, one to win the Stanley Cup in 1980.

If you were caught in the goal crease,
see page 285.

developed woodworking skills under his father's tutelage while growing up, Noel was able to craft such items as desks and headboards for the people in the Fort Collins community.

But by 1995, he had developed a yearning to spend more time with his kin, so he returned to Quebec. He is now semi-retired and living about seventy miles outside of Montreal in St. Damien de Brandon. "I come from a family of ten children," he related. "So it's great to have them in the area."

Noel's immediate family is more spread out. His daughter, Annie, lives in Chicago while his son, Danny, is in the United States Air Force in Portland, Oregon. Noel is particularly partial to his grandson, Andrew, who occasionally comes up from Oregon to do some fishing with his grandfather.

Pilote, Pierre: *Played defense for Chicago and Toronto from 1955-1969. Born: Kenogami, Quebec, 1931.*

Pierre Pilote was much bigger in his deeds than he was in physical size. He consistently deceived his adversaries by extending himself beyond the limits of his 5'10", 178-pound frame through the use of visualization techniques. One of the first hockey players to consciously employ such methods, he would imagine himself successfully shutting his opponents down in advance of actual games. Such imagery enhanced his already ample supply of tenacity and grim determination.

Pierre served a four-year apprenticeship with the Buffalo Bisons of the American Hockey League before receiving a green light to join the Blackhawks in 1955. He quickly evolved into a finesse player, respected for his playmaking skills, superior skating and leadership.

By 1961, he had become a frontline defender who lead the league with 165 penalty minutes, scored fifteen points in twelve playoff games to win his lone Stanley Cup and accepted the team's captaincy—a post he held until he was traded to Toronto in 1968.

All told, Pierre's talents were acknowledged

to the tune of three straight Norris Trophies as the league's best defenseman from 1963-65 plus five consecutive first-team all-star awards culminating in 1967.

In 1968-69, he played one final season in a somewhat unsuitable Maple Leaf blue before retiring with the comfortable knowledge that his second career as a businessman and investor was already airborne and rapidly gaining altitude. In the years that followed, he owned and operated a car dealership, a series of laundromats and he established a small luggage-and-tote manufacturing company called "International Travel Products".

In an effort to contrast the intensity of his life in business, Pierre purchased a farm just outside of Milton, Ontario. "I've always loved farming so I picked up ninety-four acres," he recounted. "But it really started with the children in the family. We wanted to be out in the country and the kids wanted horses. The next thing you know I had a lot of hay. Some would spoil and you'd say, 'Oh I'll get rid of that...' "

So his pursuit of a country life lead him to a third career as a hobby farmer. In addition to a few horses, his main focus was on raising Angus cows. "There was a guy not far down the road who I got to be friends with," Pierre related. "He was into Angus [cows]. The next thing you know, I'm into Angus. They're for beef. I breed them and I try to upgrade their standard so I can sell them as registered cattle and I sell the bulls as breeding bulls."

Having a past as a hunting man, he also raised pointing dogs known as German Short Hair Pointers.

To put his operation in perspective, Pierre compared his enterprise to that of his neighbour, Lou Fontinato: "I'm a breeder whereas Lou has a feed lot, so he feeds and ships, feeds and ships. He's an actual farmer.

"There was a guy not far down the road who I got to be friends with. He was into Angus [cows]. The next thing you know, I'm into Angus."

Pierre Pilote

Mine is classified as a hobby farm because I make more outside of my farming operation than I do on the farm. I can make as much profit as I want, but I can only declare a $5,000 loss as a maximum. There are a lot of perks, but you still have to keep it going as a farm."

Back in the city, Pierre sold International Travel Products in 1985 in favour of joining the Tim Hortons coffee and donut empire. "I first started working for the organization as a supervisor because first I had to learn the trade," he recounted.

By 1988, he was ready to run his own show. He purchased a Tim Hortons outlet in Milton. "But when I owned it, it didn't fit into my lifestyle," he admitted. "It was very hard to get people to work and it took really long hours. So I backed off. Not that I couldn't do the work—the store was growing like hell ... but it just wasn't worth it to me."

He sold his restaurant and since that time has free-lanced with a variety of activities. "I've been doing public-relations work and playing in golf tournaments," he related. "I just came back from giving a speech at the Hall of Fame. Friday I was in a school doing a little thing... I just keep going all over the place. I'll make appearances and I'll do card signings."

Pierre likes to spend his leisure time on the ice and out on the fairways. "I still skate twice a week," he emphasized. "I try to get in shape for playing golf. I never played the game until four years ago. I'm trying to take it seriously. My score's coming down but it's not coming down like I thought it would. I'm not a die-hard golf nut, but I'm happy with what I'm doing!"

He and his wife have raised four children who have in turn brought six grandchildren into the Pilote family. Looking to take life at a slower pace, Pierre sold his farm in the spring of 1996. He is now stalking the sweet life of retirement in the town of Elmvale, Ontario, just south of Georgian Bay.

216

Plager, Bob: *Played defense for the New York Rangers and St. Louis from 1964-1978. Born: Kirkland Lake, Ontario, 1943.*

When the St. Louis Blues were born into the NHL in 1967, Bob Plager was there for the delivery. He stood in their defense through three straight Stanley Cup finals and watched Bobby Orr leap through the air to claim the grand prize.

A product of one of hockey's toughest families, Bob patrolled his blueline in true Plager fashion, doling out rock-hard bodychecks and rugged enforcement just like his older brother, Barclay.

Thirty years later and minus the jersey, Bob still remains a committed Blue Note. He is presently listed as Vice President of Player Development for the team; but for Bob, such designations amount to little more than party favours. "They give you all the titles... I've had them all," he decreed. "But to me they're just titles. Really, what I've done is whatever the St. Louis Blues wanted me to do. I think I've done it all except the zamboni. I keep saying, one of these nights I think they're going to let me drive it! I guess I'm more or less a company man."

During the 1977-78 season, the Blues were in the throes of their worst season to date. Head coach Leo Boivin had resigned and Bob's brother, Barclay, was brought in from the team's farm club in Salt Lake City to replace Boivin. "I was still playing here," Bob recounted. "So ... to give my brother a fair chance, I didn't want to be around with him coaching and me playing. So ... I went down to Salt Lake as the playing coach for the rest of the year."

His sacrificial departure from the NHL was not without its rewards. "I enjoyed it! I was ready to get out of hockey," he declared. "In those days, when you were ready to get out, you always wondered what you were going to do after you retired. So it was great for me to stay in the organization..."

The following season, he exercised his option to join Blues' general manager Emile Francis in learning the management side of the hockey business. "Whatever Emile wanted, that's what I did!" Bob reported. By being so flexible, he was eventually assigned to every duty on the club's roster.

He started out as a scout, evaluating players who had been drafted into the Blues' fold. In 1980, the addition of four new teams from the World Hockey Association drastically changed the league's playoff format: The best team overall now played the sixteenth team; the second best team in the league played the fifteenth team. Within such a structure, every point was vital and could make the difference for getting home-ice advantage. The Blues' management was now searching for an edge, and it was here that the concept of advance scouting was born. Once again—Bob was there for the delivery.

"I'd show up at a lot of rinks and other GM's and people ... would wonder what I was doing!" he recollected. "And we'd talk and I'd say, 'We've got your team coming up in a couple of days. So I'm here to get the lines, the power play, the penalty killing and anything I can pick up.' And now, every team has pro scouts and advance scouts."

Over the years, Bob's NHL kaleidoscope has continued to turn. He weathered the untimely loss of his brother, Barclay, as a result of a brain tumor in the early eighties and has clung to the one theme that had always been a constant—hockey. In the early 1990's, when Wayne Thomas was brought up from Peoria to help out with the parent club, all eyes were on Bob. Needless to say, he spent that following season as head coach in Peoria.

And when Blues' head coach Brian Sutter was cashed in in 1992, all eyes were on Bob again. "It wasn't something I was looking to do, to coach in the NHL," he confided. "I said I'd do it for a while... But it wasn't the right thing for me and I got out of it after eleven games."

Bob has since returned his focus to scouting and player development. Because he spends so much time on the road, away from his home in the suburbs of St. Louis, he makes a priority of maximizing his time with family in the off-season. "During the summertime, it's trailers or tents," he emphasized. "My wife, Robyn, and I have two kids, so we just get into the trailer and travel."

Nickname: *Bhudda*

"I guess I tended to be a little tubby," Bob confessed. "I used to come walking in at training camp and the guys would say, 'Bhudda's back!' Rick Wilson started all that."

Playfair, Larry: *Played defense for Buffalo and Los Angeles from 1978-1990. Born: Fort St. James, British Columbia, 1958.*

The Buffalo Sabres attended the 1978 NHL entry draft with a shopping list the read: "Wanted—one big, surly, stay-at-home defenseman." Weighing in at 6'4" and 215 pounds, Larry Playfair of the Portland Winter Hawks was their man, having accumulated a bruising 402 penalty minutes during his final season of junior hockey. Larry headed east to join the Sabres' blueline corps where he continued his tradition of bellicose play for eight seasons before bouncing to the Los Angeles Kings and then back to Buffalo by 1989.

The following season, nagging injuries dictated an end to his on-ice career—and it left him in a financially precarious situation.

"The last year that I played, I ruptured a disc in my back," he recounted. "I had the following year with a guaranteed contract. The Sabres were hemming and hawing and talking like they weren't going to pay for my final year because, even though it was guaranteed, there was no way that I could pass a physical... What they finally agreed to do was to buy out my contract at two-thirds of what they owed me and then bring me on board in a community capacity..."

Larry saw this outcome as an ideal and somewhat unique way to resolve the conflict and to ease his transition out of a Sabres' uniform. "I didn't have to go into my savings and flounder around for two or three years to figure out what I wanted to do," he emphasized. "I was able to get out of the game and try on a few different hats to see which one I liked. I know it was an opportunity that was not afforded to a lot of players who left the game."

Larry spent his first year doing public-relations work on behalf of the Sabres by speaking to young people in local schools and attending banquets. He then gradually worked his way into the sales end of the organization before finally settling in as a colour analyst for Sabres' radio broadcasts.

Three years later, the ground-breaking strike of 1994 hit the NHL. "At that point, I was employed partially by the Sabres and partially by the radio station that covered the games," he reported. "When the strike had ventured almost as far as Christmas, it looked like it was going to be a season tossed in the can! The radio station, which had paid us up until then, said that if the season didn't start by a certain date, we were not going to be paid anymore, which made sense. At that point, I had been looking into the tool-rental business and even though the season got back underway, I had already made a commitment to [it]. So once the season ended, I went into my business venture full-time."

Larry had taken the plunge, establishing two separate outlets under the name "The Rental Store". He has taken a hands-on, frontline approach to make his business a success. "It's an opportunity here in Buffalo ... to do well," he said. "Nobody has really grasped the market. There are a lot of mom-and-pop operations, but nobody's taken the bull by the horns."

Larry and the bull are now face to face in a field that requires great diversity to keep the customers happy. "We rent things that folks maybe need once in a while and don't necessarily want to go out and buy," he explained. "That ranges from a Bobcat, to a floor sander, to a chain saw, to party goods and tents."

He and his wife, Jayne, are happily raising a bustling crew of two daughters and two sons. Larry is a dad from the peel to the core, coaching the kids' baseball and hockey teams.

He is also not at a loss to share his thoughts about today's brand of professional hockey: "I think a little bit has been lost in the amount of money the players are making," he concluded. "And I don't mean anything derogatory by that. I think that when you had the biggest paid players at somewhere around three or four hundred thousand dollars and the least paid player at around eighty [thousand], there was a lot more continuity and a lot more closeness within the teams. I'm not sure what that means other than, from a comradery standpoint, it was probably more fun on some of the teams previous to today's situation."

Nickname: *Bucko*

"The name came from a gentleman named Bobby Mongrain who used to play for the Sabres many years ago," Larry recollected. "Bobby was a French Canadian kid who barely understood English. Once he made the team, he, Lindy Ruff and I roomed together. One of Bobby's favourite pastimes was watching TV. He liked to watch *Happy Days*. If you remember, whenever Richie Cunningham would get really, really mad, he'd say, 'Listen Bucko!' and then he'd go off the deep end. Bobby was joking around one morning, pretending to get upset with me. He said, 'Listen Bucko!' with a French accent. It came out so funny, it broke the room up and the name stuck. So it was 'Bucko' from then on."

———⟿———

Plett, Willi: *Played right wing for Atlanta, Calgary, Minnesota and Boston from 1975-1988. Born: Paraguay, South America, 1955.*

As a rookie with the Atlanta Flames in 1975-76, Willi Plett scored thirty-three goals and twenty-three assists to claim the Calder Trophy as the league's best newcomer. In the process, he also made it abundantly clear that any adversary looking for trouble was looking for Willi Plett. Fisticuffs and broken rules were as much a part of his game as shooting and skating. Over the course of his thirteen seasons in the NHL, he sprang for almost 500 points on offense while serving retribution in the form of 3,038 penalty minutes.

During the playoffs of 1988, he found himself as a member of the Boston Bruins who were facing the powerful Edmonton Oilers in the finals. Only such adversaries as Mark Messier and Wayne Gretzky stood between Willi and his best crack at winning a Stanley Cup. The

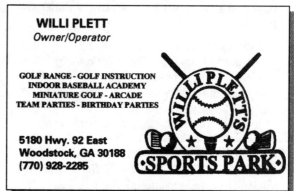
outcome was a disappointment and proved to be monumental in more ways than one.

"We ended up loosing the final game in Edmonton," he lamented. "I didn't dress ... and I knew in my heart that that was going to be the last game that I'd play because I planned on retiring... And I actually started crying after that game. That moment was kind of emotional."

Willi was at the end of the line although not at the end of his rope. "I could have continued to play, but I was burned out," he confided. Instead, he retreated with his family to their home base in Atlanta to take a year off. Regular payments from the Bruins' payroll eased his transition and afforded him the necessary time and funds to remodel his home and his weary soul.

By late 1989, Willi had consolidated his personal resources and was again up to looking at his career options. He and his wife, Robin, settled on purchasing fifteen-and-a-half acres in Woodstock, Georgia for the purpose of developing a family fun centre. They started from scratch, secured zoning and building permits and then spent the next five years learning the hard way how to have fun running an amusement centre.

"I didn't have any prior experience doing this. And it's taken me about four or five years to figure it out," he admitted with a laugh. "But that's what life is. You can read all the books you want. But until you experience it, you don't really learn... And after five years, we're starting to turn the corner, starting to turn a profit."

He now operates his centre under the name

"Willi Plett's Sports Park". Since its inception, the facility has grown to include a golf range, indoor batting cages, a miniature golf course and an arcade. He and Robin run the park as a family business, so it is not unusual for their four sons to join in the family cause when school is out.

But in spite of entrepreneurial demands, Willi carves out some spare time each week to golf with former teammates Eric Vail and Tim Ecclestone.

And amidst the hum of the NHL's planned revival in Atlanta, Willi cast a humorous glance towards his own day in the big-league spotlight: "I experienced a changeover. I ... started out where all you did was party the first seven or eight years of my career," he quipped. "And then ... it got a lot more serious. The kids coming up were in better shape—they worked out all summer. And the people who play now, they're in incredible condition! They actually work hard at being in really good shape, and that wasn't necessarily the case when I was playing. It was kind of funny, the first few years. The coach, Al McNeil, would say, 'Willi, the playoffs are coming. Why don't you ride the stationary bike for about ten minutes to help your conditioning?' And I'd go, 'Ten minutes!! Are you crazy?' Now they get on that thing for an hour and think nothing of it!

"I remember our dressing room in Atlanta had one old CCM stationary bike," he continued with amusement. "You know, one of those old tire jobs ... and it had a couple of old barbells that you get at Sears. That's all that was there! Now, shoot, the training rooms have got hundreds of thousands of dollars worth of training equipment in them."

Willi also sees today's big money as a big reason to stay in top form. "When we were playing," he explained, "guys were making eighty or a hundred grand. Ah what the heck, so your career's a little shorter. But now, if you're making a million or two million a year, you go, 'This wouldn't be very smart if I didn't take the most out of this that I can.' So it gets to the point where your business, which is yourself, is worth a lot more. It would be worth riding that bike for a little of the money they're making now."

Prentice, Dean: *Played left wing for the New York Rangers, Boston, Detroit, Pittsburgh and Minnesota from 1952-1974. Born: Schumacher, Ontario, 1932.*

In the NHL of his day, Dean Prentice was one of the most reliable left wingers in the game. Skating on a line with fellow New York Rangers Andy Bathgate and Larry Popein, he quickly established himself as a player who could effectively read and respond at both ends of the rink. After ten productive seasons in New York, Dean went on to see action with Boston, Detroit, Pittsburgh and finally, Minnesota.

While sustaining his livelihood in the major leagues, Dean also developed a parallel career teaching others the fundamentals of the game.

His desire to teach began in 1964. That year, he joined forces with well-known figure-skating coach Kerry Leitch to start his first hockey school in Galt, Ontario.

In the ensuing years, his teaching services extended to Banff, Alberta as an assistant to Glen Sather. He also had a hand in setting up the Can-Am Hockey School programme which presently

Hockey Ministries International

13-220 Salisbury Ave., Cambridge, Ont. N1S 1K5

Dean & June Prentice

operates on both sides of the border.

By 1974, Dean was forty-two years old and about to wrap up his twenty-second season in the NHL. It was at that point that Old Man Age snarled, "Enough is enough!" "Everything started to slow up," Dean recalled. "Not my skating, but my ability to read and react to things. So it was time to pack it in."

With twenty-two years in the NHL and ten years of hockey schools, Dean looked to coaching as the next logical step in his career. He started the following season as head coach of the New Haven Nighthawks of the American Hockey League. "I went there as coach," he recollected. "But as I was preparing for the season to begin, the manager, Charlie Burns, was called up to the North Stars to assist general manager Jack Gordon. I was then given the responsibility of both coach and manager. I had to learn quickly. The major dilemma was, too many players. I had players directly owned by the New Haven Nighthawks management plus a working affiliation with both the Minnesota North Stars and the New York Islanders. All owners wanted their players to play regularly and be groomed for recall to the National Hockey League. Of course the NHL scouts wanted to see their players in action. Trying to please everyone was not easy. We did, however, make it to the finals of the Calder Cup that year."

> *"We are interested in the hockey player in and beyond the arena."*
>
> *Dean Prentice*

Dean was released after two seasons and moved on to Traverse City, Michigan. There he managed and coached the team in the U.S. League in addition to managing the arena with all that that entailed. "They were long, long days," he declared.

After one year in Traverse City, he then returned to his home base in Cambridge, Ontario and accepted the positions of manager of the Ayr Community Centre plus Parks and Recreation Director.

No longer having the many-facetted responsibilities of a hockey team removed a lot of pressure. "I really enjoyed my ten years in Ayr," he declared. "It was fun."

In 1987, Dean left the arena business and along with his wife, June, joined Hockey Ministries International. This is a Christian organization with a heavy emphasis on working with youth. The Ministry operates twenty-six Christian athlete hockey camps throughout Canada, the U.S. and Europe. These camps integrate a high quality of hockey instruction with practical teaching in Christian living.

Hockey Ministries International has also developed a video called *Hockey Beyond Belief*, which Dean distributes throughout the OHL junior-A league. The video features tips on the game of hockey with several current and ex-NHL players sharing how they came to the realization of the need for a personal relationship with Jesus Christ. "We are interested in the hockey player in and beyond the arena," Dean emphasized.

Dean spends his leisure time playing golf and hitting the ice to play oldtimers' hockey with ex-NHL players.

He and June have raised two daughters who are married and also reside in Cambridge. Their seven grandchildren provide Dean and June with seven exciting reasons to spend time with family.

Pronovost, Marcel: *Played defense for Detroit and Toronto from 1950-1969. Born: Lac la Tortue, Quebec, 1930.*

The 1997-98 NHL campaign marked Marcel Pronovost's forty-eighth year in professional hockey. His first nineteen seasons were devoted to the relatively stable profession of riding shotgun against all who dared to encroach the blueline of the Red Wings and, later, the Leafs between 1950 and 1969.

Growing up in Lac la Tortue, Quebec, Marcel's dream was to play for the Montreal Canadiens. But the Detroit Red Wings' scouting staff spotted him first and tucked him securely away with their farm club in Omaha. During the Wings' run for the Stanley Cup in 1950, Marcel got his promotion to Detroit where he won his first league championship at age nineteen.

With Red Kelly as his defensive partner, Marcel quickly evolved into a smooth-skating, hard-hitting rearguard who was as tough as a lone tree on a Manitoba prairie. He would frequently bend to the pain of countless injuries but always find the resolve to keep on playing.

Since the day he relinquished his Maple Leaf Blue, however, Marcel's life has shifted from a settled existence to a nomadic journey through the backwoods and frontlines of the hockey world.

"I coached in Tulsa, Chicago, Hull, Buffalo, Detroit, Windsor ... and I worked for three to four years for Central Scouting," he revealed.

The peak of his coaching career came between 1977 and 1979, when he lead the Buffalo Sabres to a respectable fifty-two wins, twenty-nine losses and twenty-three ties. But the team lost out in the quarter finals in 1978 and got off to a slow start the following year. So in spite of a solid overall record, he was replaced by Bill Inglis.

Marcel eventually settled into a career as a scout, first with the league itself and then for his present team, the New Jersey Devils. "I cover any draftable amateur player on the North American continent," he declared. "Sometimes you work two games in a day, like say if you have a game in Guelph in the afternoon and a game in Oshawa at night—I will do the two of them."

Marcel contended that so much hockey is now being played around the continent, that a broad-based network of eyes has to be maintained at the grass-roots level.

"In scouting, you have to narrow it down," he remarked. "It's an elimination process... We have local people that kind of weed them out for us. They'll see the junior B's and the junior A's... And if there's a player here or there, then we know through their reports that these players should be seen. So it helps us to narrow things down because we wouldn't have time to go through junior C, junior B, junior A and so on and so forth."

He also pointed out that with such a large number of young players to be profiled, the entire field of scouting, including Marcel himself, has turned to the use of computers to compile their data-bases and to analyze their findings.

Scouting has become a serious business where even the smallest card up a sleeve is worth the effort to obtain. "Let's say there's two guys in Hamilton and two guys in Oakville and Oakville is playing Hamilton tonight," he explained. "So you put that in your schedule. Now you're looking at four guys plus whatever might happen to catch your eye. It gives you a head start."

And at the end of each working night, the lights go down and the rink doors close as Marcel recedes into the calm of his personal world. "Between the computer and attending hockey games, I just like to relax at home," he confided. "In the wintertime I don't do that much and in the summertime I play golf and we travel. I don't intend to become a couch potato!"

As Marcel's career on ice evolved over time, his family followed suit. He and his wife, Cindy, raised two sons and a daughter who in turn brought two granddaughters into the world. Unfortunately Cindy passed away in 1993. Now recently remarried, Marcel and his second wife, Eva, make their home in Windsor, Ontario.

Metro Prystai
CHICAGO BLACK HAWKS

Prystai, Metro: *Played centre for Chicago and Detroit from 1947-1958. Born: Yorkton, Saskatchewan, 1927.*

As twenty-year-old Metro Prystai extended his reach to the big leagues, his fingers clasped at the bottom rung of the NHL—home to the struggling Blackhawks, who during the forties sat consistently on the bedrock of league standings.

In 1950-51, however, he was swept into the open arms of the Detroit Red Wings along with Gaye Stewart, Bob Goldham and Jim Henry in exchange for, among others, Hall of Fame goaltender Harry Lumley. Metro had had the good fortune to join a Wings team on the rise. His speedy skating and deft shooting fit in well as the team rose to secure two championships before he was claimed on waivers by Chicago and then bounced back to Detroit to close out his career.

By the time he made his final landing for the Red Wings in 1958, he had four young children, a wife and limited career options waiting at the end of the runway. For Metro, hockey had been a satisfying journey. But that which had been life's thoroughfare was now becoming an endless highway devoid of the exit ramp that would lead to the one thing he wanted most: a stable career and a settled home life. So he just kept on driving—with one eye on the road and the other on the employment ads.

In the meantime, Metro accepted a post as head coach of the Omaha Knights of the Central Hockey league for the 1958-59 season. "I didn't do very well that year," he reported. "It was a farm team of the Red Wings and [Jack] Adams said, 'Get a bunch of young guys'—So I did! Well, we had trouble winning. We were losing games that we should have won. We had a good hockey club but just too many young fellas. Well I was kinda satisfied," he quipped with a laugh. "But at the same time, the owners weren't—so I got canned!"

Metro then returned to the more familiar soil of Saskatchewan to lead the Moose Jaw Canucks of the Saskatchewan Junior Hockey League. This time around, the coaching was sweet with a league championship thrown into the mix. But he and life on the road continued to clash. "It got to the point where I was away from my family so damn much," he complained.

But to be a coach is to be a wanderer and Metro and coaching seemed to be like two strangers tolerating each other in an elevator. Whether going up or down, they were going together.

In 1962, he took over the helm of the rival Melville Millionaires, also members of the Saskatchewan League. And although he was now working closer to his home in Yorkton, his ambivalence towards the profession continued to thrive. "I kind of enjoyed it in a way," he remarked. "But I don't think I was really cut out to be a coach because ... it was frustrating as hell working with the juniors. You know, one day they'd go like hell and the next day they couldn't do anything ... they were up and down.

"So I just figured I'd get out of hockey. I went to work with the O'Keefe Brewing Company as a representative. I lived in Yorkton and worked on the north-east end of the province. I was sort of a beer salesman in a way, visiting all of the outlets that sold their products: hotels and bars. I also made trips for them to father-and-son banquets. They treated me very well—it was a job."

Metro represented O'Keefe until 1970 when relentless travel nipped at his heels for the last time. It would be his way or the highway—but not both. "I was on the road a heck of a lot with the brewery," he stated. "It was kind of nice in a way but my wife was at home with five little kids by then. So I just said the hell with it!"

Metro had reasons to be so bold. In his travels, he had spotted a small insurance outfit for sale in the town of Wynard—and the advertisement had stability written all over it. "I bought the business, and it was probably one of the best moves I ever made," he declared with conviction. The Prystai Agency finally allowed him to make a satisfying living while staying close to home.

His initial transition into insurance, however, was like toting a few extra pounds at training camp. "It was tough for me because I had to ... pass my insurance exam," he admitted. "But in time, I did. And my previous hockey experience helped me ... a lot. It brought the business to me. Wynard was only about ninety miles from Yorkton and I had played ball around here previously so they all kind of knew who I was."

In addition to his name, Metro also kept his blades in the picture by running The International Hockey School in Nelson, British Columbia. "It only went for a month or six weeks during the summer," he recalled. "I looked after the book work and getting the students. Glenn Hall, Andy Bathgate and I were in it together. Then they got out and I got in with a fellow from Moose Jaw who originally started it."

Metro retired from Prystai Agency and his hockey school in 1985. Unfortunately his wife passed away from cancer at about the same time, thus nixing their plans to savour the rewards of retirement together. In the ensuing years, he also endured the loss of his eldest daughter who died as a result of an asthma attack.

But with time he eventually weathered the ordeal to marry his second wife, Mavis, in 1994.

Together they are relishing a life of retirement in Yorkton in the company of two grandchildren plus three surviving sons and a daughter.

Raleigh, Don: *Played centre for the New York Rangers between 1943 & 1956. Born: Kenora, Ontario, 1926.*

In 1943, with World War II raging in full force, seventeen-year-old Don Raleigh was not old enough to enlist in the Canadian Armed Forces, but he was good enough to join the NHL.

After a three-month taste of life with the Rangers, he returned to the junior ranks until he was eligible to join his comrades in the fight. He had been trained and en route overseas when the war ended in 1945.

While being discharged from the military, Don made a few mental notes about the void that he and many of his fighting mates were stepping into upon their return to civilian life. Ten years later, after having banked 331 career points in Ranger Blue, those mental notes resurfaced in the context of his retirement from the NHL.

"One of the things about hockey in any time is that it's like getting out of the army," he stressed. "There's not a whole lot you can do. You have no trade... You've got no vocation. The only thing you can do is sell and so I went into the insurance business because I was well-known."

After leaving New York in 1956, Don set up shop in Winnipeg, Manitoba. He specialized in selling group insurance on behalf of Crown Life and later, Royal Trust until 1960.

"Then I went to work for a brokerage house ... till about 1971. At that time there was a takeover and it didn't work out very well for me," he disclosed. "I found myself redundant and that was very traumatic... So I did the only thing I could do. I just said, 'Well, instead of selling for someone else, I'll manage it on my own'."

Shortly after getting his pink slip, he opened his own insurance agency called "J.D. Raleigh Company Ltd." "I would go out as a broker to companies and assist them with their employee benefit programmes," he explained. "Then I sold life insurance and general insurance..."

While putting his new agency on the map, Don gave the company shingle a lift by appearing on Winnipeg Jet broadcasts as a colour analyst. "There were about five or six of us former NHLers, like Bill Juzda and Charlie Rayner... We each did five or six games a year," he explained. "We commented during the periods and then selected the three stars."

He also gained notoriety for his benevolent work within the Winnipeg community. He is past president of the Winnipeg Lion's Club; a former member of the Misericordia Hospital board of directors; and for the past twelve years, has served as the chairman of the Manitoba Hockey Foundation. "We sponsor the Manitoba Hockey Hall of Fame," he noted. "It's a hall and wall of fame which acknowledges successful players in various leagues who originate from Manitoba. As well, we offer scholarships to hockey players that are in need and we help players if and when a situation occurs."

By 1993, Don had made the rounds of the working world and was ripe to retire himself and his agency. "I'm still active as a consultant, but in a lesser capacity now," he affirmed. "I decided that fifty years was long enough to make a living."

And although now leading a life of apparent retirement, his lifestyle is as brisk as ever. "I play a lot of golf, a lot of tennis, I play badminton and I curl," he declared. "So I keep pretty active and I'm in good health. I'll be seventy-one next summer. I'm just lucky because staying in good health is Russian roulette at best."

Don also keeps his mind engaged in the manner of a three-on-one rush. "I save some Canadian stamps on occasion," he related. "And I enjoy some of the modern television programmes like the History Channel especially. There's some incredibly good stuff on there. I'm a bit of a war buff too... I went over on the Normandy tour in '95. I also visited some of the WWI battlefields which I enjoyed."

He and his wife, Janice, divide retirement life between their cottage in Sandy Hook, Manitoba and their home in Winnipeg. It is there that they receive occasional visits from their daughter and son, the latter of whom became a doctor in Kingston, Ontario.

Nickname: *Bones*

"The name 'Bones' was coined by a New York sports writer named Barney Kremenko," Don recollected. "It was strictly because I was skinny. I was going on six feet but I only played at about 145 pounds. From the time I left Winnipeg until I got back home, I never did hear the name Don."

Ramage, Rob: *Played defense for Birmingham (WHA), Colorado, St. Louis, Calgary, Toronto, Minnesota, Tampa Bay, Montreal and Philadelphia (NHL) from 1978-1994. Born: Byron, Ontario, 1959.*

During his final season of junior hockey with the London Knights in 1977-78, Rob Ramage was chosen as an OHA first-team all-star. He then jumped to the Birmingham Bulls of the World Hockey Association for one season before joining the Colorado Rockies as the NHL's first overall pick of the 1979 entry draft.

In Rob Ramage, the Rockies' management saw a 6'2", well-rounded blueliner with offensive smarts and a propensity for dishing out tough defense in his own zone. Over the course of his sixteen years in professional hockey, he corralled 662 career points while being charged for 2,609 penalty minutes. After Colorado, he made stops in St. Louis, Calgary, Toronto, Minnesota, Montreal and Philadelphia.

During his final season in 1993-94, Rob played a total of only twenty-one games on behalf of the Canadiens and the Flyers. He knew his career was drawing to a close and the press box and players' bench became his place for contemplation. It was there that he began fine-tuning his vision for the future.

"There was a preparation that was ongoing in that last year," he disclosed. "It was a decision of where, what, when and how. It boiled down to going back to Tampa which we'd really enjoyed; moving back home to London where both my

Over the Glass & Into the Crowd!　　　　**Ramage. Rob**

225

wife and I are from; or going to St. Louis where I'd spent the longest time in my career. After evaluating all the pluses and minuses, we settled on St. Louis. And then the wheels moved very quickly.

"I took a job with A.G. Edwards which is a brokerage firm based in St. Louis. It's the largest brokerage firm in the U.S. based outside of New York City. We moved back the first of August. I started training about a week and a half later and was up and operating as a broker later on that year."

An important plus that swayed Rob towards St. Louis was his association with Blake Dunlop. "When I came to St. Louis in a trade from the Colorado Rockies in 1982, Blake was a teammate here in St. Louis," Rob recounted. "He became a very good friend. Both he and his wife really helped my wife and I get acclimated... And then when he retired, he became my broker for ten years. So he was a major impetus for getting [me] into the business. In fact now he's not my broker, he's my manager! We work at the same branch in Clayton, Missouri... So it's a nice tie there."

Such a firm alliance has helped Rob sustain a sensible link between his hockey past and his civilian present. "It was a long, long time that my life truly just revolved around hockey," he emphasized. "So it was a drastic change. Did I miss the game? Of course! That goes without saying. I guess I was fortunate in the sense that the players were locked out my first year out of hockey. So I really didn't have anything to miss till they commenced play again in the new year. And then it really hit home! I remember my wife and I were going to an event in downtown St. Louis. We stopped off to get a bite to eat. The TV was on and the Blues were opening up their season in San Jose. And that, I felt, was the first time the thought really kind of hit me: The game is going on—the season's started and

"I enjoyed the physical activity when I played and I've tried to keep that up as time will warrant... I don't want to end up with broker butt (laughs)!"

Rob Ramage

I'm not there! And there was a little bit of sadness. But heck, that all passes and you realize, there is life after hockey. And there's a very good life!"

This is not to imply that Rob's existence is now without hockey. A useful part of his adjustment off the ice has been to gradually work his way back into the sport.

For the 1994-95 season, he did a post-game radio call-in show after all of the Blues' home games. The following season he switched to television, serving as a between-periods host for forty-two Blues' outings at home and on the road.

Rob's transition into broadcasting was not unlike the first leap into the deep end of a swimming pool—it may not have looked smooth but there was considerable savvy behind the frantic kicking and paddling.

"Heck, it seems like everything I've done since I retired from hockey has been an incredible learning curve, and the broadcast work was no different," he admitted. "I look at some of the interviews and work I did earlier in the season and it's horrifying! But what you do is you take it back to something you know so well. Boy some of my games as a rookie with the Colorado Rockies were pretty horrifying too! There are a lot of nights I was in front of the camera that I would have far rather been in the corner with skates on getting put through the boards (laughs). But I've thoroughly enjoyed it and I hope to continue on with it."

Rob and Blake Dunlop also joined forces along with three other investors to bring a junior-A hockey team to St. Louis at the start the 1996-97 season. "Another tie to the NHL is that our coach is John Wensink," Rob reported. "He's coaching full-time for us. This is the great thing about hockey. The people you meet and the friendships ... you carry on, not just through hockey but after your hockey lives.

John and I were teammates with the Colorado Rockies back in '81."

But clearly, a more stable family environment is the most significant benefit Rob has garnered through retirement from the NHL. "I don't have to get my wife to be a single parent for the hockey season," he stated with relief. "So often they have

to carry the burdens of both moms and dads."

These days he and his wife, Dawn, share the responsibilities and pleasures of parenthood more evenly. They have two daughters, Tamra and Jacqueline, and one son, their only Canuck, John. "They're all very, very active in sports," Rob reported. "It keeps my wife and I hopping, chauffeuring them around. It's a lot of fun watching them compete."

Rob himself also has a serious reason for staying in shape. "I'm active in all sports. I'm an avid scuba diver. I enjoyed the physical activity when I played and I've tried to keep that up as time will warrant... I don't want to end up with broker butt!" he joked.

Nickname: *Rammer*

"I have a brother who's five years older than me," Rob explained. "He was known as 'Rammer', so I think I just followed in his footsteps."

Rayner, Charlie: *Played goal for the New York Americans and the New York Rangers between 1940 & 1953. Born: Sutherland, Saskatchewan, 1920.*

It takes an uncommon mettle to stand before an advancing rubber missile; to be the final straw that refuses to bend; to say to the opposition, "You've come this far but you'll go no farther." Young Charlie Rayner was inspired by such acts of solitary valour and he was more than ready to enter the fray.

"When you're brought up in the prairies," he explained, "one of the big things in life was to grab a stick and get out there on that frozen pond and play hockey. I always kind of wanted to be a goaltender. I caught a little glimmer in the eye watching these goaltenders play with the Saskatoon Quakers. They were always an idol of ours. I thought, 'Maybe some day I could play in Saskatoon for the Quakers.' And of course listening to Foster Hewitt and the NHL all the time as a kid—you'd hear these goaltenders making the big saves the way Foster used to announce it. I thought, 'That was the spot for me'."

Nickname Challenge #22

Huey, Louie & Dewey

"When I turned pro in Boston, I had a couple of roommates. We were all single. Dave Forbes was one and Al Secord was the other. There weren't too many young guys there, so we used to always hang out together. We were always getting into some mischief. And so whenever one of us was involved, everybody figured, 'Well there's Huey, Louie and Dewey. They're always together through thick and thin'."

Who is he?

Clues

a. He played centre for Boston, Colorado, New Jersey and Detroit from 1977-1987.

b. He was a first round-draft choice of the Boston Bruins and wore #27.

c. His initials are D.F.

If your backhand shot was gloved, see page 285.

By age fifteen, Charlie was tending goal for the Saskatoon Wesleys along with centreman Sid Abel. A local scout named Johnny Walker spotted Charlie's resolve and signed him on with Red Dutton's New York Americans.

Charlie cracked the big-league line-up in 1940. "I'll never forget my first game," he recounted. "It's something you dream of as a kid. You sit down after the game and say, 'I've made it. I played my first game!' You kind of pinch yourself to see if you're still alive."

Charlie remained very much alive propping up a near defenseless Rangers team for eight seasons after his return from World War II. His acrobatic style and courage in the face of injuries won him a Hart Trophy as the league's most valuable player in 1950 plus three straight selections as a second-team all-star between 1949-51. In all, he racked up ten Hall of Fame seasons spread over thirteen years. By 1953, when he gloved his final drive, it was as though his association with hockey was just getting under way.

He headed west to British Columbia to coach a senior-league club called the Nelson Maple Leafs. "It was quite a change," he said of his transition into coaching. "It had its ups and downs, but I enjoyed it."

Two years later, Bud Poile, who was coaching the Edmonton Flyers at the time, took on a new post in San Francisco. "So Sid Abel phoned me one day and asked me if I'd be interested in going to Edmonton," Charlie recollected. "I said, 'Sure!' So I went."

He served as the Flyers' head coach and he added the general manager's hat to the mix. "It was quite a challenge really," he stressed. "At that time it was kind of frustrating because we were a farm club for Detroit. You never knew from day to day how many players you had because if they had injuries in Detroit, why they'd pull directly from the Flyers. So it made it pretty tough, but I enjoyed it. We had Billy McNeil, Charlie Holmes and John Muckler with us at that time."

After two seasons with the Flyers, Charlie became head coach of an intermediate club called the Thistles, in Kenora, Ontario. The posting was ideal since he and Jim Henry had been running a summer camp called "Hockey Haven" in Kenora since 1946. "We were at the camp all summer and then we used to coach the team all winter," Charlie related.

Hockey Haven was not unlike the goal crease that Charlie tended in New York: a popular place for people to hang out and a lot of toil to keep clear. "Jim Henry and I had that camp for twenty-one years!" he remarked. "It was a new experience too! We met an awful lot of nice people, but it was a lot of work. We had the people coming and going all the time—it kept us pretty busy."

Many of those people included teammates and opponents from the NHL. "A lot of the boys from the West like Glenn Hall and the Bentleys used to drop in to say hello on their way back from the East," Charlie related. "We had them stay for three, four or five days at a time. Allan Stanley and Zellio Toppazinni spent their honeymoons there."

One can just imagine the likes of Max and Doug Bentley, Neil Colville and Alf Pike sitting around a campfire telling stories that were embellished a little more with every round. "There were lots of lies told on that one," Charlie affirmed with a twinkle in his laugh. "Lots of lies!"

After eight seasons with the Thistles and twenty-one years of battling the elements in the service of his camp, Charlie closed down his Kenora-based operation. In its place, he went to Winnipeg to do public relations and sales work for Molson Breweries and, years later, for Carlings as well.

Throughout the next twenty years, he reentered the public eye on occasion by doing colour commentary for Winnipeg Jet broadcasts and by representing Molson and Carlings at various functions. "We went to the hotels and to the golf deals and all the entertainment in the summer months like the rodeo," he explained. "It was just quite a job really. It kept us going and I met an awful lot of nice people."

These days, with his knee having been

replaced and golf now out of the picture, Charlie enjoys spending his leisure time following a variety of sports like hockey and football.

In 1991, he and his wife, Ina, resettled in Langley, British Columbia where they presently live in retirement.

Reid, Tom: *Played defense for Chicago and Minnesota from 1967-1978. Born: Fort Erie, Ontario, 1946.*

Over the course of his eleven seasons with the Chicago Blackhawks and later, the Minnesota North Stars, defenseman Tom Reid was as steady and reliable as the blueline itself. As the action scrambled from end to end, his coaches always knew where to find him—firmly anchored to a defensive posture. And although he was not known for his scoring prowess, he did once leap beyond his calling to score on a penalty shot against Canadiens' rookie goaltender Ken Dryden in 1971.

By the mid-seventies, Tom was firmly established as a career North Star. All was normal until one day he noticed a small red spot about the size of a quarter on his biceps. It seemed harmless enough at the time, but in fact, that spot marked the beginning of the end of his playing career.

"In the mid-seventies, a number of players in the NHL had problems with allergies as related to the equipment," he revealed. "The perspiration and the friction actually removed the skin. It started out very small but after three years, getting up to the '77-78 season, I had some terrible problems with it. I was spending a lot of time at the doctors, trying to combat this thing and it was getting progressively worse. When I finally had to quit playing in 1977, I had no skin basically from my neck to my waist... But fortunately also, I'm the only one

"I had no skin basically from my neck to my waist... Unfortunately it ended my career much sooner than I had planned."

Tom Reid

who had to retire because of it. Rick Vaive ... Lou Nanne, Dennis Hextall ... and I think Jacques Lemaire had it as well. There were players all around the league who were experiencing it. We went through great pains working with the people from the 3-M laboratories, having different components analyzed. I went through a number of patch tests to find out what the problem was but they could never isolate it. We changed materials. We changed equipment. I would take off a t-shirt after each period. I would use a barrier of creams. I tried everything! But there was no relief. The only way I got relief from it was by not playing."

Tom found himself forced, by his worsening skin condition, to make a career change much sooner than he had planned. "It was not easy," he admitted. "Fortunately for me I had worked every summer in Fort Erie in the recreation department. So working certainly did not bother me. Also, the North Stars recommended me for a radio position with Al Shaver. I worked with Al until 1990. In 1980 I was also doing television broadcasts with Bob Kurtz. We worked together up until 1990 when Norm Green came to town..."

Tom stepped into the field of broadcasting the way a child enters a haunted house. "It's scary," he laughed. "I had no training... And it's much more difficult to interview than it is to be interviewed! We were what they call I.F.B., which means we can hear the people in the control truck so they can tell us how much time before the commercial or the break. But no one prepared us for that. I thought it was just so I could hear myself talk! So all of a sudden I was doing my first interview and somebody started talking into my earpiece ... and I said, 'What is this? Who is this and where are they?' But I picked it up pretty quickly, although I was very, very nervous when I started. But I thought, nothing ventured, nothing gained. It's turned out to be a big plus in the opportunities it's given me down here."

And in spite of the North Stars removal by the roots, Tom has continued to keep his hand in broadcasting as a colour commentator for the Minnesota Gophers who were recently ranked number three in the NCAA. He also does colour analysis for a state-wide high-school hockey tournament which runs for four straight days each year.

With broadcasting as a sideline, Tom used his days to develop career interests outside of hockey. "I got into a chemical business with a product that was developed by the H.P. Fuller Company," he related. "Ed White, who played for the Minnesota Vikings, and I became friends and then partners in business down here. I tried that for a while but it didn't work out."

In 1982, Tom was hired by the Olympic Print Company which is based primarily in Minneapolis. He is now their national sales manager promoting such products as stickers, static clings and packaging.

Within the community, he has worked steadfastly to assist in the founding of a Make A Wish chapter in Minneapolis. The Make A Wish Foundation was created to provide the fulfillment of special wishes expressed by children who are either seriously or terminally ill. "Our first wish was done in the fall of '82," he recalled. "We did five our first year. Now we'll do over a hundred a year... In fact we just celebrated our one thousandth wish here a week and a half ago and I was co-chair of the event. It was a way of saying thank you to the people of Minnesota. We had live bands and a thousand motorcycles. Each one represented a child and each biker carried a piece of cloth with that child's name on it and a wish number. They skirted the Twin Cities ... and then came into one main area. And then we built what we call the 'Wall of a Thousand Wishes'. Each one of those pieces of cloth was put in position until we had all the thousand pieces up there."

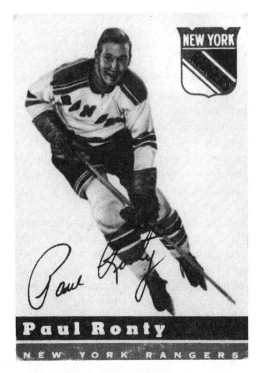

Paul Ronty

NEW YORK RANGERS

Ronty, Paul: *Played centre for Boston, the New York Rangers and Montreal from 1947-1955. Born: Toronto, Ontario, 1928.*

Paul Ronty entered the NHL as a young farm hand of the Boston Bruins in 1947. The tall and slender centreman played a clean game between wingers Ken Smith and Johnny Peirson. It was in such company that Paul attained his best offensive output in years two and three, scoring a total of forty-three goals and sixty-five assists. In 1951, he was traded to the New York Rangers, where he excelled as a feed-man for his prolific right winger, Wally Hergesheimer.

All was unfolding like a well-told story until 1955 when Paul saw a first-rate example of how the little things you say can amount to more than the big things you do.

In three-and-a-half seasons with the Rangers, he had notched more than 150 points. And yet it took only a fleeting comment to change the course of his career. "When I was with the Rangers, we were always struggling," he confided. "We had a tough team. And I think Carson Cooper was the scout for the Rangers at the time. We were sitting in the Royal York Hotel in Toronto and I said, 'Jeez, the way things are going, I think I may retire at the end of the year.' I guess he promptly went up to the front office and the next thing you knew, I was on waivers to go out to Vancouver which was the farm club. Then Montreal picked me up on waivers. So I went there and played in a few games. It was pretty much at the end of the season and they were fighting the playoffs with Detroit. In fact, if I remember correctly, it was the time when [Rocket] Richard was suspended and he couldn't play in the playoffs."

At the conclusion of that season, Paul and his wife, Natalie, were making plans to settle in Montreal. "My son was going to be six and his first year in school was coming," Paul recollected. "We thought it would make a lot of sense to move into an English-speaking community like Westmount so he could go to school. But [the Canadiens' management] advised me that they never sign anybody's contract until after training camp. So I just decided I wasn't going to take the chance of moving my family down to Montreal and then end up in the minors."

Paul's brazen resolve to call his own shots in a league that did all the shooting came from the fires he'd been stoking outside of hockey. "You're talking about a family man and I knew I couldn't play hockey forever," he remarked. "I thought there was more involved in the future. That's why I was trying to think of some business that I could do during the summer months and then let someone look after it during the winter months."

Paul had settled on the insurance business a few years before his retirement from the NHL. He set up Paul Ronty Insurance on a part-time basis, and then in 1955, he said *adios* to Montreal and went at it full-time. "It was general insurance, but we also offered life and health," he explained.

He ran his agency until 1982 when he closed shop and hooked up with Deland Gibson Insurance Association in Boston. Today, he is the agency's vice president, but seems unaffected by the prestige of his title. "Ah, everybody's a vice

president," he remarked. "You're your own man really."

Paul stays fit by savouring a vigorous round of squash during the winter and golfing with his former teammate, John Peirson, during the summer. He and Natalie have raised two sons and one daughter over the years and continue to make their home in the suburbs of Boston.

Nickname: *Chew*

"Growing up in Toronto, I played for a team called 'Chewies Aces' which was coached by Les Chew," Paul recollected. "I was playing against my future teammate, Ed Sanford. Ed gave me the name 'Chew' because of my association with the team."

Ruskowski, Terry: *Played centre for Houston, Winnipeg (WHA), Chicago, Los Angeles, Pittsburgh and Minnesota (NHL) from 1974-1988. Born: Prince Albert, Saskatchewan, 1954.*

Terry Ruskowski was a fiercely determined centreman who could light things up in all facets of his game, whether it was goal scoring, assists, penalty killing, power plays or fighting. During his final season with the Swift Current Broncos of the Western Junior Hockey League in 1973-74, he squeezed forty goals, ninety-three assists and 243 penalty minutes into a sixty-eight-game schedule.

Although drafted by the Chicago Blackhawks in 1974, Terry opted for the World Hockey Association where he played five seasons for the Houston Aeros and Winnipeg Jets. He finally joined the NHL in 1979 where he saw action with Chicago, Los Angeles, Pittsburgh and Minnesota.

During his final season with the North Stars in 1987-88, Terry read all the signs along the road to retirement—yield to oncoming injuries; slower moving players keep right! He knew his exit ramp was just ahead.

"That last year ... I didn't play very much and I knew age was catching up to me," he revealed. "I'd had knee surgery the year before, so I felt that it was the end. I was an aggressive type of player. I did not want to look bad to my teammates, or to my fans, or even to myself! If there was a challenge, I had to meet [it]. If that meant having an altercation with somebody on the ice, then I had to... At the end of my career it got to the point where I was having trouble sleeping. I kept thinking, 'Who are the guys on the other team that I may have to face, to meet the challenge with?' It just got to me after a while. And when the time was up ... the good Lord said, 'Okay Terry, time to look onward and upward to see what else is out there for you instead of playing.' Hockey has been my life ... ever since I grew up on a farm back home in Saskatchewan, starting from eight years old. The other alternative to staying in hockey is to coach which is exactly what I did."

To that end, Terry caught his first break as head coach of the Saskatoon Blades of the Western Hockey League. "The first year I had a great time," he recalled. "I had character guys on the team that played hard. We weren't supposed to do well and we did very well...

"But coaching junior was a challenge for me. When you're coaching young guys you have to be a coach ... a baby-sitter and ... a guidance counsellor for school. And I was a real stickler on school. If you didn't go ... you didn't play. I missed the boat by not going the college route because it wasn't there for me in my particular situation."

After two years with the Blades, Terry travelled east to coach Columbus of the East Coast Hockey League. "I really enjoyed Columbus," he emphasized. "I had complete control of trades, contracts, who to play and who not to play. I loved the whole scenario! The general manager there let me do what I wanted to do."

At the end of his third season in Columbus, Terry caught wind that the Houston Aeros, his former team, were entering the International Hockey League while in search of a new head coach. For Terry the potential to step back to nostalgia while moving up the ranks was too great to ignore. So he applied and landed the job. "I loved Houston and I always will love Houston," he declared with conviction. "Our fans

are terrific. We're still drawing ten thousand a game. It's a great turnout for our league."

"I coached last year and had a very successful season," he reported. "This year I had some tough luck. I got to a point where the day of the games I was as nervous as when I played. That's not a bad point—it's just obvious that you're getting keyed up to do the best you can at game time. But it was just one of those things. Nothing seemed to work."

By the midway point of that second campaign, action was taken to replace Terry with his assistant Dave Tippett. *The Hockey News* quoted Terry's candid thoughts on such a rude awakening: "It has been a great honour for me to coach the Houston Aeros. It was like a dream come true for me. I kept pinching myself when I got the job. Lately, I must have pinched myself too hard and woke myself up. I found out it was a nightmare."

But as the cold sweats subsided and clear minds prevailed, Terry agreed to remain with the Aeros as an assistant general manager. He now does promotional work on behalf of the team by making personal appearances in the community and by making commercials for the big corporations.

On the leisure side of his life, he revels in playing golf and riding horses. "Just recently I got together with the trainer from the [Houston] Rockets, Ray Melkiori," Terry reported. "He has some cutting horses. I used to live on a farm in Prince Albert and had my own horses so I love riding... And I like to spend as much time as I can with my family."

Terry's wife, Carol, hails from Lubock, Texas and during the mid-seventies, was voted Miss Texas. Their two teenage daughters are very active on the local sports scene and frequently require the usual chauffeuring to their events. "So it's Ruskowski Cab on top of the vehicle and let's go," Terry joked. "All I'm missing is the metre!"

Nicknames: *Ruski; Ski; Rosco*

"When I played junior hockey, the guys called me 'Ruski'," Terry reported. "When I made it to Houston they called me 'Ski' and in

Chicago and L.A., they started calling me 'Rosco' which is more or less what everybody calls me nowadays."

***

Sabourin, Gary: *Played right wing for St. Louis, Toronto, California and Cleveland from 1967-1977. Born: Parry Sound, Ontario, 1943.*

While sitting in his wooden school desk, Gary Sabourin was the kind of lad who possessed immense powers of imagination which, rather than being applied to Miss Crabtree's lessons, were instead reserved for transforming his desk top into a rink, his pencil into a stick and his eraser into a puck. The opening face-off came each morning at precisely the moment Miss Crabtree announced, "Now children, take out your math books."

By the time he had made high school, Gary's imaginary game had become the real thing. "I was consumed with the idea that I could play hockey and make it," he recalled. "At that time, I would have skated on a two-foot patch of ice if it was frozen! That's all I wanted to do. And as a youngster, nobody ever thought I could make it because a lot of junior guys were more talented. But I had a burning desire. I became a better hockey player than anybody ever thought I could, and it was all work. I then improved to the point where for a time, I was above average in the NHL, scoring twenty-five, twenty-eight goals. I got there and I lasted for ten years—it was a dream come true!"

By 1977, the Cleveland Barons were merging with the Minnesota North Stars and Gary's dream had almost played out its course. Retirement came at the end of the season. "In a sense, I think I was glad it was over," he confided. "When you get to be thirty-two, thirty-three, hockey becomes real tough because of the back-to-back games and the travelling.

> *" When you get to be fifty-five ... you feel everything that happened to you. Your body is hurting—your shoulders, your knees—you take so much beating!"*
>
> Gary Sabourin

You were sore and the fun was going out of it. So for the most part, I was glad when it was done because I didn't have to be physically abused anymore. And I'd suffered some bad injuries the last year or so."

But as the curtain was closing on his career in hockey, physical pain became secondary to Gary's concern for his future. "It was the uncertainty of what comes next that was the hardest part to deal with," he revealed. "When you were done, there was nowhere to turn as there is today. Now the league counsels players. There are other avenues they can pursue to help them in business or whatever. But back then, it was, 'No we don't need you anymore. Good-bye!' And here you come out and you're not trained for anything.

"I had no job, but I was lucky in that I had deferred monies. I still had a $20,000-a-year scouting contract with Cleveland-Minnesota. I had put it in my last year's contract that if I couldn't play because of this knee injury, they'd pay me my last year's salary over three years. And I had a home already built up in Britt [Ontario] that was paid for, so I could get by. But I can't imagine what it would have been like if I hadn't had that."

Gary's initial plan was to purchase his uncle's marina business in Britt. He knew the enterprise well, having worked there as a young man. But his uncle's son bought it and Gary found himself as the odd man out.

Instead, he settled on purchasing a Buns Master franchise in Chatham, Ontario. He sold his house, packed up the family and launched himself into the new venture.

"It hasn't been easy," he admitted. "It's been a tough business. But every business is tough. Chatham was forty-one thousand when I came here and it's still forty-one—so it hasn't been conducive to a growing business. I just had to build up a core of loyal customers and hope they'd keep coming back. It hasn't been too bad, but there have been tough years too.

"A lot of people think, unrealistically, that if they buy a business, they've got it made. But it's not like that at all. You don't just pop in for an hour and then leave. I put in eight or nine hours a day. But that's fine with me. It's a physical type of work. You're always moving. So I like that part because I could never have been a person who sits in an office all day."

At home, Gary credits his wife, Nancy, for having worked so diligently on the front lines of raising their four children and coping with the ups and downs of his career. "The wives, they play a big part in it too," he declared with respect. "They have to because they're raising the family while we're playing. It leaves a lot of responsibility on them. I mean you go through slumps and they suffer with you. If the team's losing, it's tough on everybody because you bring the game home..."

Gary's take on hockey twenty years after the fact is now more engaged by off-ice litigation than breakaways on ice. He followed the recent pension lawsuit initiated by the Professional Hockey Pensioners' Association with great interest. "When I was young, I just didn't give a (bleep) about any part of it but playing," he recalled. "We didn't have enough smart guys who could see through what happened through Eagleson and the pension issue. They were really screwing the players. I'm really bitter about that part. Thank God we had some guys who saw through it—pretty brilliant guys like Carl Brewer and Bobby Baun. They knew something wasn't right—then we found out. Eagleson started out with all these good intentions. He did a lot for the game, but he really abused his position. I just can't forgive that—it really hurt. Even though we had this pension settlement, I just think the present NHL should reach out and do something monetarily for a lot of these retired players."

Since Gary's day, NHL players have progressed from lone prospectors, panning for gold dust to a precious-metals cartel—and he is pleased as all get out to see the Association's newly found prosperity.

"It's crazy but it's great for the players because I always said, 'Once you're done, you're done'!" he exclaimed. "And I hope they all make a million because you give so much of yourself for those years you're there. It takes a helluva toll on you. When you get to be fifty-five or whatever, you feel everything that happened to you. Your body is hurting—your shoulders, your knees—you take so much beating! If you played eight, ten years, it's a lot of stress on your body and you feel it all when you get old. So you can't be paid enough as far as I'm concerned."

St. Laurent, Dollard: *Played defense for Montreal and Chicago from 1950-1962. Born: Verdun, Quebec, 1929.*

Since there was no such thing as a warranty on the career span of an NHL player during the league's so-called Golden Era, a hard fall into the boards or the errant twist of a knee could bring an instant end to the financial lifeline of a player and his family.

With a wife and seven children to look out for, Dollard St. Laurent was acutely aware of the need to be insurance minded. Four years before he retired from professional hockey, he had begun working with his brother in Montreal to establish Lorenzo and Dollard St. Laurent Insurance. When his time was up, whether by fate or by his own choosing, he'd be ready.

In the interim, his on-ice career was still thriving. He'd made his mark as a stalwart of the Canadiens' blueline corps for eight seasons. His tough bodychecking and adherence to defensive-zone fundamentals helped his team to three straight Stanley Cup victories before he was traded to Chicago in 1958. As a Blackhawk, he lasted an additional four years and cherished one final league championship in 1960-61.

At the close of the following season, Dollard was sent to the minors to play for the Quebec Aces of the American Hockey League. "I enjoyed it but we didn't make the playoffs," he said of his time in the AHL. "I also felt that I was in good enough shape to keep on playing in the NHL. Doug Harvey was in New York at the time and he wanted me to go and play there. But through circumstances I could not get to New York to play for the Rangers."

But the issue of big-league viability was soon rendered irrelevent. A hard fall to the ice broke his leg and any hopes of an extended career in pro hockey. Before the Aces' season had ended, he was forced to the sidelines. And although he was offered a contract for the following year, he decided it was time to pack it in and gear it up for the start of a new career.

"It was very difficult to adjust from the way of life I had been used to, to a person going into work which I had never done before," he admitted. "But in the summertime, I used to work with my brother ... building up the business for the day I retired. So I was already blended into the insurance field, which made it easier for me than other guys. But I still found it tough—a different kind of life. And having a family, I think I did the right thing. I could have hung on, playing in the American League, doing this and that and travelling. But I had seven kids," he quipped with a laugh, "and I thought it was time to quit the game and do a little bit of work."

Dollard and Lorenzo managed their life and general insurance agency for more than a decade until they sold it to investors from London, England in the mid-seventies. Dollard stayed on for a few additional years before shifting to insuring financial premiums. On the subject of his new line of work, he explained that instead of borrowing money from the bank to pay insurance premiums, his clients could obtain the necessary collateral directly from his company and then defer the payments over a period of time. "I worked for different people from 1978 to 1990," he recounted. "I enjoyed it and I did well at it."

Since retirement, Dollard has savoured a gratifying blend of society and tranquility. "During the summertime, I've got many golf tournaments to play in from the National Hockey League Players' Association and from many other organizations," he noted. "Plus I have ninety-two acres in Cèdres. It's an area around St. Lauzare and Hudson. I go out there a lot. I enjoy gardening, flowers and so on. It's quiet and really peaceful."

Dollard also attends an occasional hockey game at the Molson Centre. "It's a completely different game today," he stressed. "It's big business. The price of everything is so expensive—the boys are making nothing but millions! And it's the fan that has to pay for everything. But what the hell! What can you do? That's the sport right now. I enjoyed my days when I played and I'm sure the kids are enjoying their days today, money-wise and hockey-wise."

St. Marseille, Frank: *Played right wing for St. Louis and Los Angeles from 1967-1977. Born: Levack, Ontario, 1939.*

Frank St. Marseille was a top-notch defensive forward whose unselfish play brought him two assists for every goal he scored during his ten seasons shared between the St. Louis Blues and Los Angeles Kings. Combining speed and heads-up intuition, he excelled as a penalty killer and playmaker, banking a total of 470 points by career's end.

After skating his final shift for the Los Angeles Kings in 1977, he accepted a post as player-coach for the Halifax Voyageurs of the American Hockey League. "It was a little confusing ... when I was playing and coaching at the same time," he admitted. "At the beginning of the season it was very hard. But as the year progressed, it pretty well became automatic."

He stayed on with the Voyageurs for an additional year before returning to the Los Angeles Kings as an assistant coach to Bob Berry. "It was very exciting," he declared, speaking of his return to the NHL. "I would have probably stayed on except that I had a little misunderstanding with the general manager [George Maguire]... He and I didn't see eye to eye on some things and I just couldn't work under those conditions. That's the only reason I left there. As a matter of fact, I never lost a game when I coached," he joked. "I coached one game and I won it. I'm undefeated!"

Frank had the conviction to leave professional hockey on matters of principle because, although he loved the sport, he knew that the world of hockey was revolving within a greater universe of options. "I miss it once in a while," he revealed. "But not to the extent that a lot of players do. A lot of them can't live without it. But I can."

After L.A., he, his wife and three children packed up and returned to their home base in Sudbury, Ontario. Frank went to work selling gas products for Northern and Central Gas Company and settled into his new job as a salesman quite comfortably. "As a matter of fact, it's something I'm quite good at," he declared. "So I didn't have any problems."

But after four years with Northern and Central, his life got bumped through a cloud of upheaval. "I went through a divorce in Sudbury," he confided. "Things didn't work out and so I moved out of town."

He eventually found a haven in Ottawa, Ontario where he started his present job as a salesman with United Auto Parts in 1987. U.A.P. specializes in providing parts for service professionals in the area. As a liaison, Frank is required to have a broad-based knowledge of mechanics in order to provide correct products for his customers. He originally obtained this experience out on the farm. "I owned a farm the whole time I played hockey," he reported. "I used to repair all my own equipment. Farm machinery and cars are pretty basic. They end up not really being any different. So I'm very, very handy with mechanics."

Now settled into the rural surroundings of Ashton, Ontario, Frank has remarried. His new wife works for the Federal government and together, they are raising two sons.

As a sideline, Frank looks forward to playing tennis and oldtimers' hockey with the Ottawa Senators' alumni team.

Nickname: *Saint*

An abbreviation of his last name that Frank picked up while playing in St. Louis.

Ed Sandford

B O S T O N   B R U I N S

Sanford, Ed: *Played left wing for Boston, Detroit and Chicago from 1947-1956. Born: Toronto, Ontario, 1928.*

Ed Sanford shows up for work at 7:15 to 7:30 each morning. He reads *The Wall Street Journal* and an occasional *New York Times*, attends a few meeting at 8:30 and then hits the phone to solicit and service his clientele for the remainder of the day. Over the past forty years, he's been as dependable and consistent in executing his work as the company he represents, H.C. Wainright & Co., occupants of State Street in Boston since 1862.

Ed's steady approach to life accrued with age, but its foundation was laid early on in his NHL career as a trusty left winger for the Boston Bruins. "It goes back to the first year I played," he revealed. "I always wondered what I was going to do when I was through. I knew I wasn't going to be in the game forever and ever. I talked to some of the players who were with the Celtics at the time. I was impressed with some of those fellas who were college graduates—they were thinking about what they were going to do when

236

they got through. I remember meeting some of the New York Giants at training camp in Hershey—they also impressed me. These people gave me enough of a spark to do it on my own. I didn't need an awful lot in a sense because it was just right in front of me. You could play hockey as long as you were young and strong. I saw veterans who were being cut from teams and some of them had nothing else to do. I'm always amazed that more of them weren't looking beyond."

The real issue for Ed then was to find an alternative to hockey that would blend his creativity with his need to make a living. "I always had an interest in investments because at that time I was investing my own money," he recounted, describing his search. "I was learning the stock market on my own, so I thought, 'Try a business you like and see if you can be successful at it.' And that's how I worked it out. So I had a job to go to the moment I retired from hockey."

Ed's big day came when he left the Chicago Blackhawks at the end of the 1955-56 season. It would be full speed ahead with Wainright from that moment on. "Like anything else, it was a brand-new business," he remarked in describing his transition into the world of financial advisors. "I knew a little bit about it. But I didn't know as many things as I should, so it was slow and difficult for a few years. I wondered whether I'd made the right decision. But I always knew that I liked what I was doing. The transition was difficult and I think this is why it's so hard for professional athletes to face up to reality and to step out of that cocoon they're in when they're with all the other guys in the dressing room. That's a safe haven, but eventually you've got to face the new world."

At home, Ed and his wife, Patricia, have raised five children along the way. Their oldest son is a scoring official with the Boston Bruins.

As a pastime, Ed savours a round of curling in the winter and golfing in the summer. He has also been supervisor of off-ice officials for the Boston Bruins since 1968. As such, he has witnessed a steady outgrowth of open doors in professional hockey.

"I think it's still an awfully good game," he concluded. "I think for a young boy today, there are a lot of opportunities. A lot of colleges down here have very good hockey programmes. They're looking for boys to come and get a scholarship and a great education. You can go to Harvard, Dartmouth, Boston University, take any courses you want. And if you happened to get drafted, you've got two avenues going for you. You've got a good education and your skill in hockey. I think these are wonderful times for young people."

Sasakamoose, Fred: *Played centre for Chicago from 1953-54. Born: Sandy Lake Reserve, Saskatchewan, 1933.*

On the night of March 5th, 1954, Moose Jaw Canucks' general manager George Vogan entered his team's dressing room. He projected his voice over the post-game hum of conversations. "I don't want anyone to move just yet," he affirmed. The players looked to one another with faces of curiosity and anticipation. Then, there was more commotion at the doorway as a man holding a telegram entered. The room fell silent: "Attention Fred Sasakamoose, stop. You are to report immediately to the Chicago Blackhawks, stop!" As a sense of excitement animated the room, still more carfuffle stirred in the doorway as two suitcases were brought in and placed at the feet of the newest Chicago Blackhawk—the first full-blooded Indian to ever play in the NHL. "Fred," they stated, "these clothes are for you—suits, a watch and everything you'll need to look respectable as the professional you are about to become."

That night, Fred caught a train bound for Toronto's Maple Leaf Gardens. A two-day journey brought him to Carleton Street where the short stroll from the sidewalk to the dressing room matched the immeasurable span of a life-long dream. "You talk about a young Indian! You talk about the thrill of a lifetime!" he proclaimed. "Just looking at big stars like Bill Mosienko, Doug Bentley, Bill Gadsby, Al Rollins and Lee Fogolin. And then I put on that sweater with the logo—that's an Indian! So here I am, a real Indian wearing an Indian sweater that fit me to a tee!

"Then I hit the ice and that's an experience I'll never forget. Huge...huge...people...full! As I looked around at all these guys, I thought, 'How the hell was it that a man like me should be able to step onto this ice after hearing about it so many times on *Hockey Night in Canada*?' I felt nervous because I was a different breed altogether. I was walking on air..."

As he circled the ice during the pregame warm-up, he was ushered back to partial reality by a teammate who flagged him down. "There's a guy over there who wants to talk to you right away," the teammate stated.

Fred eased his way towards the box. "Here was old Foster Hewitt himself!" he exclaimed. "He wanted to know how to pronounce my name. He said, 'Are you Saskatchewanmoose or Saskatoonmoose'?"

Perhaps no moment in Fred's professional career better symbolized the distinctions that lay between the big-city realm he was entering and the reserve from which he had come. His name was indeed unique at best, but his cultural heritage, unlike the world of big-league hockey, was grounded on a completely different rock.

In 1933, Fred, like all of the Sasakamoose children, was born into the arms of a midwife at his parents' twenty-by-twenty-foot log cabin on the Sandy Lake Reserve in Saskatchewan. Electricity, telephones and cars were no part of his early beginnings, although since hockey required none of the above, he was soon off and gliding.

"When I was six years old, my grandfather gave me these bob skates," he recollected. "They're like little sleighs that strap onto your shoes. My grandfather would get a team of horses and clear the snow from the slough—which is like a little lake where we'd water the horses. That's where I started to skate."

After mastering some basic moves, Fred's

Fred Sasakamoose accompanied by his mother during his induction into the Saskatchewan Indian Hall of Fame in July of 1994

grandfather—a man of resource—took him to the next level. "I remember he used to make a hockey stick out of a willow branch for me," Fred explained. "He would shave it down to a hook. Then he'd make a puck for me by cutting a disk from the trunk of a poplar tree.

"Now I couldn't really skate with those bob skates, but it was all we could afford. But after a while, my grandfather finally got me a little pair of real skates. They had half-inch thick blades and were about a mile long. And after some time, I did pretty well with them."

1940, however, brought an abrupt change to young Fred's home life. The clergy at St. Michael's School at Duck Lake had convinced his parents that a good Catholic education would do wonders for their son's soul. Henceforth, Fred's annual routine became ten months of hard work, strict control, a tinge of academics and plenty of sports—especially hockey. In between soccer, baseball and boxing, Fred began to develop into a respectable young hockey player. His physical development was greatly enhanced by lots of old-fashioned hard labour.

"We farmed about fifty acres of vegetable

gardens at the school," he recalled. "And we had to milk eighty cows in the morning and eighty cows in the evening. There were forty of us kids in there milking—so we'd each do two cows. And I remember the priests always telling me, 'You've got to work hard! Your wrists will become strong by pulling the tits on the cows all the time'."

But all of the skating, milking and hoeing that St. Michael's had to offer could never replace the familial glow of summers spent back on the reserve. Even victory in the provincial midget hockey championships did nothing to dissuade Fred from his primal link to Sandy Lake. By age fifteen, and in spite of his growing on-ice notoriety, he came home to stay.

"I didn't want to go anyplace!" he asserted. "I just wanted to stay here with Mum and Dad because the reserve was my whole life. But as you'll see, things didn't work out the way I planned.

"One day in September I was out in a field thrashing and stoking for these farmers along with my mum and dad. We stopped our work as we saw a car pull up a couple of hundred yards away. I noticed it was Father O'Saul and Father Chevrier and a third guy I didn't know. They sent me away a distance while they talked. After a while they called me over and Dad asked, 'Do you want to go son?' I said, 'Where?' He answered, 'This guy is the general manager of the Moose Jaw Canucks junior team. He wants you to try out for the team.' I said, 'No! I'm not leaving Dad! I'm not going anyplace.' But the priests continued to press me to go. So finally I said to Mum, 'Okay, two weeks and that's it—I'm coming back'!"

Shortly thereafter, Fred hopped on a truck and was delivered to Moose Jaw—the biggest conglomeration of people, architecture and science that his eyes had ever beheld.

"It wasn't easy for me to fit in because I'd never seen a city," he admitted. "I'd never seen city people nor did I know about their way of life."

George Vogan, the club's general manager took Fred under his wing to ease the culture shock that, in spite of his best efforts, possessed a current all its own.

"George would take me to the dressing room to be with the white kids," Fred revealed. "And I'll tell you, I felt out of place. Some of them tried to talk to me, but I hesitated ... because I was embarrassed for what I was—to be an Indian.

"But after four or five days, I got more confidence in myself as I realized I could skate with the other players—I was on the same level."

To stay there, however, required more than just hockey skills. He also had to convince a few of his teammates that the colour of his skin made him just as diversely human as them.

"When you were trying to make the hockey team, you damn well had to fight," he affirmed. "Some of the white kids in Moose Jaw disliked me because of what I was. They'd call me names and I didn't like it a damn bit! Oh I had some sufferings! I got beat up. But in my younger days I was trained tough as a boxer, so I was able to hold my own. I remember one time I got into a fight with the Huckle brothers—both of them! And they were bigger than me. The three of us went at it and nobody stopped us. And by golly, afterwards, I started crying. I didn't want to be like that, but I just got fed up with being called names. After that we became friends—they learned to respect me."

Two weeks of rookie training camp passed quickly, and respect or no respect, Fred stood resolute on his promise to return to Sandy Lake. "How are you getting home?" George Vogan enquired. "I'm just taking my clothes and walking," Fred replied. "When George was gone, I just snuck out of there and hit the road. I made it as far as a town called Chamberlain when he caught up with me and took me back to Moose Jaw. I said to him, 'George, I told you I was only staying for two weeks and no more.' 'Well,' he said, 'you made the team!' He asked me to stay with him and because I'd gotten pretty used to him, I did. He treated me really well—I loved the man."

Fred spent the next four years refining his skills with the Moose Jaw Canucks. He also signed a C-form with the Chicago Blackhawks which opened the door to their training camps each fall. It was there that he centred one of the more racially diverse lines in hockey history.

"Did you ever take a close look at my hockey card?" he queried. "Look at my skate laces. On the left side is a yellow skate lace and on the other is a black one. My right winger was a black man named Al Laycock and my right winger was a Chinaman named Jimmy Chow. And in the middle is an Indian—me!"

During his final season with Moose Jaw in 1953, Fred became team captain and won the Western League MVP award. He also earned a two-game tryout with the Hawks. The first time he stepped onto the ice at Chicago Stadium, the organist played *Indian Love Call*. And love him they did, promising to bring him back at the conclusion of his junior season.

> *"I told the judge, 'Here's the keys to my truck, it's here in the parking lot. You phone my wife and tell them to come and pick it up. You're taking me to jail, now'."*
>
> **Fred Sasakamoose**

After that momentous telegram had arrived in the spring, Fred's NHL stint was underway. And although his stay at the top was short, he managed to squeeze so much living into so little time. He was renowned for having introduced himself to Gordie Howe by raising his right hand—Indian style—and saying "How". He sat with heavyweight boxer Jack Dempsy at the latter's restaurant in New York City, and he worked out with George Capone's boxers in Chicago.

Life seemed so full of promise that Fred purchased a sparkling new De Soto for thirty-nine hundred dollars. "I was the only one on the reserve who had a car at the time," he recounted. "There were no highways in there—nothing but wagons, horses and my De Soto. It only lasted for three months for God's sake. It was ripped apart by all the roads! I told Mum, 'Don't worry about it, I'll buy a couple more of them next spring, so I can give you one too.' But I didn't listen right to Mum and Dad

because it never happened. Instead, I was sent to the minors to play in Chicoutimi, then New Westminster and then Calgary."

It was at that point that Fred's association with professional hockey boiled to the top and over the sides. Recently married, he wanted his wife to join him in Calgary while he was skating for the Stampeders. The club's management offered him two plane tickets, but a twenty-four-hour wait was too long to hold loneliness at bay. Fred was leaving immediately.

"I hired a taxi to take me 600 miles from Calgary to the reserve to get my wife," he explained. "I got there at five in the morning and went to my wife's place. She said, 'What do you want?' I said, 'I've come for you.' 'No, I'm not coming,' was her answer. So I went back to Calgary alone.

"Later, when I was playing a game in Saskatoon, a bunch of Indians, including my mum, dad and nephews came to visit—but no wife! She wasn't there. Well that night, I went back to my room and told my roommate, 'Don't tell anybody, but I'm leaving. I'm calling it quits right now. I love my wife and I want to go home'."

Fred caught another taxi back to Sandy Lake, this time to stay for good. "I was sick of being kicked around," he stated. "In hockey, you're not your own boss. You're told where to go, when to practise, how much to weigh and what to eat. But us Indians have got to be free. My freedom is like an animal.

"And you know a lot of people ask me, 'Did you make the right choice?' Especially white men because they think differently: He thinks prosperity. He thinks of greatness. He thinks about money to be made—his athletic name. So did I make the right choice? I say I did. I have a wonderful family now. And if I hadn't made that choice then maybe I would have lived in a lost world—I don't know."

In the years that followed his defection from

Calgary, the Blackhawks attempted to control Fred's future by refusing to grant him the amateur status he needed to play senior hockey in Western Canada. To escape their grasp, he exercised his local star power to generate a career outside the confines of organized hockey.

"When I came back to the reserve," he recounted, "the people in all the white neighbouring towns knew about it. They wanted to watch an NHL player and they wanted to watch an Indian. So they'd invite me to come and play and I ended up on a schedule like a star on a guitar that sings every night. I was motorized all over the place. In one month I'll bet I played thirty games. I was a performer. I could dance on my skates. I could handle that stick and I could fire that biscuit! When I lifted my hockey stick between the red line and the blue line—look out! I remember one time in Meadow Lake, the goalie took off—he left his net! He knew I was going to shoot that puck and he got out of the way."

The lack of an amateur card, however, cost Fred a harvest of ripe opportunities. He received countless invitations from as far away as Jacksonville, Florida and as meaningful as a chance to win Olympic gold with the Warwick brothers and the Penticton V's.

They all fell wide of the goal post until the management of the Kamloops senior club paid $10,000 to secure his release from the Blackhawks' organization. He returned their favour by playing for the next seven years, at which time he got a chieftain's send off.

"I told them that this was my last year," he recalled. "Well a man named Gus went up to the mountains and made smoke signals. He called all of the Okanagan Indians in British Columbia to join them in Kamloops. They brought Fred Sasakamoose to the middle of the ice and do you know what they named me? Because I could shoot a puck like nobody had ever seen, they called me 'Chief Thunder Stick'."

Since that momentous time, Fred has devoted his life to raising his family and improving the quality of life at Sandy Lake. He was elected as band chief in 1980 and the responsibilities of the job changed his life in a big way.

"Being chosen as chief saved me from being an alcoholic," he confided, "or going further—to be a drunk. After my election, a bunch of people came and said, 'Freddie, come to the party—you're chief now. We'll have a drink for you!' So I went and opened me a bottle of beer and half a bottle I drank. Then I thought about our previous chief, Alan Ahenakew, and how he had told me that one day I would be a leader. So I stood up and I told them, 'Friends, my career of drinking is over right now! I have to look after my people.' I left that bottle on the table and I said good-bye. That was the turning point of my life—one of the greatest things that ever happened to me."

Fred immediately applied himself to the profoundly problematic issues of alcohol and drug abuse on the reserve. "My hope is that one day we'll have a reserve free of drugs and alcohol," he stated. "But I know it's a long struggle. Alcohol has been a real killer in our lives and we have to get away from it. Our young people are being destroyed left and right. And government welfare is a big part of the problem. Thirty years ago, people had to work at four dollars a day—they were too proud and too busy to drink. But then welfare came and it's no damn good! It kills our pride. It has made the Indians into the laziest son of a buggers ... and it's a bunch of bullshit."

By 1987, the pressures of leadership had taken their toll on Fred's health. He resigned his post as chief but has continued his cause as a volunteer member of a reserve support group that counsels youth on issues of alcohol and drug abuse. And although not officially an elder, he sits at the top of the request charts among school children who are eager to hear firsthand of his groundbreaking exploits.

Now in his sixties, and at an age when most people recede, Fred continues to attract notoriety the way a puck attracts a stick. In 1994, his livelihood of catching and selling fish fell under the lens of provincial law. With television crews in the wings, Fred battled the Saskatchewan courts over the issue of his freedom to catch and sell fish without a permit. He argued his own case with simple elegance:

"I told the judge, 'I will not accept any handouts from the government! If I'm able to put food on the table with my own hands—I'll do it. You're not going to stop me from fishing. I've been doing this for the last thirty years. Besides, I'm a treaty Indian—I don't need a permit to sell fish. I did not steal that fish. I went out onto the lake when it was thirty below and caught them. And the nets I use belong to me. I didn't steal them either'!"

On April 4th of 1997, the judge weighed provincial policy against Fred's concerns and then levied a fine of $4,000. Fred rose to his feet and with the grace of conviction, made his stand: "I told the judge, 'Here's the keys to my truck, it's here in the parking lot. You phone my wife and tell them to come and pick it up. You're taking me to jail, now'."

The judge's frustration grew as Fred repeatedly refused to accept the fine. "During the last three years," he told the judge, "you and I have been fighting over this situation and you understand my position. If I pay the fine, then my treaties are all gone to hell—I'd no longer believe in them and I'd have to destroy them."

Finally the judge conceded and told an unremitting Fred that he could go. "When you're ready to pick me up," Fred continued, "you'll know where to find me!

"I haven't heard a damn thing since! They've left me alone so far, but the next time you call, you might be talking to me from jail!"

But the courts are not the only group with an interest in the life of Fred Sasakamoose. Recognition for his achievements has been on the upswing over the past few years. Television crews, autograph collectors, VIP invitations and bags of mail have marked a steady stream to his door. In 1994, he was inducted into the Saskatchewan Indian Hall of Fame. Most recently, he was invited as a VIP to attend the Indigenous Summer Games in Victoria, British Columbia. "I walked in the Parade of Athletes at Commonwealth Stadium," he recounted. "There were about thirty thousand people in there... They were yelling and clapping hands. There were

8,600 athletes from across North America, South America, New Zealand and Australia. I was able to walk among them—huh, an old guy like me. And to think that I was once an athlete and now I'm walking with the champions—that was one of the biggest moments of my life!"

Schmidt, Milt: *Played centre for Boston between 1936 & 1954. Born: Kitchener, Ontario, 1918.*

In all facets of his career, Milt Schmidt can be characterized as a deep well of spring-loaded energy whose containment has yet to be achieved. In the old days, opposing defensemen leapt into his path, stopping him only half of the time. Chicago Blackhawks' general manager Tommy Ivan literally threw Phil Esposito and Ken Hodge in his way and it only raised him higher. These days, at age seventy-nine, only age seems to be able to slow Milt down, although he continues to hold out for the final word.

At the time of his interview, he was convalescing from hip replacement surgery. Being confined to the couch in front of the television is not his usual station in life, but his beloved Bruins are on the tube and he's got a chance to talk shop, so he makes do.

As a player, Milt has been regarded, particularly by his opponents, as one of the greatest centremen to ever play in the NHL. As a member of Boston's "Kraut Line", he garnered 624 points in 864 games. And although his numbers were not astounding by today's standards, his intangible qualities were. His endurance, gritty determination and creativity lifted his team to two Stanley Cup victories and brought personal acknowledgment in the form of an Art Ross Trophy as the league's leading scorer in 1940; a Hart Trophy in 1951 as the league's most valuable player; three first-team all-star awards; and his induction into the Hockey Hall of Fame in 1961.

In the midst of his sixteenth season in 1954, Milt figured his usefulness to the team would be better served behind the bench. To that end, he replaced Lynn Patrick as the team's head coach and embarked on the long and slow process of setting Bruin fortunes on the rise. By the late fifties, Boston was within a five o'clock shadow of winning the Cup. But the lack of a strong farm system and the exodus of key players such as Terry Sawchuk and Allan Stanley set the club spinning downward for years to come.

Milt had to tough it out through the thin years before he finally got creative control of the team in 1967. As general manger, he had a nucleus of young talent in the form of Bobby Orr, Gerry Cheevers, Derek Sanderson and Wayne Cashman. And he wasted little time in wheeling and dealing this base of talent into an empire. His career night came when he convinced Blackhawks' general manager Tommy Ivan to accept Gilles Marotte, Pit Martin and goaltender Jack Norris in exchange for Ken Hodge, Phil Esposito and Fred Stanfield. By 1969, the Bruins held their first Stanley Cup in twenty-nine years.

> *"I've had my fill in all walks of life as far as hockey is concerned— as a player, coach and general manager—and I enjoyed every minute of it."*
>
> *Milt Schmidt*

Milt eventually left the high mount of the Bruins in 1974 to descend into the deep, dark valley of expansion as the first general manager of the Washington Capitals. Head coaches Jim Anderson and Red Sullivan tried in vain to move the team forward. Milt himself finally jumped into the flames to squeeze his players to a record of five wins, thirty-three losses and five ties.

"That's an adventure that I want to forget about!" he declared. "It was tough going. It was an expansion club and you didn't get the personnel years ago like you can get today. That was my final job with hockey and I haven't been associated with it since. I've had my fill in all walks of life as far as hockey is concerned—as a player, coach and general manager—and I enjoyed every minute of it. So I've been very fortunate that I participated in all phases of the game."

For the first time in many, many years, Milt found himself working outside of the NHL. "I went into the steel business for a couple of years along with a friend of mine, but that didn't work out," he related. "So then the opportunity to be the manager of the Boston Madison Square Garden Club came along in 1979. It was a godsend! It gave me something to do and I had Marie, my wife, working for me during the Bruins' games, so it worked out very nicely.

"It's a private club and I was the manager. We served cocktails and dinners and we had tickets for all the events that went on in the Gardens."

Some time before the Garden Club was moved to the new Fleet Center, Milt decided to retire. He brought Don Marcotte on board, taught him the ropes and handed him the reigns. But Milt disliked the taste of life in the retirement lane, so he made a quick U-turn and hastened back to the Gardens. "Now Donny Marcotte is the manager and I work for him," Milt explained. "And that's what I'm still doing and I fully intend to go back just as soon as I get rid of my crutches!

"So my job with the Garden Club has certainly been a blessing as far as I'm concerned because the hours are short and I can enjoy golfing in the summer. But I'm seventy-nine years of age now so I don't *move it* the way I used to. I'm playing at eleven handicap right now and I used to be a four. But I do play a lot of golf and I enjoy it very much. And I usually go on a week's fishing trip in the spring, going after some landlocked salmon. And my wife and I usually take a trip up to Canada, to Waterloo, to visit my two sisters. We get up there at least once or twice a year. That's still home you know. We're American citizens but we still look at Canada as being home."

Shand, Dave: *Played defense for Atlanta, Toronto and Washington from 1976-1985. Born: Cold Lake, Alberta, 1956.*

Dave Shand is the type of person who strives to make a little bit more than the most of any situation within which he finds himself. His eyes will inevitably gaze over the shoulder of the obvious in search of the unexpected spinoff, something new to learn, something new to see.

He entered the NHL in 1976 from the University of Michigan's hockey programme. It was as a Wolverine that he acquired course credits and a relationship with the institution that would one day stand his future in good stead.

While playing for Team Canada in 1978 and 1979, Dave received invitations to play in Europe. Still at the peak of his NHL career, however, he filed their hospitality away for future reference.

When the end came with the Washington Capitals in 1985, he dusted off his European rain

checks and headed to Klagenfurt, Austria for the next four seasons, two as a player and two as a player-coach.

Dave Shand: full-time lawyer and part-time Red Wing oldtimer

"Training camp used to start in July," he noted. "We started the season in September. We had a thirty-eight game schedule and then we had what they called a super playoff for ten games. Then we went into two best-of-seven series and finished around the second week of March. I'd stay over there and my kids would come over at spring break. We'd do some touring and they'd have a blast!"

In an effort to ease his ability to live and work amidst foreign cultures, Dave used his four years of opportunity to learn German. "I read, write and speak fluently," he reported with pride. "I was in an area in Austria where there isn't a lot of English. So if I wanted to eat, I figured I better learn how to speak!"

Years later, his second language has escaped fossilization through occasional outings at the office. "I did work for a big corporate law firm," he related. "We did a lot of transactional work involving banks around the world, and I've been able to sit down and translate a fax or a document without having to go outside the firm. So it's been a big asset."

Dave returned from Austria in 1989 and went to work as an assistant coach to Red Berenson at the University of Michigan. Dave capitalized on the scholarly setting by first completing his undergraduate degree and then graduating from Michigan Law School.

"It was a challenge," he admitted of his return to school. "I don't think I'd written anything besides Christmas cards for thirteen years. But I'd always been a good student. So once I got in there, I really enjoyed it. I think the pro hockey experience really helped: the discipline, the drive and being goal oriented. They are the same habits and patterns you use in law school."

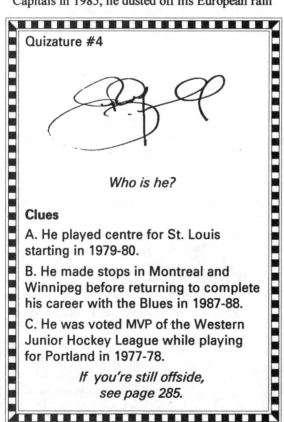

Quizature #4

Who is he?

Clues

A. He played centre for St. Louis starting in 1979-80.

B. He made stops in Montreal and Winnipeg before returning to complete his career with the Blues in 1987-88.

C. He was voted MVP of the Western Junior Hockey League while playing for Portland in 1977-78.

If you're still offside, see page 285.

Shortly after his graduation in 1994, Dave passed his Law Board exams and then joined a crowded legal firm of a hundred attorneys. "I do primarily employment law: litigation, wrongful dismissal and sex-race harassment suits," he explained. "We're not a plaintiffs' firm, we defend companies."

In his practice, Dave has observed that a spirited courtroom workout is not unlike clearing a goal crease in the NHL. "I'm used to being competitive and litigation is a competition," he reasoned. "I enjoy it except that the results are a little longer in coming than you're used to on the ice. You don't get to sit there like after a game and measure your success. Going to trial and getting the result is great, but it takes a long time in getting there."

He has also concluded that gearing up for a courtroom showdown requires some of the same pre-game rituals as lacing up in the dressing room. "All the things you do to prepare for a hockey game, you do to prepare for a trial," he revealed. "You have to take care of everything you have control over and then, expect the unexpected and know how to deal with it."

As it stands, Dave is one of the few lone mavericks of the NHL alumni to obtain credentials to practise law. "I don't know why there aren't more of them," he enquired. "I think there's going to be, as more college-educated players come out and go to school. It's so difficult if you've played junior hockey and all you've ever done is finish high school. You have to go back and face seven years of school if you want to practise law. It's a lot easier to go back if you only have to face three years."

Dave's legal expertise has also opened doors in the field of player representation. "I represent about a half-dozen players who are playing in the minors right now," he explained. "I didn't plan on going into representation, but players approached me because they know and trust me. So I've stepped that up a little bit too."

Any thoughts Dave had of indulging in legal ease with his spare time were quickly dispelled by Dennis Hextall and his roving band of oldtimers. "In '91, Dennis approached me about joining the Red Wings' alumni," Dave recounted. "So I've been playing with the team and now I'm the attorney for their alumni organization. It's nice for ... Dave Debol, Kris Manery and guys of our era who get to play with Gordie Howe, Alex Delvecchio, Bill Gadsby and Ted Lindsay. We sit there and listen to their stories. We're as enthralled as if we were just fans."

Dave and his wife, Sue, maintain their home in Ann Arbor, Michigan where the wonders of parenthood abound. "I was married and divorced early in my career as many of my contemporaries were," he confided. "I got remarried in '91, so I have a nineteen-year-old, a fifteen-year-old and eight-month-old twins. It's called really poor planning. There's really no other word for it."

Nickname: *Sugar*

"I got that name when I was with the Leafs," Dave recounted. "There used to be a song called *Sugar Shack* and they used to call Eddie Shack by that name. So I just kind of fell into it when I got to Toronto."

Skov, Glen: *Played centre for Detroit, Chicago and Montreal from 1949-1960. Born: Wheatley, Ontario, 1931.*

When Glen Skov speaks, his smooth and articulate voice surrounds you as though you're the only game in town and he's got season's tickets. In dealing with people, he is a sincere and consummate professional who excels at sales the way he excelled as a defensive specialist at centre ice.

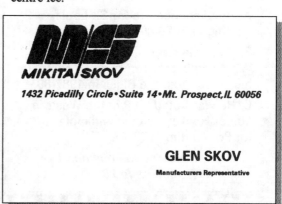

He first joined the NHL in 1950 via the Detroit Red Wings, although he didn't play a complete season until 1951-52. By then he had established himself as the designated gadfly to the opposition's number-one centre. In the process, he also picked up three Stanley Cup victories before moving to Chicago where he continued his tradition of defensive acumen.

Three years prior to seeing his final action in the NHL, Glen had embarked on a second career as a sales rep in the plastics industry. As in hockey, he was quick to develop an effective scoring touch around the sales circuit.

After the lights had dimmed on his final NHL game in 1960, he was then faced with the dilemma of whether to follow through on his interest in other facets of the hockey business or to make the leap into the world of plastics.

The Canadiens forced the issue by offering him a shot at coaching their farm club in Ottawa. With two cards in hand, he could afford to negotiate on his own terms.

"My goal was to stay in coaching," he asserted. "But in the end, we couldn't get together on salary, so I moved on."

Returning to his original training ground in Michigan, Glen resumed his sales career with Plastic Moulder's Supply. "We provided colour for plastics and we supplied plastic moulders, injection moulders, extrusion houses and things of that nature," he explained.

Shortly after his return to P.M.S., he was shipped off to blaze new trails at a company outpost. "I came to Illinois to open up their state division in 1961," he reported. "It was a very, very small company at that time. After I had been with P.M.S. for twenty-five years, we had sales in excess of fifteen million dollars! So it was a very successful venture for me."

By the mid-eighties, Glen had accumulated almost three decades of experience in the plastics industry and felt it was time to break out on his own. "So I severed with the company," he disclosed. "Stan [Mikita] and I had summer condos in Florida. We were down there and he had just left Kemper at that time. He asked me what I was going to do and I said, 'Well, I've just

Glen Skov

DETROIT RED WINGS

started a reping business of my own and I'm not going to work for another company. Whatever I do, I'm going to be my own boss!' Stan, at that time, wasn't sure what he was going to do. I said that the two of us together would make a good team. He called in a few months and said the other things he was looking at had fallen through and asked if we could still get together. I said certainly and we've been together now for over ten years."

Glen's partnership with Stan Mikita is still thriving. As a well-tuned ensemble they operate Mikita/Skov from their company base in Mt. Prospect, Illinois. "We are manufacturers' reps for different companies," Glen explained. "An example of an application would be McDonald's sauce containers. We provide the plastic sheets for producing these containers. We also sell to big candy companies, injection moulding for plastic jars and so on."

When spare time beckons, Glen relishes a round of golf and spending time with his wife, Shirley. Together they have raised a daughter and have recently embarked on the wonders of grandparenthood. He and Shirley reside in the same town as their business, Mt. Prospect, Illinois.

Nickname: *Sam*

"I got that name while I was playing junior hockey with the Windsor Spitfires," Glen recalled. "The assistant trainer of the team had just seen the movie *Good Sam* starring Gary Cooper. He said that I looked like Gary and the name 'Sam' stuck."

Nickname Challenge #23

Raw Bone Jut Jaw

Our subject had a large jaw and was often called Popeye. "I was slim too. I didn't have much fat on me. Wally Cross, who was a sports writer in St. Louis, nicknamed me 'The Raw Bone Jut Jawed ———.' My wife didn't like it (laughs)."

Who is he?

Clues

a. He played left wing for Toronto, St. Louis, Buffalo and Philadelphia between 1961 & 1972.
b. He was born in North Bay, Ontario and was drafted from St. Michael's College by the Leafs.
c. His initials are L.K.

*If you hit the goal post,
see page 285.*

Smith, Rick: *Played defense for Boston, California, St. Louis, Detroit, Washington (NHL) and Minnesota (WHA) from 1968-1981. Born: Kingston, Ontario, 1948.*

"The life that I love is the life that I went back to after hockey," Rick Smith stated. "And that's on Buck Lake, north of Kingston, Ontario. The skating on the lake! cross-country skiing!.. Last night we were making maple syrup, sitting beside a fire with the stars, having a beer and eating steaks. That's what it's all about!"

Life among the wilds of Buck Lake was a striking contrast to Rick's uproarious existence in the NHL. Over fourteen professional seasons he consistently performed as a solid and steady rearguard who always attended to the homework of his own zone.

When he retired from the Washington Capitals in 1981, he knew that his adjustment from the NHL's fast lane to a rural side road would take some getting used to.

"I had a definite intent to take a year and try to enjoy life," he recounted. "And also to give myself time to allow the transition to occur and with that, some thinking time to decide where I wanted to go. I could afford to sit there without having to worry about where the paycheque was coming from because I was able to collect a deferred salary from the St. Louis Blues for five years."

While with the Bruins, the Golden Seals and the Fighting Saints, Rick had accumulated course credits during spring and summer sessions at Queen's University in Kingston. By 1975, he had completed his bachelor of arts degree which paved the way for a run at higher learning—in this case to the steep incline of a Master's programme in computer science. "I anticipated the growth of computers in our society and business world and I wanted to be part of that," he asserted.

But Rick had been away from school for eight years and, as such, found the early stages of his studies to be the equivalent of a first sprint at training camp. "Hockey players aren't used to failing other than when they fire you at the end, demote you to the minors, or when you decide to quit," he reasoned. "Typically we've never failed at life, so to be a student and have trouble with my studies was quite an experience. Simply said, it was difficult."

But he persevered and by year three had his Master's thesis underway. "I was trying to develop a database for the National Hockey League," he reported. "I thought that there was a natural match between new computing skills and my old hockey knowledge. I expected the league to require people with those talents... Boy was I wrong—I got there too early! I spent about two years trying to get in the door. Many people liked the idea, but I couldn't get them to commit. I was never able to make a profession out of working in computing and hockey in particular."

The degree, however, was a different story. Rick was determined to bring his project to fruition. He found fertile ground in conjunction with Hockey Canada, the Canadian Hockey Association and the Kingston Frontenacs of the OHA. Within two years, he had his Master's degree in hand.

But with his deferred payments from St. Louis having lapsed, Rick found himself facing a career dilemma: He had very respectable credentials but no income.

Nine months of humility awaited him as he searched for opportunities to exchange know-how for hard cash. Eventually, good fortune surfaced in his own backyard—he landed his current job as an instructor for the Computer Services Department at Queen's University.

As an instructor, Rick found great pleasure in the process of teaching. To that end, he took full advantage of the University's offer to provide one free course per semester. Term by term, he chipped away at a degree in education. He saved a computing course, like a cherry on a dessert, as the final credit he'd need to graduate. But once that course was underway, a conflict

> *"And of course being a strong-willed hockey player, I didn't think it was appropriate to back down. I had enough confidence in myself to say, 'Wait a minute, I disagree with this academic'."*
>
> *Rick Smith*

with his professor threw his entire programme into jeopardy.

"I couldn't believe what that person was saying!" Rick protested. "It became quite a personal disagreement as opposed to an intellectual disagreement. And of course being a strong-willed hockey player, I didn't think it was appropriate to back down. I had enough confidence in myself to say, 'Wait a minute, I disagree with this academic.' Most students don't have the nerve."

In spite of his professor's insistence that multimedia could not be a subject for a required term project, Rick insisted that it was his right and that he would proceed with the forbidden topic. When the big day came, students were invited by the professor to make their presentations—all except Rick. He later brought his grievance to higher authorities within the university; but in the end, the professor prevailed and he missed his education degree by one credit.

Apparently academia can be a tougher crease to clear than a goal-mouth scramble in the NHL. And although bruised, Rick emerged as a winner. "All in all, I feel much better about myself to have stood up and made my point," he remarked. "I probably did more in life by letting those other students see another point of view. That was more important to me than the degree..."

Nicknames: *Panda; Rick Nifty; Harpo*

"I was sleeping on an airplane and Teddy Green said I looked liked a panda," Rick recalled. "I had another one, 'Harpo', because I had very long, curly hair at the time.

"And in the early seventies, Gerry Cheevers and I went to see a movie. One of the guys in the movie was called 'Rick Nifty'. So Gerry Cheevers came out and called me 'Nifty'. Then I was traded from the Bruins and in the meantime, Rick Middleton arrived. So Gerry Cheevers called him 'Rick Nifty'. Then I got traded back to the Bruins and so then there were two 'Rick Niftys' as named by Gerry Cheevers."

Smith, Sid: *Played left wing for Toronto from 1946-1958. Born: Toronto, Ontario, 1925.*

Sid Smith and the city of Toronto are as the maple is to the leaf, inseparable. The teeming vitality of Yonge Street flows as much through Sid's heart as it does through the city itself. It was only natural then that he aspired to represent his hometown in the NHL.

He achieved his goal by 1946, just in time for the Leafs roll towards three straight Stanley Cup victories. Over six seasons between 1949 and 1955, he buckled down to become one of Toronto's most potent scorers, piling up a total of 154 goals and 130 assists. In 1955, he also entered an exclusive club by donning the captain's *C*. Sid stayed true to the Maple Leaf blue throughout his entire career.

On the eve of his finale, however, he was tempted by a potential trade to the Detroit Red Wings—a move that would have extended his time on NHL ice. But Sid was of no mind to sever himself or his family from their Toronto roots. He declined the offer.

Besides, he had other options he'd been nurturing. "I used to play hockey for Stafford's Foods before I turned pro," he recalled. "When I first made it with Toronto, I got into doing sales for them in the summertime. Then in 1951, Labatts came after me and I went as a sales rep for them. I mean you couldn't live on the money you made in hockey in those days for the rest of your life—so you had to discover what else you were going to do with yourself! I got into sales because that's what I liked to do. A lot of players got into sales because playing hockey got you into a lot of doors. You could get in some places that the average guy couldn't because of your name. But I still had to sell. I mean it wasn't just a case of relying on my reputation. I had to know my products."

By refusing the Red Wings' offer, Sid cleared the way to sign a two-year deal as an amateur with the Whitby Dunlops. He eased his way out of hockey by serving as their player-coach. He also maintained a sideline of selling truck tires throughout Southern Ontario on behalf of Dunlop Tires.

But he eventually found that selling rubber tires was not very lucrative, so in the early sixties, he made a leap into the paper business. His brother was a printer and through that connection, he became a jobber representing Roland Paper, a mill based in Quebec. For the next twenty-five years, he sold fine paper bonds and offsets to printers and lithographers under the name "Fine Papers".

Although he was no longer front and centre with the Maple Leafs, Sid still found the afterglow of his association with the team to be beneficial for making business contacts. "The Leafs were starting to win the Cup again with Punch Imlach," he recollected. "So there was a lot of hockey talk around Toronto. People would meet me and say, 'What do you think of ... Mahovlich and Keon?' So I got to talk a lot about what was going on."

By 1976, Sid figured that a quarter of a century in the paper business was plenty. So he quit to go to work for a photo studio. "We had contracts with Woolco and Canadian Tire," he explained. "We'd do layouts, set up props and colour schemes for some of their advertising flyers."

Sid retired from the work-a-day world six years later, but soon discovered that puttering around the house and playing golf was insufficient to occupy his energies. On his brother's advice, he went to work for the Newmarket Courthouse, and to this day, serves as a court services officer on a part-time basis.

"You're committed to take the judge into court," he explained of his duties. "As for the trial, it's whatever one you're assigned to. Some of the cases are boring and some of them aren't. It could be a murder, a sexual assault or some civil matters... It makes it interesting if you keep an ear open."

At age seventy-two, Sid remains an

unwavering testament to the athletes of the old-time era. He was as steady in holding the Stanley Cup while a nation cheered as he was in selling tires or leading the judge to trial. For Sid Smith, ostentatiousness is as foreign as quitting when there's a job to be done.

Stanfield, Fred: *Played centre for Chicago, Boston, Minnesota and Buffalo from 1964-1978. Born: Toronto, Ontario, 1944.*

The frontline fan of the NHL loves the speed and wizardry of the best; but their deepest line of respect is often accorded to the guy who shows up *every* night with two skates in hand instead of one.

While playing in Boston, Fred Stanfield caught the eye of fans who had a lot to distract them in the likes of Bobby Orr and Phil Esposito. "They nicknamed me 'Steady Freddy' because I showed up every night," he recalled. "I guess that's why I won the Seventh Player Award there... They choose a player on the team that plays above his ability and plays every game as hard as he can. He's maybe not going to be on the all-star team, but he's an all-star as far as the fans of Boston are concerned. So if you needed an extra player, he'd be the seventh player—the unsung hero. And that was nice because I walked away with a new car, or I should say, I skated away with it."

Fred's consistency on ice is a reflection of an inward character that permeates all aspects of his life, whether affecting family, friends, business or hockey.

By 1978, he had battled through 1,020 games, racking up a respectable 672 career points on behalf of Chicago, Boston, Minnesota and finally, Buffalo. In the midst of his fourteenth season, the old warrior finally had to give in to the reality of covering less ice with more strides. To make way for faster, younger men, he began a gradual withdrawal from the game to avoid the jolt of changing horses in the middle of a stream.

To that end he eased his way down to Hershey of the American Hockey League to serve as player-coach of the Sabres-Capitals' affiliate.

After one season with the Bears, he then cut his ties with the pro ranks to coach the junior-A Niagara Falls Flyers. He found himself in charge of such future NHL stock as Steve Larmer, Steve Ludzik, Mark Osborne and Kevin McClelland. At season's end, however, the Flyers moved to North Bay, Ontario—a distance too great to travel from his home in Williamsville, New York. So instead, Fred opted to exchange coaching for a full-time crack at his business, all while limiting hockey to a side order on the oldtimers' circuit.

He and his wife, Anita, already had Stanfield's Office Furniture underway in Amherst. They were into supplying desks, files, chairs and computer tables to residential and commercial markets in their area. "I started my business with just my wife and myself in the first year," he recounted. "Then I brought in a fellow named Steve Summers. He's been with me fifteen years now, so that's really helped with our business."

To ensure Stanfield's success, Fred made ample use of his streetwise smarts—accentuated and tempered by occasional pieces of external advice.

"You talk to so many retired players and you learn from them, the good and the bad," he remarked. "And some of the guys get together and form their own businesses—maybe three, four, five or six guys. But I just figured it would be easier if I went out on my own—make my own decisions, make my own good things happen and make my own mistakes.

"What helped me too was that years ago we

used to negotiate our own contracts. We never had these agents all the time. I did towards the end of my career, but I was always with my agent anytime there were any negotiations going on. So I learned the other side of the business."

Stanfield's has been a reality now for over sixteen years—a fact of little surprise considering Fred's stamina.

"One of the toughest things is to get through junior and then try to make the NHL," he remarked. "But then the hardest thing to do is to stay there. You're out there fighting every day and that's like being in business. You're always trying to prove that you should belong where you are. Instead of selling your talent, you're now selling whatever product you're into. There's an advantage to having been in the pressure world too as far as competition in the sport of hockey... If things get a little tough in business, you can handle it better than maybe the guy off the street. And it's been sixteen years now and you know the old story, if you're still open, you must be doing something right."

At home, Fred and Anita have raised a son who is a salesman with Lifttech National Co. in New York and a daughter who is a special education teacher in Amhurst.

These days he spends his free time playing racquetball, golf and oldtimers' hockey with The Greatest Legends of Hockey as well as with the Sabres' alumni team—the latter of which is the offspring of the Buffalo alumni association which he founded some years ago as a forum for reuniting former players and to support various community causes.

"We've helped Brian Spencer's two boys with scholarship funds," Fred cited as an example of their work. "After Brian got killed, their mother, Brian's wife, died of cancer. So her sister took the two boys in. And they're doing really well for themselves. We're helping them through their four years each at school. They're both in college now. One's at Madison, Wisconsin and the other one's out in Minitonka, Minnesota. We had the two boys fly in and we presented them with their scholarship funds on centre ice before one of the Sabres' games last year. They're doing great, I'm really proud of them.

"We've also helped Larry Mickey's daughter and son. He died quite awhile ago. So we set up a scholarship fund for them. They're now seventeen and thirteen."

Nickname: *Fritz*

"I think it was when I was in Chicago that Phil Esposito called me 'Fritz'," Fred recalled. "Then when we went to Boston he just carried it on. I think he got the name from the movie, *Fritz the Cat.*"

Nickname Challenge #24

Sugar

"I got the name when I was two or three years old. There was a field between our house and our neighbour's house. When I was just out of the baby stage and able to waddle over there with my soother, they'd dip it in a sugar bowl and I would suck the soother with the sugar on it. So the girls who lived there gave me the name 'Sugar ——'. Then I couldn't get rid of it."

Who is he?

Clues

a. He played goal for the New York Rangers, Chicago and Boston between 1941 & 1955.

b. His initials are J.H.

If you hit the crossbar, see page 285.

Stanley, Allan: *Played defense for the New York Rangers, Chicago, Boston, Toronto and Philadelphia from 1948-1969. Born: Timmins, Ontario, 1926.*

Allan Stanley was originally a Boston Bruin farm hand with the Providence Reds when New York Rangers' general manager Frank Boucher paid big money to acquire his services in 1948-49. Boucher heralded Allan as a panacea for all Ranger ailments, past, present and future. By the time the big man first stepped onto Madison Square Gardens' ice, his 6'2", 191-pound frame looked like a Lilliputian when held up against the expectations of fans. For six relentless seasons, he endured the scorn of Ranger enthusiasts who failed to appreciate the virtues of his plodding, defensive style. In 1954, he was traded to Chicago where the tradition of criticism continued.

It was not until he reached Boston in 1956 that his game came to fruition as a hard-hitting, intelligent defender with a knack for well-placed poke-checks. By 1958, however, the Bruins' management figured Allan was near the end of his prime. They unloaded the old warhorse to the Toronto Maple Leafs where general manager Punch Imlach had a hunch that Allan Stanley was just getting warmed up—and he was right. When paired with Tim Horton on defense, the opposition was hard pressed to squeeze ice shavings between the two rearguards. Leafs' fortunes soared and by 1967, Allan had four Stanley Cup victories to his credit plus two second-team all-star awards. In 1968, he was taken by Quebec in a reverse draft and eventually resurfaced with the Philadelphia Flyers for his twenty-first and final major-league campaign.

During the summer prior to joining the Flyers, Allan and his wife, Barbara, were vacationing at a golf resort in the Bobcageon-Fenlon Falls area of Ontario. While there, Allan was approached to be a partner in a local hockey school. He declined the offer, but by then, the hockey-school bug had been placed in his ear and before long, he had a whole hive of ideas buzzing in his head.

"Barbara and I started talking about it the last weekend of the summer," he related. "And I was saying, 'If you want to go into the hockey-school business, we know the right location because we were customers there during the summers.' That was the Beehive Resort on Sturgeon Lake. And once we started talking about it, we never stopped...

"So when I went to Philly, I told the manager, Bud Poile, that I might have to make a special trip up to Bobcageon because it was something to do with my future... He was very obliging. So I flew up here four times during the year for discussions to purchase the property. And finally, on the forth time, we came to an agreement. I needed an option on the property and I needed an option on the local arena. One without the other wasn't good enough for all my ideas. So I got both options."

When the Flyers were dispensed with by the powerful Blues in the playoffs, Allan returned straightway to Beehive to launch his second career. "It was a resort with a golf course, a dining room and a coffee shop," he explained. "We inherited all of that without any experience other than sitting at the table in the dining room or sitting at the opposite side of the bar or playing golf. So it was completely new to us."

But Allan was bent on moulding the Beehive Resort to his plans. To succeed, he had to summon all of the internal fortitude and cunning that sustained him during his lengthy stay in the NHL. He also needed an opposition against which to pit his determined will. The previous owners of the resort would do just fine.

"Actually, the people that owned the resort, sold it to me to get the down payment back because they didn't think I could handle it," he revealed with a glint in his eye and gleam in his voice. "And I proved them wrong! Even years after that they couldn't figure out how the heck I did it!"

In truth, there was no magic in Allan's formula, just good old-fashioned slave labour. "There's nothing to match what Barbara and I had to go through," he declared. "I always figured that if I took the worst days of my whole life and put them together, they couldn't match my first three years in business. All that Barbara and I knew about it was, we liked to look after people. Hey, we wanted to spoil them! So that's what we based our whole business sense on."

Their first step was to ensure that the resort could sustain itself while they set about converting the place to a boys camp. "Ever hear of a crash course?" Allan queried. "This was the biggest crash course anybody had in a lifetime! Like I say, we didn't have any experience at this. So I tried to set up each area so it looked after itself. The previous owners stayed on to look after the dining room, but halfway through the season I had to let them go. I came down one night and the wife was leaving with a case of vodka and the husband had his fingers in the till. So Barbara and I took over the dining room ourselves, and that was besides all the other responsibilities around the place like the hockey school and the golf course. We started on a shoestring and the only thing we realized early was that you couldn't spend anymore than you took in."

That shoestring must have been a skate lace with sufficient strength and length to hold things together while they got the conversion process underway. "At one point we were a quarter boys camp and three-quarters resort," he recounted. "Then we progressed to half boys camp and half resort till we had filled the whole place with kids... I could handle 136 boys plus all my staff which was made up of counsellors, camp

directors, coaches and their families. And I was feeding maybe two hundred people three times a day!"

With sheer force of will, Allan drove his hockey school to its full potential. In the early going, such schools were rare, so the Beehive Camp thrived as a novel idea. "But from that point on, they just sprang up all over the place!" he exclaimed. "They advertised big names and then half the guys didn't show up. And the ones that did show up were just there to sign autographs! But here, I had good coaches—they were family-oriented men. They took a great interest in the kids, worked with them on the ice and played with them off the ice. We taught them more than golf. We taught them how to get along in society. And I received letters from parents who couldn't even recognize their kids when they came home!"

Allan ran his hockey school for about nine years before the market bottomed out. "At that time, they started building artificial ice in every little hamlet with Wintario money," he explained. "And then they started building rinks all across the northern States. When they built a rink down there it would cost them two million dollars, so all the rinks were losing money. Then the coaching fraternity and the amateur body got together ... and said, 'Let's keep the kids at home.' In some areas, they told the kids, 'If you go to a Canadian hockey camp, you're not on the team!' The final death knell came when they started having their tryouts for the next year in July and August on all these artificial ice rinks—and our season was July and August. I went on for three years trying to turn it around in some way—but I wasn't going anywhere. I was running fifty-five percent American kids and bang! just like that, in one shot! with no warning! no nothing! I was running half full. I thought they had locked the doors at the border. So I closed and converted back to a resort."

Motivated by such trials, Allan took a half-forgotten kettle off the back burner and turned up the heat on his simmering idea. "I had close to two hundred acres," he recounted. "The northeast corner was a beautiful walk through

"I always figured that if I took the worst days of my whole life and put them together, they couldn't match my first three years in business."

Allan Stanley

hardwood bush. It was sixty acres, and I always had it in the back of my mind to develop it some day. So I started early, laying the local groundwork, talking to council members, to the Reeve, to see if it was a good idea and hey, I got a good response! So I had the piece severed from the property. I ended up with sixty one-acre lots. I put in over a mile of township roads... Of course that took money. So I went all over Ontario to all those institutions just looking for money with a good idea. It all depended on cash flow. If you didn't have cash flow, they didn't remember your name by the time you'd left. And my cash flow was going the other way ... all the time. We were just scrambling to keep our nose about water. I looked for two years and finally it came through one of the local banks.

"I think the saviour of this whole thing was the subdivision—it just turned out absolutely

beautifully! I think it's the most prestigious development in our area. You can look out any window and it will take you right back to nature. We still have deer running around the place, running through your backyard and fox, man, you name it, we've got it. I had one person who wanted to buy a lot and take all the trees out. I wouldn't sell him the lot. I told him, 'Hey, you want that, you can go find a field with no trees on it! But not here'!"

In 1988, Allan and Barbara sold the Beehive Resort and reaped the rewards of their labour. "I retained my lot in the subdivision," he reported. "Right now I've got the high ground and I overlook the whole resort, the golf course and Sturgeon Lake. I overlook everything the new owner is doing in more ways than one," he joked. "You couldn't paint a better picture and I haven't gotten tired of it in twenty-seven years."

Wally Stanowski relaxing at home in Etobicoke, Ont.

Stanowski, Wally: *Played defense for Toronto and the New York Rangers between 1939 & 1951. Born: Winnipeg, Manitoba, 1919.*

Known as the "Whirling Dervish" on Leafs' defense, Wally Stanowski was a marvellous skater and skilled bodychecker who, by his second season in Toronto in 1940-41, was chosen as a first-team all-star along with Boston's Dit Clapper. Wally was a serious rearguard with a humourous streak that sometimes found its outlet during delays in game action. To divert restless fans while injured players were removed from the ice, he would perform his best impersonation of a figure skater spinning and gliding with mellifluous grace.

After returning from a two-year stint with the Canadian Armed Forces, Wally resumed his position on the Leafs' blueline where he enjoyed four league championships before being traded to the New York Rangers for Cal Gardner and Bill Juzda in 1948.

His career in professional hockey came to a premature end, however, in 1951. It all started with the team doctor's misdiagnosis of his injured knee. "I was on crutches and my left knee was swollen," he recounted. "The club doctor said it was probably just a cyst or something. But I was two months hobbling around. Then one day a Japanese doctor who used to fill in said, 'Are you still hobbling?' I said, 'Yeah.' So he said, 'Come on, we'll go in the dressing room.' So he felt my knee, pressing it here and there and I jumped. And he said, 'I could make you hit the ceiling if I wanted to. You're going to the hospital! You've got a bad cartilage.' So he took it out. But I was out of shape by that time. The playoffs were just starting, but I just couldn't get back in time.

"So the following year, they sent me down to Cincinnati to get in shape. I finally started to move again and I started to play well. The Rangers were in a bit of trouble, so they said, 'Send Wally back—we need a defenseman.' Clint Smith was our coach in Cincinnati and he decided to hold me over for another game. And that was the game where I broke my leg. The puck was sliding over towards the corner and I

He and Barbara now spend seven months a year in Fenlon Falls and the remaining months at their getaway in Venice, Florida. On the subject of family, Alan joked: "We don't have any kids. I always say that I took my hockey seriously—and that was hard on the legs years ago and I'm very impressionable."

In retirement, Allan is free to do something he never did as a hockey player or a businessman. "I'm a floater now," he confided with a hefty laugh. "I have one hobby. I want to be talked about and remembered as a golfer. Hockey is in the past. The business is in the past. Now I'm dedicating myself to playing a reasonable game of golf. I tell you, when I leave the golf course, they're going to be talking about me one way or another! I used to be the longest ball hitter on the course but the farthest in the bush! And it hasn't changed much either."

forget who the other guy was, but I was going to beat him to the puck and all of sudden my feet went from under me. Someone must have thrown something on the ice, the way I fell. My left leg took the whole brunt of it. I broke the board there and in those days it was over an inch-and-a quarter thick!

"So that's what finished me. I was advised not to play anymore. If I ever broke it again ... I'd be crippled for the rest of my life. This way at least I could salvage my leg.

"So I had a cast all the way from my toe right up to my hip for six months and I wasn't supposed to depress even a break pedal. And I drove to Vancouver from Cincinnati (laughs). You know, in one of those old cars with the clutch pedal. So I rigged up a little hockey stick and I used it to push the pedal down with my hand."

Wally managed to stall his car on a steep hill in San Francisco while heading up the West Coast. But thanks to his agile foot and effective stickhandling, he deked his way out of a jam. "I think I left half my tires on that hill!" he exclaimed.

After convalescing, Wally eventually resettled in Toronto where he embarked on a new career. "I used to know a chap who was involved in the heavy-construction industry," Wally recounted. "He was selling heavy equipment, big bulldozers and earth movers. He said, 'Come on down!' And they hired me. So I started selling heavy construction equipment with Sheridan Equipment. I worked there for about seventeen years.

"But I never made big money over there. And when I did, they generally said, 'Well we can't give you the full commission.' Like I sold one crane for $250,000—which was a lot of money in those days—and they'd say, 'Well we had to drop the price so we can't give you a full commission.' And then I had a sale for a million dollars worth of trucks and I got peanuts out of it! So I finally left them and joined another outfit called 'Allat's Tractor Parts'. I worked there for about two-and-a-half years and then I retired."

Throughout Wally's working life as well as in retirement, fishing has been his great recreational passion. His exploits range from fresh-water fishing in Ontario to deep-sea and surf fishing off the coast of Mexico.

Once while on a fishing trip up on Lac Suel, north of Dryden, he got a little closer to the fish than he would have liked. As part of a crew of three boats headed out to a hunting camp, Wally's boat was overloaded with supplies and a forty-five gallon drum of gasoline. "Our boat was

Wally Stanowski in St. Catharines, Ontario for the Leafs' training camp of 1942

riding low and it got rough," he recollected. "The boat started filling with water. Fortunately we were about a hundred feet from shore. If we'd have rounded the point and been out in open water we'd have never made it. So I said to the guy ahead of me, 'You better start bailing!' So he started to bail and then he stepped back towards me. Then the water just flowed a little more from the stern and we started to go down—and our stuff just floated away! Fortunately we didn't lose that much. So we had to camp there and it started to rain—it was a horrible night. We finally got a fire going and we just stood there all night! The next morning I think I had a small case of hypothermia because we had had to swim to shore."

Perils and misadventures, however, are a small price to pay in exchange for serenity. "I have a fondness for the outdoors and fishing takes me there," Wally explained. "It's a quiet atmosphere: Solitude, peace and quiet."

Stapleton, Pat: *Played defense for Boston, Chicago (NHL), Chicago, Indianapolis and Cincinnati (WHA) between 1961 & 1978. Born: Sarnia, Ontario, 1940.*

In literal and figurative terms, it seems that Pat Stapleton was born to plant seeds and nurture living things to fruition. He's good at it because from the outset, no matter how small the seed, he sees in that tiny speck all the essential ingredients of a complete existence. Without such optimism and anticipation, the farmers and creators of this world would never plant.

Pat got down to some serious cultivation of his own in 1978 after closing out his seventeen-year career in professional hockey. On the ice he had been a success as a jovial, hard-working defenseman with a flair for rushing the puck and setting up goals. It was now time to translate his creative energies into something new. "I went straight back to Strathroy [Ontario] and engaged in farming," he reported. "I was into general farming, growing wheat, corn and raising cattle although I'm out of cattle now. I did this from 1978 to 1990."

Pat also developed an interest in supporting young people. Amongst his own clan, he and his wife, Jackie, raised three sons and three daughters and currently have ten grandchildren. But his commitment to youth extends well beyond the farm.

In 1980, he established the Minor League Hockey Association. "It was a skills-development programme for minor hockey designed to develop the compete athlete," he related. "I visited 1,300 communities across Canada, the U.S. and even in Germany. We used about thirty-one different former pros. We delivered a drill programme with five segments and each segment was presented on an annual basis."

But with the loss of sponsorships in 1987, Pat was forced to close his travelling school although not before having fashioned a clear vision on how to reach young aspiring hockey players.

He now uses the insights gleaned from his experiences as the basis for his frequent speaking engagements. "I talk about what I feel it takes to be a complete hockey player," he explained. "I've divided the concept into three different categories:

- Fundamentals: moving forward, backwards and laterally.
- Conditioning: seeing and visualizing yourself as being successful; being in good physical shape; and having spiritual awareness which is ultimately believing in yourself.
- Strategy: playing effectively in the offensive zone, the neutral zone and the defensive zone.

"I also encourage kids to recognize the life skills they are exposed to in playing hockey such as discipline, persistence and courage. I also talk about what I refer to as the 'largest room in the world'—the room for self improvement. I use this statement because it's intriguing. People wonder, 'Is it heaven?'

"In talking to high-school kids, I encourage them to think about goals using the following analogy: *The closer you get to the net, the more people try to keep you from your goal.*

"I also emphasize the strength in young people and the need to find things they can improve on without being negative. I see the number-one issue coming up for young people in hockey is seeing reasons to fail. 'I'm not fast enough. I'm not big enough.' Whereas really it's all in the belief system."

In recent years, Pat has simplified his life by handing the farm operation over to younger members of the family. He now has more time and energy to enjoy his family, puttering around the farm, encouraging high-school kids and coaching the Strathroy Rockets junior-B club. "I never have a bad day," he affirmed. "These days, that's all I'm in charge of—having a good day!"

Nickname: *Whitey*

"I picked up the name on my first day ever at school," Pat recalled. "A grade-eight boy named Bill Lamb called me 'Whitey' and it stuck with me ever since. And as I say, you can call me anything but don't call me late for lunch!"

Stasiuk, Vic: *Played left wing for Chicago, Detroit and Boston from 1949-1963. Born: Lethbridge, Alberta, 1929.*

The Stasiuk family heritage was hewn in the rugged climes of the Ukraine, where people pulled together to make ends meet. In the company of other hearty clans such as the Bucyks and the Horvaths, these families eventually found their way to the equally rigourous climes of Canada. There, their children played hockey and some of them even made it to the NHL. Vic Stasiuk, Johnny Bucyk and Bronco Horvath were three such tough customers who made it to the top to form the "Uke Line" in Boston during the late fifties.

With Bronco in the middle and Johnny on the right, Vic's game rose to its summit in terms of goals, assists and hits. Together, they raised each other's play and brought the Bruins to within a skate blade of winning the Stanley Cup.

Most good things eventually pass however—including the "Ukes" who were disbanded by 1960. Vic moved on to Detroit where he closed out his playing days in 1963. He was then promptly dispatched to coach the Red Wings' farm team in Pittsburgh of the American Hockey League. "It was an opportunity to stay working in hockey and being close to the action," he recounted. "I think that was the attraction for me. And, it provided approximately ten more years of contributing to Uncle Sam!"

After two seasons in Pittsburgh, Sid Abel and the Red Wings' brain trust decided to make a coaching switch, feeling that Vic was better suited to work with the younger players in their system. So Eddie Bush came over to Pittsburgh while Vic went to Memphis.

"And then I got into a little disagreement about a couple of players, Gerry Abel, Sid's boy, and Greg Pilling, as to their eligibility or ability to play," Vic revealed. "We got into a little argument as far as managing the team and on who should be playing. So I spent just one year there and then Sid let me go. We met two or three times after that and we were still friendly, so it was just the occasion of that season."

Vic's subsequent stay on the open market was brief. With the NHL on the brink of expansion in 1967, he was recruited by the fledgling Philadelphia Flyers' organization to coach the New Jersey Devils of the Eastern Hockey League. His assignment was to generate regional interest in advance of the Flyers' inaugural season.

Once Philly was up and running, Vic was granted the helm of their principal farm club, the Quebec Aces—and he didn't mince words about the challenge he faced. "I had some rough moments not being able to speak French in Quebec," he revealed. "You know this English-French thing is always in the dressing room. Anybody who says it isn't is full of prunes! It's there, but I managed it okay."

After two seasons of cultural juggling with the Aces, he then caught the ultimate bounty—a summons to replace Keith Allen as head coach of the Flyers. "It was fantastic! I couldn't believe it!" he exclaimed. "We drafted pretty well. It was a defensive team. We couldn't score freely ... but the one thing I'm proud of is that I was in on the scouting and evaluation of those players. We were the first expansion team to win the Stanley Cup and I feel proud that I was part of that."

Vic had an indirect hand in the eventual success of the "Broad Street Bullies." Had his judgment been held in higher regard, however, it might have been Vic instead of Fred Shero who was around to claim the biggest prize.

"I remember going into the office and making the recommendation that we've got to bring up Brossard, Schultz and Saleski from the Tidewater team," he explained. "And Keith Allen, who was the manager, said, 'Well, we can't just take those players, we've got to supply [Tidewater] with American League calibre players and what are we going to do with the players we've got? We can't send them down.' We missed the playoffs by a point! Then the next year, Bobby Hull blew us out. Then I was let go and Freddie Shero was brought in and he missed the playoffs. The next year, they brought up all three, Brossard, Schultz and Saleski and won the Stanley Cup!

"But I think it was also some sessions I had with our goaltender, Bernie Parent. I think I developed some of the character he needed to lead the Flyers to the Stanley Cup. He and I had it out a couple of times after two seasons of frustration. The guy had such great talent but he wasn't mature enough... He didn't want to accept the responsibility of the position he was in. In front of the team, publicly, I just said, 'For Christ sake! Why don't you grow up?' He would just sort of laugh it off."

Vic eventually jumped to the West Coast outpost of the California Golden Seals, where shootouts and wafer-thin defense were a way of life. "That was quite an experience!" he exclaimed with a laugh that said more than his words. "With Charlie Finley, oh my God! I could sit here for hours and talk about Charlie Finley and the white skates. And I had another good young goalie there in Gilles Meloche. God I'll never forget the game where he beat Boston 2-0, right in Boston. I think they must have had eighty shots—and he shut them out!"

At the administrative level as well, the Seals sometimes resembled a frontier town where the shake of a hand and the nod of a head could dispense with any cumbersome fine print. Vic joined the club based on what he perceived to be a two-year verbal commitment. When the team's management refused to follow through, he packed his bags and went north to Vancouver.

As head coach of the Canucks, he pushed his charges to a record of twenty-two wins, forty-seven losses and nine ties before being replaced by Bill McCreary in 1973. "I don't know what it is in Vancouver," he queried with a perplexed tone. "It's a good hockey town, but they just couldn't put a winner together."

Vic then decided to close out his career in hockey by coaching the St. Louis Blues' farm club in Denver for one final season.

"I figured that was it," he asserted. "I'm going to make a living farming... I've been farming since I was a little boy, irrigating sugar beets, crop land and breaking land." So Vic returned to his native Lethbridge where he had purchased a spread years earlier while coaching the New Jersey Devils.

His long-range plan, however, was not to till the soil forever. He bided his time until the community of Lethbridge spread out to his area and then he negotiated for approval to develop his land into a golf course. The lengthy process of construction started in 1989 and lead to the opening of Paradise Canyon Golf & Country Club in 1993.

"I think God made our site for a golf course," he contended with pride. "There are golf sites and then there are *golf sites!* Anybody who comes to play is impressed to no end. Stadler, Finch, Grady and Barr all expressed quite a surprise about the uniqueness of our layout."

Vic humourously linked the origin of Paradise Canyon to his days with the Detroit Red Wings. "I used to go golfing with Gordie

Howe quite often," Vic recounted. "He and I used to go just about everywhere in Detroit, mainly as an excuse to get out of after-practice socials! Sometimes the socializing overextended itself. The beer was sweet as honey, but Gordie and I didn't drink, so our excuse was, 'We've got to be on the tee at one o'clock!' So I think our weekly golfing sessions sort of led to Paradise Canyon."

With his course now fully operational, Vic has retired to pursue his passions: enjoying life with his wife, Mary, and their ten grandchildren plus the sacred rituals of breathing, discussing, playing, and watching the game of golf.

Nickname: *Yogi*

"I didn't have a real nickname," Vic reported. "But when I was in Detroit, I used to always eat yogurt with the fruit on the bottom to keep my weight down and to stay in shape. So the guys started calling me 'Yogi'. Johnny Bucyk continued with the name when we got to Boston."

Gaye Stewart enjoying the old days and the new at his home in Burlington, Ontario

Stewart, Gaye: *Played left wing for Toronto, Chicago, Detroit, the New York Rangers and Montreal between 1942 & 1953. Born: Fort William, Ontario, 1923.*

Gaye Stewart politely paused to turn down his radio in an effort to screen out any external factor that might diminish his intent on being completely present in the moment. As he spoke, his voice rang with a grounded, steady tone that conveyed reverence for his listener and a pleasurable regard for the details of his life.

He was born knee-deep into the hockey culture of his native Fort William, Ontario where names like Chummy King, Curly Stover and the Port Arthur Bearcats dotted the oral and visual scape of the town. At every turn, his young senses were absorbing such scenes that, as a mosaic, would assemble to fire his ambition on ice.

He took his first crack at the art of skating on local outdoor rinks and later, on the frozen waters of the Neebing River which bordered his backyard in Fort William. "As a kid, I was out there every day after school until it was dark," he recollected. "We kept two or three shovels stuck in the river bank behind our house so anybody could clear the ice when needed. I mean nobody ever worried about things being stolen in those days. And we had a permanent hole off to the side so we could flood the ice with a bucket. Even when I was playing junior, I was still out there playing pick-up hockey after school until my dad or uncle would take me over to Port Arthur to play that night."

Through the magic of radio, Gaye also became aware of hockey on a national scale. "We listened to Saturday night games with Foster Hewitt," he recounted. "That was the big thing in those days. I also remember in 1937, Detroit and Toronto went west to play an exhibition series after the season was over. Since Fort William was a divisional stop, their train would have to pull in to rewater the engine and fill the hopper up with coal. My dad took me to the station at about ten o'clock that night. Charlie Conacher,

Busher Jackson, Joe Primeau and all those guys got off the train for about thirty minutes. There were quite a few people there. I mean we didn't get too many celebrities in town... I remember getting an autograph from Charlie Conacher—he seemed to be so big. I was enthralled just like the kids of today getting an autograph from Lemieux or Gretzky!"

With his imagination on the boil, it took Gaye only three years to evolve from that awestruck lad on the train-station platform to a *bona fide* member of the Toronto Marlboros junior club. All was progressing as expected in Toronto until he caught hold of a meteor at the start of his second campaign. "I started out playing junior with the Marlies until Christmas time," he related. "Then they moved me up to the Marlboro seniors. On March 8th, I turned pro and they sent me down to play in Hershey, Pennsylvania. I got down there and played about four games before the playoffs. After we lost out to Indianapolis for the Calder Cup, I came up to join the Toronto Maple Leafs and was on the roster when they won the Stanley Cup in 1942. That's the only time that somebody ever played junior, senior, minor pro and the NHL all in one season—and I got a Cup on top of that!"

The following year, Gaye played the entire season with the Leafs, popping home an impressive twenty-four goals and twenty-three assists to claim the Calder Trophy as the league's top rookie.

With World War II as a raging backdrop, however, he had little time to savour his success. At the close of the 1942-43 season, he left the NHL to join the cause. "I was in the Navy for two years," he recalled. "I did some mine sweeping between Nova Scotia and Newfoundland. That was a port of entry where the submarines came through into the Gulf of the St. Lawrence. They had a big ferry that ran back and forth there so they didn't want German submarines dropping mines off in the area."

In 1945-46, Gaye returned to the Maple Leafs and picked up even more than he had left off. With no signs of rust on the blades, he skated his way to a first-team all-star award, having scored

thirty-seven times to lead the league in goals scored—the last Maple Leaf to accomplish such a feat.

In 1947, he won his second and final Stanley Cup before being traded to Chicago along with Ernie Dickens, Bob Goldham plus his "Flying Forts" line-mates, Bud Poile and Gus Bodnar—all for Max Bentley who went the other way.

Gaye found life in Chicago to be eventful down the middle and a hazard on the edge. "You were in the gangland capital in those days," he remarked. "I remember we were leaving practice one morning and we saw a guy get shot right on the sidewalk, a common daily occurrence—didn't hear anything more about it.

"We stayed in a place called the Midwest Athletic Club ... and it was interesting the people we would see. George Capone, Al Capone's brother, lived there—he was a real nice guy—and Ray Jones, who ran the whole syndicate for the Midwest, lived there too. They were all great sports fans and of course, they were all betting. Just like at Maple Leaf Gardens in those days. They used to call the area up behind the blue seats, 'the Bullring'. That's where all the betting went on ... the gamblers just loved to be involved in sports, so they were always around the fringe."

Gaye played three seasons in Chicago before moving on to see action with Detroit, New York and Montreal. After only six or seven games with the Canadiens, he was sent to play for Punch Imlach's Quebec Aces of the Quebec Senior League. "From a monetary standpoint, it was quite worth it," he revealed. "Senior hockey was big in those days. We were putting in full houses all the time at the old Colisée, so they gave out big incentives. I made more money playing down there than I ever made playing in the National Hockey League!"

Having a young Jean Beliveau with the Aces didn't hurt either. "He was getting a big offer from Quebec to stay as an amateur," he related. "So he was all set. He even drove around with a license plate that had 'B2' on it—'Beliveau 2'. I'm not sure but I think the premier of the province, Duplesis, had 'B1'. Of course the next year, Mr. Selke, who was running the Canadiens, practically turned the league professional so he could get Beliveau up to Montreal."

In 1953-54, the Canadiens sent Gaye to play for the Buffalo Bisons of the American Hockey League where he remained for two seasons before resigning his position as the club's coach in favour of working full-time for Molson Breweries. "I had only worked for them for ten months when Mr. Selke came back into the picture," Gaye related. "He wanted to know if I'd be interested in becoming a referee. So I stuck my head into the ringer."

The officiating business was flowing along smoothly until January of 1958 when his career took a perplexing nose-dive. "I was a victim of circumstances," Gaye confided. "I was working a game between the Chicago Blackhawks and the Boston Bruins. It was a tight game. The play swung out of the Chicago end and I followed the play up the ice when I heard a big roar. I turned around and saw a guy laying on the ice by the goal. I whistled the play down and went back to find Doug Mohns with blood coming out of his ears, nose and everywhere else. I thought, 'Holy Jeez, what's this?' It turns out that Mohns and a fella named Ian Cushenan had both lost their sticks and they had both grabbed the same one. After a tussle, Mohns dropped his end, moved towards Cushenan while going to the boards to pick up the other stick. But as he went by, Cushenan slugged him, a blind blow, and broke his jaw. So I just gave my report as it was and later, I got back home to Fort Erie and Mr. Campbell, the *presidente*, was on the phone. I told him what happened and he said, 'You know in all my years in the league, we've never had a call like this.' I had given Cushenan a game misconduct and a deliberate attempt to injure and this was a no,no. I had all of my National League assignments taken away from me for the rest of the year and I just worked the American League."

Gaye was unhappy with the arrangement, so at the close of the season, he retired and returned to Molson where he remained for the next twenty-eight years. "I got into management after two or three years with the company," he explained. "It was very pleasant. I always seemed to get a pretty good staff together. We had a lot of hockey players come on in the summer to do PR work like Al Arbour, Jimmy Roberts, Billy Dea and Bep Guidolin. I operated an entire area in Hamilton ... and then in Toronto. Then I ended up managing all of the sales projects. I was in on putting together the original Molson Indy."

Nickname Challenge #25

Leapin'

He drew a total of 1,289 career penalty minutes in the NHL. Feeling that many of the calls were doled out unfairly, he developed a patented response. "I got the odd few penalties in my day and I used to leap up and yell, 'What for?' to the ref. Rex Steimer, who did the radio announcing for the St. Catharines Tee-pees, noticed and started referring to me as 'Leapin' and it stuck."

Who is he?

Clues

a. He played defense for the New York Rangers and Montreal Canadiens from 1954-1963.

b. His career ended in 1963 as a result of a broken neck.

c. His initials are L.F.

If you fanned on your shot,
see page 285.

Gaye retired from Molson in the late eighties and has since enjoyed a quiet life with his family in Burlington, Ontario. His living pattern has changed little over the years although he does enjoy vacationing in Florida in the thick of the winter.

In reflecting back upon his numerous accomplishments in professional hockey, he found satisfaction in the time he played. "I was fortunate to go through the league in an era when some of the old guys were still around like Dit Clapper, the Colvilles and Bill Cowley," he recalled. "And, I was still there when guys like Howe and Richard came along. I'm very proud of the fact that I managed to play ten years in the league when there were just six teams and only ninety players."

⟨⟨⟨ ⟩⟩⟩

Sullivan, George (Red): *Played centre for Boston, Chicago and the New York Rangers between 1949 & 1961. Born: Peterborough, Ontario, 1929.*

In 1954, the Topps Bubble Gum Company issued hockey card #42 featuring Red Sullivan digging his blades into the ice the way a child digs into an ice cream—with a smile from ear to ear. "When you get paid for something you love doing," he remarked, "you're a very fortunate guy!"

Although not overly gifted in the stickhandling department, Red was a tenacious forechecker who developed a special brand of poetry which he frequently used to needle the opposition. Wherever he played, his fans loved his leadership and flair for prying his way into the thick of trouble.

When it came time to clear the ice for good in 1961, Red was like a kid in a candy store who figured that one empty jar was no reason to leave the shop. "I always loved the game of hockey and hockey was really good to me as far as playing," he reported. "And then I decided that I'd like to stay in it in some capacity, preferably in the coaching ranks. And I'm very pleased now that I made that decision because I loved the game..."

Red hung on with the Rangers' organization

to coach the Kitchener Beavers for the 1961-62 season. "I was a playing coach," he recounted. "I had a good bunch of guys like Rod Gilbert, Jean Ratelle and Jimmy Neilson... I got along real good with them. We won more than our share of games. And I said, 'This is not a bad job.' Actually, it was a joy!"

At the start of the following season, the Rangers took over the Baltimore Clippers of the American Hockey League. So they brought Red in to lead their charges. "Again, we had a good bunch of guys and we were winning our share of games," he related.

But three months into the season, Muzz Patrick and the Rangers were struggling. The team's management looked to Red as their solution. "So that's when I started my tenure with New York," he recalled. "And I think I did a credible job with the team. They were at a rebuilding stage. But we eventually got over the hump and I don't have to tell you about the Rangers from then on. We had younger players like Gilbert and Hadfield and ... some of the older players like Bathgate and Howell who blended in nicely with the younger guys. I never made the playoffs but I think it was because ... in those days, Detroit, Montreal, Chicago, Toronto—they really had some great hockey teams. You know there's a difference between good and great hockey players—and a lot of great hockey players played in that era."

By the 1965-66 season, the Rangers were on the sub floor of the standings. And as such, Red got bumped in favour of Emile Francis who inherited a team ready at last to move up the ranks.

His tenure on the sidelines was short-lived however. The newborn Pittsburgh Penguins came knocking and enticed Red to put his neck on the line as the club's first head coach. "That probably had to be the toughest!" he exclaimed. "To be frank, there weren't a heck of a lot of good hockey players made available to us. We missed winding up in first by [six] points and still lost the playoffs. That's how close it was. But I had to take my hat off to the players ... they gave me 110% and without the full support of the players,

I think a coach is dead."

The Penguins continued their struggle into the following season. By year's end, the team was embroiled in a last-place shootout with the North Stars. And as the smoke cleared, so was Red—straight to the NHL's bread line in search of a new job.

But his free agency was quickly caged by his old friend and mentor, Milt Schmidt. "I had the opportunity to play with Milt in Boston and I really thought the world of the guy," Red recalled fondly. "He was a centre-iceman and so was I. I saw him go out there night after night after night and he was hurting—but he'd still give it his 110%. In my opinion, he was the best all-around centre-iceman that ever played the game!

"Milt asked me if I'd become chief scout of the Bruins, so I jumped all over that. Here I am, the chief scout of the Bruins and I'm working for a great guy and consequently we won the Stanley Cup.

"Then Milt decided to go into Washington as general manager and he asked me if I'd go along as chief scout. So again, I didn't think about it for a minute. I said, 'Wherever you go Milt, I'd like to go with you.'

"It was an expansion team and we struggled! I was chief scout when they really had a rough start. So Milt phoned and wanted me to go down there to see what I could do. He put me in as coach to see if I could get them rolling. I was reluctant, but I thought it was my duty to go and see what I could do and I didn't do a helluva lot to be honest. The guys were great, we just lacked talent.

"After things didn't work out in Washington, I tried to get another job in the National Hockey League in any capacity. But I couldn't get to first base in that department. So I phoned Jim Gregory who was the ex-GM of the Leafs. Jim was heading up the Central Scouting [Bureau]. He said, 'Meet me in Lindsay at a certain restaurant and maybe I can do something for you.' So I went up and met with Jimmy. He said, 'Here's what I'm prepared to offer you Red. It's not a great deal but you'd still be connected with the National Hockey League.' I said, 'Jimmy,

"Red" Sullivan
CHICAGO BLACK HAWKS

hockey's in my blood! That sounds good to me.' I had to take a real cut in my pay, but I took it in order to stay in the game and it was the best thing I'd ever done."

By 1984, Red's patience paid off, having worn a path to more prosperous ground—this time within the Philadelphia Flyers' organization. "While I was out west on a scouting trip, I had the opportunity to have lunch with Bobby Clarke," he recollected. "We seemed to hit it off pretty well. So lo and behold, they said, 'Are you interested in joining us?' Naturally I said yes and I was never treated better in all of my hockey career."

Seven years later, however, all the respect the Flyers had to offer couldn't hold Red from taking his final bows. "With all the expansion teams and junior teams you had to look at and whatnot, I found that I was on the road a little too much," he confided. "I wanted to spend a little more time at my home in Peterborough, Ontario with my wife. And to be honest with you, I had had a long stint at it as a player, a coach and as a scout and I thought it was time to step aside and let some younger guy have a crack at it..."

Since his retirement in 1991, Red has focused on enjoying the simple basics of life. "I like my golf and I like to fish," he remarked. "And since I retired, we're doing a fair amount of travelling to places I never had a chance to go to."

Over the years, he and his wife, Marion, have raised three daughters and a son. They now make their home in Indian River, just outside of Peterborough. "I built a new house here four or five years ago," he reported. "I don't farm, but I have nine acres and we just love it!"

Taylor, Dave: *Played right wing for Los Angeles from 1977-1994. Born: Levack, Ontario, 1955.*

Once a upon a time in Los Angeles, there were three Kings who rode together as the "Triple Crown Line", pillaging the offensive zones of rinks across the NHL. Marcel Dionne, Charlie Simmer and Dave Taylor ruled the Fabulous Forum with soft hands and big sticks.

But one day, Marcel and Charlie renounced their crowns and headed east to wage battles in distant lands. Only Dave Taylor remained to uphold the tradition of kings. Known for his hustle and aggressive style of play, he made effective use of his puck-handling skills to bag a career-high forty-seven goals and sixty-five assists in 1980-81. By the end of his reign in 1994, he had racked up an impressive 1,098 points in 1,100 games.

"During the years that I've spent here, I earned a reputation and I have the respect of the fans and the people that work in the organization," he asserted. "I played my whole career with the Kings ... and it was always my desire to stay with them in some type of management capacity and fortunately that's worked out. I'm currently working in the front office as assistant general manager of the team."

Now three years removed from NHL action, Dave is as pleased with his future as he is with his past. "I think that I was fortunate to play as long as I did and I think I got my fill," he admitted. "Don't get me wrong, I thoroughly enjoyed my days as a player. There's certainly

nothing like it! It was my dream to play in the National Hockey League and I was able to do it for seventeen years! But I knew I was at the end. I wasn't able to compete like I wanted to day in and day out. When you get to be thirty-eight-years old, it's hard to go out there and perform every night. The little injuries turn into bigger injuries ... so it was time to move on to something else. The transition of moving into the front office was ideal for me..."

Dave works closely with general manager Sam McMaster and team president Rogie Vachon in managing the Kings' day-to-day affairs. "Part of my duty is to oversee our affiliation with our farm team, the Phoenix Roadrunners," Dave explained. "At any time we'll have eight to twelve players down there. So I stay on top of those players and their development.

"I also keep close tabs on players that we've drafted who are playing either junior hockey in Canada or in the European leagues. I try to see them a couple of times a year. I talk with their coaches and monitor how they're coming along."

Although Dave's transition into the front office has been smooth, the front office itself has experienced a few tremors in recent years. Bruce McNall lost controlling interest in the Kings and since then, the franchise has changed hands twice. "The new ownership that took over this year has been very solid," Dave reported. "They're going to build a new building here by September of '99. And considering the way the salaries have skyrocketed the last few years, you can't compete in this league without the revenue that comes from a state-of-the-art building with luxury suites. It's pretty well a gate-receipt-driven industry!

"Unfortunately some of the smaller towns in Canada are the ones feeling the crunch. I remember going into Edmonton to play all those times during their glory years—they had the Gretzky's, the Messier's, the Kurri's, the Coffey's and Grant Fuhr. Now they have to battle just to keep the team afloat ... and that's sad."

Dave and his wife, Beth, are currently in the thick of parenthood, raising two daughters.

"When I have time off, I generally spend a lot of it with them," he remarked.

He and Beth also participate in a series of Kings' community-outreach programmes. Their family of charities is comprised of three non-profit organizations: The Kings' Wives For Kids Foundation; Kings Youth Hockey; and Kings in the Community. Dave also hosts an annual golf tournament to raise funds to combat cystic fibrosis.

(*Editor's note: Shortly after his interview, Dave was promoted to general manager of the Kings in the wake of Sam McMaster's dismissal in April of 1997.*)

Nickname: *Stitch*

While playing against the Atlanta Flames in 1979, some pregame press notes referred to Dave's scoring success as "a stitch in time". "So Charlie Simmer picked up on it and started to call me 'Stitch in Time'," Dave explained. "Then it was shortened to 'Stitch'. Now that's pretty well what everybody calls me."

Tkaczuk, Walt: *Played centre for the New York Rangers from 1967-1981. Born: Emstedetten, Germany, 1947.*

As rambling souls find a special place in this world to call home, they unite their earthly comforts and family to plant a few roots deep into the soil. Walt Tkaczuk found his sacred place in St. Marys, Ontario where he purchased a farm along the Thames River in 1970. He too united his family and proceeded to set—not just one root deep into the soil—but thirty-five thousand roots! Walt Tkaczuk is not your average soul.

"When we bought the property, we weren't into farming," he explained. "It was more of a pasture farm with rolling hills. So we planted thirty-five thousand trees on the property besides what was already there!"

Walt left his trees to grow while he spent a total of fourteen winters wearing Ranger blue. Known for his rock-solid durability and toughness, he endeared himself to Ranger fans as a well-rounded centreman who could take out the opposition and stand his ground in the crease.

Walt Tkaczuk instructing Magnolia the llama on the finer points of serving as a caddy at his golf course near St. Marys, Ontario

"He's the strongest man I've ever seen on a pair of skates," his former teammate, Ab Demarco, affirmed. "He was short, 5'10", 5'11" and stalky, but that meant dittle—a 6'5" guy couldn't knock this man over! It's like he had lead in each foot.

"I remember one night when we were playing in Madison Square Gardens against Toronto. Bobby Baun, the Leafs' short, stalky defenseman known for his powerful hip checks was on the ice. Now Walt Tkaczuk could never really see that well and, he was a bit of a lumbering centreman. He picks up the puck inside our blueline. He had one hand on the stick, pushing the puck ahead of himself, circling up centre. Now Bobby Baun sees him coming and lines him up for one of his patented bangers. As Walt hits the centre-ice line, Baun takes a run and *nails* him! Now just visualize this: Walt Tkaczuk didn't even break stride as he ran over Baun like he wasn't there! There wasn't even a ripple as he kept lumbering up ice."

Walt continued his juggernaut ways until an eye injury forced an end to his on-ice career in

Walt Tkaczuk surveys the rolling hills and fairways of
River Valley Golf and County Club

1981. He retired as a player but hung on as an assistant coach under Craig Patrick and later, Herb Brooks. "It started off slowly," he reported. "I was asked to look at the players and tell them what I saw while I was behind the bench. I would talk to them individually as they came off the ice. From that point it went to changing lines and running some practices. I didn't realize it was going to be that much fun! You still get excited! You get disappointed! You get happy!—the same feelings I had as a player!"

By 1983, Walt had weighed the pros and cons of staying in professional hockey, and after a brief struggle—the cons prevailed. "I think some players love the game to the point where they can't get out," he concluded. "But I thought for me it was time for a change. I was there for fifteen years. And besides, I wanted to come back to Canada. My family enjoys the kind of life we have here in St. Marys."

Walt made the leap, settling into a sales position with Nasco Plastics in nearby New Hamburg. "They were a company out of the States that had an arm here in Canada," he explained. "They did some manufacturing of sterilized sampling bags for quality control labs."

On the surface, Walt appeared to be a typical Nasco sales rep over the next three years. Below the surface, however, he was devising something much more ambitious—plans to convert his farm into a golf course. There was one major problem though—he couldn't see the fairway for the forest!

"We had to remove about fifteen thousand trees to cut our fairways!" he exclaimed. "It took us about nine months. We had D9's, dozers, 7's and high-hoes in here because we had to ... pull those trees out by the stumps—and some of them were sixty, eighty feet high! So it was a big job. I remember when I started with the removal of the trees, I weighed about 205 pounds. In nine months, I lost about seventeen pounds just working on the property, eating well with no formal exercise."

By June of 1995, Walt and his partner, Danny Séguin, were ready to open River Valley Golf and Country Club. "It's a challenging course cut out amongst some thirty-thousand trees!" he attested. "It's scenic, hilly and mature."

To keep the place flourishing during the winter, he added River Valley Winter Tube Slide—the first of its kind in Ontario. "It features a big hill with a lift," he explained. "It takes a minute to go up and about thirty seconds screaming to go down! The people from Mt. St. Louis and Collingwood have been up this past winter looking at it, taking pictures. They're thinking about adding it to their places. I think they liked what they saw."

Walt is now into his second full season of operation. The tube slide has been a big hit and principal bread winner in the early going. Golf, on the other hand, has been more like an acorn striving to become an oak. "It's been growing steadily but it's not real busy," he admitted.

"We're just starting to get a membership drive going for next year because when you don't have any members, you're busy and then you're quiet. It's on the whim of the weather and the people out there. So at least with memberships, we'll have some kind of base."

To grease the golf-cart wheels and catch a little local publicity, Walt and Danny hooked their brain waves together to cook up a novel and exotic idea: to relieve all those burdened golfers of their weighty clubs, why not use llamas as caddies? With the help of their neighbour, a llama breeder, they did just that—and the ensuing publicity jumped from St. Marys, across the continent and all the way to Japan where the likeness of Walt and his llamas are smiling at waves of potential tourists.

Walt's wife, Valerie, is described as River Valley's project manager. With her finger on the pulse of daily affairs, Walt and Danny are free to do maintenance work around the course and to stay true to their rituals of fishing every Tuesday and knocking off nine holes at the end of those balmy summer days.

─ ⬥═══ ─

Tonelli, John: *Played left wing for Houston (WHA), the New York Islanders, Calgary, Los Angeles, Chicago and Quebec (NHL) from 1975-1992. Born: Milton, Ontario, 1957.*

John Tonelli was eighteen years old when he turned pro with the Houston Aeros in 1975. And through the perspective of his youthful eyes, life's fortunes appeared as an endless rink upon which he could glide, shoot and score forever. But John was not so naïve as to overlook the signs of mortality posted along the highway of professional hockey.

"I can remember one of the first road trips we took," he recounted. "I was looking at one of my fellow players, Larry Lund. He was doing all kinds of work on the plane, studying. I asked him, 'What are you doing?' And he said, 'This game is not going to last too much longer. I'm getting ready to enter the real world.' So it hit me very early. I thought it might be wise for me to be prepared... To make sure I'm ready to do

something when I get out."

By the mid-eighties, John and his wife, Karen, were immersed in the fleeting delights of raising two young children. With ten years of planes, buses and hotels under his belt, John's desire for a more stable lifestyle began to surge. As he pondered his future there were certain conclusions that were inescapable. "One thing I never ever wanted to do was to stay in the game after I was done!" he asserted. "I was looking forward to the fact that I could stay at home every night and hang out with my family."

So, to seal a fate of his own choosing, he went to work on a part-time basis in the title-insurance business. "We did property searches in relation to real-estate acquisitions, real-estate restructuring or refinancing," he explained. John's employer offered real-estate buyers protection by searching property titles to ensure that they are clear of any legal hindrances such as liens.

"I was really prepared," he affirmed. "I wanted to make sure that as soon as it was over, I could get right to work with my next career. And fortunately, by that time, I had built up a certain base..."

The big jump came in 1992 as John skated his final shift for the Quebec Nordiques in 1992. It marked the end of a career that spanned seventeen professional seasons, four Stanley Cup victories and 1,126 career points. On ice, he had been an intense competitor who could dig deeply into every aspect of his game. He was strong on positional play and could grind along the boards like a boulder with soft hands. In retirement, his life off ice would now become the centrepiece of a well-laid plan. He returned straightway to his home in New York and began to pursue his options.

One of his close friends owned a title-insurance agency called "Titleserv", based in Plainview, Long Island. "The first day I knew I was not going to be playing hockey," John recounted, "I called him up and I said, 'Hey, can you use a guy like me?' And he said, 'Sure, come on over.' He's been a tremendous supporter and backer. He knew he was getting someone who would go out and work for him. And for me, this job is a promotion from playing hockey. I don't mean to downplay hockey at all. I grew up dreaming about playing the game. I was very fortunate to be a part of Stanley Cup championship teams—it was a major stepping stone towards what I'm doing now. I'm very happy and I really like what I do."

As a sideline, John coaches his son's bantam hockey team. Last season, they won the national title over powerhouse clubs from the hotbeds of

Nickname Challenge #26

Herbie & Smitty

Herbie

"We had Hooley Smith and myself, and if somebody would say 'Hey Smitty', why both of us would answer to it. Dit Clapper was always quite the guy to give everybody nicknames, so he used this comic strip to separate one of us from the other. Do you remember *Herbie & Smitty* in the funny papers? Hooley Smith was much older than I was, so Clapper called him 'Smitty' and they called me 'Herbie'. I got that name in about 1936, '37."

Who is he?

Clues

a. He played centre for Boston between 1936 & 1955.

b. He won the Art Ross Trophy in 1940 and the Hart Trophy in 1951. He was a first-team all-star in 1940, 1947 & 1951.

If you're bottled up in your own zone,
see page 285.

Detroit, Chicago and Minnesota. He also enjoys hitting the golf course. "I like to play good golf," he confessed. "Right now though I'm going through a stage of playing ugly golf ."

He and Karen maintain their home in the rural setting of Brookville, Long Island where life has subsided to a slow and steady pace. "I have a nineteen-year-old daughter in college," he reported, "a sixteen-year-old son who plays hockey on my team and a six-year-old daughter. She's the one who gets a lot of my attention. My oldest two never got the benefit of me being around all the time. It's not that I can say I'm around all the time now either because it takes a lot of hard work after hockey to be successful... "

Nicknames: *JT; Johnny T*

"I can think of some pretty nasty nicknames, but you're not going to get anything out of me!" John insisted.

"While I was with the Islanders I was pretty much 'Johnny T' of 'JT'. Pretty boring, huh!"

Turnbull, Ian: *Played defense for Toronto, Los Angeles and Pittsburgh from 1973-1983. Born: Montreal, Quebec, 1953.*

Place an issue of *The Hockey News* and *The Wall Street Journal* on Ian Turnbull's coffee table and odds are he will reach for Wall Street and use *The Hockey News* as a coffee coaster. At any stage of his career, mortgage rates and the Dow Jones held more personal significance than "goals for" or "goals against".

While playing junior hockey in his late teens, Ian began to take courses in business administration at the University of Ottawa. His ultimate destination was to work in business and finance—but the NHL got in his way.

"I wouldn't say unfortunately, but sort of unfortunately I got drafted," he disclosed with a chuckle. "Of course I made the decision to take that road—wherever it took me—which lasted just about ten years. So it wasn't all bad."

As he toiled on the NHL's blueline corps, Ian continued to hone his business skills on the side. In the mid-seventies, he established Grapes tavern in Toronto. Years later, he also got certified to sell real estate. On ice, he had quickly developed into one of the league's better rearguards. He was a willing bodychecker blessed with mobility and puck-handling skills. His best campaign came while with the Maple Leafs in 1976-77. On February 4th of that season he set a league record by scoring five goals in one game against Detroit. He finished the year with a personal-high twenty-two goals and fifty-seven assists.

By 1983, however, Ian had delayed his real life's calling for long enough. He and the NHL were through and it was time to get on with business.

"It was actually quite refreshing," he stated of his transition. "I never really took hockey as a career. It happened to be something I did quite well as a kid but I never really thought of it as a vocation."

With his blades now gathering moss, Ian, his wife, Inge, and their son and daughter shifted straightway from Pittsburgh to California. "I just happened to have had a house in L.A.," he remarked of his decision to choose the West Coast as a home base. "My kids had started school there. So it was as good a place as any."

Once settled, Ian pursued his new livelihood in a logical progression. "Basically I just started selling real estate and then it slowly evolved into financing," he explained. "I found that, quite naturally, a lot of the deals I was involved in had to be financed. With the trickier transactions, I found it was easier if I got involved with that end of things. Then I just sort of fell in love with financing real estate and that's basically all I've been doing since.

"I have a company called 'King Harbor Financial'. We fund mortgages here in California. We'll put a group of loans together and sell them off to pension funds, institutions or private investors. It's my company, but I work with other companies. You can't fund everything, so you're always working with other groups."

Now a middle-aged financier, Ian has taken to toking on the quintessential symbol of the pin-striped banker—cigars.

"I have some buddies who have a cigar club

King Harbor Financial Inc.

Ian W. Turnbull

**8251 Westminister Avenue
Suite 100
Westminister, Ca 92683
(310) 374-5195**

---

here where you can just smoke away," he quipped with a laugh. "We do cigar dinners and wine tasting. It's a very social group. Most of the cigars I like come from the Dominican Republic and Honduras. A lot of people do get their hands on Cuban cigars, but it's illegal as hell! So I stay away from them. It's not worth the aggravation."

Nickname: *Hawk*

"It was way back in the seventies," Ian recounted. "I moved up to left wing where I was pretending to be Bobby Hull...

"Now I used to play with Howie McKenny and we'd laugh because Bobby Hull had a characteristic where one finger would hang out of his glove. It was like a dead finger that would hang down all the time when he skated along the wing. So I started imitating him and the first shift I played on left wing, I blasted one past Gerry Cheevers! So the fellas started calling me 'Bobby Hawk' after that."

Turnbull, Perry: *Played centre for St. Louis, Montreal and Winnipeg from 1979-1988. Born: Rimbey, Alberta, 1959.*

Perry Turnbull's life has been an adventurous progression from the frozen ponds of Rimbey, Alberta to the arenas of the NHL. Along the way he was voted MVP of the Western Hockey League during his final year of junior with the Portland Winter Hawks in 1978-79. As a first-round draft pick of the St. Louis Blues, the 6'2", 200-pound centreman hit NHL ice the following season. He was an excellent skater with an effective shot who leaned towards a robust style of play. His most prolific season came in 1981-82 when he notched thirty-three goals and twenty-six assists.

Over his nine major-league campaigns, he balanced 1,331 penalty minutes with 364 total points.

By the late-eighties, the only frontier left to explore was in Europe. Like blades on ice, the numerous offers coming from overseas made their impression on Perry's mind. In response, he effected some creative bookkeeping to spring himself from his final year under contract with the St. Louis Blues. Next stop—Italy.

Starting in 1988, he played three seasons on behalf of teams in Asiago, Aleghe and Bolzano. "I personally loved it!" he exclaimed of the experience. "But my wife hated it. She's a real go-getter and likes to be busy all the time... She was just sitting on her duff washing dishes and cooking because there's not a lot of recreation over there. What they do is something that we're not that big on—going out to eat and to drink a bunch of wine!"

By 1991, Perry's voyage around the frozen side of the world was complete. He retired from professional ice hockey and resettled in St. Louis where he'd purchased a small travel agency while still in the NHL. His plan was to make West Travel a bigger kid on the block. "I went out and purchased another agency and merged the two which, being a little guy, got us over the hump," he remarked. "Then we started to get all the good stuff. The question then was, 'Do we go out and buy a bigger one and get twice as big'?"

He inevitably decided that anything larger than the present edition of West Travel would result in a loss of control over the facility's management—a situation he prefers to avoid.

"It's been a good little business for us," he professed. "But after I got it built up, my job wasn't busy enough—I was bored! So that's when I started to look into creating something else."

Perry's mind began to synthesize a little bit of Europe with the potential market for youth hockey in St. Louis. "Ultimately, I wanted to build an ice rink, but I really couldn't afford to at that time," he explained. "So instead I tried to create a low-cost alternative to get more kids [involved]. I got this idea from the rinks I played

on in Europe—I put a roof over a rink and I started roller hockey. I did the whole rink for about four hundred thousand bucks! We went in and put down the concrete, put up the boards and put down the floor. We use a floor called Sport Court which Bernie Federko sells. It's great to skate on and the puck moves a lot more like on ice.

"It's worked out quite well. We have what I think is the most people playing at one roller-hockey rink in the United States. I have fourteen hundred at one and about a thousand at the other!"

Perry's in-line success is attributable to choosing the right wave at the right time. "It's just taking the country by storm because it's accessible," he asserted. "There are twenty-one rinks that are playing roller hockey in St. Louis right now. We've got something like 118 teams that play through the week. It's the only game in the world that's fun to practise!

"It's fast, fun and exciting! I mean the [kids] are out playing baseball and they're picking their noses, throwing their gloves in the air and pulling their shorts out of the crack in their butts! They're not paying attention to what's going on! But when they come to the rink, whether it's roller or ice, they're paying attention. They're ready for their next shift."

In 1993, Perry joined with a group of investors, including Bernie Federko, to establish the St. Louis Vipers roller-hockey team. "I got involved initially ... after a couple of beers," he confided with a chuckle. "They said, 'You could still play!' And I said, 'Yeah I could.' So I ended up playing the first two seasons the team was here. Last year I took on the coaching duties and now I'm coach and GM. I've also just been asked to coach the North American roller-hockey team in Europe. We're doing a tour with Team Europe versus Team North America in April."

Outside of his business activities, Perry savours spending time with his wife, Nancy, and their young son and daughter. He also likes to hunt and fish. "I bow hunt quite a bit and I still play hockey every Monday night with the Blues' alumni team," he related. "And Mike Zuke and

I coach the mite double-A team out here in Chesterfield. We spend a lot of time at it. It's fun."

Nicknames: *Percy; Bull*

"They called me 'Percy' forever," Perry recollected. "I got it when I was twelve. I was playing at a tournament and they misspelled my name on the programme.

"When I got to St. Louis, if they wanted to say something nice, they'd call me 'Bull' and when they were on my case, they'd call me 'Percy'."

Ververgaert, Dennis: *Played right wing for Vancouver, Philadelphia and Washington from 1973-1981. Born: Hamilton, Ontario, 1953.*

Many professional athletes experienced their careers in the same manner as a boy who constructs a jigsaw puzzle on a kitchen table. Piece by piece, the image is assembled until at the moment of its completion, the lad is told that the table must be set for dinner. With no time to savour the view, the boy must apply all of his ingenuity to move and preserve his creation.

In 1981, Dennis Ververgaert found himself facing a similar conversion as the world seemed to close in on him with a fury too fast to be processed.

"Nobody wants to retire," he asserted. "I just had a real bad training camp and I wasn't scoring the year before... A young guy named [Gaetan] Duchesne, a right winger, came in that year and had a super camp. I had two real bad groin pulls and I couldn't afford not to skate. It's not like today where if you get a groin pull, you don't play. I was out there bandaged like a mummy!

"So they wanted to send me to the minors—which looking back—maybe I should have done because at that time, Quebec was looking for a right winger. They took Wilf Paiement and from what I heard, they were interested in me too. But with personal problems on my mind and the groin pulls—I don't know if I lost interest or my mind was just confused—but I said, 'The heck with it. That's enough!' It was a lost feeling. The worst feeling of my life."

After packing up his bags in Washington and closing out affairs in Philadelphia, Dennis reunited with his wife and returned to British Columbia. In his receding wake he left a career that spanned eight NHL seasons and 395 total points. His most productive campaign came in 1975-76 when he posted thirty-seven goals and thirty-four assists plus a trip to the All-Star Game where he popped in two goals. But then that was all in the past and in its place, he would have to grapple with the uncertainty of immeasurable change.

> *"I was one of those players who had to find himself. It was a real tough time ... Those are the sad parts of reality. I can bullshit you and tell you other things, but those are the truths."*
>
> *Dennis Ververgaert*

"I was one of those hockey players who had to find himself," he confided of his transition out of the game. "It was a real tough time. I took a year off. My wife and I skied and did the whole thing. But we did eventually split up and that took me awhile to get over... Those are the sad parts of reality. I can bullshit you and tell you other things, but those are the truths. That's what happened."

In the meantime, Dennis began his search to get a second career off the ground. While with the Canucks in years past he had made numerous contacts around town. A logical starting point was to cash in those connections.

"When I came back to Vancouver, you realize all of your so-so, good friends at the time are not around anymore," he remarked. "You go to those people when you retire and no one wants to give you a job. They have all the excuses."

Through persistence, however, Dennis found a friend of substance who introduced him to the insurance industry. "With the desire and the things I learned in hockey," he affirmed. "I'm now very successful. So it's all coming back."

For the past nine years, he has been selling

commercial, residential and auto insurance in the greater Vancouver area. "I compare it to hockey," he explained. "I'm in the minors just ready to go pro. I'm not right there but in the next year or two I should be in insurance—like hockey—back at the pro level."

And in any profession, as Dennis knows well, intense commitment and self-motivation are the currents that raise the foreman above the journeyman. "I'm in the type of sales position where you can take off and golf all day and do whatever you want," he declared. "Insurance is not the most exciting thing in the world. It's pretty dry. So you've got to get yourself going by setting goals like in hockey. I don't just want to settle at an average. I want to be one of the best in the insurance business with knowledge and volume. I guess you could compare the volume to scoring goals."

Since his turbulent departure from the NHL, Dennis's family life has gradually evolved into a stable and fulfilling experience. He and his second wife, Becky, are raising three sons at their home in the town of Abbotsford. And if and when he can escape the uproarious marvels of fatherhood, he likes to play golf and oldtimers' hockey with the Canucks' alumni team.

During his time in the big league, Dennis stood a respectable 6'0" with 180 pounds of weight to throw around. By today's standards, however, he's starting look on the small side. "They're all pretty well monsters!" he exclaimed. "Especially the defensemen. They're 6'4", 6'5" and they're fast skaters for their size. In the old days, if you saw a guy like Pat Quinn—they were big, but they were slow... We loved them! We'd dump the puck in their corner because they were a little slow turning and getting to the puck. None of those guys could compare with fast guys like Wayne Gretzky coming down on a wing, making a move. But now the guys are so big and they *can* turn with those fast guys. They can also skate and come up into the play, so times have changed."

Nickname Challenge #27

Shakey

"I put names on a few guys in my time, so I thought they'd catch me one day. I gave nicknames to Harry Lumley, Sid Abel, Marty Pavelich and Gordie Howe, so they were trying to figure out something for me. At the old Boston Gardens the railroad station, the hotel and the rink were all in one building. And when they were playing the National Anthem, the train came in and you could actually feel the building shake. And of course I'm a nervous guy anyway. I figure somebody must have looked over and saw me shaking. So that's how I came about being called 'Shakey'."

Who is he?

Clues
a. He played right wing for Montreal, Boston, Detroit and Chicago from 1945-1954.
b. His son has the same name and played for Detroit and Los Angeles between 1965 & 1975.
c. His initials are J.P.

If you're going head-long into the boards, see page 285.

Vickers, Steve: *Played left wing for the New York Rangers from 1972-1982. Born: Toronto, Ontario, 1951.*

For Steve Vickers, NHL fame came with a label that read: Warning, the brighter the spotlight the greater the blindness. And as such, he was more than happy to skate in the wings where only the second-hand limelight shone.

"It's never easy," he admitted of the transition out of hockey. "But I think the superstars have a rougher time with it than somebody like myself because they're held in such esteem. When they do walk away from any sport, people just don't pay them the same attention that they were used to.

"One good thing about living in New York was that you were never really held in much esteem by anybody anyway. You walked away from Madison Square Gardens and you were just another person out there—which had its advantages... You didn't have to worry about where you were going or being hounded. Whereas in Toronto or Montreal, you can't look sideways without somebody knowing who you are and being hassled..."

On the ice, however, Steve was very recognizable. His opponents knew him as a rugged customer with an obstinate tendency to double-park along the opposing goal-crease line. From such a vantage point, he chipped in an impressive 270 goals and 365 assists during his ten seasons in Ranger blue.

As his time in the NHL was winding down, Steve looked to the insurance industry as an accessible alternative to life on ice. "I had friends in the business that seemed to be doing fairly well," he recalled. "And I knew you didn't have to have a degree to get into it—you just had to have a license in New York state. So one summer, instead of hanging out at the beach, I went to school."

By the time he packed in his blades in 1982, he had his insurance-brokers license in hand. He stayed on in New York and spent the next five years insuring lives, homes and small businesses.

But by the late eighties, he and his wife, Joanne, had three children on the rise and felt that Canada was the place to let them branch out. "I didn't want to live in Scarborough where I grew up," he admitted of his choice of towns. "Maybe after living in New York all those years, it was time to step back and get some space. Aurora seemed like a nice little community and I thought it would be a good place to raise children."

Once he was settled into his new home, Steve began his search for a job. "I knew some gentlemen I met in Aurora," he recounted. "They recommended applying to Yellow Pages. They were hiring like crazy then. So I went in one day and dusted off a suit, got a haircut and found a real job!

"It's been nine years now. And like any job, you put the effort in and the results will be there. We got hurt like a lot of companies in the early nineties with the recession, but we're back on track again."

As an NHL spectator, Steve is a kettle on the boil with thoughts about the league's evolution. "I don't think there's as much respect for one another out there," he observed. "There seems to be a lot of running from behind and sticking around the head. But I guess that goes with the visors and the helmets. Everyone who wears them feels they're bullet proof.

"In our day, if you hit somebody over the head, you were getting it right back—no matter who you hit—whether it be Ross Lonsberry or Bobby Clarke. You lived by the sword, you died by the sword!

"But they seem to have gotten away from that. The Players' Association should step in and say, 'Hey we're all in this together. Let's stop hurting each other.' There's no respect. Especially two or three players like Ulf Samuelsson and [Claude] Lemieux—they could care less! I think that one or two players in the league have got to take it upon themselves to fill these guys in. It doesn't seem that management or the league is disciplining them enough. To get two games for that hit [Lemieux on Kris Draper] was a disgrace! It was a black mark in hockey as far as I'm concerned. That guy should have been out for half a season. But like I said, maybe

somebody will get him. I hope they do!"
(Editor's note: Somebody did.)

Nickname: *Sarge*

"Steve and I used to live together on Long Island along with Stemmer [Stemkowski]," Ab Demarco said. "We would drive into practice together. Steve showed up one day wearing a shirt with some sergeant stripes on it. That's all Stemmer needed. 'Hey, Sarge! What's happening?' So that stuck for fifteen, twenty years."

Villemure, Gilles: *Played goal for the New York Rangers and Chicago between 1963 & 1977. Born: Trois-Rivières, Quebec, 1940.*

While in his prime with the New York Rangers, Gilles Villemure shared the Big Apple with Eddie Giacomin, Vic Hadfield, Harry Howell and Jim Neilson to name but a few. One by one, however, they drifted away to other worlds, leaving only a tiny corps of survivors.

"There's no one around here!" Gilles exclaimed. "Just Peter Stemkowski, but he's only here in the summertime and Ron Greschner. But we only see him about once a year. He moves around with his wife who's an actress. And I do a few clinics for the Rangers with Rod Gilbert. That's about it."

The late fifties, though, were quite a contrast as a young Gilles Villemure came of age in professional hockey at a time when original-six teams carried only one goaltender. Patience would be the keyword as he toiled for ten seasons in the minors. During his final two years in the American Hockey League he drew attention to himself as a league leader and MVP. His determination had paid off. By 1970, his cool, standup style and ability to play the angles earned him a sizeable piece of the action in the Rangers' net alongside Eddie Giacomin. But in 1975, he was sent to the Chicago Blackhawks where, as a backup to Tony Esposito, ice time became scarce. Two years later, retirement came knocking. "I didn't have a choice," he stated of his departure. "The team didn't pick up my contract and that was it. When you're thirty-seven years old, it's

about time to quit."

Gilles traded one passion for another as he returned to New York City to pursue a career in harness racing. "All my life I was with horses," he recounted. "That goes back to when I was ten years old. Throughout my career I used to go home every summer to drive horses. It's like hockey—it's all reflexes. I guess I was pretty sharp when I played hockey for eight months and then I'd drive horses. I did well with it, so when I retired, I went at it full-time. I did both the training and the driving."

For the next eight years, he groomed his horses and circled the tracks of the Meadowlands, Yonkers and Roosevelt Raceways.

"This game has its ups and downs," he explained of the business. "I did very well for a few years but then I sold this good horse I had. I bought a couple of cheap horses that didn't do well at all. So I said, 'Forget about it, I quit!' I didn't want to invest more money into it."

In 1985, Gilles sold his horses and sulky, put his life's second passion to rest and settled into a more stationary job with Consolidated Electric Corporation in New York City.

"I'm an electrician right now," he reported. "I'm with local three here, working in the supply house. We have about one hundred men working for us. As the men are sent out to do various jobs, I coordinate insuring that they receive the necessary materials to do their work."

Gilles' memories of hockey and harness racing have now found their place on the fireplace mantle. Amongst the mementos, he still guards Opee-chee hockey card #248 from 1971. Eddie Giacomin stands to the left and Gilles stands to the right of the Vezina Trophy. "As you know," he related, "I didn't win a Stanley Cup with the Rangers who hadn't won for fifty-four years. But Eddie Giacomin and I won a Vezina Trophy for the best average in the NHL. And I made three All-star Games and spent ten years in the big leagues which means I did something right I guess."

Walton, Mike: *Played centre for Toronto, Boston, Vancouver, St. Louis, Chicago (NHL) and Minnesota (WHA) from 1965-1979. Born: Kirkland Lake, Ontario, 1945.*

When Mike Walton first entered the NHL in 1965, he stepped into more than just a Maple Leafs' jersey, he waded waist deep into a system that would demand conformity and obedience—even if it meant compromising his own values. In the early going, he gave it his best shot, winning a Stanley Cup in 1967 and netting thirty goals and twenty-nine assists during the campaign that followed. Over time, he had become a firmly established member of the Leafs' family—on ice as a player and off ice as the husband of Conn Smythe's granddaughter. From the outside in, he and the system appeared as a cozy fit until problems began to emerge in 1969. In reaction to riding the bench more than he felt he deserved, Mike was no longer willing to suppress his convictions. He walked out on coach Punch Imlach and the Leafs—thus putting his career on the line. His departure was temporary, but the fallout was permanent. Mike Walton the outspoken, non-conformist had now bubbled to the surface to rock the boat—and there he would remain as an early reminder of what a player could do outside the rules of serfdom. His detractors labelled him as unstable while his supporters saw him as a colourful man who, at times, had been painted in black and white by those who stood to lose the most through the assertion of player rights.

The Leafs eventually sent him packing to Boston in 1971 where he slowly regained his confidence and scoring touch, winning another Stanley Cup during his second season as a Bruin. When the World Hockey Association came calling with an open chequebook in 1973, Mike made the leap into financial prosperity as

MIKE WALTON

2255 Bloor St. West
Toronto, Ontario M6S 1N8

a Minnesota Fighting Saint. There he won the league scoring championship during his first campaign, potting fifty-seven goals and sixty assists. Two years later, he made his return to the NHL via the Vancouver Canucks where he remained until his final season in 1978—a campaign which was based more on a travel plan than a game plan.

"That year I was traded back and forth," he recollected. "I went from Vancouver in the summer to St. Louis; from St. Louis to Boston; Boston to Chicago; and then I retired. It was hard on everybody including my family and myself."

Mike couldn't pack his bags fast enough to catch yet another flight. This one was headed for Europe where he had agreed to play for an A-division team in Cologne, Germany.

"The main thing was to get away from it all," he revealed. "To have a year or eight months to make a decision about what I was going to do once I came back, in my case, to Toronto. Being over there took my mind off the home factor. What were the teams doing? How were the Leafs doing?"

After one season in Cologne, Mike resettled in Toronto to lay hockey to rest and launch a new career. "The transition was very difficult," he admitted. "Whether it's dealing with the fact that you're no longer a professional—you're no longer ... a star ... or the celebrity. You no longer have a job that was paying you good money. Now all of sudden you're out in the real world, looking for work."

In 1980, he began to sell real estate, representing several local companies before going solo with Mike Walton Real Estate. Six years later, however, a recession struck and he read the writing on the wall—"Caution: slow-moving market ahead!" He began instead to diversify his options. "I was selling a restaurant," he recounted. "I sold it a couple of times and the deals fell through. So I decided to buy the bar myself. It's called "Shakey's" on Bloor Street West.

"When I originally bought it, I had no restaurant experience which made it very difficult. But I had friends in the business that came in and helped me out. I also counted on my managers who basically knew what they were doing."

Mike worked hard in the ensuing years to give Shakey's the right feel. "It's sort of like a sports bar," he explained. "I've got two to three hundred pictures on the walls of great hockey players like Richard and Howe that I've gotten personally signed. You can't see any wall at all—it's all pictures! I've also got my two miniature Stanley Cups and my scoring

championship from '74 with Minnesota. I've got a cabinet of sticks downstairs. I recently acquired a Brett Hull stick that he signed for me and a stick from Jagr. I've got Gilmour's as well."

Following an intense ride on the learning curve of the food-service industry, Mike has begun to initiate changes. "To be a good restaurateur you basically have to spend all of your time there," he remarked. "Over the last couple of years, I just got tired of it. I originally bought it for my family to run and for me to stay in the real estate because that's what I love doing. So I've got a couple of people coming in as partners which is going to take pressure off of me. Now I don't have to get phone calls at two or three in the morning!"

In 1993, he reentered the real-estate business with a local company called "Country Wide". "I'm doing residential now," he noted. "I sold Dougie Gilmour a house and I sold one to Tie Domi."

As Mike's life has evolved, so has his family experience. "I was married twenty-one years and I got separated and divorced six or seven years ago," he confided. "I got custody of the three girls and my middle daughter had a baby girl, so I'm a grandfather now."

To keep himself in shape, Mike engages in a variety of sports. "I love tennis and I just came back from Tahoe where one of my favourite sports is skiing," he reported. "I play a lot of squash and I love swimming. I used to be a pretty good golfer. But then I didn't have time to play, so now I'm basically brutal."

Nickname: *Shakey*

"Of course everyone thinks it was 'Shakey' because *I* was shaky," Mike observed. "But the reason I had that name was because my dad [Bob Walton] was called 'Shakey'. He played over in England. He'd shake his head one way and go the other. Today we call it a deke, but back then they

Mike Walton calling the play-by-play at Shakey's Bar & Grill on Bloor Street West in Toronto used to call it a shake. That's how he got the name. Of course every reporter across Canada and the United States would ask, 'Well Shake, how did you get your name?' Everybody was looking for a big story but there was no story. I just inherited the name through my dad."

Trying To Shake Shakey

George Tokar is Mike Walton's lawyer, business partner and close personal friend. He's also a keen observer of the game and related the following story.

The most devout of Montreal fans has an equal love of his Canadiens and a hatred of the Maple Leafs. So you can imagine back in '66-67 when I followed my beloved Canadiens and the old Leafs' team had this upstart, this kid on the team, #16, Walton. I hated him because I couldn't hate Sawchuck. You couldn't hate Tim Horton. You couldn't hate the old guys.

And back then, there was no Players' Association. The players weren't allowed to have an opinion of their own. They were indentured slaves. And this guy, Walton, had the audacity one night to get off the train in Brockville on the way to Montreal and take a taxi back home, after being told by Punch Imlach that he wasn't dressing him the next night . And if you think about it, in those days you could be condemned to life in the American Hockey League. So that was a pretty brash move.

So now imagine that this same guy has himself certified as being unfit to play in Toronto because of the pressure and gets traded to Boston. And at about the same time, my beloved Canadiens are having their great Dryden-era rivalry with Boston. So it just seemed that I couldn't shake this guy.

So you can imagine then about thirteen years ago, because of a common friend, we were going out to a dinner party and we weren't told who the other couple was. And "Shake" walks through the front door of my house, sticks out his meaty paw and says, "Hi, I'm Mike Walton." And I said, "I know who the (bleep) you are. I hated you then and I hope you're better now." And then because of that introduction, we became best of friends.

Watson, Bryan: *Played defense for Montreal, Detroit, Oakland, Pittsburgh, St. Louis, Washington (NHL) and Cincinnati (WHA) from 1963-1979. Born: Bancroft, Ontario, 1942.*

It isn't hard to find Bryan Watson in Alexandria, Virginia. Dial any local number and you're apt to get someone who can help you out. In misdialing my call, a businessman answered, saying:

- May I help you?
- Yes! Is Bryan Watson there?
- This is Burke & Herbert Bank. But I think I know who you want. Armand's right?
- How'd you know?
- We're just down the street from there. We order pizza from Armand's all the time. The food's great! I heard that Bryan Watson, the former hockey player, owns that place. You mean he's really in there all the time?

The fact is, when it comes to Armand's, Bryan Watson is the main man—front and centre. But long before he made his transition from the cold ice to the heat of the kitchen, his life had taken many a twist and turn.

His NHL career first opened with the Montreal Canadiens during the early sixties, although he didn't catch on full-time until joining the Detroit Red Wings in 1965. It was with the Wings that he earned the moniker that, in one word, best defined Bryan Watson as a player. "I was always driving Andy Bathgate and Gordie Howe crazy," he recalled. "I was buggin' the hell out of them. So they started calling me 'Bugsy'!" Throughout his career, Bryan was a designated shadow, appointed to hound, cajole and pester the game's big stars. Bobby Hull, a frequent recipient of Bryan's attention, once referred to him as "Superpest". Over sixteen professional seasons, the hard-hitting defenseman was caught with his hand in the till to the tune of 2,340 penalty minutes.

By 1979, the Washington Capitals had bought out his contract. And after seven trades and so many years, he was not adverse to the idea of retirement and stability for his family.

There were, however, general managers out

there who had other ideas. The Cincinnati Stingers of the World Hockey Association were making a run for the playoffs that year. Floyd Smith recruited Bryan to play twenty-four games, including a shot at post-season play.

The following season, the phone rang again. This time John Ferguson of the Winnipeg Jets was on the line. "He wanted me to come to play that year, but I just didn't want to move Lindy and the kids one more time," he related. "Winnipeg is a nice city but we were living in the Washington area and it was just time to get the hell out."

With his mind firmly resolved, Bryan was putting his gear in storage when the phone rang again—this time it was Glen Sather in Edmonton. "Glen talked me into going to coach, which was a fiasco!" he exclaimed. "It lasted six weeks and then I was fired. But actually I think it was a godsend, being fired and getting out of it. I look at some of these guys who coach—Christ they age—and you know that as soon as the team starts to go bad, the first guy to go is the coach, regardless of whether he's doing a good job or not. I think you have to take that job with the understanding that coaches are hired to be fired."

Having rented out his house in Bethesda, Maryland, Bryan and his family retreated to their cottage on Eagle Lake in the Haliburton area of Ontario. "We spent a year in Canada, which was really terrific," he recounted. "We kind of licked our wounds a little bit. I'd never not succeeded in anything before, so it had a different feel.

"While we were there, we researched what we wanted to do. I was still under contract with Edmonton for two years, so they had to pay me which was great. It gave us the luxury of finding out what we really wanted to get into."

After his year on Eagle Lake, Bryan chose Alexandria, Virginia as the site of the next chapter in his life. "As it turned out, we got into the pizza business, which at the time was really taking off," he explained. "We've been at it now, thirteen years. And as you know, pizza has taken over as the number-one fast food in the United States. We have a great location in the old town—it's an historical area of Alexandria. We

were lucky enough to find a great property and we got a great product. It's a deep-dish Chicago-style pizza."

He and his wife, Lindy, now employ eighty-five people to help run their two-story operation. The main floor features Armand's Chicago Pizzeria while the second floor is home to a sports bar called The Penalty Box.

"It's fun to be involved in meeting people," he declared. "I'm really lucky. I like the business a lot."

Bryan and Lindy have a daughter, Lisa, and a son, Stevie. "Stevie's with a band in Austin, Texas," Bryan reported. "He's loving music. That's where all the budding young guys go who are writing. Stevie Ray Vaughn was his hero as he was ours. Lindy and I are really big on the music."

As a contrast to the fast pace of sports bars and pizzas, Bryan maintains a home in St. Michaels, Maryland, along the Chesapeake. "The hobby that I like the best is gardening," he noted. "I like fooling with flowers. I get that from my father. Also, my real love is the Chesapeake, finding out about it. It's a magnificent body of water."

Watson, Harry: *Played left wing for Brooklyn, Detroit, Toronto and Chicago between 1941 & 1957. Born: Saskatoon, Saskatchewan, 1923.*

As the reflexes slow and the rust begins to grow, the seasoned player glances over his shoulder to see younger men flying in the wings. An inaudible hum circles the rink—a rumour here, some trade talk there. The phone rings. The tense anticipation breaks as a voice says, "We've got an *opportunity* for you!"

Harry Watson got *his* opportunity when the phone rang at the close of the 1956-57 season. His fourteen-year career was hanging in the balance at the other end of the line. In his prime, the 6'1", 203-pound left winger was as strong as a prize fighter with a gentleman's temperament. His greatest prosperity came during the mid-forties while in the company of linemates "Wild" Bill Ezinicki and Syl Apps. Together, they helped propel the Leafs to two of the four Stanley Cups that Harry enjoyed during his tenure in Toronto. In 1954, he was sold to Chicago where he skated for two-and-a-half seasons before the knell of retirement began to toll. "Tommy Ivan decided that!" Harry exclaimed. "He called me one day and asked me if I wanted to go to Buffalo or Calgary to be a playing coach. I said, 'I don't even get invited back to training camp?' He said, 'No, we've got Ted Lindsay and Ron Murphy.' So I said, 'I'll take Buffalo, it's closer'."

Harry Watson enjoying some fresh air just outside his office in Markham, Ont.

Sporting a fedora on his head and a stick in his hand, however, was not an agreeable experience for Harry. "It was certainly different," he recalled. "I'd never be a playing coach again though. It's too tough to do both jobs and do them properly. And then the management didn't want me to be associated with the players off the ice—we all lived around each other in Fort Erie. Frank Eddolls was one of the managers there at the time. He didn't even want me to ride to the rink with them. So it was a little bit much."

Harry returned to Canada, laid his stick to rest, and embarked on a succession of coaching jobs. After stints with the Unionville Jets and the St. Catharines Tee-Pees, he became head coach of the Windsor Bulldogs in 1962.

"When I went to Windsor," he recollected, "all my friends told me I was crazy because with senior hockey, a lot of guys have been up with the pros and then they're on their way back—they won't work for you! But I had no problems in Windsor at all. I had a great hockey club!

"In fact we had a little Christmas party and they called me over to the corner and said, 'All the other coaches we've had have given us hell all the time. They would pay for a case of beer if we won and if we didn't, there'd be no beer!' But I put a case of beer on the bus for every trip when we were out of town."

By 1963, Harry had handed the Bulldogs' leash over to Joe Klukay and made his exit from the world of hockey. "I had three kids at home and I didn't want to start moving them all over the country," he explained. "So I decided to get out."

He and his family settled in Markham, Ontario where he set up his own shop. "I went into the bowling-alley business which was a mistake," he lamented. "I didn't have too much business experience. All of the projections of the people around here indicated the area was going to grow real quick. But it took ten or fifteen years before it really started to grow. So we went too big, too soon."

Harry eventually joined with a partner in the operation of Pioneer Label Inc., based in Markham. "A friend of mine had a chance to take this little business over and he asked me if I would join him," Harry reported. "There's no pressure, so it's worked out really well for both of us."

At age seventy-four, Harry is still a working Joe, supplying pricing machines to local retail businesses. "I prefer to keep active," he stated of his working longevity. "It's a reason to get up in the morning. I tell all my friends I'm practising for retirement!"

In 1994, Harry was joined by his wife, Lillian, and their three sons for his induction into the Hockey Hall of Fame.

"It was a long wait for me to get in," he admitted. "It was really a nice surprise. The ceremony was just super! I was pretty uptight though—I'd never been on national television before! You have to give a little blurb when they give the presentation. Anyways, we managed to stumble through it all right."

Wensink, John: *Played left wing for St. Louis, Boston, Quebec, Colorado and New Jersey between 1973 & 1983. Born: Cornwall, Ontario, 1953.*

On January 1, 1985, a plane touches down in Holland. With family and members of the media in wait, the exit platform is wheeled in place. The doors open and out steps John Wensink, his wife, Rhonda, and their two daughters. "It was kind of neat," John recounted. "My aunts, uncles and grandmother were there. I got off the plane and all of a sudden I'm conversing in Dutch—the media, they were amazed! I can speak and understand the Dutch language really well."

John grew up in the Cornwall region of Ontario with the Dutch culture as a backdrop within his home. When an invitation came to play hockey in the homeland, the chance to sport the blades and mingle with his ancestral kin was too rich to refuse. "I was over there for three-and-a-half months," he reported. "I played, had a good time and then resumed my construction business in St. Louis."

A year and a half prior to Holland, however, John's course in life was a little less certain.

At the end of the 1982-83 season, the New Jersey Devils backed off from resigning him. "I think that Jersey was grooming me a little bit to become an assistant coach," he surmised. "Whenever I didn't dress for a particular game during that year, they had me behind the bench. But unfortunately for myself, I expressed my opinion and they closed the door. You say it, you've got to live by it!" he affirmed with a laugh. "It was uncharacteristic of me to do what I did, to go public with what I said. I guess I just had my limits."

As a free agent, John put his marketability to the test. He gave the Detroit Red Wings a try only to be sidelined by the club's preference for youth. Five other clubs also made inquiries with the intent to retain him in the minors. But with a young family in tow, John wasn't about to subject them to the instability of life on the road. Instead, the quintessential "Big Bad Bruin", called it a career.

But as retirement brought a manner of closure, it also unveiled the accruing dilemma of where to resettle—Boston, Denver or St. Louis? In Boston, John had experienced his highest level of success. Denver had his friendship with Mike Kitchen and their interest in establishing a lawn-sprinkler business. But St. Louis had the strongest ties and as such, won out as the Wensink's permanent home.

"My wife is from St. Louis. I met her when I was with the Blues," he explained. "We had bought a house there right after we got married. We rented it out for about six years, so we had a house to move back to. And St. Louis is a good place to raise kids—it's a big city with a small-city attitude and lifestyle."

John's first career move was to fall into the construction business. "The guy across the street owned a construction company," he reported. "He came over one night, had a beer and one thing lead to another: I said, 'I'll work for you instead of sitting around doing nothing!' Besides, I'd always been kind of handy with my hands in that department."

Over time the flying sawdust and singing skill saws proved enough to his liking to prompt a shot at going solo with his own company. "I'm still doing my construction business," he stated. "I'm not very big. Once in a while I hire a high-school kid during the summer, but basically I work all alone. It keeps me pretty busy. I don't really advertise. I get a lot of work from the Blues' alumni. I'm not getting overly rich in the construction business—but that's my choice."

As a sideline, John has also been a bastion of support for the once-beleaguered minor-league hockey programme of St. Louis. "I've worked really hard at helping to establish credibility for youth hockey here in town because the St. Louis hockey scene wasn't respected by the rest of the country."

Along the road to reform, John caught a serious bout of coaching fever. His condition has now progressed to higher ranks as head coach of a newly arrived junior-A club compliments of his former teammates Rob Ramage and Bernie Federko.

Construction, needless to say, has now been eclipsed to simmer on the side. "I don't plan on closing down totally," he explained. "I mean job security in pro sports is not that good... So I'll just be a little more selective. I might have to start doing strictly decks or basements—something that won't tie up a kitchen or a household—because instead of taking me a week, it might take me three weeks to complete the job. So that's my game plan."

Nickname: *Wire*

"I had a couple of nicknames when I first started, 'Burr Head' and 'Buffalo Head' because of my afro," John recalled. "But when I got to Boston, I had an afro, *Fu Manchu* look. 'Cheesy' [Gerry Cheevers] was trying to figure out something. He was joking around after practice one day. The next thing you know the word 'wire' came out. You know, barbwire hair? And he also described it as the way I would shoot the puck—it went along with 'Wire' Wensink.

"Every once in a while, even now, if my wife really needs my attention in a social gathering, I'll hear this word 'Wire' come out and I know who's calling me. So Gerry Cheevers gets credit for that one."

Nickname Challenge #28

Jethro

"I got that name my rookie year. I was living in a hotel and Eddie Westfall, who was our captain at the time, said, 'Where are you staying?' And I said, 'Right now, I'm staying in a hotel.' He said, 'You're going to come and live with us.' So I lived with Eddie Westfall and Craig Cameron. I was just a young kid, so I spent most of my time hanging around the house and a lot of times, I'd be sitting there watching TV when these guys came home. And it seemed to be inevitable that whenever they walked in, I'd be watching *The Beverly Hillbillies* (laughs). Eddie Westfall said, 'No wonder you watch *The Beverly Hillbillies*, you look just like Jethro'."

Who is he?

Clues

a. He played left wing for the New York Islanders and Buffalo from 1974-1988.

b. He played on a line with Bossy and Trottier.

If you're still offside, see page 285.

Wharram, Kenny: *Played right wing for Chicago between 1951 & 1969. Born: Ferris, Ontario, 1933.*

Ken Wharram speaks in soft tones that are almost transparent. But those listeners who extend themselves gain a view of a man who gives modesty the good name it deserves.

As a career Blackhawk, his deeds on ice were also transparent—their visibility often obscured by Stan Mikita and the flight of "the Golden Jet".

But behind the scenes, Ken used his "Skooter Line" speed and intelligence to quietly amass 579 career points, a Lady Byng Trophy and two trips to the All-Star Game as a first-team right winger.

At the start of the 1969-70 campaign, Ken was thirty-six years old and looking forward to at least four more seasons in the NHL. His first workout of the year, however, would be his last.

"I had a heart attack the first day of training camp," he recounted. "I ended up with an infection in the heart. They call it *mio carditas*. This type of thing was very rare and they really don't know how it came about. It's an infection in the heart muscle itself. I was close to cashing in all my chips. For a couple of nights, they didn't think that I was going to make it through.

"I was in intensive care for about twelve weeks. But then I eventually came around. I had to go to the Cleveland clinic the following August where they did that dye test on me to see if I had any damage done—which I did.

"When I got out of the hospital, I couldn't come back to North Bay. I had to stay in Chicago for three months. Then I was allowed up ten minutes on the hour. It just gradually built up. Even when I came home that summer, I played one hole of golf per day... It took me all summer before I built it up to eighteen holes."

With his vertical momentum on the rise, it became only natural for Ken to wonder if he might one day revive his career in hockey. But a further exam laid any such hopes to permanent rest.

"When I went to Cleveland to have the dye test done, they said I could live a normal life as long as I didn't play hockey," he explained. "I could dig a ditch or climb a mountain—and that news was better than any medicine I could get! I was through playing hockey but, with leeway like that, at least I could live a normal life."

> *"I was close to cashing in all my chips. For a couple of nights, they didn't think that I was going to make it through."*
>
> Kenny Wharram

Such a splurge of normalcy eventually brought Ken, in concert with a former teammate, to sell hockey sticks on behalf of Northland.

"Moose Vasko used to work with me and we would go to the [NHL] training camps," he recalled. "We had a trailer and a craftsman with us. We'd come out with a bunch of blades with the handles—they were blanks. Our tradesman would cut them down and fix, sand and even bend them—that was when the big hooks were in. He'd make the stick to the player's specs. Then, hopefully from that point on they would use a Northland stick."

Over the next three years, Ken tried to establish a distributorship for Northland sticks in Canada. But he couldn't compete with domestic brands while shouldering the increased cost and red tape of hauling his goods over the border. So, to avoid the market squeeze, he slipped out of the business and back to his home in North Bay, Ontario.

Once resettled, he forged himself a new career by dispensing with the hockey while retaining the lumber. "I used to work with a contractor when I was a kid," he related. "I built my cottage and did a lot of renovations on my kids' houses. So my hobby, and really my trade, was carpentry."

Ken soon found an outlet for his hammers and saws with the Nippissing Board of Education. "We had a maintenance shop," he remarked. "We used to build cupboards and cabinets for the different schools."

Nine years later, Ken finally took a stab at retirement from the working world—at least until boredom reared its stilted head. "You just can't golf all the time," he asserted. "I wanted to have something to do. That's really why I eventually started a part-time job with Greco Paving. I was doing estimates on driveways and small parking lots ... just in the summertime. The rest of the time I didn't work at all. I enjoyed doing it, it kept my mind active."

These days, Ken is retired and living with his wife, Jean. They have raised a son and a daughter and are now grandparents four times over.

This time around, Ken and retirement seem to be getting along just fine. "I'm out golfing and taking it easy. I'm sixty-three now so that's enough," he quipped with a laugh.

Nickname: *Whipper*

Ken is uncertain of the origin or meaning behind his nickname. He speculated that it may have been his style of skating or shooting.

White, Bill: *Played defense for Los Angeles and Chicago from 1967-1976. Born: Toronto, Ontario, 1939.*

As a professional athlete, Bill White was raised on the edge of the roaring crowd. Its waves of sound washed over his mind, sculpting a perspective hewn from uncommon stone.

"We react differently to different situations," he concluded. "A lot of trivial things don't bother us. I see some people making mountains out of mole hills. When you go out to a hockey arena though—every time you perform in a game—you're putting your courage and ability on the line! You've got to do it for sixty minutes and there's nowhere to hide. There are seventeen thousand people looking at you. Not everybody goes to work each day like that. So you develop a kind of character."

Early in his career, Bill encountered his first major-league character in ex-Bruin defensive pillar Eddie Shore. It was under Shore's tutelage in Springfield of the American Hockey League

that he obtained his degree in the art of defense. League expansion in 1967 then paved the way for his entry into the NHL with the Los Angeles Kings where he remained until being traded to Chicago midway through the 1969-70 season. As

Nickname Challenge #29

Howie

"One night we were playing in Montreal and I was killing a penalty by lugging the puck. I don't remember for how long, but I was looking pretty good out there. When I came off the ice, Eddie Johnston called me 'Howie' as in Howie Morenz. Later, Tom Johnson of the Canadiens said they didn't try to get the puck away from me because they were winning 5-2 and there were only about four minutes left in the game. They said, 'Let him kill the penalty, we don't care.' (laughs)—so I just couldn't win on that one."

Who is he?

Clues

a. He played centre for Chicago, Detroit, Boston, Philadelphia and Toronto between 1956 & 1969.

b. At 5'8" and 185 pounds, he was as fearless as a runaway train in lining up his bigger opponents.

c. His initials are F.K.

If your stick was lifted,
see page 285.

a Blackhawk, Bill blossomed into an all-star blueliner who kept a tidy house in his own zone and could effectively advance the puck when the rush was ripe.

After retirement as a player in 1976, he developed even more character as head coach of the Chicago Blackhawks for a brief spell before returning to Canada to enter a new line of work.

He eventually settled in as a manufacturers' representative for Armco Agencies Inc. in Toronto. "We represent manufacturers from the U.S. and Canada," he explained. "We do a lot of leg work for people who don't have the stuff to do it themselves. We supply wholesalers and many supply houses with lots of things to do with the plumbing industry like copper fittings ... thermostatic mixing valves for tempered water in hospitals and Sunrock drinking fountains. We work on a commission basis and some of the products we buy and sell are stocked in our warehouse."

It is when Bill leaves the office, however, that he unleashes his greatest concentration of creative energy. "I got into photography, taking pictures and developing them in the darkroom," he stated with a spark of enthusiasm. "It's a great way to create a lot of satisfaction. I like black and white—it shows the most emotion and tone.

"Then I got into building furniture—another way of creating. I was making the old-fashioned screen doors about ten years ago. I was trying to develop a kit that you could buy as a consumer and take home to fit to your door. But it couldn't be done because you have to build a screen door to fit a door frame. But I did quite a few screen doors, hutches, tables and mirrors.

"After that, my son and I got into building radio-controlled cars and speed boats. The cars get up to 100 km an hour! They're like a mini formula-one car. They look just like Graham Hill is sitting in one."

Bill and his wife have raised four daughters and one son, Kameron White, who played junior-A hockey for the North Bay Centennials of the Ontario Hockey Association. "He's in his last year of junior," Bill noted. "He was drafted by the Leafs two years ago. So he really wants to be a hockey player."

Nickname: *Whitey*

"Of course playing with Pat Stapleton, he was known as 'Whitey'," Bill explained. "And I was known as just Bill White. But all my friends throughout my life call me 'Whitey'."

Nickname Challenge #30

"Mikita"   &   "Mikita"?

Mikita

"Stan Mikita's my favourite hockey player. So when I was a young kid, I used to see him smoking Larks in the Gardens' coffee shop—so I'd smoke *Larks* too. I don't know, maybe Red Kelly found out about it because when Red was coaching the Leafs, he made me a fourth line centre. I'd be playing against Stan the odd time and it would be like, 'God this is heaven! I don't care if I do anything else again. I got to play against him head to head!' Roger Neilson and some of the guys used to laugh about it. They'd say, 'The way you handle the puck, they call you Mikita? Forget it'!"

Who is he?

Clues

a. He played defense for Toronto of the NHL and Vancouver and Cincinnati of the WHA from 1967-1978.

b. His initials are M.P.

If your open-ice pass was intercepted, see page 285.

1. Allan Stanley
2. Stewart Gavin
3. Bobby Leiter
4. Armand "Bep" Guidolin
5. Doug Mohns
6. Bill Hollett
7. Rick Martin
8. Metro Prystai
9. John Anderson
10. Grant Mulvey
11. Leo Labine
12. Reggie Fleming
13. Johnny McKenzie
14. Danny Grant
15. Jerry Korab
16. Jim Lorentz
17. Marcel Dionne
18. Jim Dorey
19. Frank Brimsek
20. Joe Klukay
21. Bob Nystrom
22. Dwight Foster
23. Larry Keenan
24. Jim Henry
25. Lou Fontinato
26. Milt Schmidt
27. Jim Peters Sr.
28. Clark Gillies
29. Forbes Kennedy
30. Mike Pelyk

Quizature Answers

1. Jerry Korab
2. Jim Dorey
3. Ian Turnbull
4. Perry Turnbull

Resources

- *The National Hockey League Official Guide and Record Book* ©1995.
  — Compiled by the NHL Public Relations Department.
- *Fischlers' Hockey Encyclopedia,* Written by Stan & Shirley Fischler.
  — Published by Fitzhenry & Whiteside Limited © *1975.*
- *The Complete Encyclopedia of Hockey, Fourth Edition*, Edited by Zander Hollander.
  — Published by Visible Ink Press © 1993.
- *Hockey's Golden Era: Stars of the Original Six.* Written by Mike Leonetti.
  — Published by MacMillan/Shaftsbury Books ©1993.

ABOUT THE AUTHOR

The author—where it all began.

Brian McFalone is a free-lance writer and an avid hockey fan who specializes in celebrity profiles. He developed an early interest in hockey while practising with his brothers on the back ponds of Aurora, Ontario. At the age of 5, he was drafted by his father, the coach of the Aurora Atoms—thus launching an on-ice career that became more notable in his mind than in his deeds. Since taking an early retirement from hockey, he has developed a keen appreciation for the human side of the game which has fuelled his research and inspired his writing.

Between periods, Brian has become a graduate of the University of Waterloo and Lakehead University. He is presently a teacher with the Wellington County Board of Education based in Guelph, Ontario.

Over the Glass and Into the Crowd!

Life After Hockey

Order your copy today!

Over the Glass & Into the Crowd! is the perfect gift for any member of your family or social circle who is a hockey enthusiast or who would simply enjoy revisiting some of the colourful personalities of hockey's past.

Over the Glass & Into the Crowd! is also an excellent career-planning tool, providing a wealth of insights, inspiration and reality checks for the benefit of those individuals contemplating their futures.

Special prices apply for quantity purchases of 10 or more copies. For more information, contact MainStreet Press at (519) 766-4756 (phone & fax) or by e-mail at mainst@freespace.net

Visit our web-site at: http://www.freespace.net/~mainst

There's more to come...

If you would like to receive information about future editions of the *Over the Glass & Into the Crowd!* series, please contact us a MainStreet Press.

This is a Test!

You've read the book—now it's time to pit your knowledge against *Over the Glass...The Mother Of All Exams!* Find out where you rank in the voting for hockey's cerebral Hall of Fame. Are you

1. an MVP (Most Valuable Pundit)?
2. a bulger of twine?
3. a mere scoring threat?
4. a journeyman? or,
5. an overrated draft pick?

Drop us a line to obtain your free copy of our final exam and graduate with honours!

To order your copy of *Over the Glass & Into the Crowd! Life After Hockey*, send $24.95 Can./$19.95 U.S. along with $5.00 in the currency of your country for shipping and handling. You can also place your order by phoning or faxing our office at (519) 766-4756, or via e-mail.

(Canadian residents add 7% GST)

MainStreet Press
10 Suffolk St. W.
Guelph, Ontario, Canada, N1H 2H8
e-mail: mainst@freespace.net

VISA

Please make your cheque payable to MainStreet Press.

Name _____

Street _____

City _____ Province/State _____

Postal or Zip Code _____ Telephone _____

Number of copies ordered _____ Amount enclosed _____